THE HEROIC PATH OF THE HEART

The Arthurian Quest will inspire you, challenge you, and ultimately transform your life. This book draws together information from a wide variety of sources—historical, mythological, psychological, and magickal—to reveal how these legends can be used as a catalyst for personal evolution and empowerment.

Unlock the ancient Celtic wisdom at the heart of the Arthurian legends to reach higher realms of thought, philosophy, and magick on your personal quest for meaning.

Enter the mythic realms of Camelot for yourself through beautifully written guided journeys and experiential exercises that will deepen your connection to the archetypal forces of the Arthurian legends. Awaken the transformative power within yourself as you undertake your own mythic quest through the enchanted realms of the Otherworld. Open yourself to the Divine through unique ceremonies derived from the Celtic roots of the Arthurian tales and enrich your life with the gifts of self-understanding and balance.

The Arthurian Quest reveals exciting new insights into the spiritual mysteries of Avalon, the re-emergence of Celtic consciousness, and the true nature of the Grail. Experience the magickal current of energy associated with Merlin—the Archmage of Celtic mysticism—and learn to apply the secret knowledge within these stories for positive self-evolution and growth.

Reconstruct the spiritual ideals of the Round Table within the realms of your own consciousness. Gain a deeper understanding of your personal quests and life patterns by using the Arthurian myths as a catalyst for personal and planetary change. Learn new ways to tap into the elemental energies of the Earth to create your own path to power and fulfillment.

Journey to the magickal realms of the Arthurian legends and find yourself within a world of unparalleled spiritual adventure.

ABOUT THE AUTHOR

Amber Wolfe is a master-level educator and psychotherapist in private practice. She follows an American Shamanic path, using the wisdoms found in the Celtic forms of Craft, Church, and myth that are her heritage. She also honors the sacred teachings of Native American medicine elders who have shared their knowledge of the nature of this land.

Amber Wolfe calls herself a Ban Drui, a term that has several meanings. Among them are Wise Woman, Druidess, White Oak Woman, and (as described by William Butler Yeats) a "Faerie Doctor." These titles represent her style as a writer, teacher, and therapist, whose work emphasizes the magick qualities of self-transformation and personal evolution.

Amber is a Solitary practicioner of the Celtic tradition of the Craft of the Wise. In addition to two earlier books published by Llewellyn, she has created guided imagery tapes designed to evoke and support the quest for spirituality and Nature awareness. She is currently working on several books drawn from her work with both Celtic and Native American sources.

TO WRITE TO THE AUTHOR

If you wish to contact the author or would like more information about this book, please write to the author in care of Llewellyn Worldwide, and we will forward your request. Both the author and publisher appreciate hearing from you and learning of your enjoyment of this book and how it has helped you. Llewellyn Worldwide cannot guarantee that every letter written to the author can be answered, but all will be forwarded. Please write to:

Llewellyn's New Worlds of Mind and Spirit
P.O. Box 64383-K806, St. Paul, MN 55164-0383, U.S.A.

Please enclose a self-addressed, stamped envelope for reply, or $1.00 to cover costs.
If outside the U.S.A., enclose international postal reply coupon.

FREE CATALOG FROM LLEWELLYN

For more than ninety years Llewellyn has brought its readers knowledge in the fields of metaphysics and human potential. Learn about the newest books in spiritual guidance, natural healing, astrology, occult philosophy, and more. Enjoy book reviews, New Age articles, a calendar of events, plus current advertised products and services. To get your free copy of *Llewellyn's New Worlds*, send your name and address to:

Llewellyn's New Worlds of Mind and Spirit
P.O. Box 64383-K806, St. Paul, MN 55164-0383, U.S.A.

THE ARTHURIAN QUEST

Living the Legends of Camelot

AMBER WOLFE

1996
Llewellyn Publications
St. Paul, Minnesota, USA 55164-0383

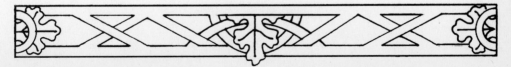

FIRST EDITION, 1996
First Printing

Cover and interior art by Carrie Westfall
Cover design by Tom Grewe
Interior design and editing by Connie Hill

Library of Congress Cataloging-in-Publication Data
Wolfe, Amber, 1950–
    The Arthurian quest : living the legends of Camelot / Amber Wolfe — 1st ed.
       p.   cm.   — (Llewellyn's Celtic wisdom series)
    Includes bibliographical references and index.
    ISBN 1-56718-806-0 (trade pbk.)
    1. Celts—England—Religion—Miscellanea. 2. Britons—Kings and rulers—Religious aspects. 3. Arthurian romances—Miscellanea. 4. Spiritual life. I. Title. II. Series:
  BL980.G7W65   1996
  299—dc20   95-48324
                                                  CIP

Llewellyn Publications
A Division of Llewellyn Worldwide, Ltd.
St. Paul, Minnesota 55164-0383, U.S.A.

LLEWELLYN'S CELTIC WISDOM SERIES

At the core of every religion, at the foundation of every culture, there is *Magick*.

Magick sees the world as alive, as the home that humanity shares with beings and powers both visible and invisible, with whom and which we can interface to either our advantage or disadvantage—depending upon our awareness and intention.

Religious worship and communion is one kind of magick, and just as there are many religions in the world, so are there many magickal systems.

Religion and magick are ways of seeing and relating to the creative powers, the living energies, the all-pervading spirit, the underlying intelligence that is the universe within which we and all else exist.

Neither religion nor magick conflict with science. All share the same goals and the same limitations: always seeking truth, forever haunted by human limitations in perceiving that truth. Magick is "technology" based upon experience and extrasensory insight, providing its practitioners with methods of greater influence and control over the world of the invisible before it impinges on the world of the visible.

The study of world magick not only enhances your understanding of the world in which you live, and hence your ability to live better, but brings you into touch with the inner essence of your long evolutionary heritage, and most particularly—as in the case of the magickal system identified most closely with your genetic inheritance—with the archetypal images and forces most alive in your whole consciousness.

OTHER BOOKS BY THE AUTHOR

In the Shadow of the Shaman: Connecting with Self, Nature and Spirit

Personal Alchemy: A Handbook of Healing and Self-Transformation

FORTHCOMING

Elemental Power: Celtic Faerie Craft & Druidic Magic

THE ARTHURIAN QUEST
is dedicated, with honor,
to the
Sovereignty of the Lands
and to all
of
Celtia's Clan

ACKNOWLEDGMENTS

The Arthurian Quest could not have come into being without the support of many of my friends, family members, and fellow explorers in the mystical realms of myth, legend, and magickal consciousness. Although those who have helped, each in their own special way, are too numerous to list here, I want to acknowledge several specific people whose wisdoms and efforts formed the keystone for the construction of this book:

My Family—who have guarded me well while I was in "Cave Perilous" writing this ever-expanding book.

Kara, Jon, and Jonathan Starr—and "The Old Boy," to whom they graciously introduced me in a manner which continues to bring me multi-dimensional gifts.

Pech Rafferty and Jay Veneer—who brought their gifts as master wizards and guardian warriors to the experiences of crafting this project, as well as to so many other parts of my own quest.

Jean Underwood—my dragon-ken, who kept me going and treated me with kid gloves in the process.

Lady Elspeth—whose good heart and great confidence brought me strength, courage, and inspiration.

Nancy Mostad—who knew when I was truly ready to emerge from "self-imposed domestic exile," and to all those at Llewellyn who continue to enlighten us with new worlds of wisdom.

A most special thanks goes to:

Jeanne Tiedemann and "Essie Mac," my techno-scribe and her most wise machine (which some may consider simply a computer, but I know is far more magick in Jeanne's competent hands). Thank you for continuing to hold the line while *The Arthurian Quest* tripled in size, with its subsequent requirements of time and effort.

For those not named here, and especially for the readers who continue to encourage me in my work, please know I am grateful for the many positive contributions you make to my life.

Ceud Mile Taing! (100,000 Thanks!)

Amber Wolfe
Summer Solstice, 1994
Savannah, Georgia

CONTENTS

GUIDED ACTIVE IMAGERIES

THE WEAVE OF THE REALM

Opens wide the Ashwood door,
New landscapes now revealing,
With fern and tree and flowers galore,
And bird song most appealing.

A meadow's sweet grass for a floor,
Clear skies to form the ceiling
Oak and Ash and Pine restore
Clear senses, and smooth feeling.

Enter now, the Bards so fair
Harp and Muse-song garb they wear
To dance, to sing, to laugh, to care
To weave the rhymes, replete or spare.

Of knights so bold and maidens fair,
And wizards caught in their own snare;
of kings and queens, the trumpets blare,
And do express with time to spare.

We reflect this form, this bloom, this flare
We craft the tales of destiny, and dare
To pass the visions from heir to heir.

Retain the wisdom, and not impair
The truth so sacred, so fine, so rare
In poetry finds its place to fare.
Without it, none, the world could bear.

So weaves the gossamer fabric there
With fibers strong, yet still so fair
And threads of Light beyond compare.

So open wide the clear mind door
To realms which are revealing
With treasures fair and gifts galore
And powers most appealing

A crystal cave to form the floor
And towers for your ceiling
The branches of your mind restore
bright visions and deep feeling.

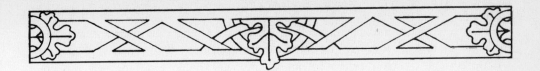

PREFACE

EXPLORING THE REALMS OF THE CAMELOT LEGENDS

You don't have to go far off the interpreted paths to find yourself in very difficult situations. The courage to face the trials and to bring a whole new body of possibilities into the field of interpreted experience for other people to experience— that is the hero's deed.

Joseph Campbell
The Hero with a Thousand Faces (Princeton: Princeton Univ. Press, 1973)

To enter the realms of the Arthurian legends is to find yourself within a world of unparalleled spiritual adventure and mystical wonder. It is an experience that is, simultaneously, one of reaching into the shared dimensions of Western, Celtic tribal memory, and of finding a uniquely individual dimension of the Self. It is a sacred quest—and a quest for the Sacred—on a heroic path of the heart.

There are no real maps for this quest, nor are there any books of rules. All that each of us can do is listen to our own inner voice, which is our truest guide, while we explore the sacred legacy left to us in the forms of myth, magick, and legend. Having heard the tales of wonder that ware the Camelot legends, and having heard the experiences of others who have gone questing before us, we can then begin to make our own journey into these ageless realms of power. We must make this journey on a path that is uniquely our own, with the full knowledge that if there is an already existing path, it is a path belonging to someone else.

To follow another's path into these realms is invariably to be led astray. This is true of many forms of mysticism and wisdom; but is particularly true of the Arthurian traditions. It is a theme constantly repeated in the wealth of legends that have come to us as a mythic legacy of power. The foundational message of empowerment in these legends and traditions is the full development of independent, personal potential.

It is this right of individualism upon which the mythic and magick traditions of the West are formed. It is an especially Celtic/European tradition that emphasizes the Divine powers of each individual heart to empower the personal journey, the inner quest for authenticity of Self. In the realms of Arthurian myth and legend we find our own codes for personal spiritual growth. In these realms we find the rights—and the rites—of individual consciousness, choice, and self-determination.

The Arthurian legends have been called the most transformative catalyst for the Western mind. They are the crystallization of the ancient Celtic ways of Nature and the renaissance of self-nature, both of which emerged relatively unscathed in spite of centuries of misconception and political manipulation. These legends are the source of reclamation of Nature and self-nature which is the hallmark of the Celtic mind, and it is with that same heroic, fiercely independent Celtic mindset that we must approach these sacred realms. No other approach is either wise or worthy.

It is with this same mind and purpose that I have approached and explored the realms of the Camelot legends. It is with the intent to inspire the quests and explorations of others that I have chosen how to express my experiences of these mythic realms. To do so in any other manner, I feel, would not be of true service to the Source from which these realms emerged.

So, I say to you as an individual, share in the experiences this book provides. Learn from the material presented and the opinions expressed; but do so with an unwavering conviction that you have the right, as well as the heroic responsibility, to choose only what you need for your own quest. It is ultimately up to you to enter these realms, as their mythic characters, who, while questing, have entered the enchanted forests time and time again—"at a place where there was no path."

As it is my intention as a writer, teacher, and psychotherapist to prepare you for that personal journey into these enchanted realms, I want to begin by helping you understand the transformational course of experiential instruction I have prepared. To this end, the following is an overview of the format of this book.

You might say that *The Arthurian Quest* is a field guide for working the frequencies, or the energy channels, found within the Arthurian matrix. It is quite important to know that these legends are direct connections to significant lines of power. They are, in essence, the "tales" of the dragons' powers—the elemental energies of the Earth herself.

One of the primary reasons we approach, acknowledge, and activate these ancient powers with the formal overlay of myth and legend is so we may "ride" those dragons with honorable mastery. We do this as an ally in the shared service of Sovereignty, the Goddess of the Earth, the Lady of the Land—and her Lord of Light—however we may know them within our hearts and minds.

Because of the importance of being fully prepared for working with the power sources of the Arthurian traditions, it is my intent to introduce and instruct you in as many aspects of these traditions as possible. Therefore, we will begin with a little school work, and then move into some investigation of the primary messages in these myths. After that foundational course work, we'll enter the "enchanted forests" of these legends in order to make more direct connections with these realms. By doing this, we'll find these realms to be reflective of ourselves—then and now.

We will explore the powerful truth that myths are the personifications of ourselves, reflecting Nature and self-nature, the inseparable alliance. Having strengthened that alliance, we will become familiar with the process of translating the messages of the myths into forms applicable to the empowerment of our personal lives. We will make in-depth, effective connections with the specific lines of power that the legends and their primary characters represent.

Progressively, as Ban Drui—wise woman, Druidess—I will present you with sets of specific enchantments. This is a collection of techniques for the evolutionary enhancement of Self. Once again, I stress that the methods and the systems I present here are of my own design. As they have incorporated the designs of others before me, I hope you will use them to design systems for yourself. Let them serve as a catalyst for your own experience.

If this all seems like work, well, it is work. All adventures require work in preparing for them, as well as in experiencing them. Otherwise, neither the adventure nor the adventurer is able to reach the dimensions of quality that are life-transforming. Just remember that we are all still in training. Why else would we be here?

Or, as The Merlin put it to me plainly when I was being particularly temperamental about training and retraining for quality magick working:

Amber Wolfe: "Work, work, work all the time. If this is life, then life is hell!"

Archmage, The Merlin: "Life is not hell, Lass. Life is school."

And, yes, I am working with what I call The Merlin Current—or I might also say—the current Merlin. The Merlin is that multidimensional frequency which, I stress, is absolutely accessible to anyone willing to make the earnest efforts to reach it. In fact, if you are especially anxious to make that connection right away, feel free to check the Table of Contents (which is your course outline) for specific chapters on ways to accomplish this. Go ahead if you want to—I'll wait.

Of course, you might be surprised to find yourself right back here sooner than you thought. There are a number of reasons for this; the most important being that this text is neither linear nor structured according to any format that assumes you know nothing at the beginning, and everything at the end.

Indeed, you may find it is difficult to say with any real certainty just where the beginning or the ending is located. That is because this text is designed as a Celtic weave, interwoven to signify both strength and interrelatedness in life, as well as in learning. That is the way of the Drui, the druidic way in general, and specifically the way The Merlin Current operates. It is, most importantly, the way the paths into and within the sacred realms of the Camelot legends will lead. "Best get used to it now," as The Merlin says.

This is not to say you must follow the format of this text as it is presented. Written material is bound by dimensional limitations and must be expressed linearly. This realization is one of the reasons the ancient Druids stressed the less limiting forms of the oral traditions. Modern Druids have to compensate by using forms presenting the material with an interwoven design in an effort to duplicate these extremely effective, ancient forms. This is why there are materials in this text, as there are traditionally in the telling of these legends, which weave in and out, over and around other materials, as does a Celtic weaving.

The Norman French who wove and rewove threads into the pattern of these legends called this process *entrelacement*. This lacing between the lines is—and was—done for the specific purpose of strengthening the weave and the wisdom found within the realms of the Camelot legends. This same "entrelacement," incidentally, is found in the flow of energies arising from the dragon lines of power, preserved and manifested in the minds and the myths of the Western Celtic consciousness. This you may already know; and, if so, you also know there will be far, far more to know. That is the true knowledge of the Drui. As Caesar said of the Druids he encountered: "And the wisest of them said, 'This we know—that we know nothing.'"

So I say to you, yet again, that I also know nothing. I claim to know nothing more than the personal path provided by experiencing these realms, and by virtue of years of training, the techniques by that I will endeavor to provide the catalysts for your own experiencing. All I have experienced I will earnestly try to share, unless I feel it has somehow enhanced my own experience in a manner which may impede your progress. I will strive also not to influence your choice in a way that would lead you astray. The only suggestion I will make is for you continually to choose and rechoose for yourself, and constantly keep a free and open mind.

Additionally, I will admit to being decidedly biased against any interpretation of these myths or applications of their powers in any form that is exclusive, separatist, or hierarchical. Whether or not that was ever the druidic way is highly debatable. Regardless of how it may or may not have been then, it simply can't be that way any longer. Hasn't a millennium or two of these arbitrarily imposed structures been enough to show the dangers they bring to the development of our personal consciousness—and that of the planet? I know I've had quite enough of it.

Another admitted bias is my resistance to the efforts to reclaim the ways of magick and the messages in these myths in order to recreate exactly how it was, or might have been, then. Certainly this is a valuable effort. It provides the foundation stones upon which we build our own systems of magick for the present. Those present systems will, in turn, be foundation stones for the future.

The developers of systems of magick are the keystones in the structures of power at all times, so long as what they construct has current and creative application for the times. The length those "times" entail depends entirely on how well those systems inspire the individual to develop independent power paths. To constantly strive to create what-has-been-as-far-as-we-know is to create a rut, not an evolutionary path to wisdom. This approach, used exclusively, will impede progress and sidetrack the process of personal evolution.

I believe R. J. Stewart, that fine and current interpreter of The Merlin materials and Arthurian lore, expressed this best when he said: "Such mythic and dynamic structures may be kingdoms of unbalanced force if they are aroused without a spiritual or ethical awakening within each individual."

Once again, the emphasis is on the personal path, the personal work, and the personal experiencing of these realms. That is what makes them current and conscious in the mind of the Western Celt.

As we are exploring realms that are essentially Western and Celtic, it seems important to stress that, in activating these realms individually, we are also activating what The Merlin defines as the "time of doing." It is true we cannot set out to rescue, nor make another's quest for them. However, we can set out to restore the lines of power that will help in the rescue of this shared planet—our true Sovereign.

We can courageously conduct our own quests with grace and honor that will inspire others. As the legends have for us, we can be for ourselves, for others, and for our evolution as a species. Each, in our own way, can be a part of this time of doing what must be done for the preservation of Nature and her people. As we activate the powers found within the Arthurian myths, I believe we will activate powerful tribal codes that will power our actions (our destiny, in effect) to make the transformational changes we and our world require.

We, as Celts, were once people of Nature. We still are. Fortunately, we have the added benefit of learning from native peoples around the globe—people who have never forgotten, not even for a moment—what our essential relationship to Nature is—and must eternally be. On an expanded scale, we can consider that the Celts specifically, and Western peoples in general, have been on a very long quest. As such, I believe we can now begin to awaken to what I see as the purpose of our shared quest—the protection and preservation of our sacred connections to Nature. We can claim the lands we share—not for ourselves, as we did in the past—but for Sovereignty's sake.

We begin, one at a time, each on his/her own path, questing for that which is Right and True, each awakening to his or her own "dream of the proud." It is a vision of hope to which I hold fast. We can restore the Wasteland we have unwittingly created. Whether we did so by living our lives inauthentically, or by providing inadequately for our Sovereign lands, we must do what we can to make it Right again. We are now remembering the ageless truth that applies to us all as "royal" children of a shared Sovereign, Mother Earth: "You and the Land are One" (from John Boorman's "Excalibur").

As we make our personal quests, exploring the realms of the Camelot legends, we can best do so as conscious allies in the service of Sovereignty. My British "cousins" will forgive me for being so bold, but I take my revolutionary heritage quite seriously. I believe that the "Matter of Britain," which is the name given to the powerful source reflected in the Arthurian lore, is a matter for the entire world to consider carefully. As such, I suggest we may also, in an honorable fashion, refer to this as the "Matter of Sovereignty." After all, we are dealing with a shared "Sovereign Mater," the planet Earth. Much, if not all, of whose lands we of Western Celtic heritage now inhabit.

Furthermore, may I also now be so bold as to suggest that each of us, continental Americans or otherwise, have the rights and responsibilities to approach and activate the sacred mystical powers preserved in the Arthurian legends for the good of all. Remember what that great secular humanist, Thomas Jefferson, wrote in the Declaration of Independence:

> Let us now, as individual inhabitants of a shared world "assume among the powers of the earth the separate and equal station to which the laws of Nature and nature's god …" entitle us all as human beings.

We can, each and all, be the catalyst for the construction of a new, albeit improved, form of Camelot. We are, in essence, the mind of The Merlin, and the awareness of Avalon. Our honorable efforts can result in the realization of the Round Table. Together we can implement that Arthurian vision of unity and glory that is the Western foundation for Truth and Light.

Moreover, we can design our own new systems, based on those ancient traditions that help us all in the pursuit of knowledge, self-evolution, and understanding. In so doing, we are following, in true druidic fashion, the lines of power set down for us, since time immemorial, by "pioneers on the frontiers of consciousness" (Timothy Leary, from "Down the Genetic Runway").

Can we not now live up to our shared legacy, and carry on in the true traditions of the wisdom seekers and evolutionary catalysts who came before us? Can we not now be the inspiration for those who will come after we have gone? I believe we can, simply by accepting, with gratitude, the gifts with which we entered this world. I believe we begin by accepting fully who and what we are—*Homo sapien, sapiens*. Wise, wise humans. Let us begin now our evolutionary quests—each where there is no path.

INTRODUCTION

MIND, MYTH, AND LEGEND

Myth is a directing of the mind and heart, by means of profoundly informed configurations to that ultimate mystery which fills and surrounds all existence.

Joseph Campbell
The Power of Myth (New York: Doubleday, 1988)

 The development and the endurance of any myth is an intricate, complex process which would require volumes to explain. Since the Arthurian materials are so transformationally reflective of Western Celtic consciousness, it is helpful to understand how many aspects are affected by—and affect—the development of such a powerful myth.

These are the aspects of legends, myth, and human mind. For our present purpose, these are the realms of the Camelot legends. From these aspects we can understand the effect such myths have on our lives. In turn, we can use these to effect a change, a transformation of our Selves, as we will explore later. They are the threads, the fibers of the Celtic Weave.

Aspects of Legend, Myth and Human-Kind (nonspecific order)

- Personal—individualization, self-identification
- Psychological—self-mind, personal patterns of behavior, emotions
- Familial—kinship patterns, relationships defined
- Ecumenical—religious practices, ways of recognition of the Divine
- Sociological—blended tribal and cultural patterns, rules, laws
- Anthropological—primitive, original patterns of cultures
- Historical—observed, communicated, and recorded forms

- Archeological—physical structures and effects
- Mythological—symbolic representations of natural forces and forms
- Mystical—higher consciousness, sacred wisdoms, prophecies
- Magickal—activation and manifestation of natural forces, metaphysics
- Multidimensional—evolutionary transformation of consciousness

Joseph Campbell said, "Myths are the clues to the spiritual potentialities of the human life." As such, we could interweave the aspect of Spirituality with all the other aspects of legend, myth, and Humankind. It is truly the nature of spirit and the Spirit of Nature from which myth comes as a liaison to the Light on behalf of humanity. As we continue to evolve in heart, mind, and spirit, our myths will evolve along with us. This is because myths represent the mystery of who and what we are. Like a mystery—a good one—the clues are often seen as such only after we have discovered the source of the mystery itself.

Because myth and mind are so integrally linked, we may define their combined aspects as the Mystical Mind. This is the mindset from which we derive the transformational magick for our lives. It is the Mystical Mind that activates our unconscious, as well as conscious, aspects and brings evolutionary enlightenment. Most of the time, we're not even aware of when or how it is working; but we have learned to have faith in the fact that it does. It is the Mystical Mind we're referring to when we say, "Do you believe in magick?" It is the Mind connected to Spirit.

That which capitalizes Mystical Mind is its emphasis on the Right use of Spirit and Light. These functions of the mind are "the means by which consciousness obtains its orientation to experience," according to Carl Jung, the great Western mystic and psychoanalyst. Basically, these functions give you the validating reality of your experience. Because of these functions working together in synthesis, we are able to achieve valid experiences from the spiritual transpersonal experience, as well. This means if we actively bring these functions together in the creation and experience of imagery, then with active imagery, we can access expanded dimensions of personal consciousness.

When we combine our active imagination with mythic and symbolic images, we can access expanded dimensions of tribal, cultural, and universal consciousness. This is Jung's "collective unconscious." We can draw from it like a sacred well. We activate the collective unconscious in order to deepen our connection to the myth and symbols we use. Still, we are basically unconscious of its actions. We are conscious of its effects.

Therefore, when you're experiencing deeply powerful images and mythic visions brought "up" into your consciousness, please remember, as a rule, these are not external in origin. You've just made a clear connection to the deeper realms of your conscious mind, and your collective unconscious "feels" that, too. After years of dealing with this personally with friends, as well as with clients—and with those who work with the mythic, symbolic realms of collective unconscious using active imagery—I've determined there are a few things that are important to understand.

First: Almost all those extremely real experiences you have of the mythic realms and their characters are the result of your own mind internally connecting with the archetypes—the original patterns—forces or sources from which that mythic symbol emerged.

Second: Very few of those extremely real experiences of characters come from actually having connected with a person who is now in Spirit. These Spirit guides are undeniably real. They are also undeniably rare, particularly as a "channel" for you—or anyone else, for that matter. It is possible to pick up on such a spirit guide who is in the service of the Light and is working within the realms or aspects of the mystic wisdom you wish to access. This, I am certain, many of you already know. However, all of us would do well to remember to be wise in such matters. Choose a guide as carefully as you would a true friend. Be open, but be wise.

> Don't expect it; but don't reject it.
> Don't deny it; but don't rely on it, either.

Always, always view your experience as a wonderful activation of your expanded potential. It is far more sacred when you realize just what a Divine gift your Mystical Mind truly is. We will explore the realms of this as we proceed; so for now I'll also say that I realize it is often confusing, at least at first, to hear mythic characters discussed as though they were personal spirit guides. For example, "I talked with Nimue today," or "Gawain told me to tell the Green Knight story," or "Merlin woke me up this morning."

This is a personification process that is very similar to the creation of Celtic tribal gods. It is an acknowledgment of a personal relationship. It is an intrapersonal connection of internalized aspects of myth and inner mind within your self. (Emphasis on within!)

It is also an acknowledgment of an interpersonal relationship between your self and another person working with very similar frequencies of the same myths. It's also very much easier to say, "When Arthur came to me, he gave me a gift of power," than to say, "While I was activating imagery that I have classified as encoded to the Arthurian myths, I realized I could use a specific symbol as a mnemonic device (a cue!) to stimulate an appropriate response in a variety of correlated environmental, verbal, and subverbal conditions."

Finally, when we personalize our myths, we are personalizing aspects of our self-nature as well as aspects of Nature, herself.

This is precisely what our ancestors did. We assume they didn't know much about the psychology of the mind at that time. I believe we assume that to make ourselves feel advanced. Here is a good grid of the way the mind works with and within itself.

Jungian Functions of the Mind

1. Sensation: perception by the senses, "tells you that something exists."
2. Feeling: response of emotions, "tells you whether it is agreeable or not."
3. Thinking: associating, process and analysis, "tells you what that something is."
4. Intuition: integration process and analysis, "tells you where it probably came from, and where it may go."

(from Carl Jung, *Man and His Symbols*, Doubleday, 1969)

To this I add:

5. Synthesis, as the transcendent function that brings the other four into an alliance in the active use of imagery for the evolution of Self.

When we explore these realms of the Arthurian, Camelot archetypes, we do so most effectively by using "special glasses" as an image or cue that we are experiencing the realms of our inner vision. Archetypes come into our realms of vision and consciousness wearing the legendary garb of the myths we are exploring. The archetypes themselves are elemental contacts with the realms of Nature's and self-nature's mind. They are the mystical representation of energies and sources of energy we are often unable to contact either directly, or consciously. Their images, however, come to us through the functional synthesis of our own Mystical Mind. We really have no further need to try and track their origins for ourselves. Suffice it to say they are encoded.

PART I

THE LIVING LEGENDS

With elements of air
She does conspire.

White Goddess whispers
Of Her desire.

To Bard and Muse-singer
To inspire,

Harmony's note
For harp and lyre.

Poetry, prose
The chorus entire,

Gives She this to all
And then does retire

Into Spirit
Water
Earth
Air
And Fire.

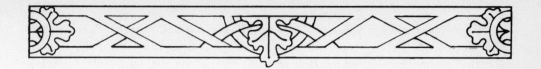

CHAPTER 1

THE ONCE, FUTURE, AND ETERNALLY PRESENT POWER

Myth is only true "revelation" so long as it is a message from heaven—that is, from the timeless and nonhistoric word—expressing not what was true once, but what is true always.

Alan Watts
The Essential Alan Watts (Berkeley: Celestial Arts, 1974)

 Most of us, drawn to the Arthurian myths and legends, are unaware initially of what attracts and holds us to them so steadfastly. We know we love the legends and feel somehow connected closely to their familiar characters. We know these mythic characters and their stories awakened something deeply personal from within each of us. At the same time, they give us a sense of kinship with others who hold these legends dear also. Still, for the most part, we are unable to express why these have endured collectively for ages within our hearts and minds.

Moreover, few can explain why those legends, whose variations have been many, can evoke in such a great number of people such a mutually shared experience. It is as though we are all a part of a great conspiracy, one of which we are not aware entirely, with codes we cannot understand completely. Despite this, we are compelled by these myths to acknowledge that something extraordinarily special exists within them. It is a force that draws us into a part of ourselves that seems fine and rare.

When we encounter the legends of Arthur and Camelot, we catch a "fleeting glimpse of glory" that we recognize, yet cannot define. For "one brief shining moment" we are illuminated by these legends. Then, for most, that moment passes, and we continue our lives, relatively unaware of what we have touched upon, and what, in turn, has touched us.

For those who may have questioned why that glimpse comes and then passes away, their answer would most likely be that these are legends of the past; stories of a mythic time that is no longer here. Nothing could be further from the truth.

The illuminating experience shared by so many through the medium of these myths emerges from the unconscious recognition of their power. It is a power that belongs to the timeless, eternal realms of heart, mind, and spirit. It is truly this once, future, and eternally present power that conspires to keep us closely connected to ourselves, as we are now, and, authentically, to our origins.

These Arthurian legends have such a profound impact on us because they are, unquestionably, the central, unifying myth of Western civilization. These myths represent a codified spiritual experience and philosophical ideal that is uniquely Western and Celtic. Spiritually, they represent our essential connection to Nature. Philosophically, they represent our deep respect for individualism.

These may not seem much like revelations when we hear them now. Yet it is due, in no small part, to the endurance of the Arthurian myths, that we now take our connection to Nature and our rights as individuals as simply a matter of course. In order to understand this fully, we will need to recognize the conflicts that affected the Arthurian myths historically. Then we'll see that while they have endured, the process was never simple.

Currently, in the new times of the Transformational Light Age, it is easy to forget the times that were dark, when change was systematically controlled. Fortunately, the true evolution of mind and spirit cannot be controlled for long. The Light invariably shines through, and its illumination is the catalyst for natural growth. This is so in Nature, as well as in self-nature. One of the great Lights that continued to shine throughout the darkest of times was the illuminating legend of Arthur and Camelot.

The Arthurian legends essentially reflected as a constellation, or synthesis, of far more ancient mythic materials existing on the European continent and in the British Isles long before the Eastern cultural system imposed itself upon the newly emerging religion, Christianity.

However, it is not really true to say it was the tenets of the Christian faith that were responsible for these unfavorable changes. In other words, it was not the doctrines, but the dogmas, that sought ways to change the legends—and so attempted to change the Celtic mind. This oppressive orientation arose from an Eastern cultural philosophy that ran counter to the philosophy of the West.

This created a conflict between what I will call the Orthodoxy of the East and the Individualism of the West. It was a conflict that would emerge time and again. It would be reflected in the Arthurian legends until it reached a starting point of resolution in the Grail legends.

Basically, those differences between the East and the West are as follows:

Eastern: Emphasis on the group. Individual valued only insofar as it values the group or society as an organized whole. Stresses rituals and laws of power governing spirituality. The Divine is viewed largely as external, with limited access only through strict adherence to set rules.

Western: Emphasis on the individual. The group value is determined by the quality of individuals by whom it is formed. Stresses independence and humanistic philosophies that hold that true spirituality, the Divine power, is operative in one's own heart and one's own life.

It was the Orthodoxy, and not Christianity, which with military force beginning in the fourth and fifth centuries A.D., pushed the separatist dogma of the East. In essence, the social order that arose in the Dark Ages was imported, and summarily implanted in the Western, Celtic mind. While this process had some effect, it never truly flourished in the mind of the Celt. To understand this, we need to look briefly at the evolution of the Celts and the development of the Western, Celtic consciousness.

In Europe, prior to the Celts, the inhabitants were a relatively peaceful, Nature-connected, agrarian people who reverenced the Earth as the Mother Goddess, and the deities of the lands on which they lived. Then, about 2000 B.C., a group that has been called the Battle-ax Aryans came into Europe from the areas surrounding the Black Sea. These people, having emerged from a harsh, arid environment, brought with them a culture that was more warlike and patriarchal. Luckily, as happens sometimes when people from arid regions impose themselves onto lands that are rich and fertile, these Battle-ax Aryans then absorbed the ways of the lands and the people already living there.

Naturally, this did not happen overnight, but it was the beginning of the independent, nature consciousness in the European mind. From this blending, a breed was born that would give rise to the tribes called *Keltoi* by the Greeks—a tribe we now call the Celts.

The Celts were (and still are) a breed of proud, aggressive, fiercely independent and tribally loyal people who had learned to reverence all the aspects of Nature. Admittedly, these Celts held their tribal gods in highest esteem, but this reflected their emerging independent spirit. Also, as many of these tribal gods were, in effect, spirits of place, or *genus loci*, they were still reflections of Nature, as well as of the nature of the Celtic peoples. The syncretistic, or mutually shared, gods of Nature, the Celts held second in esteem. The multitude of tribal gods of place and the relatively small number of syncretic, shared gods found repeatedly throughout Europe gives evidence of this particularly Celtic trait.

The Celts, as we know them, came from Bavaria. In time, they made their way into France and Switzerland, where archeological evidence reveals the high points of their culture on the European continent. The Halstatt, Celtic Culture (about 800–500 B.C.) were the ox-cart people who then made their way from what is now Austria into the European wilderness. The La Tiêne, Celtic Culture (about 500–50 B.C.) were the chariot warriors who made their way from what is now Switzerland, across Europe, and into the British Isles.

Those chariot-warrior Celts who migrated first took a more southerly route, some of them settling in France and Spain, in regions called Gaul by the Romans. Others proceeded into Ireland, Scotland, and the Isle of Mann to become what we now call the Gaelic, or Gallic Celts. Those ox cart Celts who migrated later took a more northerly route, many of them settling along the way across northwestern Europe. Others went into Wales and Cornwall to become what we now call Britons, or Brythonic Celts. Later, some of these Britons migrated back to France to establish themselves in Brittany, as the Bretons.

In the process of this migration, the Celts spread their culture across nearly all the European continent and the British Isles. As they did, they brought with them their sacred deities, the Earth Mother and the Sky, or Tribal, Father. While these two distinct god forms were interwoven with attributes reflecting the varied aspects of Nature, there seems to have been a profoundly simple form upon which the foundations of Celtic spirituality were constructed.

All female deities were the reflections of one Earth Mother goddess, yet her most mutually shared form was that of the triple goddess, *Les Trois Matres*. The male gods all had the qualities and attributes necessary for the needs of the tribe. The shared god form was called All-Father, or *Dis Pater,* by the Romans. However, Roman understanding of the essentially nonhierarchal Celtic gods was influenced by their own belief in an organized pantheon of Greco/Roman gods.

It would perhaps be more appropriate to view the Celtic gods as we view the Celtic tribes—as a confederation. These deities arose from Nature, personifying the forces of Nature. They were there to protect, defend, and empower the people with the qualities they needed most as Celts.

When we consider the flexibility of these ancient Celtic god-forms we can begin to see how a character such as Arthur could take on the qualities of both a Celtic tribal god, guardian of the tribes, and a newly energized syncretic god, a Solar Lord of Light. This becomes even more understandable when we know that Lugh (also Llew, Llud, or Lugos), the shared Celtic god of Light, represented a solar active, sun king god. He was consort of the Earth Mother, who was, in turn, consort to him. All in all, it appears to have been a fairly egalitarian situation—as is the way of Nature.

When we begin to see Arthur as a Celtic Lord of Light in relationship to the Sovereign Lady of Nature (in her many aspects), we also begin to comprehend how the Arthurian legends reflected this ancient spiritual alliance. Indications of this are found in stories of Arthur in relationship with women throughout the legends. That there are far more aspects of women in these myths than is generally known will be discussed in later chapters. They, too, have managed to shine the light of their nature through the dark shadows of misconceptions cast on them by an Eastern desert Orthodoxy that held women, and Nature, in very low esteem.

That Arthur's knights were, in their own way, reflections of the qualities of the Celtic tribal gods is also a point that we may consider to be a Celtic, encoded process. For now, we can begin to consider the more recent form of the Celtic confederation of gods. We can briefly introduce the sacred images currently reverenced by those more modern Celts seeking to connect with the Light and with the Land as the inseparable alliance that we may call the Divine Source.

The goddess, in her three aspects, reflects as Maiden, Mother, and Crone. These are the primary forms of the Earth's seasons, the cycles of the moon, and the cycles of a woman's life. The god forms two basic aspects, the Solar King or Lord of Light, and the Otherworld Lord of Mystery and Shadow, also called the Dark, tanist, wizard. When we understand that "Dark" does not imply negative here, but mysterious, we can begin to see how the figure of The Merlin may relate to Arthur. Arthur is the extroverted energy; up front and obvious. The Merlin is the introverted energy; behind the scenes and subtle. Together, they reflect a mythic balanced polarity that echoes the active forces in Nature—and, of course, in self-nature, as our next section will explore.

The section we have just completed should help you begin to see how the Arthurian myths evoke the deep tribal consciousness of the Celts—and the deeper consciousness of Nature. As we proceed through this book together, I will point out these connections ... but not always. To do so would prevent you from making those discoveries on your own. This exploration of the realms of the Camelot legends is also a quest for you. It isn't all just in the lessons. It's in the experiencing.

I'll close this section of the chapter with a guided imagery exercise that will provide you with a useful item for your quest through this text (there will be others later, as well; I promise). You may make this exercise as ceremonial or as casual as you choose, and, of course, you may keep indefinitely the gift it brings to you.

THE PENDRAGON'S EGG
An Activation Catalyst Imagery

Take a long, slow, deep breath. Now, slowly release your breath, and pause for a moment before you breathe—deeply—again. Repeat this sequence several times until you feel yourself becoming relaxed and receptive. Let your thoughts and expectations float away as you free your mind for an inner quest.

———

You are climbing up a rugged cliff rising majestically from an untamed coastline. Beneath you the sea waters swirl in shades of blue, green, and gray. You can feel cold spray just reaching your feet as large ocean waves splash against the cliff on which you are climbing, steadily upward. The rock face of the cliff is cool and damp, but not slippery. There are many small crevasses created by ages of wave action. You use these to make your climb with ease—moving steadily and securely upward.

Near the top of the cliff you find an especially large crevasse, more like a cave, really, which is large enough for you to enter. As the Western Sun is moving slowly into the sea, its rays slant into the cave, illuminating your vision.

One sharp ray of sunlight falls upon an oval object about the size of your head. It is an egg of some sort, covered with a complex design of dots, lines, and swirls. It is almost the color of the rocks upon which it rests, so you do not notice at first that it is shaking slightly.

You reach out to steady the egg and it begins rocking harder. Concerned that the egg might rock off its position and fall into the sea, you pick it up. You find the surface is smoother than it looks—and it feels soft, more like leather than shell.

The egg is fairly light and flexible. As you examine it more closely, you find on one side the surface appears to be peeling away in layers. You glimpse something through a tiny opening that reaches down through all of the layers.

You are compelled to make the opening larger. Carefully, you peel through the layers of the egg until you can reach what is waiting for you inside.

As you reach the inner chamber of the egg, you are surprised to find inside it a long, cylinder-shaped object—somewhat like a wand. As you pull the object out of the egg, you see it is covered with flat round disks, each with something written in small print beneath. Holding the object up to the light, you can see clearly that it is a remote control, with buttons indicating, according to your own design, what the functions of this truly magick "wand" are for you.

Looking back at the egg, you see a small, narrow strip of paper sticking out of the opening you have created. On the paper are words, also written in very small print. The sunlight in the cave is sufficient for you to make them out: "Whosoever carries the weight of too many expectations upon their head shall soon find themselves with egg on their face."

Taking the remote control and the message along, you make your way out of the cave and down the cliff. When you have reached a place where the ground is level and the sea is calm, you exit this landscape in your inner vision. All the while you wonder—but try not to expect—what you will do with what you have found.

CHAPTER 2

LIGHT AND SHADOW REFLECTIONS OF THE LEGENDS

Where do we place Arthur? Malory believed he lived in the fifth century since he had Galahad take the Siege Perilous in 454 after the birth of Christ. He then proceeded to put his knights in fifteenth century armor and impose twelfth–thirteenth century codes of knighthood against a curious depopulated and ruined countryside which reminds us of England after the first plague and ruined as the Wars of the Roses made it.

John Steinbeck,
The Acts of King Arthur and His Noble Knights
(New York: Farrar, Straus and Giroux, 1977)

While it is probable that there are a few, it is possible there are no truly restricted access channels to images of myth and realms of wisdom. All that is required is a Light exploratory attitude and the right "remote control," as you have now. So we begin.

It is from within the realms of our own mind that we may explore the Mystical Mind of the All. Bearing this in mind, let's turn our attention back to that magick remote control wand which you found inside the Pendragon's Egg in the last chapter. Realizing the remote control is a visual image, you may now "see" what possibilities it may bring into view within your inner vision.

We'll start our exploration of this with a visual imagery exercise. This exercise will allow you to "see" what you already know, and what you are still learning in a newly compiled form—like a movie. In this case, the material for your inner movie has been developed—"docu-mentally."

RECLAIMING THE LIGHT
A *Visual Imagery Exercise*

For this exercise, I want you to imagine yourself inside a theater of inner vision in which there is a wide screen. Later you may wish to make this screen surround you, cycloramically. For now, I'd like you to make this a flat screen. The images I will be presenting will flash by quickly. When you repeat this exercise, you may freeze-frame these images and explore them in greater depth. For now, please let them flow by freely. Also, you will need to turn up your visual perception channels, and turn down the distractions of sound, taste, touch, and smell. You may turn these up later as experiential amplifiers when you choose to repeat the exercise or explore specific aspects that caught your eye.

Breathe deeply and release your breath slowly; repeat, pausing briefly before inhaling and before exhaling in order to focus your mind. Repeat this breathing sequence until you are relaxed and receptive to your inner vision.

Breathe naturally and focus on the screen within the theater of your mind.

———

A title emerges on the screen. It says: "The Journey of Reclamation." The title fades and is replaced with clear images of Arthurian times. As these are personal images, take a moment to view them on your own. Note the aspects of your Arthurian images as they emerge for you now. These may change as you explore the realms of the Camelot legends.

Now, breathe deeply and release your Arthurian images. Let the images fade away into gray. For a time there are only undefined, misty shapes on the screen. You may wonder if your inner movie is already over.

Then, suddenly, you see lights emerging onto the screen. You are presented with images of Medieval times:

Castle fortresses with dragon banners flying; a tournament of champions in progress.

Colorful pavilions surround the castle. Ladies in long dresses—rainbow hues. Knights jousting on the field, wearing their ladies' colors. Shields with images of dragons, boars, and others;

personalized for you.

A royal court, illuminated by the light of the Sun, a glorious day in Nature—for Nature.

The scene glitters, then fades away to black. New images emerge in darker tones—some only in black and white. The images are dark and light briefly; then the dark images dominate the screen and you see the following:

Monks in dismal cells writing and rewriting on scrolled paper, using dark feathered quill pens, with only a single candle to guide the lines.

Black-robed bishops arguing among themselves as they feast at a richly laden table. From time to time, they imperiously throw scraps toward the scullery.

Peasants working on barren land, wearing rags tied to their feet. Meager threads make up their woven clothes, little protection against the constant cold of the times.

Dark skies and ominous clouds over crumbling castle forts. Knights imprisoned within their own walls.

Lords and ladies unknown to each other, matched for wealth and power.

Battle scenes prevail. Red-cloaked cardinals question simple friars in an ornate hall hung with costly and rare tapestries.

Knights Templar—red crosses on white across their hearts. Crusader knights from many clans parade across the screen. A great queen rides with her king on Crusade.

The images fade away to gray. For a moment the screen is blank and dark. then the images emerge again, slightly unfocused in a dim light.

A gentle Oxford cleric presents a manuscript to a wise, wealthy British Earl. The light brightens on the screen and an image emerges clearly.

A gift for Britain, Aquitaine of France confers with her Courts of Love. Another courtly cleric writes stories for that great queen's daughters.

For a brief moment, the images are illuminated by a lovely light. Then darkness advances onto the screen with a vengeful force. Fortunately, the images flash by swiftly.

Black-robed bishops and red-cloaked cardinals in secret meetings. Richly jeweled fingers point in accusation. Gold and silver gleam greedily in this gathering.

A shadow darkly steals onto the screen. Plague and despair beset the lands. The Spanish Inquisition reigns. Fires of hell and heresy turn the dark sky blood red.

The image fades to black. It seems as though there is nothing on the screen for a long time. Looking closer, you see tiny lights emerging like stars twinkling from very far away. Then patterns of light form quickly and the images race by in a flowering of Light.

The Renaissance bursts forth onto your screen in bright living colors. Nature reveals herself in a bountiful rainbow of rebuilding.

Kings and queens unite and depart from each other, disregarding the dogmas of the Dark Orthodox. A catalyst queen loses her head; ravens come to roost in the Tower of London.

Courageous men write words of truth, and the people of their lands rise in support. The Reformation comes like a double-edged sword. Queens clash, and the holy flame of Scotland is extinguished.

For a time the images are divided and unbalanced. New lands are discovered and disputed.

Revolutions of Light sweep across the screen. Declarations of independence. Reorganizations of rulerships. Human rights, as yet, too new. Societies restructured.

The images sweep through on the screen of your inner theater—illuminating images of the present preview the future.

For a while you let these flow freely and note the patterns where they have repeated themselves. A lovely flow of gentle Nature images moves across your screen and you watch for a while until you decide it is time to return to the Light of the present day. Inside, the movie continues.

Breathe deeply. Release slowly.

Remember your remote control wand? Use it to change the channel to the present day and time. Return to a realization of your Self, where you are now. Breathe naturally.

For future reference: if an imagery or a journey into vision ever "sweeps you off your feet" and you need to feel more grounded; get up and move around, change locations, change your mindset. "Turn off the inner movie and go play outside," as Mother Nature would say. "Work with the Earth."

THE TIMES AND THE LEGENDS

This chapter ends with a general outline of the approximate times and factors that were instrumental in the development of the Camelot legends. I'll take notes for you—this time.

1500 B.C.–A.D. 500 The Celtic Expansion, particularly into the British Isles.
> A. Celtic natural and spiritual philosophies: especially that of the guardian Lord of Light and the deities of Nature spread westward across Europe.

100 B.C.–A.D. 600 A.D. The merging of Roman, Celtic, and Christian philosophies, both during and after Roman rule.
> A. The brief united peace of Britain celebrates Arthur.
> B. The stories of Arthur emerge in the oral tradition.

A.D. 600–1100 The restrictive oppression of Eastern Orthodoxy begins in 900 to influence Europe, and then Britain.
> A. The Arthurian legends remain underground, or under the veil of accepted doctrines.

A.D. 1100–1300 The Courts of Love and Chivalry emerge in France.
> A. The Norman conquest of England gives rise to the Arthurian troubadours.
> B. Reaction to Orthodox oppression brings a flowering of romance, personal value, and respect for the rights of love and choice.

A.D. 1300–1500 The Dark Times and the Reformation.
> A. Orthodox reaction to the ideas of Courtly Love and Chivalry changed some of the legends. Sides are drawn in this medieval "media" war.
> B. Religious persecutions result from the clash between natural, Celtic philosophies and arbitrary structures of Eastern thought.
> C. Divisions in religion were first sign of choice (even in chaos).

A.D. 1500–1800 The Renaissance and Ages of Revolutionary Explorations.
> A. The Light of European consciousness reemerged.
> B. Printing presses, and more freedom of expression allowed greater expansion of the Arthurian legends.

    C. New lands, new nations, new independences and new rights continue
       emerging.

A.D. 1800–Present The New Renaissance, expanded reason, consciousness, and
awareness begin.
    A. Ecological awareness reconnects people to Nature.
    B. Global consciousness connects people to each other, to others' mythologies
       and philosophies—*and to their own.*
    C. Greater spiritual expansion and explorations of Self lead to a new accep-
       tance of the many Ways of Light. An Age of Light draws from a clear
       horizon. Another cycle is progressing.

I will close this chapter with a few comments on the "common standard" forms
of the Camelot legends. In the next chapter, we will explore their themes and discover a powerful, ancient pattern within the realms of the Camelot legends.

There are countless themes within the Camelot legends that shine through to
each of us, clearly illuminating our individual perception of what they represent.
Not only do these legends enlighten us, they reflect us like spiritual mirrors. They
represent us, in our many aspects. Some are direct and straightforward; reflecting
our strengths and vulnerabilities. Other forms of these legends are ornately embell-
ished with symbolic overlays, obstructing our view with confusing meaningless
diversions. Still others are two-way, veiled and smoked, presenting us with a deceptive reflection.

Some are simple. Some are silly. Some are sneaky.

Many are fine and beautiful as befits a magnificent mythology.

When we look at these legends from a cultural and mythological point of view,
their various styles begin to have more meaning for us as individuals. When we wish
to see their mystical, spiritual, and psychological significance, we have to look
beyond the styles and find their true Spirit. When we can recognize the simple, direct
reflections, ignore the fancy overlays, and make faces at the not-so-subtle messages
evangelically presented through the legends to us, we can see the mythic themes
more naturally.

The Camelot legends portray the cycles of Nature and personal nature. They
reflect the elemental aspects of our lives, in alliance with Nature to empower our personal quest.

Many of these myths depict their characters—and thus our characters—as
brutish barbarians or simple-minded seekers, stuck in endless patterns with no purpose, from which they cannot seem to escape. These depictions are far more representative of the times of disorder in which they were designed than valid
descriptions of Celtic cultural and tribal characteristics during the times the legends
claim to describe. Had we been as evolutionarily debased as some forms of the myths

maintain, we would be nothing more than a memory now, or a reference in some volume on evolution:

Celts: the descendants of a mutant offshoot species, too savage and too stupid to survive; now extinct.

Just as not every man in the wild, wild West was a hired gun, not every man in Arthurian times was quick to swing a sword or throw a lance simply because he encountered someone he did not know. Far too many legends present these men as mindless and aggressive killing machines—in the forests, in the courts, in the enchanted castles, or even on the tournament fields.

Just as not every woman in Biblical times was a deceptive Jezebel, not every woman in Arthurian times was determined to tempt or seduce or to entrap their prey by means of dark sorcery. In most of the legends the depictions of women are little more than politically contrived, accusational portrayals. Adverse effects are still being felt as Western Celtic women seek to reclaim their natural gifts of power. Because of modern women's research, and evolution, great strides have been made in changing the way the women of Camelot are presented. This in turn has allowed for a more balanced expression of the men to emerge in current versions of these legends. For the most part, though, the women are still shown as either pale and weak, or dark and "witchy"... in the forests, in the courts, in the enchanted castles, or even in the more gentle playing fields of the bedchambers.

The last seventy years have seen continuing intense activity in the reworking of the Arthurian Stories. In many ways, they have taken the place of the classical (Greco-Roman) myths which once dominated European literature.

Richard Barber
The Arthurian Legends: An Illustrated Anthology
(USA: Littlefield, Adams and Co., 1979)

CHAPTER 3

THE ELEMENTAL THEMES OF THE CAMELOT LEGENDS

An important point to bear in mind in studying Arthurian Legend is that each force, or human character, is presented in the round, not as an ideal archetype of perfection, but as a pattern ...

Gareth Knight
The Secret Tradition in Arthurian Legend
(Northhamptonshire, England: Aquarian Press, 1983)

 Joseph Campbell, the incomparable mythologist and self-described "storyteller" stresses that the two greatest themes in Arthurian mythos are those of: Courtly Love—which brought forth the right of individuals to choose, for themselves, specifically in regard to "matters of the heart," which are the most personal "issue of life"; and The Grail—which restores the individual's right to connect with the "divine power operative" within "each of our hearts" and personally reach "that vessel of inexhaustible vitality" by virtue of our own spiritual quests.

The themes of Courtly Love and of The Grail are undoubtedly important in the evolutionary reclamation of Western independent consciousness and personal choice. It is likely that we could fit all the themes in the Arthurian myths under those two categories alone. In a truly current mode, we also see Courtly Love as Rights of Alliance, and The Grail as Personal Quest. Other themes emphasized by Arthurian scholars are those of Otherworld, (or Fey) encounters, and those of Sovereignty, the Goddess of the Lands. Others stress those themes having to do with the numerous battles, usually personal and internal, and wars that are more tribal and external. Still others value the mystical and esoteric themes within Arthurian lore.

Fortunately, these legends freely lend themselves to individual interpretations of their themes. This quality of clearly mirroring meaningfulness reflects the heart of the wonder found within these Arthurian Wonder Tales.

THE PATTERN OF THE CAMELOT LEGENDS

This system of representing the elemental themes of the legends is based on active imagery with them and research into the intricate realms they represent. I hoped to develop a system that could work with the myths' archetypal images to encourage spiritual and psychological growth. In doing so, I came to understand the importance of seeing these legends as a whole pattern, first and last. This gestalt viewpoint is important for working on personal, spiritual, or psychological issues. A positive view about the whole of any pattern is fundamental to seeing the parts positively as well.

The Camelot legends are like an ancient mythic tapestry created using personally unique threads in order to preserve the pattern of our collective culture.

Most simply put, the Camelot legends represent an alliance of all the elements of Nature, and, therefore, self-nature. When the elemental woven themes within these legends are explored, we will better understand the elemental themes of our lives.

Remember the list of "Aspects of Legend, Myth, and Humankind" in the first chapter? The Tapestry of Camelot, as we may call its collective legends, is woven from all those aspects, as well as others of which we may not yet be evolutionarily aware. It is a Western, Celtic tapestry in style, but its threads are spun from fibers shared by all. It is a tapestry of life woven according to a pattern representsing All of Life, the specifics, the generalities, and that which is Universal.

Since we will continue to explore the Arthurian themes throughout this book, I will begin with some basic categories. You can use these as the grid on which you may build structures for your own system of understanding these hallowed legends.

The Circle of Camelot—Categories and Directions

You may wish to chart these themes on a large piece of paper and add to the chart as we continue on our course. Start by drawing a very big round circle (see chart on page 20). In the center, put the first—and foremost—theme; then proceed:

1. Arthur—in the Center
2. Merlin—in the East
3. Battles—in the South
4. Avalon—in the West
5. Camelot—in the North

Encircle your circle with:

6. Sovereignty—the Circle encircling

Now, we'll go around again, Sunwise, like our Solar King, Arthur.

7. Otherworld—SE
8. Hallows—ESE
9. Courtly Love—SW
10. Quests—WSW

11. Grail—NW
12. Lands—WNW
13. Round Table—NE
14. Chivalry—ENE

And around again, for the third time:

15. Forests—SSE
16. Isles—SSW

17. Caves—NNW
18. Castles—NNE

Finally, we mark off the quarters like so:

N–E = Winds
E–S = Flames

S–W = Mists
W–N = Tides

The Elemental Themes

1. Arthur—Center—Ether
2. Merlin—East—Air
3. Battles—South—Fire

4. Avalon—West—Water
5. Camelot—North—Earth
6. Sovereignty—The Circle—Spirit

Although you are working on paper just now, you will find that working with Arthur in personal ceremonial circles has some interesting effects, especially at first. Arthur (ether) has a powerful archetypal quality that makes him a very magnetic energy point, due to his widespread recognition, and our feelings of kinship to him.

This magnetism does not change in the sense of decreasing. It does become more balanced by increased familiarity with the other archetypal characters on their themes. Your experiencing this will explain it far more effectively in your personal work. What this means, for now, is that the magnetism of the solar/royal archetypal force that is Arthur will place him naturally in the center of your circles. This is so, regardless of where you may have thought you placed him in the first place.

Camelot Themes, Aspects, and Elements

1. Arthur—The activating key for your ideals: primary activator of all the themes; catalyst for the realization of ideal-self; energizer of self-potential through aspects of self, represented by the themes and their elemental energies.

2. Merlin—East—Air: The Evolutionary Illuminator: energies for abstracting knowledge and wisdom from experience, even when there is chaos; stimulation of brain and intellect; development of personal philosophies.

3. Battles—South—Fire: Training and Guardianship: energies for developing strength, will, faith, courage, self-motivations, and drive; experiences of self-purification for physical improvement; intensifies personal, environmental awareness. (Makes you sharp to what's happening around you. You have to be sharp in battle, you know.)

4. Avalon—West—Water: The Healing Initiators: energies for gaining wisdom from within yourself; deepening of intuition, psychic skills, and dream interpretation; experiences of healing through cycles of release and renewal; clears the flow for ceremonial and journey quests.

5. Camelot—North—Earth: Connection and Manifestation: energies for the practical application of wisdom and knowledge; establishes personal systems for empowerment, rank, position, and prosperity; experiences of kinship with the mundane and the mystical, connecting the self with the sacred; brings form to ritual purposes and designs.

6. Sovereignty—Spirit—The Circle: Synthesis: the supportive alliance of all aspects and elements of Nature and self-nature; evolutionary environmental attunement; experiences of Grace, acceptance of legacies, heritage, and destinies designed for the greater good of all; path of service, physical preservation and spiritual partnership with the land.

Note: You may choose also to draw an additional circle or two, or several, beyond the Circle of Sovereignty. These may represent your spiritual philosophies and views of the extended realms, such as planetary, stellar, and universal. My service is to the Sovereignty of the Lands. I'm here for Mother Nature, and I'm willing to leave the esoteric realms for someone else to explain. I refer simply to the extended, endless circle which we cannot truly explain. I see this as the reflective Source from which Light emerges and returns. (Creator, Creatrix—Heavens Above). We have a lot of names for that which we cannot seem to define mutually.

The Supportive and Symbolic Themes

The next twelve themes are not primary; nor are they secondary in their significance. I call them the supportive and symbolic themes. They support the primary purpose of our spiritual evolution and give us symbolic keys to the patterns or paths we may choose to follow. They are also supportive, in that they symbolize the processes involved in being human. I will not discuss these in depth yet. My intention in introducing the elements and aspects of the primary themes is to make you more aware of the messages that are found in—and have been written into—the myths. For now, just a little bit more on these themes.

The Supportive Themes—Concepts and Aspects

7. Hallows—ESE: The Sacred Gifts of Power, representations of natural potentials and powers.

8. Otherworld—SE: The Catalyst Allies, mystical guidance from elemental domains.

9. Courtly Love—SW: The Choices of the Heart, emotional responses from the individual psyche.

18

10. Quests—WSW: The Perilous Searches, developmental processes of personal transformation.

11. Grail—NW: The Vessels of Restoration, representations of inner resources and abilities.

12. Lands—WNW: The Changing Terrain, reflective developments in the forms of personal growth.

13. Round Table—NE: The Honorable Order, unified qualities of wisdom, philosophy, and intellect.

14. Chivalry—ENE: The Codes of Conduct, systems representing that which is right and ethical.

The Symbolic Themes—Settings and Aspects

15. Forests—SSE: Perceptive images and experiences of the natural environment.

16. Isles—SSW: Intuitive impressions and experiences of the inner realms of consciousness.

17. Caves—NNW: Shamanic visions and experiences connecting natural and supernatural wisdom.

18. Castles—NNE: Structures and systems of knowledge, experiences of bringing form to wisdom.

The Themes of the Quarters—Natural Actions

N–E = Winds: Directional shifts in attitudes, philosophy, perceptions of Mind and conscience.

E–S = Flames: Inspirational catalysts for creative development, actions of Mind/Body.

S–W = Mists: Intuitive experiences of Self for transformational healing of Body and Emotions.

W–N = Tides: Efforts to work with the natural cycles and patterns of life to establish structures of Self, Mind/Body/Emotions.

The Circles: Within and Encircling—Lines of Power

Center—Arthur: Catalyst core of individual self, personal potentials, and experiences.

The Circle encircling—Sovereignty: Harmonic attunement with natural, environmental energies of the Earth (dragon lines).

Extended Circles—Source: Spiritual influences, essential creative life forces, Universal Light, illuminator of all Life, the Divine.

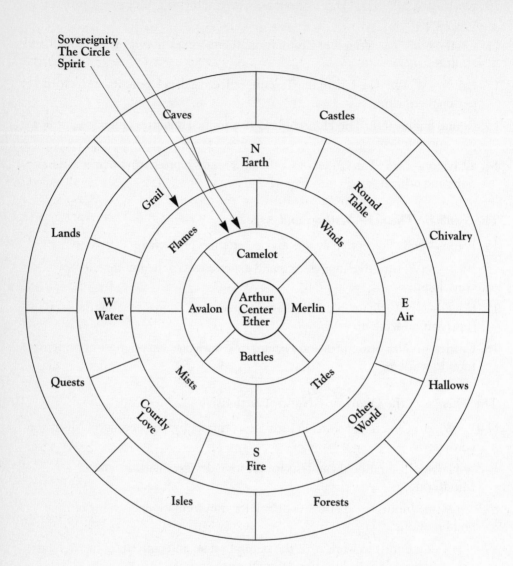

Sovereignity
The Circle
Spirit

Caves

Castles

N
Earth

Round
Table

Grail

Winds

Lands

Flames

Chivalry

Camelot

W
Water

Avalon

Arthur
Center
Ether

Merlin

E
Air

Battles

Mists

Tides

Quests

Courtly
Love

Other
World

Hallows

S
Fire

Isles

Forests

The Circle of Camelot

If this all seems like a very complex collection of themes, remember that it represents a very complex process. That process is the evolution of the nature of Western, Celtic mind and consciousness. All you really need to know for working with this now is in the first list of themes: The Circle of Camelot encompasses Arthur, Merlin, Battles, Avalon, Camelot, and Sovereignty. All the rest of the themes are encoded within those primary aspects, as you may have guessed.

Besides, we have only just begun this expedition, questing through the realms of the Camelot legends. Your explorations thus far have made you familiar already with the central theme, Arthur, and the encircling theme, which is the Circle of Sovereignty. Familiarity with the rest, with all the rest, will come as we continue our quest.

For the time being, you may wish to use the sets of themes—elemental, supportive, and symbolic—to stimulate active personal images for yourself. Consider what these represent in your own life and mind. Be positive. Express your experiences as the early authors of the Camelot legends expressed their own evolutionary images. Make yourself your truest evolutionary ally.

I'll close this chapter with an assignment that I believe you will enjoy. It is an exercise that can be as experiential as you choose. I suggest you try it once, even if you feel that you don't have enough information. There is also a homemade version of the "Right wise Borne, true King" story in the appendices if you want a convenient reference.

THE SWORD IN THE STONE
An Experiential Exercise

Here are the historical grid lines on which you may design your own version of how Arthur pulled the sword from the stone and was proclaimed the "Right-wise, true-born King of all Britain."

First: An historical fifth-century (A.D. 400s) British warlord, called Artorius, Dux Bellorum, Comtes Britannarium, was credited with having unified the warring factions of the inhabitants of Britain for a period of three or four decades. During that time, the birth of Britain, as it is known, was made possible by the caliber of that warlord (Arthur in Celtic form), and the superior quality of his weaponry and methods of warfare.

How would you, in bardic, druidic fashion, craft a tale that links the ancient rights and/or rites of kingship to this heroic warrior? Imagine that you will have to tell your version to other people and teach it to other bards, as well. How else do you suppose the oral traditions accomplished their tasks and their purposes?

Second: These are the primary, elemental themes that you need to give your version the "whole-story," balanced pattern it needs to survive and to thrive.

1. Arthur—Ether
2. Merlin—Air
3. Battles—Fire

4. Avalon—Water
5. Camelot—Earth
6. Sovereignty—Spirit

You may use these elements in whatever proportions you choose, so long as they all are represented in your Wonder Tale about this mythic yet historical king, Arthur. You may use any of the supportive and symbolic themes presented earlier in this chapter. If you are so inclined, you may also refer to my version, "The Right-Wise Born, True King," in the appendices.

Naturally, you are free to use your own mind and will to create this version. If these themes aren't reflective of your images, use your own elemental images, or include others that you prefer. Also, if you have a particular philosophical message to convey, you may weave that into the pattern, as well. Enjoy yourself being a bard.

CHAPTER 4

THE MYTHS AND LEGENDS
IN THE ROUND

*Peoples throughout the world accept their sacred tales, or myths, as a statement
of a primeval, greater and more relevant reality by which the present life, fates
and activities of mankind are determined, the knowledge of which supplies man
with the motive for ritual and moral actions, as well as with indications as to
how to perform them.*

Alwyn and Brinley Rees
Celtic Heritage: Ancient Tradition in Ireland and Wales
(London: Thames and Hudson, 1991)

Because we are a balance of both linear and nonlinear, our cultural
philosophies and myths invariably reflect a continual balancing of the
linear and the nonlinear. We may also call this a balance of the probable and the improbable, and of the literal and the symbolic—a catalyst for both our linear, structured and our non-linear, creative
aspects. This is one reason why myths are evolutionarily important to our development; individually and collectively. Legends and myths emerge to express or explain
aspects of Life.

The input of legends and myths causes us to make personal associations with
their similar aspects in our lives. From this process of association, we accept or reject
the mythic messages presented to us in the forms of legends and wonder tales. What
we accept, we then integrate, or incorporate, in our minds.

Due to this process of integrating mythic messages and meanings, we are able to
select our actions and reactions. The output of actions and thoughts results from the
processes of input, association, and, in particular, the process of integration. We

choose based upon what we believe. We believe based upon what we perceive. We perceive based upon what we experience. We are guided, constantly, by myths we don't even think we know.

We experience the mundane aspects of life as a rational, linear, and concrete reality. We experience the mystical as a revelational, non-linear, and flowing or abstract reality. Both are essential, as both are reflected in myth and legend; we are also guided constantly by a blend of the mundane and the mystical, bringing meaning to our lives even if we don't always remember to be aware of it. We know this to be true. When you think about this, you can see what an amazing and mythic process this is— quite naturally.

It is perhaps more important for us, in modern times, to understand clearly this process than it was for our Celtic ancestors. The Celtic spiritual philosophies were already based upon their acceptance of the connection between the mundane and the mystical. Much of our current spiritual philosophy has been indoctrinated with the separatist philosophy of the Eastern, desert Orthodoxy.

However, we are shaking off the effects which have been limiting to us, and we're recalling what we had thought was forgotten. We're doing this at an impressive rate, too. What we are remembering now, our ancestors could not have conceived of forgetting, because it represented an inseparable alliance to them. Their relationship with Nature was not something with which to question or barter. Nor was it dictated according to the needs of a structured Orthodoxy. Nature and Humankind were one—an alliance that our myths and legends continued to reflect—even in disguise.

If you're wondering how we managed to forget what we all once "knew," I'll give you an image to help you understand what happened. It's a comic image, making it all the more powerful, from Monty Python's "The Holy Grail," which was a brilliant, scathing parody reflecting our needs to keep all these factors in perspective, no matter how sacred or mysterious it may be.

It is a scene in a Dark Ages, poverty-stricken village. Plague has been on the land, and now it is a Wasteland. There is a procession of hooded monks trudging through the mud. Chanting in unison, they pause, and, in measured sequence proceed to hit themselves in unison with what look like books—or possibly stone tablets! And where do they hit themselves? Right in the middle of their forehead. There it would do the most good—orthodoxically speaking. This would shut down the areas of the brain that are the catalyst to enlightenment and evolution. This is the area the mystics call "the third eye," the physicians call the prefrontal lobe, and those who work with the mind call the point of synthesis. This is the point at which we evolve into knowledgeable, sapient, human beings.

Having given you those images, let me now proceed to tell you more about how I see the images and themes in the Camelot legends. I'll start by giving you a few more aspects of these themes which you may use in association with your own ideas and imagery work. Then from these you may create your own integrated philosophy about the meaning of these sacred myths. Of course, you have all the time you need for learning what you need from this. Work and experience can be shared or separated. Learn and enjoy at your own pace, by your own cycles. That is natural.

NATURAL CYCLES OF THE CAMELOT THEMES

The cycles of Nature and self-nature are clearly reflected in the pattern, or the round, of the Camelot legends. Although probably most of you are already familiar with the cycles of Nature, we'll review the concept briefly here. This is for those who may be coming into the study of these legends from spiritual traditions that do not utilize this particular round pattern of the wheel of Nature.

For the purposes of this round, we will begin in the East, the place of the Vernal, or Spring equinox. In the Celtic way, the beginning of Nature's cycle was more often seen as Samhain, or So'ween, which means summer's wane. This has come down to us in modern times as All Hallows Eve, Hallowmas, or Halloween, symbolizing the end of the growth cycle in Nature and the beginning of the fallow or dormant period of the next cycle. Thus the new year beginning, naturally. However, the East is a universal point of new beginnings—so we'll start there.

In most Arthurian literature, Arthur is depicted as taking the sword from the stone at Yule or at New Year's. This New Year could represent the old Celtic way; but more likely reflects the times in which the legends were told. Arthur is also said to have done this at Easter, or the Vernal Equinox, thereby assuming the title of King of All Britain. In both Christian and pagan traditions, this is the time of the Light resurrected. Therefore, the assumption of the kingship of Logres, the mystical Kingdom of Britain, is clearly presented in correlation with Nature.

The Cycles of the Wheel

First, we'll review the cycles, or the wheel of the year.

E—Spring Equinox/March 20 = time of renewal and rebirth of Light
SE—Beltane/May 1 = time of fertility, catalyst for growth.
S—Summer Solstice/June 21 = time of full growth, summer harvests
SW—Lammas/August 1 = time of first fall harvest, growth still
W—Autumn Equinox, September 23 = time of second harvest, growth slows to rest
NW—Samhain/October 31 = time of final harvest, fallow, rest starts
N—Winter Solstice, December 22 = time of Light, signaling promise of Spring
NE—Candlemas/February 2 = time of first growth, signals Spring

Next, let's take this 'round again; relating it to the primary pattern in the legends of Arthur. The cycles wheel is your key, naturally. Note: Remember it is the pattern, not the period, of time, which counts.

Arthur: 1st cycle

E—Arthur takes kingship in balance with Sovereignty
SE—Arthur takes Guinevere as Queen
S—Arthur battles to unify Britain
SW—Arthur rescues Guinevere from the Underworld lord
W—Arthur and Guinevere in balance; Camelot envisioned
NW—Arthur collects knights for errantry and guardianship
N—Arthur creates Camelot as a manifest alliance
NE—Arthur and his knights form the Round Table Order

Note that SW or Lammas/August 1 is the time the last rays of the strong summer sun enter the Earth's atmosphere and bring the full force of solar energies to the crops so they may come to harvest. Mythically, the Solar King sacrifices himself to bring forth the "fruits" of the Earth Mother Goddess, the Sovereign Queen of the Land. In the original legends, it was Arthur who rescued Guinevere from Melwas, the "underworld" lord, King of the Summer Country, who had abducted her. In later versions it was Lancelot who rescued Guinevere—and we know what that led to.

Next, we go 'round again, adding Lancelot.

Lancelot: 1st cycle

E—Lancelot arrives at Camelot with a new vision of Chivalry
SE—Lancelot and Guinevere fall in love
S—Lancelot and Guinevere battle against temptation
SW—Lancelot rescues Guinevere from Melwas
W—Lancelot and Guinevere consummate their mutual dream
NW—Lancelot retreats from Camelot to avoid dishonoring Arthur
N—Lancelot quests for another source or order to follow
NE—Lancelot returns from his failed quest to renew with Guinevere

And again, to show the cycle of destruction that follows in the legends of the wounded king and the Wasteland. These are the dark cycles; therefore they do not round off in natural order in the same way.

Lancelot and Guinevere: 2nd cycle

E—Lancelot and Guinevere are illuminated by mutual love
SE—Lancelot and Guinevere are together, King and Queen not "mated"
S—Lancelot and Arthur's internal battles result in weakened king
SW—Lancelot forced from Camelot, Guinevere retreats to nunnery
W—Time of Wasteland; quests for healing source of Grail begin
NW—Grail quests fail to balance; the power struggles begin
N—Camelot falls; Arthur is killed; the power is withdrawn
NE—Excalibur awaits the time of honor and emergence

This time we'll go back to the beginning of Arthur to show how this same round can work again more smoothly.

Merlin and Arthur: 1st cycle

E—Merlin envisions Arthur; Uther fixates on Igraine
SE—Uther and Igraine beget Arthur, using Merlin's plan
S—Battles for Uther due to Cornwall's death
SW—Arthur placed in the care of Merlin, then fostered to Sir Ector
W—Arthur is taught by The Merlin, whose identity is veiled
NW—Arthur finishes childhood lessons, begins training as a squire
N—Arthur pulls the sword from the stone, unaware of its meaning
NE—Arthur is reunited with The Merlin to prepare for a new role, and again, by returning to Avalon
E—Arthur officially assumes kingship, a new round begins

Now let's use this same 'round to represent the pattern of The Merlin from "fatherless child" to acknowledged, royal enchanter. For this pattern, we use the Muse-gifted works of Mary Stewart. I remind you again not to focus on the time period or span, but on the flow of the pattern. Few things take only a year in human time.

Merlin and Britain: 1st cycle

E—British king Vortigern assumes power with new concept of Saxon allies
SE—Ambrosius and Elaine beget Merlin before Ambrosius must flee
S—Merlin endures the stigma of being a "demon's whelp"
SW—Merlin finds the sanctuary of Galapas' (or Blaise's) cave
W—Merlin trains in magick with Galapas
NW—Merlin begins his quest, unaware he will find his father
N—Merlin is brought to Ambrosius and acknowledged
NE—Merlin returns to Britain to prepare for Ambrosius' coming

And again, still with Mary Stewart's visionary novels, but now also with other traditional versions of the legends included.

Merlin, Britain, and Arthur: 1st cycle.

E—Merlin taken to Vortigern, prophesies defeat for King's Fort
SE—Ambrosius returns to Britain, reunites with the land
S—Ambrosius is victorious; Vortigern is dead; Saxons have fled
SW—Merlin returns to the Hollow Hills to resume his magick
W—Merlin quests for knowledge after Ambrosius dies
NW—Merlin advises for King Uther, brother of Ambrosius
N—Arthur is born after Merlin arranged for his conception
NE—Arthur begins to develop under Merlin's supervision

Just to remind you of the nature of this pattern in terms of personal development and of a project or a plan, let's go around twice to show how this form follows these processes. I'll add the seasonal and elemental correlations to demonstrate this more clearly.

Developmental Cycles of Nature and Self-nature
E—Air—Spring: Childhood, development of perceptions, ideas
SE—Beltane: Adolescence, sexuality emerges
S—Fire—Summer: Young Adulthood, establishing independence
SW—Lammas: Still Young Adult, courtship, commitment, marriage
W—Water—Fall: Adulthood, internal growth, external responsibilities
NW—Samhain: Middle Age, quests for balance and personal meaning
N—Earth—Winter: Maturity, crest of personal power and position
NE—Candlemas: Old Age, awaiting time of rebirth in the Light

Developmental Cycles of Ideas, Plans, or Projects
E—Air—Spring: Perceptions of a situation create new ideas
SE—Beltane: Internal alliance, conception of a plan
S—Fire—Summer: Growth and development of the plan
SW—Lammas: Living in rapport with the plan
W—Water—Fall: Reevaluating, releasing, and renewing aspects of the plan
NW—Samhain: Questing for new aspects of the plan and profiting
N—Earth—Winter: Establishing the formula of the plan for others
NE—Candlemas: Emerging time of new offshoots of the plan

By now you should have the concept and the image of this round pattern fairly well encoded. I believe it was encoded in all of us from the beginning; tribally, culturally, and mythically reflected in these legends. That is why the legends evoke a sense of awe, even in those who aren't consciously aware of the what, the how, or the why of the impact upon their lives.

As a personal exercise for your own enlightenment, take some time to chart the progress of certain aspects, events, or even adventures in your life. This round pattern can give you valuable clues about your relationships: with yourself, with others, and with life in general. If something is not progressing as you think it should, perhaps you are at a point in the cycle where this would naturally be the case. Also, you may have missed a step along the way, or this may not be truly "in the plan" for you after all.

If you recognize you are on course, this can give you the motivation to continue, as well as the patience to wait things out if you have to. If you realize something really is not in the plan for you, there will be a lot less time spent wandering in the wasteland of personal uncertainty, or time and energies invested on someone else's path straying from your own.

If you determine you have skipped a step somewhere along the way, it's far better to realign with the pattern and put yourself consciously through the process that step represents. There's no disgrace in retracing your own steps, just as you do when you're trying to find something of yours that has "gone missing." If that something is a part of your self, you'll find you'll miss it eventually. You can continue on the course without that part of yourself that is missing, and you may fare well without it, for a cycle or two. However, this is like running an engine with a missing piston. You know it will run for a while, but will it go the distance?

Of course, I realize it is tough on the ego to admit you really haven't covered all the bases or points along the way, but it takes some quality to decide to do the right thing for your personal empowerment, regardless of how it may seem on the surface. There really is no such thing as backward progress. So long as you're moving forward in your own development, it doesn't matter how many remedial courses you may be required to take. Certainly, having to crawl again once you've begun to walk is difficult to take. However, how do you think it will be if you have to do it once you've not only begun to walk but are beginning to feel you can fly? Both may be accomplished with imagery—actively. It is your mind that you are developing, after all. The rest will follow suit. You may find that a "skipped step in a cycle" gives you more than just a little step up. When you learn to "step back" and assess what you need—you are empowering yourself, indeed.

Since the steps involved in the course of spiritual and magickal explorations are so intense in their impact on our lives, I'll chart a round of this for you to help clarify the need to stay with the pattern. It should also give you the patience to endure the low points, as well as the perspective to view the high points as just another part of the pattern.

Cycles of Esoteric Explorations

E—illumination, perceptions are sharpened, exciting ideas
SE—in-depth connection to the sacred rites, primal empowerment
S—internal struggles to guard your new power, isolation
SW—personal commitment to your spiritual choices or magick
W—inward progress, periods of healing, renewal, and sad release
NW—restoration of power through further quests for knowledge
N—practical application of wisdom, but the glitz is gone, boredom
NE—new growth of power signals new illumination, return of catalysts

Cycles of Camelot Consciousness

Now, let's translate that spiritual/magickal course into terms that reflect the pattern that is the round of the Camelot legends. This time you may start at the center with the following.

Arthur—or the Arthurian legends having been your initial catalyst
Center—Arthur: A sense of wonder, awe, and reverence
E—Merlin: connection to a wizardy, bardic current
SE—Otherworld: emergence of primal, stimulating images
S—Battles: sense of training for sacred service and guardianship
SW—Courtly Love: forming a personal alliance with the realms
W—Avalon: initiatory work and dreams of the Lands of Mystery
NW—Grail: questing within for empowerment through the images
N—Camelot: developing rituals and systems of connection
NE—Round Table: applying the codes of honor to your life, and again,
E—Merlin: becoming a part of the "time of doing," by envisioning your own path as
     an evolutionary catalyst

This chapter closes with another round, the twelfth, which is appropriate for Arthurian matters: first, for his aspect as the victor of twelve battles, King of all Britain, guardian of Sovereignty; next, for his stellar aspect as Arcturus, the Pole star guarding the axis mundi of the heavens, where the center of the universe is mythically said to connect with the world, and also for his mythic associations with that number.

> It is recorded that twelve kings were slain by Arthur's forces. Merlin by "his subtle craft" fashioned a complex of tombs, each with an effigy of a slain king holding a perpetual light. Above these he fashioned an image of Arthur with drawn sword in token of being vanquisher of them. This is confirmation of Arthur in the role of Solar hero, in the tradition of Hercules, having overcome the powers of the twelve constellations of the zodiac.
>
> Gareth Knight
> The Secret Tradition

The true and lasting victory of Arthur, and of his legends, is that they have overcome the overlays and the manipulations of others. Furthermore, they have done this by incorporating these, naturally, in a round pattern which we may use as guiding myths from Nature—for self-nature.

Arthur's Cycle of Mystical Power

Our last round will reflect a more decidedly pagan and druidic interpretation of the pattern. Accordingly, we will begin in the old way: at the point representative of Samhain, the Celtic new year. Appropriately, we will use the points "between the worlds" of the elemental, cardinal points. Reflecting this pattern with the twelve supportive and symbolic themes, we can begin to trace the evolutionary aspects blending the linear, historic events with the mystical, spiritual Arthur.

Twelve Supportive and Symbolic Themes in a Round

NW—Grail: Arthur as a vessel of restoration, reempowers the Sovereign lands that were weak and divided.

NNW—Caves: Arthur, as symbol of the ancient guardian from the times of the Cave Bear, begins to be connected with both natural and supernatural qualities.

NNE—Castles: Arthur brings the structures of shared leadership and the practical systems of laws and of guardianship for the lands.

NE—Round Table: Arthur develops a nonhierarchal organization, membership by meritorious service (errantry).

ENE—Chivalry: Arthur creates codes of honor and conduct, formulates the courtly ideals and duties.

ESE—Hallows: Arthur represents the one who has the power of the sacred gifts, the potential for the position.

SE—Otherworld: Arthur is shown to have mystical guidance from the realms of magick power, The Merlin.

SSE—Forests: Arthur shows courage entering the enchanted realms of Nature to defeat dangerous beasts.

SSW—Isles: Arthur willingly undertakes perilous voyages in order to retrieve healing resources for his kingdom and his people.

SW—Courtly Love: Arthur supports his knights in their choices of the heart, despite the dangers of opposition from others who made prior claims to the beloved; and, in some cases, he himself goes to rescue his own beloved.

WSW—Quests: Arthur supports his knights in their perilous searches for a source of restoration for themselves and for the land.

WNW—Lands: Arthur returns from his expansions abroad to face the troubled Wasteland and to try to change the ominous developments that have begun to affect the growth of his ideal vision. Upon failure to do this, Arthur has the sword of power returned to its source, lest it be misused. Then, mortally wounded in the mundane world, Arthur voyages through the veils into the mystical, healing realms of Avalon.

There, as the legend goes, Arthur waits in the healing care of the Avalonians for the time when his lands and his people will call him forth again—as they do—for the renewal of their individual and collective spirit. Until then, he comes in dreams and visions to those who journey inward to find him. Now that your grid has become a full patterned wheel—you are "surrounded" with resources from which to draw as catalysts for your personal empowerment and self-understanding.

Amplify your experience of these legendary realms by crafting with images from the 'round which are currently most charged, or familiar to you. Create imagery using your "remote control" and your inner vision. Try this with unfamiliar aspects next. You may find that you have far better reception than you expected! Feel free to reshape the legends positively for yourself, and for others. You may simply express them as you see them—as the bards did.

Elemental Aspects of the Legends

For your use in exploring the rounds, I have put together a list of the five elemental aspects present in the Arthurian legends. These aspects give clues to the types of action found in the legends, sometimes very subtly.

These five elemental aspects may or may not follow a sequence or a set pattern. Once again, it is the synthesis, not the set, which is the empowering quality found in the patterns. As long as all the elements are present, the pattern reflects the magick of synthesis. Regardless of what elemental proportions are represented, the power of the Arthurian "alchemy" remains potent for a very long time.

Fire—Flames: Catalyst for actions or characters that cause the adventure to begin or deepen, test, challenge, or sometimes provide resolution. Challenging environments, requiring faith, courage, and strength.

Water—Mists: Magickal, shamanic, or ceremonial experiences, mystical interventions, prophecies, and inner experiences such as dreams, reflections, visions or emotions. Veiled environments requiring intuition and attunement with the self and the place.

Earth—Tides: Structures and codes that determine the way the encounters are managed; also the conduct and the rank of the characters involved, symbols of wisdom, power, and position. Structured environments, requiring protocol and codes of behavior.

Air—Winds: Changes in mindsets, images, and perceptions; also information and knowledge, often abstracted from chaotic events, inspirations, and illumination from allies who may or may not appear "friendly" at first. Expanding environments requiring focus, natural, devic awareness, and clever uses of intellect.

Spirit (or Ethers)—Spirit: Deities of Nature and Spiritual realms, destiny, gifts and reflections of the Light, synthesis of all elements and aspects, highest potentials of receptivity, activation, and personal reflection. Transformational environments requiring spiritual awareness, acceptance, and purest sense of purpose.

Please note these are not always easy to identify as elementally separate from each other. This is because their synthesis creates an alchemy of power greater than the mere combination of the elements can be expected, determined, or even predicted to provide. As in the concept of the gestalt, the whole is greater than the sum of its parts.

CHAPTER 5

THE CAMELOT BARDS

... but the great legends, like the best of fairy tales, must be retold from age to age: there is always something new to be found in them, and each retelling brings them freshly and more vividly before a new generation—and therein lies their immortality.

Roger Lancelyn Green
King Arthur and His Knights of the Round Table (London: Penguin, 1953)

For the last three decades, there has been a great wealth of written material covering nearly every aspect of these timeless favorites, the Camelot legends. R. J. Stewart, in *The Prophetic Vision of Merlin* (New York: Routledge and Kegan Paul, 1986) estimated that "between 1965 and 1984 over eight thousand" volumes were published on "Arthurian subjects." He also reported the output of additional materials in plays, films, television, radio, and the like "reached such proportions that one successful film, 'Monty Python and the Holy Grail' was an outrageous parody of the genre." Perhaps the most important effect of this renewed interest in the subject has been the quest by many into the "deeper psychological, magical, and mystical aspects of Arthurian lore."

Even those authors whose original intentions were the more academic explorations or the retelling of the tales in a more modern manner have been deeply affected by the mystical power of the Camelot legends. One such author was John Steinbeck, whose works have made mythic quality contributions to the world of Western literature. John Steinbeck was literally a legend in his own time. Toward the end of his life, Steinbeck was working on a book which would "bring to present day usage the stories of King Arthur and the Knights of the Round Table." In 1958–59, that would have been a rare pearl to find.

As his primary source for research, Steinbeck used the medieval works of the author Sir Thomas Malory, who wrote *Le Morte d'Arthur*. The specific version Steinbeck used had been edited for Oxford by Eugene Vinaver in 1947. This was done from a much older text which dated from the 1480s, discovered at Winchester College in 1934. Vinaver's interpretation of the manuscript written by Malory in 1469–70 still represents the modern standard for the Arthurian legends.

Malory's work was originally called *The Whole Book of King Arthur and of His Noble Knights of the Round Table*. It is thought to be one of the greatest romantic creations ever written in English. The mutually held images of the Camelot legends had their origin in Malory, whose work, in turn, was taken from a mass of older works on the subject. These Malory had compiled into a somewhat more cohesive "whole book." John Steinbeck's book, *The Acts of King Arthur and His Noble Knights,* was written primarily in Somerset, England, in 1958–59, but it was not completed.

Instead, after Steinbeck's death in 1968, his editor, Chase, and his agent, ERO, combined the unfinished manuscript with a collection of letters written to them by Steinbeck while he was in England researching and writing his version of the Malory material.

From many of John Steinbeck's letters on the subject of *The Acts of King Arthur and His Noble Knights*, we can glimpse what he experienced while endeavoring to bring this transformative myth more clearly into the times in which he lived. We may also glimpse what that process entailed for those who came before Steinbeck, and also for those who in time will have quested to voice their understanding of these sacred legends and the sacred realms from which they emerged.

THE EVOLUTIONARY AUTHORS OF THE CAMELOT LEGENDS

The backgrounds of the legend lay in pagan, specifically Celtic, myth. Its heroes were the old champions, Cuchulain and the rest, returned in knightly armor as Gawain, Perceval, or Galahad, to engage, as ever, in marvelous adventure."

Joseph Campbell
Occidental Mythology: The Masks of God (New York: Viking/Penguin, 1984)

There is no question about the original Celtic sources of the Camelot legends. The oral traditions of Celtic tales, told for countless generations before the times of Arthur, were the primary lines that the original authors followed in order to express these myths in written form. Specifically, the Gaelic regions of Ireland and Wales, with their strong traditions preserving the "magic of the goddess of the land" in its "fairy lore" (as we call it today), gave rise to the forms of Arthurian literature.

*In the Middle Ages, the mystic spell of her ("the goddess of the land") people of
the fairy hills poured over Europe in the legends of the Table Round of King
Arthur, where Gawain, Tristan, and Merlin brought the old Celtic Fianna and
Knights of the Red Branch to life again in the armor of the Crusades.*

Joseph Campbell
Ibid.

Basically, what we have now in the Camelot legends is the result of the blended
expressions of the ancient oral traditions, the transcribed "monkish tales," the
medieval literary traditions, and the modern efforts of mythologists and mystically
inspired authors, reflecting the Muse. Or we can simply say: For what we have been
graced to receive may we truly bless the bards, the priests, the troubadours, and the storytellers of the once, future, and present times. Let us now proceed to point out a few
of these authors who made the most significant contributions to the creation of our
current images of these myths. Each writer built on the images of their predecessors.

We can trace clearly this current image to the works of an historical figure called
Geoffrey of Monmouth (a Welsh-Breton cleric) who wrote *The History of the Kings of
Britain* during the 1230s.

That this was an actual historical chronicle is undoubtedly untrue. That it was
a traditional Celtic-style account is true. Monmouth cited his sources in general as
the oral folklore from the Welsh traditions and specifically he gleaned "facts" from
a sixth century source, a monk called Mennius. Using these Welsh sources and his
own imagination, Monmouth literally created the legends. The myth was, naturally, already present.

Since Monmouth was endeavoring also to link his own monarch, Henry II, to
Arthur, his accounts emphasize the warrior and his heroic battles. This was not so
much a lie as it was a labor of love, romantically creating a starting point for a
history of Britain, while using the Celtic quasi-historical or histo-mythological style.

We can thank Geoffrey of Monmouth for bringing us the figures of The Merlin
(the symbolic image of Celtic druidism and spiritual philosophy) and that of Taliesen,
the quintessential bard. In Monmouth's other significant creation, *The Prophecies of
Merlin*, there are a number of undeniably accurate, prophetic accounts which are currently being interpreted by Arthurian scholars and authors.

Although Monmouth presents these prophecies as having come down from his
literary character, The Merlin, we must consider that they are also, in some part, the
precognitive visions of Geoffrey's own mind—undoubtedly connected to that line of
wisdom I like to call The Merlin Current.

Since Monmouth wrote in Latin, and the Norman French were then quite taken
with this idealized connection between Henry II and Arthur, a French version of the
legends was soon forthcoming from Robert Wace, an Anglo-Norman poet, who wrote
Roman de Brut (circa 1205) for Henry II and Eleanor of Aquitaine. Wace's work was
a vital link in the Arthurian literary chain because it was among the first to bring

Celtic tradition into French expression. Also, Wace used a wonderfully bardic format for his telling of these tales: in eight-syllable couplets. Naturally reflecting the images of his own times, Wace gave Arthur all the finest qualities found in a true Norman noble. Thus, Arthur moved from being a mythic-quality Celtic warrior hero to being a legendary Anglo-Norman lord. Arthur was not yet a king in the literary sense, at least not in the minds of the French. After all, they had their own historical king, Charlemagne, whose exploits had been quite mythic in their own right.

Wace, therefore, did not emphasize Arthur. However, Wace did bring into being that legendary symbol of unity and alliance—the Round Table. During the time (1150–1250s) that most of the Norman troubadours were telling these tales and others inscribing them, it was the Knights of the Round Table whose adventures interested them first. The Age of Chivalry had begun, the concept of Courtly Love was in full bloom when the first Anglo-Saxon version of these legends was created by Layamon, an Anglo-Saxon poet-priest, who wrote the *Brut* at the turn of the eleventh-twelfth century. Layamon used alliterative English verses to tell his version of these tales. His work was of divided benefit. On the one hand, Layamon showed a poetic pro-English attitude in regard to Arthur; on the other, a priestly, pro-Norman justification for the Norman conquest of England. Layamon saw it as punishment for the Anglo-Saxon invasions of Britain.

This type of writing with a "forked tongue" could well have been necessary in order for Layamon to slip in the mythic truths underneath the blatant, theo-dogmatic lies. However, Layamon did succeed in creating the legend of Arthur as the King of Britain. In doing that, Layamon reclaimed the Arthurian connection to ancient Celtic kingship and to the heroic Celtic traditions of tribal gods, as well.

> *While one thinks of Wace's adaptation of Geoffrey of Monmouth as a move toward courtly romance, one thinks of Layamon's adaptation of Wace as a move back toward a more heroic age.*
>
> Norris J. Lacy, Ed.
> *The Arthurian Encyclopedia* (New York: Peter Bedrick Books, 1986)

Whether inadvertently or with brilliantly subtle intentions, Wace succeeded in relinking the British mythic image with the elemental Celtic connections to the Sovereignty of the Lands. Since a poet-priest sounds decidedly druidic to me, I choose to believe the latter.

By that time in the evolution of the Camelot legends, the orders of Chivalry and the concepts of Courtly Love were empowering the philosophies and the literature of Western Europe and Britain. Motivated by the interests of Henry II and his queen, Eleanor of Aquitaine (the parents of both Richard the Lion-Hearted and his brother, King John), Eleanor's daughter, Marie de Champagne, commissioned the creation of the bardic/troubadour tales reflecting this change of mind. She and her sister, Blanche of Castille, sponsored Chrétien de Troyes, a Norman-French court poet, who wrote a number of courtly Arthurian romances during the period between 1160–1190. While de Troyes did not invent the primary patterns of these legends, he did brilliantly render them from the Celtic bardic traditions so they would reflect then-current cultural concepts, as well as the values of the court. His works include: *Tristan, Erec and Enide, Cligés, Lancelot, Ivaine,* and *Perceval.*

It was de Troyes who first brought forth the image of Lancelot and his love for Guinevere and, most significantly, the first mention of the Holy Grail, as such, in his never-completed tale of Perceval, or Le Conte del Graal. This clearly linked the Christian Grail concept with that of the Celtic cauldron of restoration. Particularly as it was represented as a cup, this also linked the literature to the ancient Gaelic Celtic/Tuatha dé Danann "faerie gifts" or, in Celtic/Brythonic tradition, the Hallows.

For future reference, these gifts or Hallows are: the Cup, the Stone of Destiny (or Game Board), the Spear, and the Sword. These we will explore later.

The works of Chrétien de Troyes led to a flood of authors seeking to finish the Grail Quest stories and to build on what had come before them in literary terms. However, the orders of Chivalry and the concepts of Courtly Love were far too indicative of a reemerging Celtic independent spirit to please the powers of the Orthodoxy. These legends were mythically reconnecting those of Western Celtic consciousness with individualistic ideals and the rights to receive from the Divine within, as well as the freedom to choose from their own hearts—all of which did not agree with, nor require the "services" of, the Orthodox Church. This conflict led to the creation of a series of works called The Vulgate Cycle (also, the Lancelot Grail Cycle and the Pseudo-Map Cycle). Written between 1215–1235 by Cistercian clerics, ostensibly under the supervision of St. Bernard of Clairvaux (note: *Clair vaux* = clear seer), these tales were an attempt to show that the Arthurian legends were "overshadowed" by the only true source of power and redemption, according to the Orthodoxy of that time.

From the Vulgate Cycle came the legends of Joseph of Arimathea bringing the Grail to Britain, the discovery of Arthur by Merlin, and the Quest knights, such as Galahad. This also tells of the ultimate demise of Camelot due to the failure of the quests to restore the Grail to the world—which was portrayed as being too originally sinful to warrant such a divine gift. In particular, the stories of Galahad also had a divided benefit. These tales have anonymous authorship, which may have been wise in those days, but they are generally attributed to Robert de Boron, a Burgundian poet. Robert de Boron was the first to link the Grail with the sacred Christian vessel of the Last Supper. This vessel was said to have been used also by Joseph of Arimathea to collect the blood of Christ.

While this linking of the Lights in the legends of the Grail was beneficial, the story of Galahad gave rise to a reaction unexpected by the Orthodoxy. Galahad was the impossibly pure and perfect knight and the son of Lancelot by the Grail King's daughter, Elaine of Carbonek. Because of his complete perfection, Galahad not only received the Grail, he was subsequently transmuted into that ultimate, perfect Light, by his own choice, to leave the hopelessly debased world of humankind. In the legend, Galahad goes immediately to Heaven, taking the Grail with him. Seen as the ultimate reward for following their rules, the Orthodoxy probably didn't recognize the flip side of their message. That was the realization by many in the West that the Orthodox path to ultimate perfection was not humanly possible to follow—so, in effect, why not try to find other ways, other paths "where there was no path before." This led to a reexamination of the dogmas and a restructuring of doctrines that allowed for a more independent connection—an individual path to the Light. First, though, came the Dark times.

The Vulgate Cycle is also valuable as the first prose version of the legends and for introducing the literary form of entrelacement which had its origins in the Celtic, bardic-oral traditions.

For a time, best not forgotten, these legends had to remain veiled. The Spanish Inquisition had far-reaching effects for some time. However, the Light of Arthur reemerged in the work of the last author we will examine in depth, Sir Thomas Malory, an English knight, who wrote *Le Morte D'Arthur* during the years 1469–70. Malory was imprisoned, presumably because he was sympathetic to the House of Lancaster and its ousted king, Henry VI, instead of being loyal to the House of York and its king, Edward IV. Additional information from court records and the like tells us that Malory was something of a rogue and, if not actually a barbaric knight, then somewhat of an heroic one imprisoned for his part in a plot to reclaim the throne of Britain for the House of Lancaster and its sovereign king, Henry VI. I would remind you here that Henry VI was descended from Henry II. Henry II "inspired" Geoffrey of Monmouth to write *The History of the Kings of Britain* for the purposes of linking his own royal Lancastrian line with that of Arthur—the ultimate King of Logres.

So, now we're back where we began our look at some of the authors of the Camelot legends. Interesting how it seems to come full circle, time and time again. Malory's version of these Legends became the modern standard, and remained so relatively unchanged and unscathed for quite a while. This version did draw some criticism during the puritanical period of the seventeenth century (once again, the cycle repeats itself). However, this puritanical banishing of Arthur did not last too long. How could it?

The eighteenth century brought a revival of many Celtic romantic ideals and images which were reflected in the works of authors such as William Wordsworth, Thomas Love Peacock, and Sir Walter Scott. The nineteenth century brought out a more solemn, Victorian image of these transformational—and transforming—tales. Foremost among the Victorian period authors was Alfred Lord Tennyson, with his mournful *Idylls of the King,* which was—and is—powerful enough to make most advocates of Arthur go questing for him again. Other illustrious Victorian poet/bards of the Camelot legends were Matthew Arnold, William Morris, and Algernon Swinburne.

The twentieth-century audience has shown a continuous interest in Arthurian lore. There are countless novels ranging from the lyrical to the fantastic, and from the traditional to the cutting-edge styles, all of which seek to illuminate those of us whose interest in Arthur has become a sacred quest. Foremost among these novels, I believe, are the Muse-inspired works of Mary Stewart, the visionary work of T. H. White, and the impressively researched and crafted work of Nikolai Tolstoy. Countless other volumes are now found in modern fiction and nonfiction. (For a listing of many of these, I refer you to the bibliographies at the back of this book.) It is clear that the current interest in the exploration of the realms of Camelot's legends is here to stay for quite a long time to come. This is due, in no small part, to the active interest of the mystical community who are questing for evolutionary changes in Mind and Consciousness. It would appear that, for all accounts and purposes, the legends are alive and well today in the individual and the collective minds of Western Celtic consciousness.

> *If the ferment of the last fifteen years of Arthurian material is an accurate sign, then we may expect Merlin to reawaken soon, though not as a wise elder who will appear in our midst and give instructions ... Merlin will have accumulated some new developing consciousness, something which may filter through to us all if we apply to his key image ...*
>
> R. J. Stewart
> *The Prophetic Vision of Merlin* (New York: Routledge and Kegan Paul, 1987)

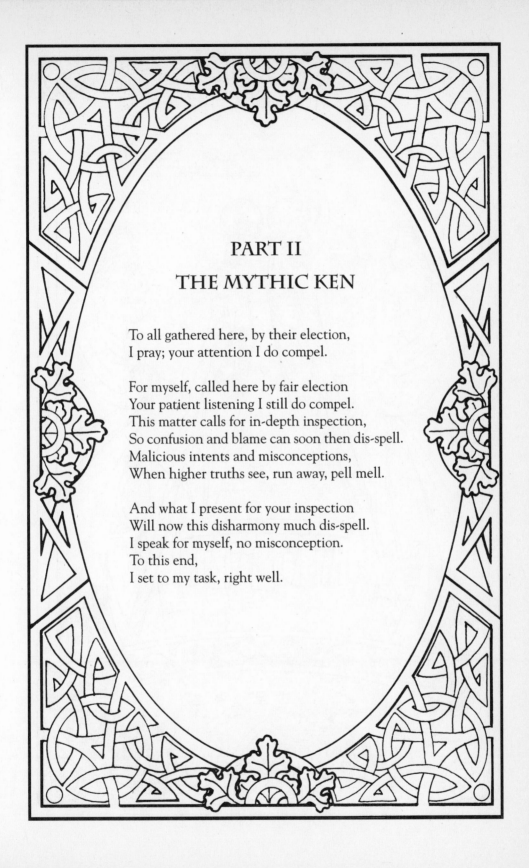

PART II

THE MYTHIC KEN

To all gathered here, by their election,
I pray; your attention I do compel.

For myself, called here by fair election
Your patient listening I still do compel.
This matter calls for in-depth inspection,
So confusion and blame can soon then dis-spell.
Malicious intents and misconceptions,
When higher truths see, run away, pell mell.

And what I present for your inspection
Will now this disharmony much dis-spell.
I speak for myself, no misconception.
To this end,
I set to my task, right well.

CHAPTER 6

ARTHUR, THE CONSTANT CELTIC KING

*Arthur's legend itself must be brought back into the investigation and taken seri-
ously. It must be sifted for clues. The right questions to ask are not the direct
ones, Who was Arthur? or Did he exist? but Where did the legend come from?
and What facts is it rooted in? If we line up the legend side by side with history,
as we know it today, the problem can be solved. It almost solves itself.*

Geoffrey Ashe,
The Discovery of King Arthur (Garden City, NY: Anchor Press/Doubleday, 1985)

 The process by which Arthur, historically defined as Artorius, Dux
Bellorum, Comtes Britannarium (Duke of Battles or Count of
Britain), who lived during the fifth century, became the "stuff of
future memory" is both intricate and amazing. It involves centuries
of expression, exploration, and excavation into the many aspects
making up the myth.

Opinions among Arthurian scholars are still divided. For some, the admittedly
scanty evidence is insufficient to validate the existence of Arthur. For others, it is sufficient to pinpoint at least the historical Arthur in such a way that the development
of the mythic-quality "once and future king" is understood. In either case, none deny
the extraordinary impact of the experience that Arthur and the Camelot legends
have had on Western Celtic culture. For all, Arthur is the true-born King of Logres,
the mystical heart and mind of Britain, and, since the expansive migration of Celtic
peoples has spread them across the globe, this realm of Logres has expanded with
them in their hearts and minds.

What is known from the Roman records is that there was a British war leader named Artorius in the fifth century who lived in either Wales or Cornwall. This Artorius, which in Celtic form becomes Arthur, was not a king according to any official Roman record. However, we must consider that the Roman Empire had no real interest in the kingship—or queenship—of the Celtic lands they had been so intent on controlling. It is recorded that Artorius, a warlord, duke of battles, or Count of Britain, managed heroically to hold the tribes of Britain together during the transitional times when the ruling power was shifting from Roman back to British.

Also, this was the time period when spiritual rules and philosophies were shifting from Pagan to Christian. Although it was not until a few centuries later that the truly oppressive aspects of that change took effect, it was a highly volatile time of shifting consciousness. Borders of land were in dispute, as were the borders defining the way the Celtic/British people lived their spiritual lives.

As if those transitions weren't enough to assimilate, there was also the influx of Saxon and Anglo tribes into Britain to consider. By that time the Romans had seriously overextended themselves and underestimated the abilities of the Germanic tribes to withstand their imperial onslaught. Rome was already in danger of losing its empire. The decision came down from Rome to withdraw from Britain. While this was certainly what most of the people of Britain wanted, it left the islands completely undefended.

The Romans had already been in Britain four centuries and had devised an internal defense structure. The regions of Britain were divided into defensible sections, each under the military leadership of a warlord. These warlords were then under the rule of specific Roman consuls. So many of these warlords were native Britons, trained by the Romans, they were naturally as territorial about their particular lands as anyone who had become essentially Celtic-Roman could be.

When the last of the Roman legions left in A.D. 407, there were natural attempts by the old lines of Celtic royalty to reestablish their claims to power. There were also a number of Romans who had intermarried with the British and had set up lucrative trade with Europe using the Roman routes. Other remaining Romans had married well, entering the aristocratic classes of the British nobility. These Romans held positions of power in the governing of the British Isles. The conflict of these groups caused further chaos in the transitional times Britain was facing. Eventually, the autonomous rule of the Romano-British was broken, and English rule began, as well stated in *The Warriors of Arthur* (London: Blandford Press, 1987) by John Matthews and Bob Stewart:

> *That this (birth of English rule) did not come about more swiftly, and with consequent destruction of both language and culture, we owe to a handful of Romano-British leaders, of whom Arthur is only one, who held back the influx of barbarian invaders and colonists long enough for them to feel the influence of Romano-British culture and become part of a new racial mixture—the Anglo-Saxons or English.*

44

The view of Arthur as a composite of all these war leaders, valiantly endeavoring to hold the lines for Britain, is a valid interpretation. This process of imbuing one person with the qualities needed by the tribes is an old Celtic method of preserving both their history and their myths. That Arthur and the other war leaders were extremely skilled in the tactics of warfare, and well equipped with the latest weaponry from Rome, would have served also to enhance their mythic qualities.

For instance, the fact these war leaders and their soldiers were able to fight on horseback would have given them a natural advantage over those whose only methods of warfare were on foot. As mounted cavalry, these troops would have been able to defeat the influx of invading tribes with a swiftness and efficiency which, in the minds of the people, would have taken on almost supernatural qualities. If we remember the ox-cart people from whom many of the new colonists of Britain descended, we can imagine the effect of encountering a force such as Arthur and the other war leaders represented. The fierce strain of Nordic invaders had not yet made its influence known in a widespread fashion, as it would do in the eighth and ninth centuries to come.

All in all, this encounter between the "warriors of Arthur" and the new colonists of Britain was very much like the encounter between the chariot warriors and the hunter agrarians in 2000 B.C. Europe. From both encounters, though, a new mythic island would result. The birth of the legendary Arthur and the birth of Britain truly may be said to have happened at the same time. For this reason alone, we may accurately grant kingship to Arthur.

The right, wise, and true-born King of Logres represents a king of such mystical, legendary quality that the Celts, then and now, naturally would weave him into the majestic tapestry that is their history. Arthur, his knights, Camelot, and Avalon have all become a part of our tribal codes, interwoven into deeper codes of Celtic nature. As such, the true power of this constant Celtic king is in his personification of the qualities and forces he represents.

Thus, in time, this constant king may well become known as a spiritual Celtic sovereign, just as the tribal gods of the Celts did before him. They, too, may well have emerged from the same process. When we view Arthur as the constant king, we need not stress either his natural or supernatural qualities. We would best view Arthur as a synthesis of the fine and rare qualities so valued by the Celts, in a Celt who is independent, courageous, wise, forthright, and born quite clearly to serve the purpose of destiny.

For the further purpose of this book, we will view Arthur and his legends as though we knew what he was and what he did actually happened historically. We will do this in order to avoid the distractions of constantly having to qualify each point made about this mythic king and his legends. As we know by now, the main point is not whether Arthur is reality or myth. The main point is the very real, very mythic effect these legends have had on each of us as individuals—and on all of us as Celtic peoples.

I'll close this section of the chapter with an imagery to help you connect with your own image of Arthur as he may have been in the time when his exploits led him into the realm of legend for all time. For the information used to create this imagery, the credit goes to Nennius, an eighth- or ninth-century monk from Wales, who is considered to be among the first authors to record the legend of Arthur—already in the oral traditions at the time he lived. Further credit, of course, goes to the scholars who preserved and translated these "monkish tales" of truth and triumph.

The form in which you choose to approach Arthur, and the form which Arthur presents to you here, and elsewhere, is ultimately your choice. These forms, yours and his, reflect essential aspects of yourself. When approaching archetypes of such a powerful, mythic quality, there is simply no other way which is either wise or worthy. As this is already designed to be experiential, feel free to determine the pace of your exploration of this realm with its legendary figures, as with all the others throughout this book.

ARTHUR AND THE TWELVE BATTLES FOR BRITAIN
A Guided Experiential Imagery

Breathe deeply and slowly release your breath. Repeat this sequence several times, pausing briefly between each inhalation and each exhalation. When you feel relaxed and receptive, begin to breathe naturally.

———

Focus your mind within the realms of myth and mystery. Open to an experience of personal empowerment. Open to a privileged experience from within.

Feel yourself drifting back through time and space to a different place. Set your inner controls for a point in History—about A.D. 500, in Britain.

You find yourself in the camp of Arthur on a clear, starlit night. There is only a sliver of a moon high in the sky.

Take a moment to get your bearings here. It is the eve of a great battle. Although it is late, the camp is still active with preparations for the coming day of destiny.

You make your way through the camp, observing the activities around you. You do so slowly, and silently, unobserved. You are not here for these others, only Arthur's kin.

Protected from the winds, as well as from prying eyes, the campfires burn low. You can smell food cooking in a large pot, and you pause to absorb the aroma.

There are hundreds of people in this camp, maybe more. Some are sleeping, resting in the forests or among the boulders nearby.

In the darkness, you can hear the sounds of troubled dreaming.

Clustered among the fires are groups of warriors. They are intently staring at a battle plan drawn in the earth by an older battle lord. The young warriors study this plan carefully.

46

There are priests and monks in the camp, and holy sisters, some wearing crosses. Others wear the ancient garb of Avalon. They are united in their prayers for the warriors.

In a stone circle nearby, you can see the Druids. Their white robes seem ghostly against the dark. Only a small center fire illuminates their faces as they watch the sky for signs, omens, and portents.

You continue through the camp until you come to a group standing around a Bard who is singing battle songs; reminding the Warriors of their past victories.

You find a place to sit on a low rock so you may hear these songs of glory.

A sturdy knight is sharpening his sword near where you sit. His eyes are wise and kind.

The songs tell the tales of eleven great battles, eleven victories, hard fought and hard won.

You hear the bardsong describing these; but it is the sturdy knight's face that gives you the sense of the costs of victory.

First, the Battle of Glein, where the Frisians fell, and the River Glen in Northumbria turned blood red. This battle marked the first victory against Octa, the son of an old adversary king, Vortigern.

Then the River Dublas flowed with the blood of four more fierce battles near Lindsay.

The warriors of Dalriadian, the Ulster Scots were not so easily defeated in battle.

You notice the warriors around the Bard. They nod in agreement with his words; honoring their worthy foes—many of whom were now friends—as is the Celtic way.

Then the sixth battle is celebrated in song. The Bard sings of a Pictish chieftain whom Arthur killed that day by the River Bassus.

"And the ravens cried Caw, Caw, Caw," sings the Bard.

You notice an imposing figure in dark robes. He is carrying a staff with dragons intertwined. You know him at once, for his fame is great.

It is The Merlin, here in his role as War Druid.

The Bard directs his next verse to The Merlin as he sings of the ancient Caledonian Forest, site of the seventh battle at Cat Coit Caledon—fought well, close to Arthur's Seat and Hart Fell, The Merlin's Sanctuary.

"Hard fought, hard won, so close to home."

You are aware The Merlin has noticed you; but you see wise acceptance in his eyes. Listening together, you hear of battles eight and nine. Caerguidn, Lands End, against the Saxon Cerdic and the battle at Cair Wisc, the City of Legions, some say.

The Merlin has moved away from the Bard and sits beside the sturdy knight with kind eyes.

You hear The Merlin ask if the knight knows you are here.

The knight glances at you directly and nods his head.

He is amused that you have not recognized him. Then you know it is Sir Kai, foster brother of Arthur.

Sir Kai motions for you to join him, and you do so.

The Merlin indicates that you should hear the rest of the song—of the tenth battle on the River Tryfwyd and the eleventh victory on Mount Agned, at Brent Knoll.

The Bard continues to sing his assurances of victory in the coming conflict.

"Eleven victories, hard fought, hard won, with the twelfth at Badon Hill, the fighting will be done."

The Merlin rises from where he is seated and stretches.

Sir Kai puts away his sword, now sharpened to his satisfaction, and stands up slowly.

They look at you expectantly, and you rise to join them.

As The Merlin and Sir Kai make their way through the camp, the warriors and the others stand aside respectfully.

Unnoticed, you follow in the clear space behind them.

Together you make your way toward a large tent. It is placed in the center of the camp, with all the others surrounding it at a respectful distance.

This is the royal tent of Arthur, Dux Bellorum, Contes Britannarium (Duke of Battles, Count of Britain).

You approach this tent with a sense of awe. It is illuminated from within and glows golden against the night sky. Above it, you glimpse a shooting star. There are banners flying in front of this tent, and its sides are painted with designs of Celtic weave.

The Merlin enters first with a serious glance in your direction.

You respond with a solemn nod.

Sir Kai holds the tent flap open for you, kindly.

With courage you weren't aware of, you enter the royal tent of Arthur—and behold him within. Arthur is busy conferring with his battle lords. His head is bent over maps strewn on an oak table.

You wait with outward patience, but excitement inside.

The Merlin whispers to Arthur, and he looks up at you with intensity of purpose in his eyes.

Face to face, you know him now, and you recognize him well ... as he does you.

Arthur finishes instructing his battle lords. They leave his tent, each with a nod of acknowledgment as they pass by you.

Arthur sits in a carved wooden chair of Roman design, with Celtic dragons and tartan robes thrown over it. He motions for you to sit beside him, on a bench covered with bearskin furs.

You do so gratefully, realizing you are most welcome. Arthur gazes at you with eyes like an eagle. You wish to return the stare, but do not dare.

Arthur sees this, and laughs—a glorious laugh.

Relieved, you find you are relaxed and secure, comforted in the presence of this Constant King.

The Merlin and Sir Kai study the battle maps as you and Arthur share your thoughts with each other—in the warmth of kinship.

Moments pass like hours, each bringing strength and power to your own purpose.

Then the time comes when The Merlin taps his staff on the floor to signal that it is time for Arthur to rest.

Arthur bids you stay for one more moment. He has messages for you to which you listen carefully. Then, with a wave of his hand, he issues a command which you know you must heed.

Arthur instructs you not to stay for the coming battle; although he sees in your heart and mind you truly want to help him. His face is calm, serene and assured. It is the face of one who knows his destiny well.

He dismisses you with gentle resolution; honoring you for having come to visit. He bids you to return to him again when battle flags no longer fly on the horizon and his kingdom truly has been won.

Sir Kai urges Arthur to rest a while and brings him something warm to drink.

The Merlin leads you out of the tent, and through the camp of Arthur toward a small hill.

As you leave the camp, you can see the Druids on the hill inside the circle of stones. They are illuminated by the first rays of dawn, and their white robes glow with a golden light.

You notice there are twelve of them, women and men, in a circle, with hands joined. On a stone altar, which they encircle, is a great broadsword, gleaming in the first rays of the Sun—Caliburn—Excalibur.

You wonder briefly if you might be allowed to join their sacred circle and help somehow.

The Merlin knowingly smiles and shakes his head, no—not now. He reminds you of Arthur's command and kindly tells you of its purpose.

You listen as The Merlin tells that the day of battles is only glorious when sung in Bardsong verse. This any real warrior will assure you in truth.

"The only glory in battle is doing what must be done," says The Merlin firmly.

The Merlin makes his way to the top of a grassy hill from which point he can observe the battle.

You ask him if there is some way you can know what happens there that day at Badon Hill.

The Merlin smiles tolerantly and taps you gently on the forehead with the head of his staff. You glimpse jeweled eyes in the intertwined dragons briefly before your vision is changed. You are given glimpses of the day to come. In your mind, you see the same camp after the Battle of Badon Hill has been won.

There is joyful song from the bards and a ceremony begins.

All too quickly the images flash, but you know that, too, is at Arthur's command—and The Merlin's. And you know that you have chosen this—every aspect is under your control.

There is one final glimpse of Arthur standing on a massive battle shield held high above the cheering crowd. Around him are his warriors, knights, and battle lords, their swords raised in allegiance.

Behind this circle is yet another, the people celebrating this victory, the twelfth and most decisive. You notice that both circles have people from different tribes, Bretons, Scots, Picts, Irish, Saxons, and some you cannot tell. All are united in honoring Arthur and his warriors. You realize you have glimpsed a moment of greatness—and have felt the power that a united people share.

As you consider that this, too, was the glory of the round table, you realize you are back from whence you came.

The images and the visions have faded into memory, lovingly stored within your heart and mind—just as Arthur and his messages are—sacredly preserved.

Yet the feeling and the power of this experience remains—and this is its greatest gift and privilege.

Breathe and release in sequence. Release the images. Return to the now. Return with honor for yourself. Honor yourself for creating your inner vision. Be here now, for now is where you are needed.

> *The twelfth battle was on Badon Hill and in it nine hundred and sixty men fell in one day, from a single charge of Arthur's, and no one laid them low save he alone; and he was victorious in all his campaigns.*
>
> Nennius
> *Historia Brittonum*

> *The statement in Nennius that Arthur slew hundreds of men single-handed has caused many commentators to believe that the whole matter is simply another fabrication, even allowing for the Celtic love of exaggeration. In fact, it seems clear that the reference is simply to the daring and strength of Arthur's picked band of warriors, whose prowess so impressed their fellows that legends began to grow from that moment.*
>
> Matthews and Stewart
> *Warriors of Arthur*

Now, before you proceed through the text, take a break and absorb the experience of Arthur. Perhaps you feel comfortable writing down aspects of your experience, such as how you felt, how you appeared to yourself, how Arthur appeared to you, and how the others, especially The Merlin and Sir Kai, appeared.

There is no set structure for this, but you may wish to begin a journal or a simple notebook in which to keep a record of your "experiencings." This is *your* record of your inner realms as you experience the mythic realms of the Camelot legends. As a journal may take whatever form is most reflective of your personal creativity, be personally creative and expressive. However, expressing just within yourself will also enhance your experiences of these mythic keys to the positive gifts of power.

In the next chapter, we make yet another connection to that most mythic wizard, The Merlin.

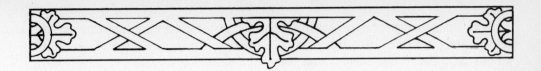

CHAPTER 7

MERLIN, THE ARCHMAGE

Present memory of Merlin is uncannily accurate when one considers the pull of forgetfulness upon the generations, as well as the loss of knowledge due to mischief and to time. Most people have heard of Merlin. Many recall him with a smile as of imagined kindred, or at least, as if he had been an unlost friend.

Norma Lorre Goodrich
Merlin (New York: Harper and Row, 1988)

 The Merlin remains one of the most illusive figures in Arthurian lore, yet, at the same time, one of the most pervasive and foundational. Perhaps this is due to the shifting times in which these legends emerged; times when a figure such as The Merlin could be neither counted, nor discounted, for his contributions to the establishment of Arthur as King, and to the subsequent creation of Camelot. The beautiful irony surrounding The Merlin is that, despite the varied ways in which he was depicted, he has come to be known by the masses in a remarkably syncretic, shared fashion. The Merlin is, as Jung called him, "the age-old son of the Mother, the Wise Old Man" and, culturally, the ultimate enchanter.

The Matter of The Merlin

The Merlin represents the highest orders of mastery, mystery, and magick found within the evolutionarily activational realms within our mystical mind. To access the realms from which the archetypal Archmage emerges is to connect with personal aspects of mastery over the elements of your life. The mystery of The Merlin dwells in the multifaceted forms and images in which he appears in the legends, as well as in our personal portrayal of him, symbolically. The magick of The Merlin is direct and draconian. It is the forthright effort and essential objectivity we utilize when we choose to manifest change in our lives.

51

It is the archetype of The Merlin that we access when, and only when, we have defined and decided on the direction of our lives. It is The Merlin with whom we connect in order to creatively master our own destinies, insofar as we are able to do so. It is The Merlin connection that allows us to accept those aspects of destiny beyond our reach and knowledge: aspects we must endeavor to experience and grace and honor.

THE TRADITIONAL VIEW OF THE MERLIN

We all know of our destiny and try to hide it from ourselves. How much easier life would be if we just allowed our destiny to unfold.

Kara Starr
Merlin's Journal of Time: The Camelot Adventure
(Solano Beach, CA: Ravenstarr Publications, 1989)

This, then, is the traditional view of how The Merlin's destiny unfolded, based primarily upon the works of Geoffrey of Monmouth, Robert de Boron, Wace, and Malory:

According to the sixth-century chronicler Nennius, Monmouth presents Merlin as being born from the union of a nun and a spirit lover. Brought up as a fatherless child in a priestly family, Merlin soon is known for his ability to foresee the future—and to see the past clearly. These abilities allow him to save his mother from execution because of her union with the spirit lover—or demon, as he was judged to have been. The Merlin shows prodigious gifts at the age of three by telling the tale of how Joseph of Arimathea brought the Holy Grail to Britain. Merlin also tells of his role as a prophet between heaven and hell, having the qualities of both.

Next, we find Merlin at the court of King Vortigern, where he was summoned in order to be the sacrifice required by Vortigern's dark Druids. It seems Vortigern's tower at King's Fort collapsed as quickly as it was constructed. Vortigern's Druids required the blood sacrifice of a fatherless child to appease the gods of the region so the tower would stand.

Instead of being sacrificed, Merlin falls into a deep prophetic trance and reveals the cause of the tower's continual collapse. A red dragon and a white dragon are battling within the underground realms beneath the tower. Merlin warns Vortigern of the coming conquest of the Red Dragon over the White—of the forces of the Pendragon, the Sons of Constantine, conquering the forces of Vortigern and his Saxon allies. Further prophetic visions so impress Vortigern that he allows Merlin to live and abandons King's Fort altogether.

In a short time, Ambrosius and Uther, sons of the great King Constantine, do indeed conquer Vortigern and drive his Saxon allies back behind Hadrean's wall. Merlin then becomes adviser to Ambrosius and later to Uther. Some versions say that Merlin inspired Uther to create a round table as a replica of the Grail table created by Joseph of Arimathea, itself a replica of the table of the Last Supper.

All is well until Uther falls in love with Igraine, wife of his much-needed ally, Gorlois, Duke of Cornwall. Merlin arranges a magickal tryst between Uther and Igraine, which results in the conception of Arthur—and the death of Gorlois. Uther marries Igraine, but on the advice of Merlin does not reveal he is the father of her child. He does not tell that it was he, Uther in disguise as Gorlois, who came by magickal help from Merlin to beget the child. The child Arthur is placed with foster parents who are not aware of his royal parentage. When Uther dies, Arthur proves himself the right-wise born, true king by pulling the sword from the stone.

Merlin is then shown to be Arthur's adviser, as well as to the Round Table and Grail Knights. Merlin is seen as having redemptive qualities, even for his own actions. As the ideals of Camelot begin to crumble, The Merlin becomes the withdrawn prophet of the Grail who was trapped into a state of eternal enchantment by the actions of Arthur's evil half-sister, Morgan le Fey, and her protégé Nimue—or Niniane.

Without Merlin's wise guidance, the Round Table falls, the Wasteland is created, and the quest knights go forth to seek the redemptive Grail. Most fail to find the grail and heal the King—as well as the land. This failure is seen to be due also to the betrayal of Arthur by Guinevere with Lancelot, the Norman-French addition to the legends. Even Lancelot in his greatness cannot attain the Grail because of his earthly desires for Guinevere. However, his son, Galahad, has such purity that he not only attains the Grail but is transmuted into the Light with the Grail.

By this time, Merlin is seen only as the tragically entrapped prophet who must watch as Mordred, Arthur's son by Morgan le Fey, destroys Camelot and Arthur. Arthur is taken to be healed, awaiting the time of his return. Guinevere takes her holy vows; Lancelot sequesters himself nearby; and Merlin remains trapped between heaven and hell, as it were, from which realm he had been fathered and born.

While that summary leaves out several subplots, or branches of the legends, it does basically "capture" the composite image conveyed by the traditional authors of these legends. It is easy to see the overlays of the Orthodoxically accepted views of the times. Consider, however, before you are too quick to judge those who inserted the overlays, that in so doing they actually preserved what could well have been destroyed outright. Whether The Merlin was seen as evil or good, dark or light, his image suited the needs of the times. Even his redemption image as a prophet of the Grail suited the needs of the Orthodoxy. The legends' authors crafted an image filled with diverting images and deliberately encoded ones, as well.

We may never truly decipher all the images—coded or otherwise—contained in the Camelot legends. However, a study of these shows enough variations created to suit the times in which they emerged to justify a reimaging of these legends in a manner more just, reasonable, and reflective of the current times. So long as the elemental themes remain in a round pattern, the implicit power of the myths remains. That is the nature of their ageless enchantment. Neither the legends nor The Merlin are entrapped by means of enchantment. Instead, we may see them clearly as being empowered by enchantment—their own and the enchanting effect their images have on us, as well.

With this in mind, we may examine our own beliefs and create our magick image of The Merlin, Arthur, and all the realms of the Camelot legends, according to our personal, current connection to the good of all that they represent.

The Merlin represents the quintessential wizard, the Archmage, whose legendary exploits give him the elemental synthesis of mythic empowerment. As such, elementally The Merlin role as War Druid shows the fire of his nature; his relationship with Avalon and The Lady of the Lake reveal his water aspects; his instruction and guidance of Arthur show the earth element; and his visionary, prophetic gifts show the element of air.

The element of spirit I see reflected in a triune, triple-aspected manner: his intricately interwoven significance in the primary aspects and actions of the Arthurian lore, his connection to the sacred Hallows, as well as to the Thirteen Treasures of Britain, and his reputed interment on Bardsey Isle, the burial site reserved for those of highest spiritual quality and contribution to Britain. Considering this, we can rightfully view The Merlin as the five-star Archmage of all times for the Western, Celtic world—one who supersedes all others, elementally, by at least one or two stars of quality.

One of the most interesting portrayals of The Merlin comes from the fantasy novel, *That Hideous Strength*, written by C. S. Lewis in 1945. In this book, The Merlin is shown to represent a bridging, both-at-once state of mind, between the mysterious, Atlantean traditions, and the Celtic, Pagan ways (which also may be seen as the blending of the Tuatha dé Danann, or Fair Folk, Fey and the later Milesian Celts practices). The Merlin is also shown as a bridge between the Celtic, Pagan ways, which had come to include the Fey, or Fair Folk ways, and those of the new ways of Christianity. Although The Merlin is clearly depicted as a Druid, he is portrayed as a helper to the Christian knights and a guardian of the Holy Grail.

This image of The Merlin bridging or blending the traditions of others is a valid representation of the archetypal Archmage, accessible to all, limited to none. C. S. Lewis further portrayed The Merlin as an enchanter who worked with the neutral powers, neither Light nor Dark, but light and dark in a perfect balance. The Merlin is not portrayed as the dark, shadowy wizard, nor the clearly illuminated catalyst for creation.

This portrayal synthesizes The Merlin and helps us understand the many aspects in which he shows himself in the Camelot legends:

- Misunderstood and mistreated "fatherless child"
- Shamanic student of the hermit Blaise (or Galapas, in Mary Stewart's novels)
- Acknowledged son of the magnificent Ambrosius
- Prophet at the court of Vortigern

- Ally for the subsequent overtaking of Vortigern by the forces of Ambrosius
- Self-initiated seeker of wisdom
- Catalyst for the conception of Arthur
- Adviser to Uther
- Trainer and initiator of Arthur
- Adviser to the Court of Camelot
- Withdrawn helper who was woven in by the Avalonians
- Self-preserving symbolic source of knowledge and wisdom for seekers of Celtic magick and mysticism throughout the ages

The Merlin represents these aspects, and more—the synthesis of magick. *The Merlin is the breath of the Magician who lies sleeping in the All.*

The Merlin is the Magus between the worlds of the mundane and the mystical. He represents the symbolic source of draconian wisdom that blends the practical with the prophetic, the definitive with the Divine, and that which is necessary with that which is numinous. The Merlin is, at once, real, surreal, and unreal in his alchemy. These qualities are defined by the image and the relationship he develops with each individual who seeks to make connection with this, the quintessential wizard.

The Merlin resists being defined as fact, fiction, or fantasy when attempts are made to classify what he represents. Traditional legends of The Merlin, and modern characterizations as well, usually only succeed in presenting a few of his aspects in a reasonably developed manner. For this reason alone, it is important to track The Merlin in a manner which matches the multidimensional facets he represents. Those who seek a clear image of, and an uncluttered connection to, the archetypal powers of The Merlin are best advised to explore the realms of literature and of analyses; it is somewhere between the literary, muse-inspired images, and the linear, multi-interpretational images that the source of our personal image of The Merlin may be found. From this personal image, a personal connection may be created. For this personal connection to be made, there are four primary requirements.

Research: The willingness to research the materials, both literary and linear, which present the varied images and aspects of The Merlin. (These awaken you.)

Respect: An attitude of respect for the images others have of The Merlin, as well as respect for your own. (This is so even when you feel others' use of their image is questionable, or in conflict with your own.)

Reverence: An attitude that reverences and honors, but does not worship, the ways of mysticism and magick. (This creates a flexible, expansive relationship with that which is ever evolving, magickally and mystically, in your mind.)

Remembering: A capacity for "remembering" what is encoded and accessed through the "pathways" of your mind and your brain. (This allows you to move from the dormant to the "awakening," to the "knowing," states of consciousness.)

Before we discuss some of the materials about The Merlin, I want to share a short excerpt from *Merlin's Journal of Time: The Camelot Adventure*. This volume is an innovative account of the experiencing of The Merlin written by Kara Starr, herself a clear pathway in the collective sense of the modern mind. Incidentally, Kara Starr refers to her work as "meta-fiction," which is an appropriate classification for the personal images and experiencings each creates with The Merlin Current.

> *"What of the illusion, Merlin?"*
> *"All is illusion, Arthur. The only reality is that which your mind gives to each event or thought. We sample it for only a fragment of a second, then it passes. It is no more, but is transformed into something else. Your only hold on it was a brief imprint upon your memory. The illusion is a two-edge sword, Arthur. New events come, old ones die, the illusion has changed, and yet many remain the same, still holding their old beliefs and thinking themselves unchanged. There are some, however, who change the illusion by creating their own events."*

What I refer to as The Merlin Current is the realm of experiencing and remembering with the creative evolutionary aspects of the mind; for it is within this realm that we are able to connect, "multidimensionally" to our own image (or "illusion") of the Archmage, master wizard. With both information and intuition we can "awaken" the symbolic, archetypal Merlin, and provide ourselves with the means by which the "knowing" may be obtained. There is one aspect of the "knowing" that is fundamental to all others in regard to exploring the realms within—within which the magick that is Merlin may be found. That is—the magick and the realms are "our beliefs." It is as simple, and as profound, as that.

We will continue to track the wizard throughout the coming chapters. Now, before I present some of the "research materials" about The Merlin, you may wish to try a bit of experiencing your own image of the Archmage. Therefore, I present you with an evolutionary exercise, an imagery that you may experience, and an image that you may create—according to your beliefs.

I present you to The Merlin. This gives you a private audience with the Archmage, as you have requested.

THE MERLIN
An Experiential Imagery

You may, of course, make this as ceremonial as you choose. I suggest that you approach this realm and this archetypal source of knowing, with personal aspects of respectful quality and reverential attitude. Your own explorations thus far already show your willingness to research. All you will need now is an open mind to activate your capacity for remembering.

Breathe and release your breath slowly, in measured sequence. Inhale to a count of four. Hold your breath for a count of four. Exhale to a count of four. Pause for a count of four before inhaling again. Repeat this sequence at least eight times or more if you need to, until you become relaxed and receptive. Close your eyes for this breathing sequence; open them when you have done the breathing and feel the deep flow of receptive consciousness.

Begin to breathe naturally. Should you become distracted, repeat the measured breathing sequence until you are once more in the flow.

———

You are climbing up a winding flight of stairs in a tower that is illuminated from within. You count each step as you ascend. Feel your foot on each step you climb. Hear the sound of your footsteps echoing within the tower. The sound travels upward as you count each step you make. You are warm and comfortable here in this tower. It is no effort for you to climb the winding steps. You move easily and eagerly up the steps, counting them as you go onward and upward.

Here and there in the curved walls of the tower are tall, narrow windows that allow you a view of the surrounding landscape. It is a landscape which is most pleasing to you. It is beautiful and mystical and deeply familiar. You may pause at a window to gaze out at the landscape, if you choose to. Or you may continue ascending the steps and counting each one as you go.

Should you lose count of the steps you have taken, just laugh to yourself and begin the count again from right where you are on the steps, in the tower, moving upward. It is the measuring and not the numbering that matters here. Each step is a measure of your expanding consciousness. Each step taken opens your mind to new possibilities. Each step helps you become more relaxed and receptive. Each step awakens your mind and brings you closer to the knowing. Breathe and focus on ascending the steps within the tower.

As you come around the next curve in the tower, you see the last few steps lead to an opening at the top of the stairs. It is wide and breezy and comfortable to enter. There are three more steps above this opening that lead you securely into the room at the top of the tower and a finely wrought railing that encircles the opening, with a gate that you unlatch, swing open, and then enter the tower room.

The room at the top of the tower is circular in shape. It is clear and bright, with the light of many windows illuminating the room. You feel comfortable and self-assured in this room at the top of the tower. You may take all the time you need to examine this room while you wait for your private visit with the Archmage. There are chairs in which you may sit, if you like. Choose a chair that suits you best. Relax and enjoy the view from the top of the tower. Be receptive to the feel of the room. Be receptive to your inner feelings. Note the aspects of the room that appeal most to you.

Soon you hear the sound of footsteps coming gently up the tower stairs. You can hear the sound of laughter and the voice of The Merlin calling up to you. He assures you he is on his way. He has been waiting for your visit and would have been there sooner had he not been enjoying the beautiful mystical landscape you have chosen for the site of your visit. You hear The Merlin pause at one of the windows, and you know he is admiring the view.

You hear him speak softly; you cannot quite understand what he has said. Then, with a flutter of tiny wings, a little wren flies through the opening at the top of the stairs and perches on the railing. The wren begins whistling in greeting. It is a lovely, enchanting sound that you enjoy very much. Soon you hear The Merlin whistling the same tune as he enters the tower room.

He nods at you in greeting and urges the wren to sit on his finger. Then he brings the little wren to you. The wren settles comfortably on your shoulder, while The Merlin busies himself looking among a stack of books and papers. He

pulls out a small book and takes a writing tool from his pocket. With comfortable grace, he moves to where you are and takes a seat closest to you. He opens the book, which you see has blank pages, and poises with his writing tool expectantly.

Seeing the quizzical look on your face, The Merlin laughs and you laugh with him. He explains this is your book of lessons. It is a course of your own making—as is your connection to The Merlin. He would like you to tell him about yourself. He would like you to tell him just what of the knowing you want to know, and why. Because you are comfortable in his company, you are able to express your feelings easily. Taking all the time you need, you tell The Merlin about yourself and your quest for the knowing. You are alert, clear, and awake as you tell of your path so far. You find you can tell him anything, and he will understand your quest for knowing. He listens, nods, and notes each aspect you share. He writes quickly, and you know he is wise and accepting of whatever you say.

The Merlin asks you first to tell him what you feel are obstacles or weaknesses that you have encountered on your path—and within yourself. You tell him these willingly, openly, and honestly. You notice he does not write these down in your little book. When you ask The Merlin about this, he explains that to do so would only empower your beliefs about these obstacles and weaknesses. You take all the time you need to tell The Merlin about these aspects that you feel are obstacles or weaknesses.

When you have finished doing this, The Merlin asks that you review these in a different way. For each obstacle and weakness you have described, The Merlin helps you find a positive event or quality that resulted from what you saw then as an obstacle, or what you once considered a weakness within yourself. Insofar as you are able, you find a balancing aspect for each. These aspects The Merlin notes in your book. Those for which you have difficulty finding the balance he dismisses until another time and meeting, when he is certain you will have found the positive events and qualities that balance these aspects which began as obstacles and weaknesses.

The Merlin compliments your earnest and forthright efforts in expressing yourself clearly and openly. Then he asks you to tell him what you feel are supports and strengths you have encountered on your path—and within yourself. You tell him these as honestly and objectively as you can, knowing you are not being prideful—but purposeful in your expression of supportive aspects and strengths. You notice The Merlin does not write these down. When you ask about this, he urges you to continue, and he will explain in due time. You take all the time you need to tell The Merlin what you perceive to be supports and strengths.

When you are finished doing this, The Merlin asks that you review these in a different way. For each support and strength, The Merlin asks you to point out, for yourself, any potential problem that may arise from what you see as supportive or strengthening. This you do without any negativity or fearful expectation, for it is the way of the Mage to learn the art of clear assessment of any given situation or aspect.

Only those aspects that pose no potential problems are written in your book. If you find you have difficulty determining which aspects are completely clear, The Merlin assures you there are at least four. Then he shows you he has already noted these in your book. They are the aspects with which you began this quest for an audience with The Merlin: Research. Respect. Reverence. Remembering. These, he tells you, are inalienably right for you. He puts stars by each, and you realize the knowing has already begun.

He closes your book and asks if there is any advice or specific information you request of him. He will tell you what he can, based on your beliefs about yourself and your path now. He will pose questions that you need not answer right away. They are for you to consider as you progress along your individual pathway to knowing. Take all the time you need for this self-illuminating interchange of knowledge and information.

Finally, The Merlin tells you about aspects and events you may not have remembered at first. As he does so, you realize how clearly he helps you recall just what you need to know and understand. Take all the time you need to listen within. Listen to The Merlin as he awakens the knowing within your Self. When you are ready, you bid The Merlin farewell, knowing you may return again when the time is right and the connection is clear.

You make your way back down the stairs. You are energized and enlightened by this experiencing of The Merlin. You know this, too, will become a part of the knowing for your Self. As you reach the last curve in the stairs, you count the last three steps: 3 - 2 - 1. As you reach the last step, you release this image. You encapsulate the experience within your mind. You return to the present time and place—clear, energized, and empowered. You have begun your quest again with clarity, energy, and power. You give yourself three more stars to celebrate yourself.

Always, always the research, the respect, the reverence, and the remembering are there for you, because of your relationship to the inner realms of your own mind.

In the following chapter, I will share some of what this relationship meant to another on the Hallowed Quest.

CHAPTER 8

THE ARCHDRUID AND
DESTINY'S KING

We find that at present the human race is divided politically into one wise man, nine knaves, and ninety fools out of every hundred. That is, by an optimistic observer. The nine knaves assemble themselves under the banner of the most knavish among them, and become "politicians": the wise man stands out, because he knows himself to be hopelessly outnumbered, and devotes himself to poetry, mathematics or philosophy; while the ninety fools plod off behind the banners of the nine villains, according to fancy, into the labyrinths of chicanery, malice and warfare.

T. H. White
The Book of Merlin (Austin, TX: University of Texas Press, 1977)

 Many years ago, a close friend and teacher, Thomas John Grieves, became powerfully illuminated by the Light he saw in the legends of Camelot. Once having been in the process of becoming a Catholic priest, T. J. was well acquainted with the teachings and the tenets of the Christian religion. He decided to forego taking his priestly vows only when he recognized it would involve sacrificing his mystical philosophy and suppressing his natural gifts, which would be considered too magickal and pagan by the organized church he sought to enter.

Instead, T. J. became a teacher of the mystical ways and wisdom, and the creator of a center in which students could learn freely and independently, supported by the love and light this fine man reflected. In essence, T. J. Grieves was a true representative of the Order of the Druid, a wise-man, teacher, and true ally in the Service of Sovereignty. As he is in Spirit now, I can say these things freely. Were he still on the mundane plane, his humble, Friar Tuck-like nature would resist such praise and would further prevent T. J. from recognizing that his work and his being were worthy of high commendations. Nevertheless, the truth is the truth, and T. J. Grieves strove to reflect truth as far as he was able.

I tell you this so you can understand how reverently and respectfully T. J. approached all the Light realms of wisdom—those of Arthur, Merlin, and Camelot, especially. He felt the legends were a direct connection to the holiest aspects of the Grail—the symbol of ultimate communion with the Divine, Restoration Source. T. J., with research and remembering, made as clear a connection to the legends as I have seen any others make, with few exceptions. The connection T. J. made most powerfully for himself—and therefore for those of us around him—was to Arthur.

T. J. saw Arthur as a true Lord of Light, a part of the Kristos, the Christ Light, a reemergence of that same Light Ray on which the Galilean entered the realm of humankind. Arthur was not in any sense a competitor for the Galilean, as T. J. saw it. He was, instead, a more Western reflection of that Same Light, one which could well have supported the transition of polytheism to monotheism, while still retaining a true reverence for the spiritual values of natural forces, the deities of Nature. T. J. was as frustrated by the structures that oppressed this mystical blend in the minds of humankind as he was by the structures of the organized church dogmas that oppressed those, such as himself, who were mystically gifted.

Although this frustrated him, T. J. never lost his sense of humor, not even at the end of a lengthy, debilitating illness. Toward the end of his days, he joked that it would be wonderful to have a vast number of bumper stickers made up stating: "Arthur is Christ." Then, he would add with amused regret, that it was too bad he hadn't thought of it sooner, because since the Dudley Moore film "Arthur" had recently been released with popular success, these bumper stickers would obviously be confusing—to say the least!

From this true tale of one fine man's experiencing of Arthur and his realms, we can begin to see how very sacred the myths and their meanings could have been, have always been, and will continue to be for our lives and our Western Consciousness. To T. J., Arthur's mission was a holy one, filled with temptations and sacrifices, just as that of the Galilean, yet with a more Celtic Western reflection of the same, essential Light. T. J. truly felt that Arthur and Excalibur would reemerge in their own way as a resurrection of the Celtic Western Light, when the time was right.

While I am not certain that most of the Western world is ready for such in-depth spiritual revelations regarding the legends of Arthur, Merlin, and Camelot, any more than it is ready for T. J.'s fantasy bumper stickers, I feel it is ready to see the legends in a new light. This light has been illuminating many of the current images of the legends for some time and is growing brighter as we become more enlightened and conscious of the evolutionary messages within the myths.

Technically, the "holy mission" of Arthur that T. J. saw—and others have for a millennium or more—was not a failed mission, as the legends often portrayed. Instead, we can consider the mission of Arthur was to create an imprint on the psyche of the Western mind. This imprint then would be a seed which flourished in the future consciousness of Celtic, Western peoples. The vision of the Round Table as a unifying concept was quite new at its inception, during the time of the historical Arthur. However, the event of this unity and the symbolic Round Table legend, led to a new wave of understanding the power of that unity. Even when it was portrayed as having failed from within, the Round Table unity conceptually created the critical mass change of consciousness required then—yet represented now wherever global alliances are made for the protection and preservation of the shared, syncretic ideals of humanity.

The orders of knighthood and chivalry may be seen as predecessors of honorable attempts being made to assume stewardship of the lands and the people. Admittedly, this ideal order of chivalry and stewardship has yet to be created—but the concept is indelibly imprinted in our minds. From this imprinted—and therefore encoded mind-set—we may well be able to create realistically that which was just creatively realized by Arthur in his uniting of Britain, and by those who heard his legends.

Those legends served their purpose then. Seen and told in a new, illuminated way, these legends may well serve our purpose now, as I believe they were originally designed to do. The legends emerged in a time that was not quite ready for them. The visions of Round Table Unity, Courtly Love, and Chivalry were evolutionarily ahead of their time; yet their light led our consciousness onward, even through very dark times. How then, we ask, shall they lead us now—in a new form, a new image, and a new light? "As far as our beliefs will let them" is the answer with which The Merlin would agree. In order to personalize the archetypal connections we make with the sacred characters of the legends, we immerse ourselves in others' portrayals of them. In so doing, we craft our own image—blending all the parts that "connect" with the currents of power found within. I'll close this chapter with a sample of one of mine; taken from a blend of inspiration, experience, and information.

WART AND THE WISE OLD MAN

(Written by Amber Wolfe—with reverent respect for T. H. White,
Mary Stewart, and for Kara Starr)

It happened just yesterday ... no, today it was ... or perhaps the day after tomorrow. Time becomes so irrelevant, one forgets to check the calendar in the realms of myth and legend, you see. Yet, regardless when it did happen, it happened indeed. Ah, what happened? Ah, yes. Let me tell you as it happened to happen.

I was in my tower, busily filling my time with the timeless tasks of wizardry, when I glanced out one of the windows and saw I had company coming to visit. Using my spyglass—that wonderful name for the telescope—I saw it was the Lady Dana. She was accompanied by a rather small boy, who put me in mind to remember Arthur as he was at that age.

As the Lady Dana is a weaver of Gaelic flair, I called for my Druid sister, Ganieda, who so enjoys spending time with one of her own kind.

And so it was that we greeted our company together, and the Lady Dana told me of her purpose in making this journey to see me. She was of the opinion that the legends of Arthur and Camelot—and of myself, of course—needed to be seen in a new light, more suitable for the present—wherever that may be. She had come to me, one supposes, seeking my illumination of the matter; as she clearly saw my hand in the original creation of these tales.

Since I am an old man now, I rather enjoy the privilege of being imperious, especially when I particularly do not feel myself to be so. With great pretense of having been imposed upon, I set the Lady Dana to the task of weaving with my sister Ganieda. This was so I would not be obliged to include them in my conversation with the wise child, who was waiting wide-eyed and expectantly by my side. The young lad seemed quite impressed with my ability to command the ladies, and they, to their credit, allowed me this small self-enhancement. I suppose this was to secure my full cooperation in the matter at hand. While the ladies worked together at their craft, I began to craft, as well—another version of these tales to tell. And so I began by addressing the lad as I had done with Arthur, in kind. Come within; and listen as now I speak to Wart, (and attempt to irritate the ladies should they doze into fantasy or frolic).

"Come here, boy, and make yourself quite comfortable, for I require your full attention to what I'm about to recount and relate to you in your own time. Did I hear you say your name? Never mind. What's in a name, really?—other than what one puts there. I believe I shall call you 'Wart.' I assume you'll want to know why ... ah, you do. Yes, it is true I once called King Arthur that, as well; but he was not yet a king then, merely a small wart of a lad like you. Now, be patient. We'll come to Arthur later. We'll have to begin well before then, if you want to hear the tale newly told.

"I remember being a small boy in my grandfather's castle. And no, it wasn't as grand as it sounds. My grandfather was a king in South Wales, in a region near Armarthen where I was born. There were many kings in those days—more than one could shake a stick at—or a sword, which is what was usually happening to one king or another. I lived in the castle with my grandfather the king because his daughter Elaine was my mother. No one knew who my father was, which led to endless speculation, most of it the dim reflections of quite superstitious, unenlightened minds.

"On the surface, that was true; but there were those who knew my father and also knew his name could not be revealed. My mother knew, of course, as did my grandfather and a few of those most trusted to remain silent. My father was Ambrosius, one of the sons of the great King Constantine, who was, alas, already dead long before I was born.

"There was great turmoil in the land at that time, you realize. The Romans had begun withdrawing rather suddenly, and all of Britain was soon left to its own resources. There had been bitter disputes among the various kings concerning who would be the High King after my grandfather, Constantine, had gone. My uncle, Constans Moine, was the eldest, so he was the natural choice; but he was murdered by his own closest adviser, his seneschal, Vortigern, who had also served Constantine.

"Vortigern was quite clever, even though he was an evil man. It is folly to believe that those of evil mind are not clever, even though they are blind to truth. Vortigern had already begun to use his power and influence to persuade the Saxons to help control the constantly warring tribes. Vortigern had allied himself with a particularly mercenary lot under the leadership of Hengist, a ruthless, barbaric, blond giant of a man. As soon as Vortigern was secure enough to do so, he murdered my uncle Constans and put high prices on the heads of my father Ambrosius and my uncle Uther. Yes, Uther Pendragon is correct, but that part comes later.

"Vortigern took the throne of Britain and a Saxon woman named Rowena to be his queen. She was magnificently ruthless by all accounts given of her. I imagine she was related to Hengist in some way, else he would have had her for his own, considering she displayed those barbaric qualities so valued by that particular breed of Saxon. By the time my father and my uncle heard of this, they were far beyond being able to defend themselves. A price on their heads meant a price for their heads, quite literally, in those dark days. Ambrosius and Uther were forced to flee to the lands we now call Brittany and there determine what to do next.

"Before that happened, though, Ambrosius risked his life to be with his beloved Elaine one more time, and the result of that encounter you see before you now. When I was born, Vortigern's spies were everywhere on the lands. It was far too dangerous to let anyone know who my father really was. Vortigern and his Saxon dogs surely would have killed everyone in my grandfather's castle, if not in his kingship altogether.

"I was not aware of all this until I was old enough to wander about the countryside on my own. When I was about your age, I chanced upon the cave of an old Druidic hermit named Blaise. He taught me many things and revealed many wonders, one of which was the true identity of my father. I suspect I rather favored Ambrosius, and this was the reason my mother and her nurse decided to keep my unruly locks so long that they were forever hiding my face. Of course, all this hair of mine merely served to prove to many what they suspected or carefully had been led to believe: this was the rumor that I was the child of a demon spirit. Lovely camouflage, when you think about it—or at least I thought so at that time.

"Blaise taught me, as I later taught Arthur when he was a boy, in the old ways, the natural ways, in Nature. I do miss those days; those when I was a student, and those when I was the teacher ... those days are dear to me. I can still teach, you know, Wart? You'll have to use your imagination a bit more though—but you have a bit more imagination, don't you? You have a bit more than Arthur and a bit more than myself at your age, I'll warrant. As it should be, it is so. That's evolution, you know.

"Well, time passed, as it will, and I grew to be a man. I suppose I was not yet old enough to drive one of those infernal machines that all young men of your times covet so. Ah, yes, and women, too—I suppose that is also true. There have always been women who wanted to go about driving chariots on their own, and such as that. Still, one must expect such things from a breed who conquered all of Europe and held it long enough to make their mark in Time. But let's not discuss the ways of women right now, shall we, lad? I see that the Lady Dana has knotted a thread in her weaving just now, and Ganieda has furrowed her brow. Ssh! Mum's the word on the women, at least for the time being.

"Vortigern still held Britain in his ruthless grasp, but Ambrosius and Uther were raising an invasion force in Brittany. This information came to us, even in our remote little region of South Wales. My mother's brothers, my uncles in Wales, brought this message to my grandfather, the King. My uncles were soldiers in Vortigern's army, as most young men were forced to be in those days. But you see that was where Vortigern was not very clever. He expected his weapons and his forces of fear to control what was inside the hearts of men—and women, naturally. Vortigern, it seems, did not know the hearts of the Britons very well, and especially those of the Welsh—a fierce, proud breed they are—but I assume you know your history, don't you?

"As you can tell already, we had spies of our own. Soon the news of Ambrosius and Uther's coming invasion spread like wildfire across the lands. Then we were ablaze with excitement and plans were being made—secretly, of course. I was thrilled. My grandfather and my mother had already admitted to me the truth about who my father was. Yet, so far as we knew, no others suspected this. The others were strangely content in considering me to be the spawn of some demon—or faerie—as others saw it. Strange. Hmmm ...

"We were content to let them continue to believe these strange tales of my conception, as we saw no harm in them at all. We certainly did not expect those strange tales to be the reason I was summoned, along with my mother, to King's Fort, the stronghold of Vortigern.

"By that time, my mother already had sought the refuge of a nunnery nearby, one of those at that time that allowed the old ways and those of the old blood, such as my mother was, to be and do what they wanted, alongside the new ways of the Christian god. My mother and I traveled to King's Fort with a great deal of fear accompanying us, I am not ashamed to admit. My mother had learned to put her faith in this new god of mercy. I had decided to put my faith in my own powers of perception. It was my contention both would be required in Vortigern's presence.

"As it turned out, Vortigern had no idea about my identity. In fact, it was the rumor that I was a fatherless child—born of a spirit who impregnated my mother—which interested Vortigern the most. There was a tower at King's Fort that kept falling down, regardless of how it was engineered and constructed.

When it fell for the third time, Vortigern's dark Druids persuaded him to use their ancient ritual of blood sacrifice to secure the building of the tower—and, one assumes, to please what they saw as the angry spirits of that location. What I saw, thanks to the teachings of Blaise, were the tell-tale signs of an underground cavern—a sinkhole, I believe you might say. Since I could easily discern their lack of scientific wisdom by the primitive nature of the measures they were suggesting to remedy the situation with the collapsing tower, I did not waste time trying to explain the causes logically.

"You've heard the expression 'When in Rome, do as the Romans,' I suppose? Well, in King's Fort what I had to do was outdo that smarmy lot of debased Druids whom Vortigern had gathered around him. They were a ruthless set of mutants, I must say. Nevertheless, I did so—speaking as they would understand me—or at least as they would understand or believe the child of a mysterious demon would speak. I had rather a lot of practice with this, you see. It was a technique I used when there were those who tried to follow me while I wandered about the countryside on some research mission or other which Blaise had set me to doing.

"In truth, I must say this time it was rather different. Perhaps fear had entranced me. Perhaps my powers of perception gave me access to a region of my brain I had not yet explored. Or perhaps, it is only fair to say, I was indeed under the protection of the new god—as well as the old ones, whom I had grown up serving in my own way.

"Being as dramatic and mysterious as I could be, I told all those self-professed sorcerers, and Vortigern as well, that there were dragons fighting beneath the tower, in a cavern deep under the ground. Then, much to my own surprise, I saw these dragons—one of them red and the other white. I knew these were visions of Ambrosius' coming conquest of Vortigern and his Saxon allies. I had seen the red dragon brooch Ambrosius left with my mother those many years ago, and I knew destiny was at hand.

"Before I could stop myself, I told Vortigern that Ambrosius was coming and he must leave King's Fort immediately. Then I continued, half in jest, half in truth, to describe the visions that kept entering my mind. Some of these were rambling constructions I made up from what Blaise had taught me and from the endless prattle I had heard from the nuns who had accompanied my mother on our journey to King's Fort.

"The rest—well, as to the rest, only time will tell—for the rest is made up of riddles, as are most prophecies, until they clearly have come to pass. By then, of course, it's far too late to do anything about the situation that was prophesied. Isn't it just?

"Strangely enough, this satisfied Vortigern that I was on his side. After all, I had warned him about Ambrosius as he saw it. So I was released, along with my mother, to return to South Wales and await Vortigern's need of me in the future. That future never came. Ambrosius and Uther swept into Britain—and through it, as well—on a rising wave of support from the people.

"In a few months, Ambrosius had killed Vortigern quite easily, it seems, since his former stronghold, King's Fort, would have been almost impossible to defeat. In time, I was able to go to Ambrosius and be acknowledged as his son, if only privately so, for fear of reprisals and jealousies that might harm me. Since I had no wish to claim my own natural rights as heir to the throne of Britain, this suited my purpose nicely.

"I served Ambrosius for a time, and later his brother Uther—by then Uther Pendragon—as you have come to know him. Uther was well aware of my rights to the throne, both before and after Ambrosius' death. Because of this, he was always suspicious of me and of my abilities, which he could not understand. Uther was a warrior. I was not. What I was you call a wizard now, and we called a Druid then, an Equites, as well: a royal Druid.

"Because of my continually having to soothe Uther's suspicions—and because I was still young and full of myself—I let Uther persuade me to arrange a liaison with the lovely Igraine, wife of the good duke, Gorlois of Cornwall. In my defense, I must say I had been beset with visions of a coming king, of Ambrosius' line, who would unite Britain as Ambrosius had begun to do before he died. I had begun to see these visions as wishful imaginings within my own mind. I could not see that Uther would father such a child—especially with the sorts of women he favored: as a rule, a passive, brooding lot.

"There was Morgawse, of course, his foster daughter; but she was quite young then. She had been given to Uther's care by her heathen northlands clan to seal an alliance and in the hope—in her hopes, for certain—that she would become his queen. But Morgawse was just a child then, no more than nine or ten; yet she was already the fierce product of her ancient warrior kin. Divide and conquer would have been more in keeping with the codes by which Morgawse was born and bred. She could not be the mother of the coming king I envisioned so clearly—and so imminently—destined to enter this world.

"Then, when Uther fixed his aim upon Igraine, I saw the chance to bring my vision into form. Perhaps it was because I did not see the danger in this. Perhaps I should have consulted with those who guarded the realms of divinatory knowledge at Avalon, as often I had done before. Still, Igraine was herself Avalon-trained, and I felt she would have known if danger were present; for she, too, desired Uther, if only for the satisfaction of her physical needs. Gorlois was a good man and an honorable one. I must say that Igraine had no intention to leave him or dishonor him publicly.

"You are young yet, Wart, and may not understand these things; but I shall try to explain. In those times, a Celtic woman, high-born such as Igraine, still had the right to choose her consorts—if not her husband—for this was done with politics and land in mind. Uther, as high king, still had the right to bed any woman he chose. It was an ancient right, and not always an unwise one. Had Uther and Igraine chosen this openly ... ah, well. The time for that had begun to pass away by then.

"Gorlois had been Ambrosius' man. He served Uther as brother to his once-loved King Ambrosius, and not as king by right. This, Uther had always known; so I suppose it pleased him to take Igraine, literally, in such a way that would show Gorlois that he, Uther, knew it was Ambrosius to whom he was still loyal, and not his rightful king, Uther Pendragon.

"There was also the matter of Cornwall, which Ambrosius, and not Uther, had granted to Gorlois. Some of Uther's knights were greedily coveting parcels of that fine land for themselves and made frequent invasions to harry Gorlois. These Uther dismissed as the natural inclinations of his warrior breed. It was during one of these battles Gorlois was killed, unforeseen by me—or by Igraine. It was, one might say, the price paid by both Igraine and myself for our role in the creation of the coming king. There was no magick other than that of the greater unfolding destiny. Uther came to Igraine disguised to avoid detection by Cornwall's guards at Tintagel Castle. There is no magick by which a man or woman may be disguised from each other when they are as one in the act of procreation, unless they wish it to be so.

"Later, when it was known Igraine would bear a child, Uther married her, but with the provision that the child be fostered out upon its birth. There would be questions as to who this child's father was, you realize. Uther or Gorlois? I must say the question crossed my mind quite often as we all waited to hear of Igraine's safe delivery of this child. One must consider that Gorlois also was a foster father to Arthur, in a spiritual sense, that is, because of his own connection to Cornwall, Tintagel—and Igraine. Igraine was, by then, well out of reach, sequestered at the sanctuary on Avalon Isle, where no one from the outside was permitted to see her.

"I was well on the outside with the Avalonians then, I can tell you. Even Ganieda had little use for me, though she did tell them of my vision of the coming king. How much of this they believed and how many of them glimpsed it, too, I had no way of knowing. I had begun to wonder about it myself during that cold, dark winter while we waited. Then at the crest of winter, Yuletide—or Christmas, we have come to call it—this golden child was born. When I was allowed to see him, I knew the visions were true. This child of light, long awaited, had his grandfather's eyes, the eyes of Ambrosius. I knew then if it were truly his destiny to be the King of All Britain, he would also be that, mythically, for All Time. And I? I would serve him as best I could in the world of men, and well beyond. I would be the Archdruid of Destiny's King for All Time."

I could see Wart was bravely trying to hide the tears welling up in his innocent, shining eyes. Ganieda and the Lady Dana had ceased their weaving craft and were watching me with the soft, gentle expressions only women of wisdom and power can express in quite that manner. It was a reverent look, one that bespeaks the deepest, most sacred remembering. We were as one, there in that tower, united by our love for Arthur, the legendary King of Light. I broke the silence first; for legendary wizards such as I, Archmage, Archdruid, and master of dragons, are not supposed to cry.

"Take care of her, Wart, and see that she brings you to visit me again very soon. There are other tales to tell, other shadows to dispel around these legends of which you shall come to know as the Lady Dana continues her teachings. When the time is right, let us meet again. Perhaps you can find me in the forest, in my favorite tree; or you might prefer my crystal cave, which reflects all you need to see—of the pathways to knowing."

As I watched them from the tower window until they were well out of sight, I knew a new age had begun for Arthur and his legends—and for myself, as well. As they started their journey homeward, I heard the Lady Dana begin to tell of these realms once again ... of the patterns of history, and myth, and time ... of the shadows cast by ancients, dancing around the center fire as they dance still today.

CHAPTER 9

THE DRUIDS' DANCE

Yet for all the antiquity of Druidism, for all the contacts between the Celts and other nations, for all the fascination they evoked, nowhere do we find a systematic account of their religion, and this stands in sharp contrast with the body of often explicit detail about Celtic life in general. The Druids, who took such pains to invest themselves and their teachings with mystery and secrecy may perhaps have succeeded better than they knew: If ever they stood guardians of the founts on an Ancient Wisdom they certainly ensured its treasures were not passed on.

Ward Rutherford,
The Druids: Magicians of the West (Northamptonshire: Aquarian Press, 1984)

 The Druids of ancient times were the spiritual leaders of the Celtic people whom they served as priests, priestesses, advisers, genealogists, and teachers. The bulk of our information about the Druids comes from Classical (Greek and Roman) writers who recorded their encounters with these still mysterious figures during the approximate period between 200 B.C. and A.D. 500. The earliest archeological record we have of the Druids comes from excavations of the La Tiêne Celtic culture in Switzerland, dating from about 500 B.C. From this we can surmise the Druids were a functional part of Celtic spiritual life from very early on, with their origins linked to the ancient Indo-European shamans.

The name "Druid" seems to have come from several sources; among them are "drus," "dervo," "daur," and "derw." Each of these words means oak, or oak tree—in Greek, Gaulish, Irish (Erse), and Welsh, respectively. In Irish, Druid is "drui"; and in Welsh, "derwydd." These names reflect the Druidic reverence for the oak tree, symbolically the most powerful, Earth-connected, growing reflection of Nature. Druids held all of Nature sacred, and trees in particular, as shamanic links between the Earth Mother and the Sky Father.

The Celtic, European Druids were influenced by the Spiritual philosophies of their tribes, their tribal deities and the natural cycles of their lands. In the Celtic forms of Druidism, the presence of women was not unusual; particularly in the more shamanic forms. These naturally followed the example set by the forces of and in Nature. The presence of women in the Druidic orders continued to develop, reaching its fullest form in Britain before the Romans.

DRUIDISM AND THE ROMAN OCCUPATION: CELTIC AND MITHRAIC

Some diminishing of the presence of women in the Druidic orders occurred during the Roman occupation of Britain. This was primarily due to the conflict between Roman practices and those of the Celts. The Roman form, which was imported into Britain, was based on the worship of Mithras, an early Persian solar deity. Mithraism had originally been brought into Western culture by the soldiers of Alexander the Great; then spread throughout Northern Europe by the Roman Army.

The Eastern desert philosophy that accompanied the Mithraic forms of druidism across Europe into Britain brought in orders that excluded women. The Celtic Druidic forms continued, some blending and some not. We can only speculate about the eventual blend of the Celtic and Mithraic forms of Druidism. This is due to the overlaying influence of Rome, first as an empire, then later as the Orthodox head of Christianity. The initial waves of Christian doctrine did not conflict as significantly with the Celtic forms of Druidism as they did with those of Mithras, "the soldier's god."

It is surmised that the original Celtic forms of Druidic orders became more involved in areas having to do with the lands, the natural laws, and the diagnostic, scientific fields, as well as those involved with teaching wisdom and establishing the centers for learning, the famous British Druidic Colleges. The Mithraic forms are seen as having taken over the orders known as the slayers, dealing with matters of war and conflict. These areas were primarily under the rulership of Rome at that time.

Eventually it was the Mithraic forms that came most heavily under fire from the Orthodoxy of the Christian religious structures. Ironically, both the Orthodox forms of Christianity and the Mithraic forms of Druidism had their origins in the East; both reflecting separatist, hierarchal philosophy. Still, it was the actions of the Mithraic slayers that caused the greatest conflict, particularly with those orders that had become debased, as greatly structured spiritual forms easily can do. Additionally, the increasingly structured and imposed Byzantine forms of Christianity had led to a weakening of the Celtic/European culture, which also diminished the powers of the Druidic orders. This was particularly true of the slayers, whose Mithraic practices had already been outlawed by the time of the late Roman occupation.

The ultimate conflict between the Eastern Mithraic forms of Druidism and the Eastern forms of Christianity was based on a very different view of the practice of sacrifice. In the Mithraic view, it was the slayer (of the bull, symbolic of Mithras), not the sacrifice, who released power in this ritual practice. In the Christian view, the sacrifice was the redeemer/empowerer. Since the tenets of the Christian religion taught that the crucifixion of Christ had been the ultimate sacrifice and no further sacrifices were to be made, the Mithraic practices were seen as distinctly in opposition. Since both Mithraic and Christian Orthodoxy emerged from set-structure philosophies, they were bound to come head to head. Unfortunately, this affected the Celtic forms, as well. To this day, the common misconceptions about Druidism still lie in the erroneous idea of the Druids—of all the Druids—having engaged in the Mithraic forms of the orders of the Slayers.

Currently, with the rapidly emerging Nature Consciousness, there is hope that the original, as well as the modern forms of Druidism, will be seen in a new light. Perhaps then the additional misconceptions about Mithras will also be cleared up. This most appropriately could come from the modern druidic forms, which still operate on the separatist policies that came from the desert, rather than the interwoven, mutually honoring alliance composed of the Earth Mother, Solar, Sky Father, and humankind, as well. Then the mutual spiritual philosophies of Light may be shared for the good of all.

Note: Sacrifices are not practiced by modern druidic orders. There are symbolic sacrifices, such as those made in the Christian practice of giving up something for Lent in order to honor the gifts of the Divine Light. No other forms that harm anyone or any living thing, nor harm or destroy anything, are tolerated.

Classical and Revival Sources

Classical sources tell us the Druids were viewed as members of the nobility. For some, their rank was equal to that of the warrior aristocracy—the equites—meaning those who rode the horses, or drove chariots into battle. In other words, the knights. Additionally, we know some of the Druids were allowed to wear six colors in their tartans, which was a privilege usually reserved only for queens. Only kings were allowed to wear seven colors.

Classical sources also tell us the Druids were classed as seers, prophets, and bards. Revival blends of Druidism dating from the late eighteenth century divide Druids into Orders of Bards, Ovates, and Druids. Both classical and revival sources allow us to better understand the functions of the Druids, which were basically as follows—with my addition, the equites, which is included in several resources on Druidism.

Orders of Druids—Revivals Traditions

Bards—the poets, signers, keepers of the oral traditions, genealogists

Ovates (or Vates)—the scientists, observers of natural laws, diviners, and diagnosticians

Druids—those who collected, compiled, and taught wisdom, organizers of the Druidic "colleges"

Equites (Eh queh tess)—these were the advisers, counsel to the King and/or Queen, interpreted natural laws and moral philosophy in order to serve the role of prime minister—or secretary of state (in more modern terms)

In some cases, the Druids and Equites were combined into one category. Revival sources designate colors for each of these categories. Bards wore blue, Ovates wore green, and Druids wore white. Presumably, the Equites could wear a number of colors, as long as that number did not exceed six.

The only classical source that indicates any hierarchal structures among the Druids comes from a reference to the Chief Druid of Gaul, who was in that position on Caesar's authority. We can assume there were other Archdruids in various regions, probably drawn from the order called Equites. Perhaps we can best view these orders of Druids as areas of expertise, rather than strictly ranking hierarchies. Each part had its own value to the whole of the Celtic tribes.

Both classical and revival sources point to Britain as the place where Druidism reached its highest point. These sources describe the efforts of the Druids to create valuable centers for learning, which we now call the Druidic colleges.

> *The Druids teach likewise many things related to the stars and their motions, the magnitude of the world and our earth, the nature of things and the power and prerogatives of the immortal Gods."*

Julius Caesar
From *The Celts* by Gerhard Herm (New York: St. Martin's Press, 1976)

The following Druidic journey uses the magick of imagery to help you experience the ceremonial traditions of ancient times. Such images can inspire your own legendary magick and give you access to tribal memory, personal empowerment, and spiritual guidance on your quest.

THE DARK FOREST JOURNEY
An Experiential Guided Imagery

Breathe, release, and relax your body, consciously. Repeat this sequence until you are receptive to your inner realms of vision. Breathe naturally.

———

It is night and you are riding through the forest on a large white horse. It is very dark in the forest and you wonder if you are traveling far too fast. Ahead of you in the dark are your traveling companions, an old man and an old woman. You can just glimpse their white cloaks flowing in the breeze as they ride, unconcerned, at great speed through the dark forest night.

As they seem to know the way quite well, and your own horse is content to follow their lead, you tighten your grip on the reins and submit to trust and faith. The horses' hooves on the soft forest floor sound like stones falling on hard ground. You can feel the muscles in your horse's neck and chest as they tighten and stretch with each stride. The long mane on your horse whips across the back of your hands as you concentrate on holding fast to the reins. The horse is strong, powerful, and confident as he races through the darkness.

You realize, with relief, that the horse is far too smart to gallop into a tree, so you relax a bit and begin to enjoy the ride. Only an occasional small branch brushes across the sides of the horse and your legs, so you know this great steed can indeed carry you to your destination—the sacred gathering of Druids from all about the lands.

It is an event you do not want to miss, and one to which you have finally been invited. Up ahead, your companions travel quickly onward, secure in the knowledge you are ready for the event. Although you still wonder if you were ready for the journey to reach your destination, you know you are ready to experience the magick that a gathering in the sacred grove is sure to provide.

You remind yourself that you are worthy, even if you are not always wise. You continue to follow your companions as they guide you toward the nemeton—the sacred grove. You whisper a prayer to Nemetona, the guardian goddess of the groves, asking her for protection on the journey. You express your thanks to Nemetona for allowing you to enter her domain, the forest surrounding the groves. You place yourself in her

care. Immediately, a deep sense of connection with these dark woodlands begins to emerge from within your heart—now touching the heart of Nature all around you.

For a few moments, you feel as if you are flying through the forest. What had appeared before to be dark, ominous shapes are now quite clearly visible. You glimpse two large clusters of boulders. As you ride quickly between them, you can see a small forest creature scurrying into a crack between two boulders. Looking back, you can see it is a fox, with glowing, reflective eyes. In a flash, you find you can see in the dark quite well—as well as a fox, in fact.

You feel a rush of excitement, for you know the magick has already begun. You can see your own hands, gripping the reins somewhat less intensely now. You can see the rings on your fingers, with their symbols of your rank clearly etched in silver and in gold. The great cabochon emerald, given to you when you came of age, seems to glow now as you've never seen it do before—not even in the light of day.

You wonder at this, but accept it as a gift of magick, a gift, perhaps, from the goddess of the sacred groves. You realize you can make out the pattern of your cloak. It is the pattern of your clan, your tartan, symbolizing the powers its colors represent, woven together with the straight lines for strength and purpose—and to signify your position.

You can clearly make out the lines of red, violet, and white in your tartan weave. Less clear here, despite your night vision, are the bands of blue, light and dark, which are also woven into the dark green background. Five colors, the tartan of a noble clan. Remembering these colors, you remember you are worthy, and the nobility of your purpose makes it definitely so.

You repeat the verses you learned as a child growing up in your clan's stronghold, the castle fort of a great warrior line. It gives you the strength to carry on through the night.

> Two red lines of fire, for courage and
>   desire;
> A royal violet line to honor the Divine.
> Three lines of white to aim with clear
>   sight,
> Bands of blue, for what is right and
>   true,
> On a rich field of green for Nature's
>   noble queen.

You become so involved remembering and recognizing the wisdom in your childhood verses that you scarcely notice your traveling companions have slowed down, almost stopping just ahead of you. Fortunately, your horse has wisely followed their lead and has slowed to a gentle walking gait that carries you toward your companion guides, close enough to see their faces in this magickally illuminated forest.

You recognize the old couple now, as if you had not known them all along. They are the Old Ones who live in the forest at the base of the hill on which your family's stronghold stands proudly. You have visited them since you were a child—and they have visited you throughout all the times of your life when you needed them most. Instead of the forest colors they usually prefer to wear, tonight they are dressed in robes of white, trimmed with Celtic braids of gold, red, and green.

You greet them warmly, with the respectful titles which show your sense of kenship with them, as valued as your kinships born of blood and family connections. You know they are as much a part of you as you are of them. You greet them in Gaelic, the language of your Celtic clanship.

"*Seanamhair, Seanair.*" (Grandmother, Grandfather.)

You ask them if you have arrived already, or are at least close to your desired destination. They laugh at your question, as the Old Ones often do at the innocent questions of a very wise child. Realizing there are no signs of anyone else here in the forest, except yourself and the Old Ones, you feel foolish at first; then you join in their laughter. You ask why you have all stopped here, when the journey had just begun to be interesting and no longer quite so uncertain.

The Seanair bids you to dismount, for the horse is tired and you both must rest and reflect on the journey thus far. The Old Ones dismount and, reluctantly, you do also. The Seanamhair motions for you to rest in the soft cool grasses at the base of a great old oak. She helps you get comfortable and listens patiently to how well you have proven yourself worthy thus far without once suggesting modesty as a needed virtue. Then, the Old Ones tell you what wisdoms you have already accepted, and worthily shared, as you rode through the dark forest.

First, you were brave, if not a little crazy, in choosing to enter the dark forest of your own mind, where there was no path to be seen. You learned to trust the strength within as you trusted your fine, shamanic steed. You submitted yourself to that faith and trust that carried you ever inward to places you have not gone before. You followed the lead of the white lights ahead of you in the dark forest night as you followed the movements of the Old Ones' cloaks, moving in the breezes of your inner vision.

You reminded yourself of your personal power and purpose to journey into the domains of Nature, to the sacred realms of Nemetona, guardian goddess of the groves and forests of Nature's wisdom. Your prayer to her and your placing yourself in her care showed your deep reverence and honor for that part of Nature that you cannot always see, at first—but can always feel in your heart.

The boulders you glimpsed were a gateway that did not present an obstacle, but a gift, an ally in the form of a fox. As the fox entered into a crack between the boulders, so you entered a deeper region within your mind. Because you recognize and honor Nature, your own natural abilities are enhanced. Thus you were able to see yourself clearly for what you are, and for what you have, a noble character with all the qualities your tartan represented to you and those that are

personally yours, as well. Whether you see them or not, these are your true colors, which you show bravely as you seek wisdom where there was no path before.

And what of the emerald? The rings of gold and silver carved with signs of rank and power? Know that Old Ones will tell you when this dark forest journey begins again ... later along the way in this, your Hallowed Quest.

For now, you may acquaint yourself more with the Old Ones, here in their aspect as the white-cloaked Druid teachers. With the Old Ones you may freely share the image you have of yourself here—now in the dark forest—illuminated by the light of your own noble character—the royal character of a wise child of the true Sovereign Queen. A child of Light and Nature you were born; a noble in the service of Sovereignty you have grown to be. The Old Ones encourage you to have patience and faith, for the journey will continue—as the Journey of life always continues, leading you to wisdom.

You choose to remain for just a brief time in the domains of Nemetona, and honor her as the guardian goddess of the sacred groves. Then you breathe and release your image of the Forest of the Old Ones; knowing they will be there when you need them.

ASPECTS OF SEEKING WISDOM
IN DRUIDIC FASHION

For now we move into a discussion of the light and shadow aspects of those who seek wisdom in their ways, Druidic or otherwise, some with a noble character, and some for whom the dark forest is never illuminated from within.

There has been a great deal written about the Druids recently, most of it based on scanty Roman records—and most of it emphasizing how things were at that time. My emphasis, and my real interest in Druids and Druidism, is how it is now. I cannot believe the Druids, then, would have wanted the Druids now to focus their quests for wisdom and their actions on what is past, but on what is present and what is yet to come.

Fortunately, there are a number of fine Druidic organizations which are well aware of the importantance of the continuing pursuit of knowledge. Unfortunately, there are others who seem intent upon maintaining their exclusive rights to "ancient Druidic wisdom" (*i.e.*, pay their fee), which they are willing to share only if you agree to adhere to their set structures. For those who decide to be a part of this type of process, we would hope that they do so by their own clear choice. Remember that *it is always the right of an individual to choose how to obtain wisdom*. So long as one is aware of what is being chosen, and that those choices may also be abandoned freely, no one can object to the way an individual chooses to find wisdom—as long as it harms no-one.

As I have stated before, my bias is clearly in favor of following a path of one's own choosing—*where there was no path before*. Certainly, it is valuable to join groups and study wisdom according to structures and doctrines. However, I have known far too many cases when these structures became restrictive. Then doctrines became dogmas rather quickly. This does not encourage learning, but controls and limits it.

Balance group work with personal work. Indeed, surround group work with personal work. Let it be known—if only to yourself—that you have the group outnumbered—all by yourself. With this philosophy, you will continue to have free mind and free will, which are your inalienable rights as a human being. Free mind and free will are essential to the seeker who is questing in the realms of knowledge and wisdom. Otherwise, the seeker is, at best, a poseur; at worst, a pawn.

Sacrificing free will and free mind to the service of someone else's path or power is sure to lead you astray into the Wasteland. That truly would be a waste for you, and a loss for the rest of us. We need all the free-minded, free-willed seekers of wisdom we have in the world—for the World.

The way of the Druid was, and is, one of open exploration of knowledge, a powerful, active process—a science. If this process is blocked, then it becomes debased. As it did in the past, so it does in the present. That is the shadow side of any structured organization. The remedy is to keep the structures open enough to let the Light of new knowledge shine through clearly. "And do be keeping your head about you," as Old Irish Biddy would tell you.

78

I stress that there are wonderful groups and organizations that have developed structures where seekers of wisdom may learn and grow to their full potentials. In fact, most are like this. Most are earnestly trying to provide for the waves of people waking up to the need to understand the ways of mystery and the ways of Earth wisdom. If these groups ask for allegiance, it is only to that which is sacred and Divine. These honorable groups and organizations never demand allegiance to, or for, themselves. That is the best key to understanding just what sort of group, or group leader, you have encountered.

An honorable group will tell you, up front, what path to wisdom they follow together in a shared, mutual quest. They will not insist that you abandon your own path in order to follow theirs—only that you respect theirs. Then, if you choose, you may let your path and theirs intersect for a time, for the good of all concerned. Your paths meet like the crossroads.

As in the ancient days, those of true wisdom still know the benefits of meeting at the crossroads. Symbolically, that represents meeting at the point where paths to wisdom converge. In the days of persecution, the crossroads literally saved many seekers of Earth's wisdom. The crossroads provided a chance to escape with their lives if they were discovered; allowing them to scatter like the winds, in different directions. Now that was truly wise and survival of the wisest is evolutionarily beneficial for the good of all. Do be wise. Please.

Before closing this chapter, I'll give you a unique imagery exercise with Stonehenge, which we will explore next.

SACRED SERVICE AT STONEHENGE
A Brief Guided Imagery

Breathe and release in sequence until you are relaxed and receptive. Open to your inner vision.

———

It is a beautiful morning on Salisbury Plain. Above you the sky is clear and blue. Beneath your feet the grass is lush and green. Standing tall on the plain is that monument of myth and legend— the great Stonehenge.

You cannot believe your luck at being alone here at such a sacred site. You breathe and absorb the powerful atmosphere surrounding you. Then, just as you begin to get a feel for this wonderful place, you realize you are not alone.

A sound which seems out of place here signals the approach of another person. It is an old man, dressed in gray, who is concentrating very hard on the Sacred Service he is performing at Stonehenge. He is doing so with an antiquated device which, nevertheless, seems to serve his purpose here at Stonehenge quite well. You can see by his expression he is honored and content with his sacred service.

He draws closer to you now, and the

vibrations from his antiquated device seem to bounce off the blue stones. He makes his way around a massive trilithon and reemerges on the other side.

You are entranced for a moment as you watch him at his work ... mowing the lush green grass on the grounds at Stonehenge!

Now you can practice your own journey work using the image of Stonehenge that emerged for you during the first paragraph of that exercise before I "shocked the monkey" of your brain. In the next chapter, we will explore Stonehenge from several different directions or, we could say, dimensions.

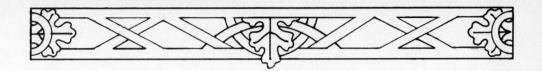

CHAPTER 10

THE GREAT STONEHENGE

All of these "people," these ancient "cultures" whose members would never have recognized themselves as such, vanished, as distinct societies, long ago, dissolved, and reassociated by succeeding waves of conquest, migration, growth and decay, the endless grouping and regrouping of racial evolution.

These dawn men left but little to tell us, their descendants, of their daily ways. But they did leave lasting memorials to their gods, testimonials of fears and hopes and deep purposes—the enduring monuments of Salisbury Plain.

And the greatest of these is Stonehenge.

Gerald S. Hawkins
Stonehenge Decoded (New York: Dell Publishing, 1965)

For centuries it was believed the Druids had built Stonehenge. This was reflected even in the later forms of the Arthurian legends that portrayed The Merlin as having constructed Stonehenge by magick. Such a profoundly amazing structure as Stonehenge would certainly seem like magick to one not able to understand the powerful magick of human mind and ingenuity. Additionally, in the days when Stonehenge was thought to have been created by some sort of Druidic magick, most people seriously underestimated the intelligence of those who had come before them. Naturally, this has been found to be a false assumption, as we will see in our exploration of Stonehenge. That Stonehenge in particular, and other henges as well, will always be associated with the Druids is not an error, really. It was wisdom, knowledge, and effort that built Stonehenge. Fortunately, those same qualities were—and are still—an essential part of what Druidism stands for.

I do not know that Merlin was a Druid or the memory of a Druid … although I suspect that The Merlin conception is far older than Druidism.

John Steinbeck
The Acts of King Arthur

Stonehenge is the most famous of the many henges or circles of standing stones found throughout Britain. In Ireland it is Newgrange that is best known. Both Stonehenge and Newgrange are of speculative origin, but both represent a feat of enlightened accomplishment at the time of construction. Exploring Stonehenge's origins is an evolutionary process to this day, as modern scholars seek to decode the mysteries of this sacred site.

Stonehenge is located on Salisbury Plain, in southern England. Its famous bluestones are precisely that, bluestone dolerite, as well as sarsen, which is a granite-hard type of sandstone. These bluestones have been traced to quarries in Wales about 130 miles away and the sarsen from a quarry about twenty miles from Stonehenge. Moving these, then, would have been a true feat.

We now know that Stonehenge was constructed in four distinct stages during a time period from about 3100 to 1100 B.C. Indications are that the first stage of Stonehenge was a circular embankment with wooden poles and upright slabs. In the second stage two rows of bluestones were added, forming a crescent at the center. In the third stage, the doorways, or trilithons, were added by placing a long flat stone atop two standing stones. During the fourth stage of Stonehenge's construction, several of the bluestones were reset, and roads were added, as well as extended around the site.

Stonehenge sat, relatively unnoticed, for centuries after the British Isles became Christian, until an English clergyman, Henry of Huntington, posed the question of their origin about A.D. 1430. This inspired Geoffrey of Monmouth (1136) to include Stonehenge in his writings about Arthur and the History of the Kings of Britain.

It was Geoffrey of Monmouth who claimed Stonehenge originated from about Arthur's time and had been built by The Merlin. According to Geoffrey, The Merlin had transported the stones from Ireland by using magick. The stones were said to have been brought to Ireland from Africa by a race of Irish Giants who had long since vanished. Since the stones had remarkable healing powers when water poured over them was used to treat battle wounds, Uther Pendragon, the fierce warrior king, and father of Arthur, sent The Merlin to get them for Britain.

Later legends tell of The Merlin being sent to Ireland to bring back the Stone of Britain. Still others have Uther, with some warriors and The Merlin, doing this by force. I dare say it would have taken all Uther's warriors to make a raid on Ireland and carry off a sacred stone from the Great Irish Henge. This, of course, would have been prevented by the Irish Drui, and the still-prevalent Irish-resistant attitude.

What I believe these legends represent is a magick feat even more powerful than the legend. I think it is likely this symbolizes at least two events. The first I see as the blending of the ancient Celtic tribes in Britain. The Gaelic Irish stone of destiny, gift of the Tuatha dé Danann, called the Lia Fiall, became a part of Brythonic mysticism. Blended, it became a Celtic stone of destiny. This blending was truly a magick tribal alchemy, as the earlier Celtic inhabitants of Britain, the Gaelic tribes, blended with the later Brythonic tribes.

The second event, I believe, represents the point at which the Celts reclaimed their mystical, as well as mundane, rulership of lands that had been controlled by the Romans for centuries. Since Rome never really had occupied Ireland, nor even tried to do so, Ireland had been able to preserve the ancient Celtic ways undiluted and undisturbed. For The Merlin to retrieve the Stone of Britain from Ireland meant reclaiming their shared Celtic destiny.

It is also possible that the Irish Drui contributed, in some way, to the reactivation of Stonehenge; that is, the reactivation of Druidic orders that had been banned by the Romans during their occupation. We know Christianity had already come into Britain during the time of Arthur. However, we also know the Druids and the Christian priests coexisted rather peacefully for several hundred years, until Orthodox edicts in about A.D. 800 forced the old ways of the Celts underground—for a while. As Steinbeck observed: "Isn't it odd that Malory, who knew the route from Amesbury to Glastonbury didn't mention Stonehenge although he had to pass it?" (Ibid.)

Finally, we have to consider that when Geoffrey of Monmouth wrote the original tale of Merlin transporting the stones, the Normans had already conquered England. (Battle of Hastings 1066—William the Conqueror). When that happened, the Normans and the British Celts had allied together against the Anglo-Saxons (the English), so the legends reflected this, as well. Later, in Elizabethan times, when Britain was in the process of conquering Ireland, the legends had The Merlin and Uther seizing the stone by force. Thus, the legends shift their shapes to show the times. Still, the deeper meanings, like the great stones, remain relatively unscathed.

In the seventeenth century, James I began an investigation of Stonehenge that was placed under the supervision of Inigo Jones, a famous architect in those days. Inigo Jones proclaimed that the Britons of pre-Roman times were too barbaric and crude ever to have created Stonehenge. Next came Walter Charleton, who was assigned the task of explaining Stonehenge's origins at the request of King Charles II. Charleton decided Stonehenge was created by the Danes, due to the fact its structures were similar to Danish/Viking burial cairns.

Still in the seventeenth century, John Aubrey theorized Stonehenge was a pagan temple built by the ancient Celtic Druids. This led William Stukeley, in the eighteenth century, to support Aubrey's theory of Stonehenge's Druidic origin. Stukeley's work was valuable in that he was among the first to present the idea of the Druids as wise scientists, mystics, and philosophers. However, Stukeley also tried to link the Druids with the Old Testament patriarchs. Wrong. Still, the idea that Stonehenge was Druidic held for years, due to Aubrey and Stukeley, until archeology developed more accurate methods for determining times.

The eighteenth century was a romantic period of revival for Stonehenge and for Druidism. First, John Wood called Stonehenge a lunar temple dedicated to Diana, and claimed it had been the sacred home of the "Archprophet" of Britain. This inspired Henry Hurle to "come out of the closet" with his own Druidism and use Stonehenge openly for rites with the Ancient Order of Druids, which he established in 1781. Druidic Revival was in full bloom.

In the nineteenth century, Sir Richard Colthoare actually excavated parts of Stonehenge and decided it was pre-Roman. This, of course, was a blow to the legends of The Merlin's magick feat with the stones, but it didn't upset the Ancient Order of the Druids—or any of the many other factions of neo-Druidic philosophy. They were too busy battling it out with the new scientific community, who maintained that the mystical ideas about Stonehenge were all nonsense. They said Celtic spiritual practices and Stonehenge were never connected.

A resolution to this battle between science and mysticism came around the turn of the century (eighteenth–nineteenth) when Sir J. Norman Lockyer, an astronomer, found some common ground. Lockyer and Penrose (an archeologist) spent several years studying Stonehenge and other henges throughout Britain. Since Lockyer had been the one to prove the Egyptian pyramids were correlated with solar and stellar tracks, the scientific community had to hear him out; but not all of them agreed with what he and Penrose said.

Lockyer claimed "astronomer priests" had constructed Stonehenge in about 3000–2000 B.C. This was getting very close to the truth in many ways. It represented an effort to blend science and mysticism, which was and is the Druidic way—the way of enlightened exploration. However, Lockyer's work was most valuable in proving that the ancient inhabitants of Britain were far more advanced than anyone had previously thought.

In the 1960s, Gerald Hawkins wrote *Stonehenge Decoded,* which is still one of the finest works on the subject. Hawkins, a professor at Boston University, used extensive computer analysis to prove the solar, lunar, and seasonal correlations with the positions of the Stones at Stonehenge. He also proved that this profound correlation could not possibly have been done by chance. Essentially, Hawkins described Stonehenge as a "Stone Age Computer." This was truly on track; still not everyone agreed.

Next, Fred Hoyle, a Cambridge astronomer who agreed with Hawkins, likened the creators of Stonehenge to great minds, such as Einstein and Newton. Then Alexander Thom, who was an Oxford professor and a Scottish engineer, pointed out the advanced mathematical concepts used to create Stonehenge. Thom showed that a specific measuring standard had been used, which he called the "megalithic yard" (2.72 feet). Additional work by Thom showed highly advanced geometric skills which were highly advanced centuries before the Greek mathematician Pythagoras ever lived.

Thom's work was so precise it forced skeptics to reconsider what they had dismissed before about the construction—and the purpose—of Stonehenge. It even led to the reexamination of ideas that had previously been thought to be far too "mystical" for the scientific community to consider. Thus, we have another catalyst for the blending of science and mysticism. This sounds Druidic to me.

By now it is certain your linear brain is vibrating with beta waves from the information you have just been given; and your head is filled with facts about the concepts and constructions of others. So let us move away from that which is concrete and stone, so to speak, and into the free-flowing abstract realms of imagination.

Let those beta waves move into the time-sharing regions of your own computer brain. They'll be there when you need them, busily working away their time. Let yourself relax and become receptive to the creative regions of your brain. Release the structures of learning and feel your brain begin to vibrate with the receptive, alpha waves of relaxed awareness.

Breathe and release in sequence until you feel the flow within shift to a more mystical frequency. Clear your mind for a visionary experience. Be open to your own active imagination. Breathe naturally and begin, again, the journey within the dark forest of your inner vision.

Thus the Journey continues through the Dark Forest toward the Circles of Nemetona.

CIRCLES OF NEMETONA
An Experiential, Guided Journey.

Your horse is rested now, and you are in the saddle, ready to ride through the forest once again. The Old Ones, spry beyond expectation, quickly mount their own horses; and, though you no longer need them to lead you—for you feel sure of yourself here, and sure of your own path—you let the Old Ones go on ahead, keeping them just within your range of vision.

Your magnificent white horse moves at a moderate and steady gait. You grasp the reins lightly, since the horse seems to know the line to follow through the forest. Although the forest is still filled with dark spaces, you know that were you to move in their direction, they, too, would become illuminated. The forest landscape is clearly in your vision now. It glows with a greenish light that may once have seemed eerie, but now seems wonderfully mystical.

You pass under the low-hanging branches of massive spreading oaks, ashes, and copper beech trees. These great towering trees present themselves as protectors, guarding lines along which your path takes you. They give you a sense of the sacred here in the forest, a sense of deep security, an acknowledgment of your connection to the Sovereignty of Nature, whom they also serve.

You see these trees as you have rarely, if ever, seen them before. Tall and stately, they reach toward the starlit sky above. Wide and well-rooted in the ground, they are, at the same time, solidly connected to the land from which they emerged. With Druidic perception, you see that each great tree is a realm of its own, with energies unique to its own kind—to your own mind. The oaks seem wiser somehow and massively strong with their deep-rooted connection to the Earth. The ashes seem to give you energy as you pass them, regenerating your self with power and purpose. The broad-branched copper beeches seem to bring forth a different sort of vitality, inspiring you with a sense of creative adventure. Each has a life of its own and dimensions of life within the realms of their illuminated power.

You can just catch sight of tiny lights flickering in the shadows of their great spreading branches and glimmering from within the dark curves of their roots as you pass by these magickal trees, so sacred to those of Druidic Nature wisdom. You make a point of remembering these trees so you may return to them sometime in the light of another day. The forest is not so dark and dense now. The trees are fewer and farther between as you move into the wide, open spaces of a gently rolling plain.

The horse picks up speed to close the distance between you and the Old Ones ahead. You are glad of this, for you are eager to reach your destination; and there are places of mystery rising up from the landscape which now you can see on this clear, open plain. A set of standing stones, some tall and pointed, others shorter and rounded, seems close enough to touch as you pass by. "Amesbury," the Old Ones tell you, answering your unspoken question, as they are wont to do from time to time. Glancing back at these pale gray stones, you glimpse an image of ancient rites performed there in times long since past. Before this circle of stones moves out of your range of vision, you see, for just a moment, the stones shape-shifting in the starlight. For an instant, they are no longer a pattern

of tall and short stones, but Lords and Ladies dancing in a circle to celebrate and empower the harvest of the lands.

The next place of mystery you seem to sense before you see. Suddenly, close and clear in your vision, is a massive circle of standing stones which glisten with blue lights, seemingly from within. You resist the urge to steer your horse in their direction and the temptation you feel to ride through the flat stone archways silhouetted against the star-encrusted sky. You sense that these are gateways to realms beyond your ken, and you want to know: to where? and how? and why? "Stonehenge," the Old Ones answer, and "Perhaps another time," as you pass by this greatest of all places of mystery along the lines which your path leads you.

Off in the distance, rising from the horizon, you can see a soft, conical hill. The night sky seems to caress the peak of this hill and starlight gently reveals a spiral path leading from the mists at its base to the tall stone pillars of the temple at the top. "Glastonbury Tor," remark the Old Ones. "Avalon," you reply. Somewhat sadly, you know you must, for now, pass it by. Watching it from the distance of the path on which you travel, you can see the mists rise to surround this place of mystery, and soon it is veiled and out of your realm of vision.

The Old Ones quicken their pace now, and you follow, suitably in step with their progress. You ride down from the high plains you have been traveling and enter yet another forest which seems to be awaiting your arrival.

This forest is brightly illuminated with firelight from within. The sounds of harp and bardsong filter through the branches of the trees, and the smells of warm brews follow on the gentle night breezes. You can hear also the sounds of many voices carried on the wind; but you cannot, as yet, understand what they say. You make your way toward the center of the forest and find a firelit clearing deep within.

Surrounding the clearing is a grove of ancient trees, even more alive to you than the ones you passed along the line. In another circle within the clearing, arranged in a round pattern, are smaller stones with intricate carvings which seem to dance in the lights of the roaring center fire. There are also gentle campfires lit here and there at the edge of the clearing. The light from these fires dances in the branches of this sacred grove, this nemeton place of power. "Vernemeton," the Old Ones tell you. "The Great Grove." Knowing yourself to be in the service of Sovereignty, of whom the guardian goddess of the groves is but one reflection, you enter this place with reverence, honoring the realms of Nemetona, protective spirit of all groves and circles of trees.

There are dozens of people here within the grove, and though you may have expected them to be behaving in mysterious ways, you find they are not. Instead, as you ride into the clearing, you see they are conducting themselves as any gathering of learned people will do. They are gathered in small groups, randomly scattered throughout the clearing. Some are laughing, some singing, some listening to the songs and stories of others. Some are studying charts and strange devices depicting the paths of the planets in the sky above and beyond. Others are describing the qualities of their alchemy, busily pointing out the various properties of the bright-colored liquids in their beautiful glass vials. Still others are casting stones and symbols in circles on the ground. Their patterns reflect in the firelight and those watching, in turn, reflect on the meanings of the manner in which the stones have landed.

It all seems like a chorus of chaos as you dismount and try to find a place for the horses. A young page hurries to your side, bows politely, and offers to see to all of the horses. Another, a maiden this time, offers food, drink, and the warmth of her family's firesite. The Old Ones seem to welcome this offer, but wait for your reply. You had forgotten for a moment, your rank and position require a suitable response. The Old Ones will not leave you as long as you have need of them; nor will they go too far, should you choose to dismiss them.

The page has returned, assuring you that the horses are well cared for. The maiden suggests that she and the page do the honors of escorting you, if you so desire. Since you do not need any introduction here, their station would be adequate to the task. Perhaps you had forgotten the intricate rules and roles required by the Celtic customs of hospitality; but you remember them now, as you have been trained in this for countless generations. No longer the wise child of light in the dark forest of the night, you remember yourself, as well. With nobility of character, you ask the Old Ones if there is something in particular they wanted you to see, and you wait for their reply.

When an answer is not forthcoming, you look to see what their faces tell you. You are surprised to see they are looking well past you. Even more surprising, you find that the page and the maiden have knelt and curtsied, each appropriate to their kind, and are doing so to honor someone who seems to have come up unexpectedly and is standing just behind you.

Before you can turn and identify this personage, you consider that their presence has evoked an even greater reverence than your own from those within this grove. You notice the songs and the sharing of wisdoms have ceased. In every direction you can see in front of you, those gathered in the circle of stones and trees are still as statues, as if waiting for a command. As you wonder if this command is yours to give, you hear a familiar voice coming from directly behind you. It has a slightly royal tone, somewhat different than you have experienced before, yet it thrills you to hear it, for you know by now what dimensions of knowledge and adventure this personage can provide.

"It's the pattern that you must perceive, young one," the voice booms out imperiously. "Come, little dragon-ken," the voice commands, "and I will point this out—this time!"

You turn to greet The Merlin in as regal an aspect as ever you have imagined. Whereas at court he seems to be, if royal at all, then quietly so, here he is magnificently regal. You see him now as the son of Ambrosius, also High King of All Britain in his own time. The Merlin, who by rights was a truer successor to the throne than Uther, brother of Ambrosius, but who chose instead to serve the lands and the coming king, Arthur, for all times, is here with you now.

You wonder for a moment what protocol is called for here in the presence of his most royal personage, an aspect you have not encountered before. In a flash, a solution comes to you, one you are sure will suit the occasion. You make a sweeping dramatic bow, according to your own style and kind. Then you greet him as Lord Merlin, Archmage of all Britain, Druid of all times, Master of Dragons, and Enchanter to the High Court of the Land.

This delights him, and he responds in kind, calling you by your highest magickal name and greeting you, in turn, as noble seeker, questor for knowledge, commander of your own realms, valued ally, and brave warrior in the highest service of Sovereignty. Then he laughs and calls you little dragon-ken once more. Dismissing the Old Ones, the page, and the maiden, you turn to follow the Lord Merlin, as he teaches you the pattern presented at this Druidic gathering.

Lord Merlin stands at the center of the stone circle in the center of the sacred grove. From there he points in each direction to give you the wisdom you are seeking. In the East, he points out the Bards and the Muse singers who both inspire and inform your creative mind. You note that Lord Merlin's own companion bard, Taliesen, is there with his harp and with parchment and pen to record the experiences—the adventures—as they happen.

In the South he points out the knightly order of Druids, the Equites, who advise those most high in matters of statecraft, ethics, and codes of honor. There are women here whom you may know already as Avalonians. You see the Lady Morgana and her protégé, the fair Lady Nimue. You are delighted to see the sturdy knight, Sir Kai, as well.

In the West are the Vates, the diviners of the Fates and the experimentalists of the Druidic sciences. Only one of these do you recognize. Though her aspect, too, is changed to reflect a more regal appearance as the Druidic sister of The Merlin, Ganieda continues her work. She is divining the causes of current worldly events and also those of your personal worlds, both external and internal. She pauses just long enough to greet you with a smile, and to grimace slightly at The Merlin's imperious manner, before she resumes her task. You note that only Ganieda, The Merlin, and yourself are active in this freeze-framed inner vision.

In the North, The Merlin points out the Druids, the professors, the teachers of wisdom, who research and share what they find for you. You see that the Old Ones are here in this company, and you acknowledge them as guiding companions on your quests for knowledge.

Even though the Old Ones are able only to do so at your command, they present an image of the most gentle guides to knowledge. Truly, you value them for their learned gifts. You also notice another woman of Avalonian garb. She is a mature woman dressed in a lavender-gray fabric of the finest quality, yet cut in the functional style of an Abbess—or a nun. When you inquire about the Lady in lavender-gray, The Merlin merely dismisses your question by saying you will meet her soon enough.

Then The Merlin unbinds the vision and those present at the gathering continue as they were when you first encountered them. You notice some stay only where The Merlin has pointed out their position to you. Others freely intermingle and blend their abilities as well as their wisdom. Some seem to be a circle within and whereof their own making—a circle unto themselves—with their own sources and resources of power, knowledge, wisdom, and purpose. As you see this, the image and The Merlin begin to fade away, merging with the forest, which merges with the sky, until only the stones on the landscape remain—and you glimpse a pattern of energy, purely reflected in lights, which fades quickly, along with your image ... for the moment.

You have glimpsed the power lines, the ley or dragon lines. In the next section of this chapter we will take a better look at this grid of energy and light on the Lands.

THE LEY HUNT: LINES OF POWER

Today, the sacred groves and mystical circles of the Druids have given way to vast monuments called churches or cathedrals. Groves, stone circles, and churches are all sacred places where religious ritual and cores of spiritual power have been generated. Such places always retain high vibrations of mystical power, which are passed on from generation to generation. If we accept that there is a special aura within the precincts of a church, we must also accept that there is a surge of psychic forces around the sacred groves and stones of the pre-Christian religion.

Sybil Leek
A Ring of Magic Islands (Garden City, NY: Amphoto Books, 1976)

That Stonehenge and the other henges are great sources created for the purpose and power of knowledge is well understood by those in the mystical community. That there are blended keys to this great mystery is what the current community of investigators is now discovering as they track the lines of power, the ley lines, or dragon lines, of Earth's energies that link science and mysticism, as well as the henges themselves.

Current investigation into these ley lines began with the work, in the 1920s, of Alfred Watkins, a Herefordshire businessman. Watkins discovered a grid of straight lines crisscrossing the meadows (Saxon "ley") of Wales and the English borderlands and linked various Megalithic sites, henges, and burial cairns. Though Watkins poetically called these grids a "fairy chain" created between 4000–2000 B.C., he also pointed out that many early Christian churches had been built precisely on these lines.

Watkins was well before his time with his work. Most of the scientific community was still in the process of determining that Stonehenge and the other henges were astronomical sites. However, Watkins did have support from other "ley hunters," some of whom already had observed similar grids in other places, such as on the Plains of Nazca in Peru and the Native American burial mounds.

When Alexander Thom's precision mathematics theories about Stonehenge surfaced, it stimulated interest in Watkins' work and began the series of investigative researches currently being conducted. Foremost among these modern ley hunters is Paul Deveraux, a scholar-explorer in the field of prehistoric stone structures. Using the latest hi-tech equipment, Deveraux and his team are isolating and identifying what he calls "terrestrial currents." These are the physical, electromagnetic energy lines we call ley lines, or dragon lines. It is most appropriate that Deveraux calls his research "the Dragon Project."

Currently, further research is being conducted, using psychometry to receive images from the standing stones. This is met with some skepticism from the scientific community, but not as much as previously voiced in regard to other theories about Stonehenge—which have proved to be true even when they were first thought to be false, or just silly. Receiving images psychically from an object is still considered to be a rather arcane practice—or Craft. However, when you think about it, carbon dating seems fairly arcane, as well. Most new procedures are viewed as suspect and arcane until they have been proven as valid and reliable. This, undoubtedly, will be the case when ancient arcane practices are seen as renewed procedures, our reclaimed Craft.

Well, these renewed arcane procedures have stood the tests of time quite well—as have the Henges of Stone themselves. No one can define precisely who built the great henges, but it is probable many different peoples did so during the two thousand years in which they were constructed.

What began as rudimentary circles in about 3000 B.C. became more and more complex as new tribes moved into Britain and Ireland. As we have discussed previously, there were a lot of Celtic negotiations going on during that time period. It is only reasonable to assume that the intelligentsia of those tribes, the Druids, not only would have availed themselves of what they found when they arrived, but they would have expanded on the knowledge contained within these circles of stone. That expansion of knowledge is a truly Druidic order of wisdom.

Whatever we have yet to discover about the henges of stone in general, and specifically Stonehenge, we are wise to remember how profoundly important their symbolic and mythic qualities are for our spiritual evolution. We may see Stonehenge as the foremost symbol of the spiritual connection between ourselves and the Land. Just as The Merlin is the foremost representative of what the Druids were, and are, so Stonehenge is the site of efforts to interpret and reverence that sacred connection to Nature.

Having reviewed the material on the explorations of the henges of stone with relatively few comments, I'd now like to share some of my own thoughts. Let me stress that this is my opinion—not my theory. Having spent more than a quarter of a century as a behavioral scientist, I am far too schooled in scientific methodology to be careless about calling an idea a theory.

What I think is that Stonehenge (and the others) was initially created by the Beaker people. These were copper-using people who came into Britain from the European continent in the late Neolithic period—around 3000 B.C.—as the Copper Age became the Bronze Age. There is ample archeological evidence to support this idea that the Beaker people, and the early Bronze Age people in Britain, constructed a new and different variety of henges and stone circles.

Furthermore, there was at that time a rather brisk trade between the copper and tin settlements in Cornwall, Wales, and Ireland, and the old Aegean civilizations, as well as the new European cultures. The trade routes would have allowed for easy passage by those skilled in engineering, astronomy, mathematics, and mining techniques to freely enter Britain. They went perhaps to oversee the building of the mines. Thus the construction of the henges, at least in their later phases, was the work of those skilled individuals in the British Isles at that time.

We also have enough emerging evidence to show deeper links between what we have called pre-Celtic Europe and the Celtic cultures to assume that the earliest Celts to migrate into Britain could well have had the wisdom, and the Druids, to do this—

in which case, Stukeley and Aubrey were right, as well, to connect Stonehenge with the Druids. Perhaps the Celtic Druids with whom we are relatively familiar were preceded into Britain and Ireland, along with the Bronze Age peoples, by an earlier order of Druids. Perhaps these Bronze Age people were really an early tribe of Celts. We know the earliest migration patterns of the Gaelic Celts took them along a southerly route, so we can assume at least some of them were influenced by the Aegean civilizations, such as the Minoan and Mycenean cultures. Since these cultures were well schooled in astronomy, mathematics, and engineering skills, the early Celts—and especially the Druids—would have absorbed a great deal of these skills along the way.

This is not to say the Beaker people (Copper Age) were not the originators of the henges. I think they were. This is to say the development of the henges expanded with the coming of the Bronze Age peoples who, I believe, were the earliest Celts. The influx of these people and the wealth of knowledge they brought with them certainly would have given them almost supernatural status among the more primitive people already there. We've already seen how this can happen when cultures combine.

This could well be the origin of our ancient Gaelic stories of the Tuatha dé Danann. The Tuatha dé were viewed as having great "mystical" skills which, in relation to the skills of the people already inhabiting Ireland, may well have been nothing more—or less—than the natural skills of very advanced, very learned human beings. The Tuatha dé, who may have traveled through areas such as Phoenicia and established outposts in the Aegean and Atlantic, were bound to be viewed as having supernatural powers. No wonder they became deified, after the fashion of creating Celtic tribal gods. With the arrival of the later Milesian Celts, who settled in Ireland, Scotland, and presumably Wales and Cornwall, the Tuatha dé were "sent underground," as their legends tell us. Now consider that if these Tuatha dé were the Druids or "astronomer priests" described by Lockyer, they would have been supplanted then by the Druids of the Milesian Celts—one of whom is known to us as Amergin. Amergin was essentially in charge of dividing Ireland after the Milesian conquest of the Tuatha dé. When we view this process of being relegated "underground" as being given the rulership of the realms of the Celtic Spiritual Otherworld, we can begin to see what Amergin's divisions really may have been all about. Of course, Amergin may have told the Tuatha dé basically to "get out of town," but I rather doubt it. Even if he had done so, it would have been a slow process, just as was the process of the Romans overtaking the Druids in Britain. Also, this process repeated itself when the Christian religion took over the old Pagan ways of the Celts.

It's a great deal like the blending of metals to make a fine sword. That process also evolved from Bronze Age techniques to those of the Iron Age, and onward. And that is my point about the merging of peoples, Beaker, Celtic, and Other Wise, who blended their knowledge of Nature and their human abilities to create the great henges of stone. The process of evolution requires a blend, a heterogeneous mixture, to succeed. Hybrid vigor is a real thing. Too much inbreeding weakens the strain. That being the case, it's no small wonder the blended peoples of the British Isles have developed into such a strong breed—like Excalibur, forged before, and since, "the Dawn of Time." That dawn of time represents the point at which we began to observe, record, and devise systems of measurement—with the Henges of Stone, of course.

We'll close this chapter with some suggestions for crafting your own experiential imagery using the archetypal sources—and the current of the mystical ley lines.

THE DRAGON'S LAIR
An Experiential Journey Exercise

Your field of inner vision opens to receive the enlightenment of a new style of journey. It is one you may construct for yourself, using the lines of power connecting you to the sacred sites of Britain, such as the Great Stonehenge, or the mystical Glastonbury Tor. Perhaps you will choose the circle of stones at Amesbury, where you glimpsed the stones shape-shifting into the Lords and Ladies in their primal circle dance honoring the Sovereignty of the Land.

If you choose the Great Stonehenge as the site of your journey, I suggest you work with the dragon lines of power there and "raise up" your own dragons. In this way the powers these dragons represent for you—and in you—also will be upraised and activated.

If you choose Glastonbury Tor, the mystical realm also called Avalon Isle, I suggest you craft the hallowed gifts that are yours by right. On Avalon Isle, these rights and craft require more ritual and ceremony. An additional dimension of formality is advised. This you may do in the manner you prefer. Also, the powers of Avalon and the Sacred Tor have more to do with your healing gifts. Stonehenge has more of the qualities we require externally. Glastonbury/ Avalon relates most clearly to our inter-nal qualities of Mind, Body, Emotions, and Spirit.

If you choose Amesbury, your journey will give you the chance to empower both yourself and someone you love. It is not essential that you take this journey with that beloved person in the physical sense. You may empower them with an etheric approach and meet within the realms of inner vision. Naturally, you may choose to let an image of someone from another place and time emerge for you in the circle at Amesbury. As long as you realize they are a balancing reflection of your self, you will benefit clearly from the experience.

Any of these journey sites and styles may be shared either in the mundane sense, or in the etheric sense of connecting with a real person through the "ethers"; that is, through the medium of mind meeting mind. All of these also allow for the emergence of an actively created image of an aspect reflected in and by yourself in journey form.

Of course, you may choose to try all three sites for your experiential journey construction. You may wish to return even to the Sacred Groves of Nemetona, with or without any or all of those present during the guided journey. You may use the formulas I give you to create or access a site which is uniquely your own.

I suggest you review the journeys of the last two chapters, and particularly the Circles of Nemetona in Chapter 10, which give you glimpses of the sites I've mentioned. I also suggest you recall your image of yourself as the noble seeker on the white horse in the dark forest. Of course you may use any allies in your journey you feel the need for, and who help the purpose and the power of your journey.

It may also help to write these down or record them. You may express them externally somehow, through art, dance, motion, or storytelling. For now, I leave you with a few "maps" in the form of verse and correlations that I believe form the basics of what you need, and upon which you may build your own quality journey work.

By the way, you may also wish to bring in the bards to develop your own ceremonial rhymes or stories of your journey. I warn you, though, it may become rather difficult to stop rhymes—at times! This, of course, you already know. Having experienced the previous guided experiential work on trouble-shooting when working with lines of power such as the elemental bards represent, you know this can be a tough access.

For your basic formulas, I give you once again the tartan verses, then the directions these colors may take for you. I will give you also some hints, in verse, which tell you how to activate, transmit, manifest, and disperse your emerging journey images, as well as how to empower them positively.

The Tartan Verses

Red lines of fire, for courage and desire
Bands of blue for what is right and true
A violet line to praise the Divine
Three lines of white to aim with clear sight
A rich field of green for Nature's noble queen.

The Suggested Directions for the Colors

White in the East for Air and the Bardic inspirational energies, clear mind, and focus

Red in the South for Fire and the Guardians protection energies, will, strength, and desires

Blue in the West for Water and the Initiators of healing energies, intuition, and sacred dreams

Green in the North for Earth and the Connectors for manifestation of your intentions, order, prosperity

Violet in the Center and Circle encircling for Spirit transformational empowerment, the Divine gifts

The Formula for Receiving and Releasing Your Journey Imagery

Spirit: As long as your source is divine, your intentions good and fine, then you'll have no trouble working the line.

Fire: Creative fires give birth to desires.

Air: which take flights, foul or fair, on ill will or clear air.

Earth: are then manifested by form in balanced quantities to avoid a swarm.

Water: are dispersed then by the streams which constantly flow within the realms only you may know.

These verses are in a counterclockwise format. This is not an indication of any negativity, as the widdershins direction is so often seen to be. Indeed, it may be said that the direction is not the important factor; but the intention truly is. However, if you have been trained so this widdershins direction causes you concern, then simply cast a sunwise, deosil, or clockwise circle before you begin your work. This will make you feel more confident about yourself and the possible effects of your journey.

Good Luck. Allow yourself time to become relaxed and receptive. Then be creative with these imageries. They are all yours, a gift via The Muse, The White Goddess of Avalon Isle, whom we shall discuss in the following chapter.

CHAPTER 11

THE WHITE GODDESS
OF AVALON ISLE

All that day, in silence, she worked, gazing into the chalice, letting the images rise, now and then stopping to wait for inspiration in the meditative flow; she worked the horned moon, so that the Goddess should always watch over the sword and guard the sacred blood of Avalon. She was so wrapped in the magical silence that every object on which her eyes gazed, every movement of her consecrated hands, became power for the spell …

Marion Zimmer Bradley
The Mists of Avalon (New York: Knopf, 1982)

 Avalon is perhaps the most mystical aspect of the Arthurian mythologies, and of the more ancient Celtic forms, as well. Avalon is the sacred isle of apples, the realm of healing wisdom which lies somewhere in the western waters, or surrounded by misty veils in an uncertain inland location. Various sources try to place Avalon in Scotland, comparing it with the Isle of Arran in the Firth of Clyde. Others suggest its location to be in Ireland, or somewhere in the Irish Sea, where it is called Emhain Abhlach or is seen to be one of the Isles of the Blest.

One of the foremost theories about the geographical location of Avalon Isle points out its similarities to Glastonbury, the original name for which is *Ynys witrin*, the Isle of Glass. The word "glass" has magical meanings in Celtic myths, meaning the crystalline, fragile veils between this world and the spiritual Otherworld. However, this is disputed by others who suggest that Glastonbury came from the name of a relatively unknown Celtic mythic figure named Glast, possibly a tribal deity or a spirit-of-place, *genus locorum*. A possible solution for this could be found in the legends of Rex Avalonis—the legendary King of Avalon, sometimes called the father of Morgana; most likely in the priestly sense or as a guardian, foster father, if at all.

97

The Glastonbury theory points to several factors to make its claim as the location of Avalon, one of the "Fortunate Isles," a place of eternal summer and blooming flowers. This is a description that fits the Celtic concept of the Otherworld, the Summerland, or in the Irish, the Happy Plain. From an archeological and historical point, this "Summerland" was the region now called Somerset, because it was a highly seasonal area.

In the summer months the people of this region moved and took their livestock from the high ground where they could find dry pasture. Most of the area in and around Glastonbury was filled with lagoons at that time and very prone to flooding. Before drainage techniques were used, starting about the seventeenth century, the area was quite marshy. When seasonal floods came, many of the hills, and Glastonbury Tor particularly, would have been almost impossible to reach for long periods of time. This could naturally give rise to the concept of an ancient Celtic sacred isle surrounded by the healing sources of water.

This encircling of the Tor by water would seem to me to have made it an ideal location for sacred ceremonies, rituals, or spiritual training—perhaps a kind of "summer camp for priestesses," as a friend of mine has suggested. Indeed, it could well have been the ideal spot for the training and sequestering of Celtic high-born daughters, both in pagan times and in the earliest Celtic Christian days, as well.

From the Celtic, Pagan perspective, Avalon at Glastonbury Tor has been depicted as one of the sacred isles or sites where the nine maidens of Bridget kept the nine sacred flames burning perpetually in the service of the Goddess, and of the lands—essentially one and the same. It is quite interesting that St. Bridget, an Irish nun from Kildare, historically placed in the same time period as Arthur (mid-fifth century) is reputed to have lived at Glastonbury. This is even more interesting when we consider her legend and the meaning of her name.

> *Brigit, or Brig (Irish brig, "power"; Welsh bri, "renoun") the patroness of poetry and knowledge, represents another aspect of the goddess and was the Celtic Minerva named by Caesar. The popular cult of St. Brigit, which carried her worship into Christian times, was represented in Kildare by a sacred fire which was not to be approached by any male and was watched daily by nineteen vestal virgins in turn, and on the twentieth day by the saint herself. Brigit, furthermore, was the giver of civilization.*
>
> Joseph Campbell
> *Occidental Mythology*

Brigid of Kildare wisely chose to set up her own sanctuary on a piece of land traditionally used for Celtic Pagan rites and kept the very Pagan symbol of the eternal flame as part of her church. This certainly would have evoked the spiritual connection with Bridget, the goddess of poetry, healing, and smithcraft. Daughter of the Celtic Great Mother Goddess, Danu (also Don), the Gaelic Bridget, in turn, relates to Brigantia, the Brythonic goddess of aspects that blend Bridget and Danu:

Brig = power + Anu or Danu, meaning land, or cycle of the land = Brigantia.

Furthermore, if we combine Bri = renown + Aine = Irish form of Anu, we can see where both words, Britain and Brigantia, also originate. All relate essentially to the power, or the renown, of the land, its cycles and its seasons. It becomes quite easy to see how St. Brigid (or Bridget, or Brigit) became interwoven with the shared, synchretic goddess of the Celtic peoples and their lands. This is, after all, how Arthur became interwoven with the ancient Celtic Lords of Light (Lugh, Llew, Llud) and with the prehistoric, Stone Age concept of the guardian deity—the Great Cave Bear.

Also, in seeking to show the connection between the goddess, Bridget, the Saint Brigid, and the sanctuary of Avalon Isle, we must refer to some of the older Pagan legends emerging about the time Christianity first arrived in the British Isles (Brigantia's Isles), which told of Brigid of Kildare as a priestess of the Old Ways, in service to the triple-aspected Goddess of the Earth. These aspects are, in some Celtic-based traditions: Brigette = Maiden, Bridget = Mother, and Bride (Breed) = Crone. Thus we have the possibility of the priestess, Brigid, who may well have either initiated or have been initiated into a tradition such as Avalon represented. Since the nine flames tradition is essentially impossible to trace, we cannot say for certain whether or not Brigid of Kildare began her own version of it, in Ireland, the result being the "cult" of Brigid which spread across the Irish sea. Perhaps it is the blend of Pagan and Christian in the aspects of Brigid of Kildare which would have made her the ideal "bridge" for the times of Arthur and Avalon. We know that Celtic Pagan and Christian traditions existed side by side for about six centuries in Britain with relatively few instances of conflict such as eventually erupted.

This change from coexisting forms of spirituality to the absolutism of the one and only way of the Orthodoxy was not essentially Christian, in any case. There was no room for the individual Christian message originally taught by the Galilean. Instead, this Orthodox shift came in the fourth century A.D., roughly a hundred years before Arthur's time. It came from the Emperor/Pope Theodocius, who issued the edict requiring all forms of Christianity to adhere to the Eastern, Orthodox, Byzantine forms. In other words, this way or no way at all. Fortunately, Theodocius was far too busy with India and the Persian Empire to bother with Britain; but his edict took effect like slow poison.

This turning of the tides certainly would have been known by the spiritual leaders of Britain at that time. Furthermore, as most spiritual leaders were, at least at that time, members of what we call now the intelligentsia, they would have had already a hundred years of watching the diminishing effect this new tide of events—and edicts—had on Europe and the Celtic people in particular.

Basically, the spiritual leaders of Britain, such as the Avalonians, would have seen the writing on the wall. There may have been relatively peaceful coexistence between the people of the old Pagan ways and those of the new Christian ways, but I'll warrant there was already significant conflict among the spiritual leaders of both factions. Remember that churches, temples, sanctuaries, convents, abbeys, and others relied on the support and protection of the kings or chieftains of the regions where they were located. Since various kings were being converted to the new ways, various spiritual leaders and their traditions had to dance fast to keep in step.

Thus, the spiritual leaders would have been in the market, so to speak, for a "bridge," if not to connect, then at least to provide shared access from both Pagans and Christians. Whether Brigid of Kildare converted to Christianity or wove some of the comparably matched new ways into her own practice of the old ways, we cannot know with certainty.

It is just as likely that the spiritual leaders of the new ways wove Brigid of Kildare—and therefore the goddess, Bridget of the Celts—into their ways; thereby converting her to Christianity, not only as a worthy person, but as a saint, and a catalyst for the conversion of Ireland and Britain. Thus, Brigid of Kildare became a symbol of the blending ways and, ultimately, the "conversion" of the Celtic lands from Pagan to Christian. We should also note that other similar catalyst converters, such as St. Patrick and St. Columba, were being activated by the same symbolic process at about the same time. They, too, were reputed to have lived in Glastonbury.

A brief look at the tales told of Brigid of Kildare's childhood will give us clues as to why she would have been considered the "right woman" to serve as a bridge. Brigid was born about A.D. 450 in the house of a Druid from Faughart, in or near County Louth in Ireland. This Druid was her guardian until Brigid was about ten years old, so she would have had her formative years in a Pagan household, although it is said the Druid had a Christian uncle and that Brigid's Druid/guardian was eventually baptized into the Christian religion because of her great influence upon him.

Brigid was the daughter of a Pagan chieftain, Dubhlach, and his bondswoman (*i.e.*, slave) who was a Christian. Dubhlach's wife made him sell Brigid's mother to the Druid whom we just discussed. When she grew up and chose to follow the ways that St. Patrick had already brought to Ireland, Brigid quickly established her own kind of blended practices we may call Celtic Christian. She also founded a convent that eventually became a double "monastery," with both men and women, co-equally, side by side.

> In its day-to-day work Brigid's convent practiced a cheerfully efficient, unself-conscious sexual equality. But in praying, as in private life, men and women must separate ... though her double monastery was a surprisingly liberal and imaginative innovation—as the strength of women and the power for good they could exercise within the framework of the Church.
>
> Katherine Scherman
> *The Flowering of Ireland: Saints, Scholars and Kings*
> (Boston: Little, Brown and Company, 1981)

It is also said that Brigid helped many similar "monasteries" become established. Brigid was a great traveler, as well; so we can assume she certainly could have crossed the Irish Sea. Stories of her travels in Ireland tell of her going about in a two-horse chariot, remarkably like her Celtic warrior ancestors before her. It is easy to understand how Brigid of Kildare, called the Bright One (as the goddess Bridget before her also had been called), could have been the catalyst for "cults" following her example throughout the Celtic lands of Britain. It also becomes possible to see her conversion into the Celtic form of the Christian Mother Mary. Here again, both historical Brigid and mystical goddess Bridget blend, then separate again, becoming St. Brigid and the uniquely Irish Celtic form of Mary, Mother of God. This Mother of all gods, as it was in ancient Celtic times, was the Earth Mother whose marriage to the Sky/Solar Father created all the other gods of natural forces and those of tribal qualities, as well.

By Arthurian times, and probably well before that, the ancient Mother Goddess, Danu, had already merged with her daughter, The White Goddess, Bridget.

Bridget, originally the patron goddess of poetry, smithcraft, and healing, was a great match for Brigid of Kildare, whose "convents" were known for the same qualities. By that time, though, the goddess Bridget had taken on the maternal qualities of her Earth Mother Goddess, Danu. Thus, as Danu-Bridget, she warmed the fires of the Earth so the plants could grow in the spring; she brought civilization to her people; and she was further correlated with the goddess of both war and wisdom, Minerva of the Romans (Athena of the Greeks).

When the goddess Bridget became the Mother Goddess, she made the first move into merging with the Christian Mother Mary. For Celtic peoples whose spiritual philosophy was as interwoven as their designs, this was a welcome, inseparable alliance— one reflected the other. This they understood. It was the separations and the hierarchies that were confusing to the Celts. These confusions they soon resolved. Danu and Bridget became The White Goddess, or Bride in the Gaelic form. When St. Brigid and Mary became confused for the Celts, then St. Brigid took on more of the aspects of the goddess, Bridget, and Mary became more closely linked with The White Goddess Bride, empowering beautifully all Her aspects.

The Goddess, served by those such as the Avalonians at the times we are discussing, already would have become the merged form for some and still would have been separated into pagan or Christian by others. This was a conflict which only now has begun to reach some aspects of resolution as the reemergence of the Great Goddess in current times seeks to reverence Her in a mutual, syncretic fashion.

Those who approach the White Goddess of Avalon today, in their spiritual and mystical ways, encounter the Great Celtic Mother, the Bright One, the White Goddess, and the Mother Mary—whose name means Light. This powerful blend becomes, in effect, Mother/Bright White Light, or Mother of Christ. In essence, the Light remains the same, Celtically speaking. The following journey in verse and visionary genre will perhaps enlighten your own experience of The White Goddess, in more than triple aspects.

THE WHITE GODDESS
A Personal Journey Account

Enters now, a celestial vision,
Triple Muse of inspiration
Healing trine for desperation
Bulwark strength against invasion.
Crafting force for all revision
Judgments source in each decision,
Safety shield against collision,
Catalyst spark for magick fission,
Power of trust 'ere free of suspicion

All merges into one,
clear Light vision
of the White Goddess.

I journey inward, seeking the source of inspiration. A single candle flame lights my way through the dark void of consciousness, directing me toward the place of visions. I focus on the halo of the flame and find myself transported into the realm of the Muse, the domain of the White Goddess.

I find myself in a meadow clearing guarded by a forest of ancient oaks. It is silent in the meadow. The only sounds I hear are whispers from the enchanted forest encircling me. I strain to catch the messages carried on the breezes blowing through the oaks; but I cannot make out the words. I let the melody of the whispers move through my mind.

A carpet of white, star-shaped flowers stretches across the green meadow grasses. A scent like jasmine rises from the ground and envelops me with its heady fragrance. I close my eyes to absorb the experience and seek deeper within myself for unspoken words of invocation. With all my heart I seek the source of ancient memory and current consciousness.

I feel the breeze quicken in the forest and come spiraling out into the meadow. A gentle chord is being played, lyrically and beautifully, on the strings of a harp. I open my eyes and see a shimmering sphere of blue-white light taking shape before me. The sphere of light solidifies into a translucent oval suspended just above the ground. The oval is vibrating intensely, compelling me to draw nearer. Its energy resonates inside my mind.

I move closer within my vision— close enough to touch the image I see before me. As I reach for the oval of light, I feel its electric vibration even before I can touch its surface. Upon contact with this electric power field, the oval opens to reveal the Source of inspiration that I seek. I behold the White Goddess as She steps from the blue-white light oval and onto the gentle meadow grasses. The white star flowers shimmer with each step She takes toward me. I wait in silent awe for Her approach.

102

She is fair and clear in Her aspect here. A trail of iridescent lights follows her footsteps, illuminating my inner vision. Behind Her, the oval of light has shifted to a deeper blue, cobalt and clear. She draws near to me, close enough for me to hear Her gentle breathing. I am spellbound by the rhythm of Her breath, and I seek to match its pace. Calmly and patiently, She waits while I attune myself to Her vibration. I breathe steadily, gaining strength as I connect with the rhythm of her breath—the Breath of the Muse.

My voice within my vision welcomes Her and requests Her blessing on my works—works in Her honor. I ask for the favor of a clear line, an unobstructed pathway that will connect my mind to the mind of the Muse. I request the Courage to clarify my visions and my convictions concerning the Matter of Sovereignty, Camelot and Avalon. I ask that She grant me the Will to see my way through the ordeals of creation and expression. Lastly, I ask for the Faith I will need to sustain me when I find myself wandering through the perilous forests of doubt and despair.

I acknowledge her as my Source for the Courage, Will, and Faith I will need. She smiles before fading away and gently touches my spirit and heart within; for within these, She tells me, are all the elements I will ever need. I return, renewed.

The most important point of correlation I see between the aspect of the Goddess served by the Avalonians and the aspect of what we call The White Goddess today comes from two essential events in the Camelot legends about Avalon. First, the sword Excalibur is crafted in Avalon and given to Arthur by the Lady of the Lake. Second, upon his mortal wounding at Camlann, Arthur is taken to Avalon for healing. Thus, we have the smithcraft and healing of Bridget (now perhaps as Brigantia) clearly connected with Avalon.

A third, somewhat less direct correlation is the abundance of the Camelot legends told, originally in poetry, then later in prose. Thus, we have Poetry, Smithcraft, and Healing. This sounds like Bridget to me. Of course, the question remains: Was Avalon serving the White Goddess/Bridget, or was Avalon at that time modeled after the profound innovations of Brigid of Kildare—later St. Brigid? Only the Goddess knows for certain. However, the indications of a blended form would make the realms of Avalon far more accessible for men who may have been told that Avalon was for the women. By the same token—and probably by the same mindset crowd—there are some who contend that the Druidic orders were for the men.

Naturally, I support the rights—and the rites—of anyone or any group to follow their own chosen course, even if it seems separatist or Orthodoxical in its forms. As the great philosopher Voltaire said, "I may not agree with a single word that you say; but I will defend to the death your right to say it." To which I must add: so long as you are only saying it for yourself and not saying what *has* to be for others.

Everyone is entitled to the healing realm of Avalon. A clear understanding of Avalon comes not from an historical or even philosophical pursuit to establish its existence definitively. It comes rather from the establishment of a personally definitive relationship with what Avalon represents. The qualities of Avalon represent the deeply sacred mystical realms of healing and self-transformation. These qualities emerge from a clear connection with personal gifts of intuition, psychic awareness, and a ceremonial relationship with that which is the inner source of Divine power for each of us as an individual.

Within the realms of Avalon consciousness, their power is clearly that of the feminine Divine. It is the Goddess in Her many aspects blended into the harmonic synthesis of Light, expressed in a receptive, nurturing, maternal aspect: thus the Mother of Light, or the Bright Mother. This is the pure white light that provides the medium through which healing and self-transformative wisdom may be received, activated, and reflected in a feminine, maternal manner.

That the realms of Avalon are more feminine in Nature and self-nature does not preclude their being reached by men, or by women whose own aspects are forthright, direct, and linear. Avalon, as an archetype, has the symbolic quality needed to develop the free-flowing intuitive gifts defined as feminine; yet which are present in every individual, regardless of gender. Just as the archetypal warrior or knight symbolizes qualities that are masculine, yet are readily found in women—and sometimes more fiercely so—the symbolic qualities of Avalon are found also in men—sometimes more reverently so. Avalon and Glastonbury Tor have been described as the realms of Gwyn-ap-Nudd, lord of the faerie folk, and as the entrance to Annwn, the realm of spirits. This folkloric tradition symbolically describes the activation of mystical gifts accessed from deep inner quests into the realms of the sacred by everyone, regardless of gender.

After a millennium or more of indoctrinations stressing the separation of gender roles and "natural" traits, both women and men in modern times are seeking to regain the truly natural qualities and traits shared, in balance, by both genders. No longer do women have to suppress the "secret warrior" within. No longer do men have to suppress their "secret" intuitive healing nature. It is a time for reestablishing balance, individually, culturally, and globally. Avalon is the realm that most clearly helps with this process of finding and maintaining balance.

Access to Avalon is a self-initiated process, and the experiencing of Avalon is a self-initiatory one. This is accomplished with a reverent, ceremonial acknowledgment of the sacred within the self. It is the development of a personal connection to the Light within, the "divine power operative" in each of us, in its maternal aspect, the empowering White Goddess. This we will continue to explore throughout the text, in relationship to the legends and therefore in correlation to ourselves.

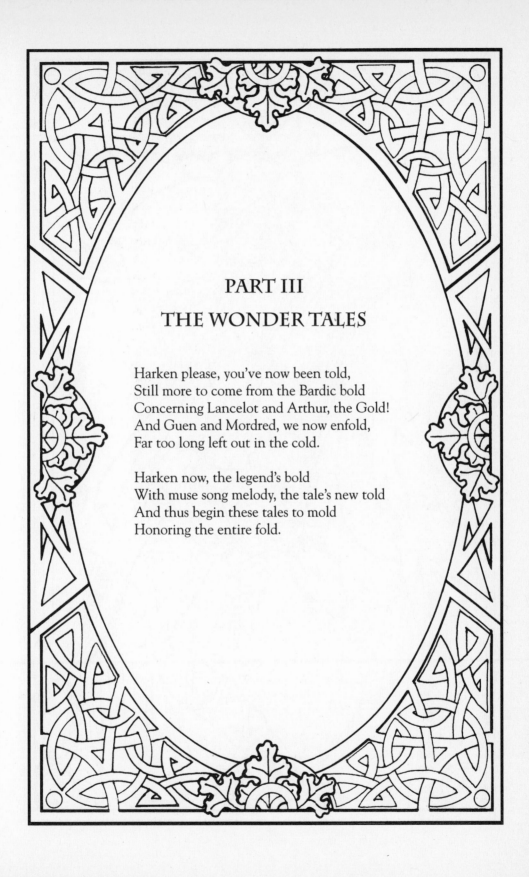

PART III

THE WONDER TALES

Harken please, you've now been told,
Still more to come from the Bardic bold
Concerning Lancelot and Arthur, the Gold!
And Guen and Mordred, we now enfold,
Far too long left out in the cold.

Harken now, the legend's bold
With muse song melody, the tale's new told
And thus begin these tales to mold
Honoring the entire fold.

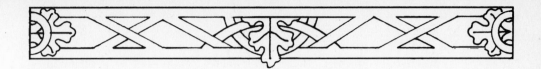

CHAPTER 12

THE LORDS AND LADIES OF LOGRES

The Knights and their Ladies who form the Fellowship are archetypes of different sorts of force as expressed through human experience, and at the same time, each one of them, as a particular type of force, is present within us all.

Gareth Knight
The Secret Tradition

 Exploring the realms of the Camelot legends is a creative, mystical experience. That is, until you come to sorting out the many characters—some varied and some confusingly similar to one another. Adding to the confusion are the numbers of different characters being cast in roles that are almost the same or exactly the same as roles featuring other characters before.

It is very much like a soap opera with its continually recurring scripts and frequent substitutions or replacements of characters. It is no wonder these legends were a long-running, popular source of entertainment for a millennium or more in Europe and Britain, and, of course, this continues to be the case globally, wherever those of Western/European, Celtic heritages have settled.

This constant matching, mismatching, and cross-matching was due originally to the blending of Celtic, Christian, Norman French, and British literary traditions. This continuing process is the result of current images being experienced and expressed. Naturally, I must include myself in that current category and express my regret at whatever confusion my versions may cause. I will do what I can to clarify my reasons for making or not making changes in the scripts or the casts of characters. I will tell you when I have created a new alchemy with the themes and characters and why I have chosen to do so. I will endeavor to keep to the elemental themes, the round pattern that we have discussed previously in this text.

I will try also to tell you when a theme or character reflects another, similar combination, and also when I see that substitutions or cross-matches have been made. Most of this I will do as we cover the chapters in Parts II and III. Initially, though, this is an overview—a playbill, as it were—to help you understand the pattern in the round. If you recognize a match or substitution I have missed—or characters I have omitted—Good for you! Though not all of the characters presented here will be discussed in this text, they are a familiar part of the mythic kin found in the Camelot legends.

I'm certain you will be able to place these omissions in the pattern I am presenting. That is the point, as I see it. Rounding up these legendary figures may not be an elementary exercise, but it is an elemental one. It is the synthesis of these characters and themes that I feel matters most in our experiencing of these legends. Just consider it to be an interwoven, star-quality performance featuring a legendary cast of stars who have been around a very, very long time. This is due, in no small part, to their symbolic qualities, which bring us lessons for our own lives. These I will point out in correlation with each character.

We will begin by categorizing these characters by their most elementally expressed qualities. This does not limit them to any one specific classification. Instead, it provides a point from which you can understand and experience their roles in the round of these legends. This initial, elemental correlation will present only their names. Their claims to fame will come later, generally defined in this chapter, and, for most, specifically presented later. For now, a field guide follows:

The Elemental Cast of Camelot's Legends

Spirit—Center—Sovereignty: (or Arthur, if you like) Sovereignty, The Lady of the Lake, and foundationally, Dagda/Bran and Danu/Don and all Her aspects.

Air—East—Merlin: The Merlin, also Blaise, Taliesen, Gawain, Ragnall, The Green Knight/Bertilak and his Lady, The Red Knight/Duke Edern, Elaine of Astolat, Queen Isolde of Ireland, Isolde of the White Hands, Brangaine, and Brisen.

Fire—South—Battles: Vortigern, Uther, Gorlois, Igraine, Melwas, Ryon, Marhaus, King Mark of Cornwall, Lot, Morgawse, Lamorak, Agravaine, Gaheris, Mordred, Balyn, Balan, Pellinore, Palomides, Aglovale, and Tor. Also, Tristan, Isolde, Erec, Enide, Culwech, Olwen, Ambrosius, Elaine, Yvain, Laudine, Gareth, Lionors, Alexander, Alice, Lanceor, Colombe and Launfal and Tryamour.

Water—West—Avalon: Morgana, Nimue, Vivienne/Elaine of Garlot, Rex Avallonis/Nentres of Garlot and Ganieda/Cerridwen. Also Perceval, Bors, Galahad, Pelles/Fisher King, Elaine of Carbonek, Dindraine, and Ector de Maris.

Earth—North—Camelot: Arthur (and also at Center, if you like him there), Guinevere and Lancelot. Also, Sir Ector, Sir Kai, Bedevere, Lucan, Uriens, Galahaut, Lionel, Leodegrance, and, foundationally, King Bors and King Ban of Benwick.

These characters are not each featured in a leading role, but they are a part of the cast. In order to define them generally, yet give you a clear image of where they are present most elementally in the pattern of the legends, I've further divided the themes to include the supportive ones, as well.

The Elemental and Supportive Cast of Camelot's Legends

Spirit—Center—Sovereignty:

Sovereignty—The powers of Nature, the symbolic ruler of the lands and the people, holds dominion over the realms of Nature, is served by alliances made with the self-nature of those whose legacy connects them to the Celtic lands and tribal, cultural codes of Logres.

Lady of the Lake—The initiator and guardian of the inner, mystical realms of Logres, the symbolic head of Avalon Isle, the Source of hallowed gifts and powers such as the Sword and the Scabbard.

Dagda/Bran—Dagda, the Gaelic Celtic form of the good god providing for his people from an endlessly abundant cauldron and with a mighty war club, as well. Bran, the Brythonic Celtic form with similar qualities, a cauldron that heals warriors and a mythic head that gives oracular wisdom to his people.

Danu/Don—The Gaelic/Brythonic Earth Mother, the syncretic, essential, triple-aspected goddess of the Celts, as maiden, mother and crone. Merged with tribal deities, the form becomes Bridget/Brigantia, the White Goddess.

Arthur—This is his symbolic role as the mythic King of All Britain, for All Time. The mythic Celtic king, blending aspects of tribal gods and heroic warriors into this legendary form. Catalyst for the Highest Orders of Right, Might, and Light.

Air—East—Merlin: The Evolutionary Illuminator

Merlin—Merlin Emrys, the Archdruid, Archmage of Britain and her peoples. The quintessential Celtic wizard, enchanter, and Druid of the Equites orders. Born of Ambrosius and Elaine in South Wales. Served three kings: Ambrosius, Uther, and Arthur. Catalyst of the pathways to Celtic spiritual codes.

Flames—Air/Fire—S/E Otherworld: Catalysts/Allies

Blaise—Druidic teacher of the child, Merlin. Guardian Initiator of the Crystal Cave of Knowing.

Taliesen—Bardic companion of The Merlin, possibly correlated to Dagonet, Arthur's court jester, one of the chief bards of Britain whose contributions to the oral traditions of the legends is considered quite likely. A Guardian of the Bardic realms, or frequencies of creative inspiration.

Green Knight/Bertilak (and his Lady)—The initiator, challenger of Gawain in the Beheading Game, he and his Lady test the powers of Gawain to uphold his codes of honor and chivalry. Guardians of the realms of personal initiation into honor.

Red Knight/Duke Edern—The challenger of Erec to prove his right of championship in the Sparrowhawk Contest. Guardian/Initiator of the balanced realms of love and honor.

Gawain—The Complete Knight, challenged frequently in the enchanted realms and passed the tests of Honor and Chivalry. Son of Arthur by Morgawse, married the Lady Ragnall, quested unsuccessfully for the Grail, was forced to fight Lancelot, who had killed Gareth when the betrayal of Lancelot and Guinevere was revealed. Gawain died in this fight but returned to Arthur in dreams before the final battle at Camlann in which Arthur was killed. Guardian/Ally of the realms of trust and Chivalry.

Ragnall—Lady of Gawain, enchanted princess transformed into a foul appearance until the love, loyalty, and gift of personal sovereignty from Gawain broke the spell and restored her natural beauty for all time. Initiator into the realms of faith and self-esteem.

Elaine of Astolat—The Lady of Shallot, would-be lover of Lancelot, died of grief over her unrequited love; her body was placed on a barge which floated to Camelot with a message citing Lancelot's failure to love her as the cause of her death. Protector/Guardian who prevents access to the deepest realms of despair over relationships and love.

Queen Isolde of Ireland—Mother of the Fair Isolde, heals Tristan/Natrist, who has been wounded with a poisoned sword point. Prepares a potion to unite her daughter, Fair Isolde, and King Mark of Cornwall. Initiator/Healer of the realms of alchemical relationships.

Brangaine—Servant of Queen Isolde, nurse for the Fair Isolde. Entrusted with the Queen's potion for Mark and Isolde, she does not keep it away from Tristan and Isolde, who drink it to seal their love. Substitutes herself for Isolde in the bridal chamber with King Mark of Cornwall. Guardian/Ally of the realms of Courtly Love.

Isolde of the White Hands—Isolde of Brittany, who marries Tristan after he is banished from the Court of King Mark, causes Tristan's death by telling him the Fair Isolde is not coming to heal him—even though she is on the way to do so. Catalyst for the prevention of entering the realms of hopeless, unconsumatable love and relationships.

Brisen—Nurse to Elaine of Carbonek, who gives a potion to Lancelot so he will believe her lady, Elaine, is Queen Guinevere, awaiting his love. Ally in the realms of love and the Grail.

Fire—South—Battles: The Guardian Trainers

Vortigern—Usurper king of Britain, killed Constans Moine, the brother of Ambrosius and Uther; used Saxon allies to control the people; had a Saxon Queen, Rowena, and summoned Merlin to be his sacrifice at King's Fort tower; was defeated and killed by Ambrosius and Uther's invasion force. Prevents access to the realms of greed and evil will.

Uther—Uther Pendragon, King of Britain, father of Arthur by Igraine of Cornwall. Foster father of Morgawse. Held Britain while Arthur was fostered out to Sir Ector and under the care of The Merlin. Guardian Trainer who shows the consequences of ruthless desires and drive.

Igraine—Queen of Britain by marriage to Uther, Duchess of Cornwall by marriage to Gorlois. Mother of Vivienne and Morgana, foster mother to Morgawse. Mother of Arthur by a tryst with Uther. Widow of Gorlois and of Uther. Guardian Trainer who develops strengths to avoid vulnerabilities.

Gorlois—Duke of Cornwall, loyal to Ambrosius, in contention with Uther and his warriors, Father of Vivienne and Morgana. Metaphysically, the foster father of Arthur. Killed while defending Cornwall and Igraine against the invasions of Uther's forces. Guardian Trainer who teaches the skills of personal environmental awareness.

Melwas—Meleagrant, King of the Summer Country, lord of the Underworld who abducted Guinevere, demanded ransom from Arthur and received negotiated terms; was unable to prevent Lancelot from rescuing Guinevere. Guardian of the primal realms of lust and drive.

Mark—King of Cornwall, uncle of Tristan, betrothed to the Fair Isolde, betrayed by Tristan and Isolde, banished both, recanted, then tested Isolde and banished Tristan forever. Guardian Trainer showing the futility of law over love, pride over passion.

Marhaus—Irish Lord, uncle of the Fair Isolde, brother of Queen Isolde of Ireland. Came to Cornwall demanding tribute from King Mark; was challenged by Tristan and killed in the process. Guardian Trainer showing the futility of greed and power over love and honor.

Ryon—Prince, King of North Waalis, enemy of Arthur who maintained forces in opposition to the court at Camelot and the Round Table knights. May well have sent the maiden to Caerleon with the Sword Unfortunate which delivered the dolorous stroke; was defeated eventually by Arthur, after the Wasteland had been created. Guardian preventing access to the primitive realms of barbarism.

Lot—King of Lothian and Orkney, uneasy ally of Arthur, and sometime foe. Married Morgawse. Father of Agravaine, Gareth, and Gaheris, stepfather of Gawain and Mordred (probably unbeknownst to Lot, these were Morgawse's sons by Arthur). Lot was killed by Pellinore, which started a longstanding battle between their clans. Guardian Trainer showing the primal dangers of elemental powers and environments.

Morgawse—Queen of Lothian and Orkney, wife of Lot, foster daughter of Uther, daughter of the barbaric northland clans, Mother of Gawain, Agravaine, Gareth, Gaheris and Mordred. Elemental queen to Arthur, instrumental in revealing the betrayal of Lancelot and Guinevere. Foster sister to Morgana, foster daughter of Igraine. Avalon-trained Druidic warrior queen. Took Lamorak as a lover; both were killed by her son Gaheris. Guardian Trainer showing the most primal forces of defense and preservation of the lands.

Lamorak—Knight, son of Pellinore, brother of Perceval, Dindraine, Agovale and Tor. Lover of Morgawse, killed by Gaheris, one of the starting catalysts of the undoing of the Round Table. Guardian showing the dangers of succumbing to lust and primal impulses.

Agravaine—Knight, son of Morgawse and Lot of Orkney, brother of Gaheris and Gareth. Half-brother to Gawain and Mordred. Married Laurel. Set up the discovery of Lancelot and Guinevere's betrayal, catalyst for the downfall of Camelot, killed in battle with the forces of Arthur. Guardian preventing access to the realms of evil will and greed.

Gaheris—Knight, son of Morgawse and Lot, brother to Agravaine and Gareth, half-brother to Gawain and Mordred, married to Linet. Killed Morgawse and her lover, Lamorak. Aided in the downfall of Camelot by the exposure of Lancelot and Guinevere. Killed in the final battles. Guardian preventing access to the realms of jealousy, cowardice, and uncontrolled actions.

Mordred—Son of Morgawse and Arthur, influenced by Morgawse and the brothers of Orkney. He allied with them to form the forces fighting against Arthur at the final battle, Camlann. Reputed to have killed Arthur and to have been killed by him. Guardian Trainer showing the need to fight one's internal battles and not let external actions be motivated by unresolved personal needs.

Balyn—Knight at Caerleon who drew the Sword Unfortunate and killed the Lady of the Lake. Questing for his own redemption, he delivered the dolorous stroke that wounded the Fisher King, inadvertently killed his brother Balan, and was, in turn, killed by him. Guardian Trainer showing the need to quest with preparation and purpose and not react with pride and rage.

Balan—Knight, brother of Balyn, defeated the Knight of the River, and then had to take his place as champion of the Enchanted Castle, inadvertently killed his brother, Balyn, and was mortally wounded in the process. Guardian Trainer showing the need to choose your own quest and determine beforehand the nature of anyone with whom you do battle.

Pellinore—King of the lost kingdom, whose duty was to follow the Questing Beast. Father of Perceval, Lamorak, Dindraine, Agovale, and Tor. Father of Palomides by a Saracen Queen. Became an adviser to Arthur after Merlin withdrew. Guardian Trainer showing the need to avoid questing just for the sake of the quest.

Palomides—The Saracen Knight who assumed the task of following the Questing Beast after Pellinore withdrew. Half-brother to Perceval, he went with him on his Grail quest and married a maiden of the Grail Castle. Guardian Trainer showing the rewards of duty for clearly determining the purpose of questing.

Aglovale—Knight, son of Pellinore, killed by the Orkneys when he was unarmed, and guarding Guinevere after she had been accused of treason. Guardian Trainer showing that nobility of action can be wasted on those not noble in intent.

Tor—Knight, Son of Pellinore, also killed while guarding the Queen, Guinevere, unarmed in protest of her innocence. Guardian Trainer showing the need to guard yourself in all events that make you vulnerable to the dark intentions of others.

Mists—Fire/Water—S/W—Courtly Love: Partners/Protectors

Ambrosius/Elaine—King of Britain and Princess of Dyfed in South Wales, parents of The Merlin from a union between them in secret as Ambrosius fled from Vortigern to regroup in Brittany along with his brother Uther. Grandparents of Arthur. Partner Protectors showing the need for Courage and faith in the higher purposes of love.

Tristan/Isolde (the Fair)—Knight, nephew of King Mark of Cornwall and an Irish princess whose love for each other caused them to betray King Mark. Separated from each other when Tristan was banished, foiled in their final attempt to reunite by Isolde of the White Hands, whom Tristan had wed when he was banished to Brittany. Partner Protectors showing the need to have faith in the power of true love.

Erec/Enide—Knight who felt weakened by his love for his Lady, quested for contests in which he could prove himself, became champion again and reacknowledged his love for Enide, who had patiently remained by his side. Partner Protectors showing the need to protect the power of a true relationship while allowing for growth and change.

Culwech/Olwen—Knight who won his Lady despite the opposition of her father and the many other obstacles in his way. Ultimately the Lady Olwen had to choose to support her lover, Culwech. Partner Protectors showing the courage and power that love brings to those who face the opposition of others for the sake of their relationship.

Yvain/Luned—Knight (of the Lion) who leaves the maiden, Laudine of the fountain, for the action at Arthur's Court, and stays overlong, not knowing that Luned is under an enchantment until he returns. Upon his return, with the help of a lion, he defends her as his Lady. Partner Protectors showing the need for patience and strength to take on the responsibilities of true love.

Gareth/Lionors—The newly initiated knight and the Lady in the tower whom he rescues after her lady-in-waiting, Linet, comes to Camelot in search of a champion for her mistress. Gareth is knighted by Lancelot and then proceeds to undergo a number of initiatory trials in order to achieve his task. He falls in love with Lionors as soon as he sees her in the tower, and they are soon wed. Gareth is killed, inadvertently, by Lancelot during the exposure of Guinevere and Lancelot's betrayal of Arthur. Protectors guiding those through the many elementally testing aspects of love and honor.

Alexander and Alice—The young knight, cousin of Tristan, and his Lady of sweetness in nature who decided, upon seeing him, that he was to be her knight, and he agreed immediately. In spite of attempts by jealous others, both remained true to each other. Partners showing the honor and rightfulness of the rarest love-at-first-sight.

Lanceor and Colombe—The Irish knight and his lady who kills herself on his sword after Lanceor is killed by Balyn, in the process of avenging the Lady of the Lake. Protectors showing the need to consider the consequences of your actions upon your loved ones.

Launfal and Tryamour—The young Breton knight and his Faerie Lady who must be protected, but instead protects him, taking him forever to her realm. Protectors showing the need to choose partners with whom you are easily able to share your life.

Water—West—Avalon: The Initiator/Healers

Morgana—Priestess, Morgan le Fey, daughter of Gorlois and Igraine of Cornwall, sister of Vivienne and half-sister to Arthur. Morgan was married to Uriens of Gorre and was an important priestess of Avalon. She and her foster sister, Morgawse, arranged for Arthur to beget two sons, Gawain and Mordred, possibly in order to ensure the line of succession and to keep the Sovereign alliance between the land and the king productive and powerful. Morgan is the healer of Arthur and waits with him in Avalon. Initiator Healer in all the realms of Avalon; brings the experience of sacrificing to yourself and your inner guidance, despite the result of being misunderstood and maligned by others.

Nimue—Novitiate, the fair Irish weaver who arranged for The Merlin to withdraw and preserve his wisdom in the realms of the Mystical mind. Parented by a union between two of the old blood lines, the Fey or Fair Folk, born to be a gift to serve The Merlin's purpose, fostered out to Avalon and trained by Morgana. Initiator Healer who teaches the craft of intuitive awareness and preservation of the psychic gifts.

Vivienne—Elaine of Garlot, Priestess, daughter of Igraine and Gorlois of Cornwall, wife of Nentres of Garlot. Mother Superior of Avalon's sanctuary, politically and personally motivated to make the realms of Avalon inaccessible due to the shifting spiritual consciousnesses and beliefs of the times. Initiator into the ways of structuring spiritual practices and the training of the clergy in their duties and services.

Nentres Garlot—Rex Avallonis, Husband of Vivienne, Priest/King of Avalon, politically motivated by Vivienne to ensure the survival of the structures of Spirituality through times of transition. Initiator Healer determining the readiness of those wishing to access the mystical inner realms and prescriptive diagnostician of specific needs for making self-healing journeys in preparation for inner quests and sacred service.

Ganieda—Cerridwen, Priestess, crone, Druidic sister of The Merlin, one of the weavers serving the Fates, the Wyrd, wise-woman companion of The Merlin, priestess emeritus of Avalonian wisdoms. Initiator Healer who reveals, through dreams and visions, the patterns of life and the prescriptive measures needed for self-renewing healing and mystical empowerment.

Tides—Water/Earth—N/W—Grail: Restorers/Questors

Pelles—The Fisher King wounded by the dolorous stroke that created the Wasteland, keeper of the Grail castle, who presents the questors with the opportunities to restore his wounds, themselves, and the lands, as well. Father of Elaine of Carbonek, grandfather of Galahad. Restorer who provides access to the Grail within the guarded walls of personal beliefs and gives those questing inward the chance to restore the Wasteland aspects of their own lives.

Elaine of Carbonek—daughter of Pelles, the Fisher King, maiden of the Grail, who became the mother of Galahad by a magickally arranged union with Lancelot, who was under the influence of a potion prepared by her nurse, Brisen. Wife of Lancelot after he served his self-imposed exile following the death of Guinevere. Restorer Questor who provides the means by which one brings the needed qualities for the Grail quest into form for the purpose of self-restoration of spirit.

Galahad—The Pure Knight, son of Lancelot and Elaine of Carbonek, grandson of Pelles, the Fisher King. Achieved the Grail and was transmuted into the heavenly realms of Spirit, to which realm he returned the Grail while the Wasteland remained unchanged. Questor who shows the need for the application of spiritually restoring powers and wisdoms to be activated and shared, first within and therefore within the world around.

Ector de Maris—Knight, Son of King Ban of Bonwick, brother of Lancelot, who seeks his brother and finds him at the Grail castle; also accompanies Gawain on his quest for the Grail, yet never understands the true spiritual motivations of either questor. Restorer of those depleted by questing; brings devotion freely given without expectation or understanding the reason for personal quests; activates personal acceptance.

Bors—Knight, the ordinary man, cousin of Lancelot and Ector de Maris, son of King Bors, nephew of King Ban, brother of Lionel; achieves the Grail for his faithful, loyal nature to the service of humanity and the everyday realms of home and hearth. Restorer who shows the practical aspects of applying Grail wisdom and inner experiences to the mundane planes of life.

Perceval—Knight, the Wise Innocent who becomes one of the three knights to achieve the Grail, after both passing and failing several tests, he quests again according to his own, inner guidance, and achieves the Grail. This act brings about the reemergence of the primal power of Bran, ancient guardian god of the lands, and restores the Wasteland. Reputed in some versions to have brought the Grail back to Arthur. Restorer/Questor who shows the need to be the Fool, ever at the beginning of the quest, which is eternal, in ever-continuing cycles of Self-renewal.

Dindraine—Lady, the Christed one, daughter of Pellinore, sister of Perceval, Lamorak, Agovale, and Tor. Accompanies the questors for the Grail and sacrifices herself to heal the Lady of the Grail Castle, thus allowing the quest to continue. Restorer of the feminine mysteries, the intuitive wisdoms, which provide the needed nurturance in our lives.

Earth—North—Camelot: Connectors/Manifestors

Arthur—High King of All Britain, Dux Bellorum, Comtes Britannarium, warlord who united Britain after the withdrawal of Rome, established and held the peace for three or four decades, giving Britain time to form its own identity during very transitional times. Legendary Celtic warrior/hero/king, son of Uther and Igraine of Cornwall, grandson of Ambrosius and Elaine of South Wales, half-brother of Morgana and Vivienne, foster brother to Morgawse by whom he had two sons, Gawain and Mordred.

Husband to Guinevere (reputed husband to one or two other queens also named Guinevere). Established the Court of Camelot and the Round Table Codes of knightly service and honor. Expanded his rulership into Brittany, thereby neglecting his Queen, who then took Lancelot as her lover. Died in battle at Camlann fighting the forces of the Orkney brothers and the Celtic clans who were seeking to regain their own rulership. Reputed to have killed, and been mortally wounded by, Mordred.

Taken to Avalon to rest in the healing care of Morgana, awaiting the call to return. Restorer Questor who provides the catalyst and the structures by which to unite the fellowship of humankind and shows the needs to wield the sword of power with honor while not forgetting the balance of the scabbard and the necessary nurturance for one's alliance with Sovereignty to be maintained.

Guinevere—Queen of Britain, wife of King Arthur, daughter of King Leodegrance of Cameliard. Foster mother to Gawain and Mordred while they were at Camelot. Lover of Lancelot, with whom she was accused of the treasonous act of betraying the King. Reputed to have brought the great round table to Camelot as part of her dowry. In the ancient Celtic sense, Guinevere is the Spring Maiden who never becomes impregnated, although she achieved her own maternal aspects in her care of the knights of the Round Table, for whom she was a source of inspiration. Later, as a sequestered nun, she may be seen as the withdrawn crone. Connector Manifestor for the ways of courtly behavior, the gentility of style and gentleness of spirit.

Lancelot—The Queen's Knight, son of King Ban of Benwick, brother of Ector de Maris, father of Galahad by a magickally arranged union with Elaine of Carbonek, whom he later wed. Reputed to have been fostered to the care of the Lady of the Lake, from whom he received the title Lancelot du Lac. The unquestioned champion of the Round Table, who quested for the Grail but failed, even though he was able to glimpse it, because his earthly desires for Guinevere dishonored his knightly vows and distracted him from his spiritual purposes. After his quest, he resumed his relationship with Guinevere in a way leading to their exposure, caused him inadvertently to kill Gareth while trying to protect Guinevere, and led to the final decline of Camelot and the Round Table. Questor showing the need to accept, at times, what destiny has brought you.

Winds—Earth/Air—N/E—Round Table: Standard Bearers

Sir Ector—Knight, foster father to Arthur by an arrangement made with The Merlin at Arthur's birth. Father of Sir Kai, foster father to Bedevere. Sir Ector brought up Arthur as his own son, only revealing Arthur's true parentage when Arthur pulled the sword from the stone. A solid supporter of Arthur's visions of a united Britain and a Round Table order of chivalry and codes of honor. Standard Bearer enabling you to bring your visions of what is Right into honorable form.

Kai—Knight, foster brother to Arthur and Bedevere, son of Sir Ector. Initially claimed he had drawn the sword from the stone instead of Arthur, who was his squire at that time. Recanted his story and became one of Arthur's staunchest supporters, his seneschal of the Court, and trusted guardian of Guinevere and the Camelot court when Arthur was away. Some versions in the older tradition suggest that Bedevere was the queen's lover, as well as her knight. Closely associated with the sword of power, Bedevere is sometimes depicted as the one who returned Excalibur to the Lady of the Lake after Arthur was taken to Avalon. Standard Bearer for the structuring of organizations with measured formulas and codes of honor.

Lucan—Knight, Lucan the Butler, subordinate of Bedevere, trusted knight and loyal ally to Arthur and to the order of the Round Table. Closely associated with the spear, Ron, with which Arthur is reputed to have slain Mordred at Camlann, when Lucan handed the spear to Arthur at the precise moment it was needed. Also reputed to have gone with Bedevere to return Excalibur to the Lady of the Lake, and to have carried out Arthur's last commands, even though he, too, was mortally wounded. Standard Bearer bringing the lessons of duty and the virtues of loyalty and honor.

Uriens—King of Gore, the elemental outlands and regions of untamed, primitive power. Husband of Morgana, father of Yvaine. Originally in opposition to Arthur's kingship of Britain, he became loyal to Arthur and acknowledged his line of descent from Uther Pendragon. Standard Bearer bringing the wisdom of structuring elemental forces into an ordered form by which their powers may be manifested with practical application in our lives.

Galahaut—The Haut Prince of the Faraway Isles, devoted friend of Lancelot who persuades him to serve the Round Table order and Arthur, whom he originally opposed. His devotion to Lancelot motivates him to keep his own needs secondary to those of his beloved friend, despite having been told that Lancelot and Guinevere will be instrumental somehow in bringing about his own death. When a false message comes, telling Galahaut that Lancelot has been killed, Galahaut dies of grief and is later buried in Lancelot's family tomb at Joyous Garde. Standard Bearer bringing the wisdom of determining for yourself the path of honor you alone follow.

Leodegrance—King of Cameliard, father of Guinevere, who gave to Arthur as part of Guinevere's dowry the great round table, which he had received from The Merlin. A loyal supporter of Arthur from the outset, Leodegrance was constant in his service to the order of the Round Table. Standard Bearer bringing the wisdom of developing specific mindsets based on inalienable truths and rights.

Lionel—The Good Knight, son of King Bors of Benwick, brother of Lancelot, cousin to Bors, who accompanied his kinsmen on their quests and adventures. Although rash at times, he served the codes of the Round Table in a straightforward manner and was later killed while fighting for Arthur at Camlann. Standard Bearer bringing the wisdom of contemplating consequences before taking action.

King Bors—King of Benwick in Brittany, father of Bors and Lionel, uncle of Lancelot, and Ector de Maris. Ally of Arthur's, bringing the support of Brittany to the cause of united Britain; his actions motivated his brother, Ban, to continue the alliance. Standard Bearer reminding of the need for allied orders of honor.

King Ban—King of Benwick in Brittany, father of Lancelot and Ector de Maris, uncle of Bors and Lionel. He strengthened the alliance created by his brother, King Bors, and Arthur, and acknowledged Arthur's kingship over all that was Britain and British. Reputed to have fostered Lancelot to the Lady of the Lake in order that he could be trained in the mystical ways of Logres. Standard Bearer bringing the wisdom of blending the mystical with the mundane to develop personal codes of honor.

Review the characters and make note of those who struck a chord of recognition or remembrance. Note the aspects and placements of these characters. They are clues to the qualities you may need in your life at the present time. Work with any or all of these characters, beginning with those who have the most appeal for you. You may do this with the skills of active imagery you have been developing throughout this text.

You may also wish to note your initial reactions and your first emerging images of these various characters. These images may well change for you as you explore these realms more thoroughly. Those changes are also the reflections of your own changes and those in your life, as well.

CHAPTER 13

THE COURTLY LOVES
OF CAMELOT

*In courtly and poetic circles the ideal of individual experience prevailed over
that of the infallible authority of men whose character was supposed to be disre-
garded. And in the Church as well, the principles of such fallibility was called
into doubt, questioned and rejected.*

Joseph Campbell
The Power of Myth

 At the time when the flowering of chivalry was in full bloom, about
1150–1250, the Norman French troubadours began rendering the
tales from the British, Bardic oral tradition into a collection which
forms the heart of the literature of Courtly Love. While the French
certainly did not invent love, despite their reputation for having done
so, their troubadours can be credited rightfully with bringing the craft of love to a
high art. In the early Middle Ages, the concept of the individual heart having the
power—and the right—to decide on such "issues of life" as love was still new, or at
the very least, renewed.

The concept of Courtly Love developed due to the support of Eleanor of
Aquitaine. Eleanor was first the wife of Louis of France, whom she left after the Crusades, and then wife of Henry II of Britain, who was himself quite enamored of the
Arthurian legends. Remembering that Eleanor Aquitaine was the mother of Richard
the Lion Hearted, and King John, as well, we can see how powerful her influence was
on Western, European consciousness. Eleanor of Aquitaine was, as Victoria was in
her time, the grandmother of the next generation of European and British royalty.
Eleanor's own grandfather had begun the troubadour tradition in the South of
France. This tradition was then continued by Eleanor's daughters, Blanche of Castille
and Marie de Champagne.

The works of Chretien de Troyes, the court poet of Champagne, have preserved the power of that transformational moment in Celtic consciousness and the rights of personal choice. Others, such as Girhault de Borneilh, went even farther and began the analysis of love which was an initial contribution to the development of Western psychology.

While the troubadours presented their aspects of Courtly Love, the Orthodoxy preached there was no such thing at all. In the Orthodox view of that time, there were only two kinds of "love": either lust, or spiritual love—*agape*. Both types of love were of the impersonal variety. The Orthodoxy failed to acknowledge the quality of love that Joseph Campbell describes as "the delight in the manifestation of the divine in another person." This concept, as well as that of "the ultimate sacrifice for a noble heart is the sacrifice of honor for love," was considered to be heresy by the Orthodox churches. Yet the concept of Courtly Love continued to flourish, waving its banner of *amor* in direct opposition to the orthodox dogmas of *Roma*!!

Troubadours such as Girhault de Borneilh endeavored to find a place of compromise. He explained that the "eyes are the scouts of the heart" which allow the individual to find the image of true love in the form of a beloved. Then if the heart of the one who is the ideal image has a true and gentle quality, Courtly Love is possible. This was Borneilh's way to show the result of blending lust (the ideal image) with spiritual love (the gentle heart) into the natural beauty of Courtly Love.

As we proceed through this chapter, I will describe the themes of other, older tales of Courtly Love. The ones selected for this chapter all share the same faerie tale quality which I call "happily ever after ... at least for a while, anyway." I suggest you note which of these tales have a theme or pattern similar to your own quests for love. It is not necessary to identify only with characters of your own gender since these legends represent patterns of human relationships in general.

The courtly tales had their origin in Celtic legends of love and honor such as the "Wooing of Emer." Emer, "the most beautiful woman in all of Ireland," told Cuchulain that she would be won by "deeds and not by words alone." Despite this, Cuchulain continued to boast about all his victories and his great prowess. Eventually, Cuchulain turned his attention to Fand, the faerie queen, wife of Mananann. At this, Emer and Fand encountered each other in a very Celtic manner. Each of the women insisted on letting the other have Cuchulain.

This encounter between Emer and Fand continued until Mananann arrived. He then passed his magick cloak between Emer and Cuchulain, causing them to forget their conflicts, to see each other as the ideal image of their own hearts' desires. This also served to remind Fand just who her ideal love really was. Thus Emer and Cuchulain lived happily ever after—for a while, anyway—until Queen Maeve of Connaught decided she must have the brown bull of Cooley, and Cuchulain decided she mustn't ... but that's another story. In the ancient Celtic forms of Courtly Love, the battle between the sexes often was quite literal.

Another courtly Celtic tale is that of "Erec and Enide." This tale, retold by Chretien, is found in the Welsh record *The Mabinogion*, originally as the tale of Gereint and Enid. Although there are some differences in the two versions, the theme remains primarily the same.

EREC AND ENIDE

In the process of establishing himself as a worthy knight in the Round Table "corporation," Erec quested for battle with Duke Edern, the Red Knight, who had insulted Queen Guinevere. In order to do this with honor, Erec needed to enter the Sparrowhawk contest and defeat Edern there. However, Erec also had to have a lady of his own to champion, so he asked his ally, Duke Yniwl, for permission to champion his daughter Enide. Erec defeated Edern and was given Enide as his betrothed.

Erec was already annoyed that this betrothal, while convenient, had caused him to miss the royal Pendragon hunt for the White Hart. Guinevere saved the White Hart's head for Enide, as the fairest, because she was avenged by Erec. Erec instructed Enide to remain with Guinevere to be prepared for marriage to a knight such as himself, while he continued questing for adventures. Despite his rejection of the idea, Enide decides to come along with Erec. Along the way, Enide was studiously obedient on the surface and patiently accepting of Erec's endless quests. Privately, she arranged to have herself mock-abducted by an earl who could not understand why such a kind, fair maiden as Enide would want to be with such a neglectful, unkind young man as Erec.

However, that plan was delayed by yet another series of adventures, some of which Erec would not have survived, except for the warnings and the watchfulness of Enide. By this time, Erec was feeling not only betrothed, but beholden to Enide. This caused him to purposefully ignore her advice. There followed a mistaken attack by Erec on Arthur's knights, done while ignoring Enide's warnings. When Erec and Enide were taken to Arthur's camp to recover, Arthur duly remarked that Erec lacked advice.

On they went, once recovered, to another set of adventures that now have taken on an enchanted nature. Mists and magick were brought in to provide a chance for the resolution of Erec's inner conflict. Between his rigid concept of honor and his growing love for Enide, Erec was knocked senseless—or perhaps to his senses—and left for dead by some giant. Along came the Earl to take Enide away. The earl offered to put an entire earldom at Enide's disposal if she would be his wife. Enide was inconsolable and refused to eat or drink as long as Erec was unable to do so. The Earl continued to press Enide—as told in *The Mabinogion*:

Earl: "You cannot fulfill that, the man is all but dead."

Enide: "I will do my best."

Then he offered her drink from a bowl, saying, "Drink this bowlful and you will change your mind."

Enide: "Shame on me if I drink before he does."

"Well," said the Earl, "it is no better being kind to you than being unkind" and he boxed her ears. She gave a loud, piercing scream and cried far more than she had before; and it occurred to her that, were Gereint (Erec) alive, she would not have her ears boxed so. With the reverberation of that scream, Gereint came to his senses.

Erec proceeded to wound the Earl and horrify everyone present, who were certain he had risen from the dead to avenge his lady, Enide. After questing on for a time, Erec encountered "a knight on a proud, high-spirited, wide-nostrilled, broad-boned war horse," which was the Red Knight of battle.

Erec bested this fierce-looking knight. As he was about to take off the Red Knight's head, the knight says: "Alas, lord, have mercy, and you shall have whatever you wish."

Erec replied, "I wish only that these games cease, and that the hedge of mist and the magic and enchantment disappear."

At that, the Red Knight told Erec to blow a magick horn, as the Champion and the games would cease.

When the horn was blown, everything returned as it was before. All of the quests and the encounters had been magickally induced when the Pendragon hunt had resulted in the slaying of the White Hart. This White Hart was a messenger from the Otherworld who signaled the start of the games, testing both Erec and Enide. The trials and tests had been the reflections of Erec's and Enide's resistance to the faerie-bolt effect of love at first sight. Enide's was of the passive resistant variety, and Erec's was aggressive resistance. Together, they canceled out each other's natural resistances and left a balanced blend. Therefore, as the legend goes on, Erec and Enide went on to their own realm, where: "From that time, he ruled prosperously, with prowess and splendor, and won praise and fame ever after for himself and for Enid."

Two other tales that combine the concept of Courtly Love with the codes of knightly honor are "Culwech and Olwen" from *The Mabinogion* and "Yvaine or The Knight of the Lion" from Chretien de Troyes' rendering of *The Mabinogion* tale, "Owein, or The Countess of the Fountain."

CULWECH AND OLWEN

In the first of these tales, "Culwech and Olwen," Arthur and his knights set off on a series of adventures in order to help Culwech win Olwen for his bride. Along the way, they encountered numerous trials and Otherworld tests in order to prove their skills and collected amazing treasures, thirteen in all. These are the Thirteen Treasures of Britain, symbols of cultural qualities, tribal skills, and the sacred forces of Nature. Since we will discuss these treasures in greater detail in the last part of this text, I will only refer to them now.

In Culwech and Olwen, the chief opponent to their love for one another was Olwen's father, Ysbaddaden (Hawthorn). His opposition was based on more than fatherly possessiveness, however. Hawthorn knew he would die whenever his daughter, Olwen wed. This theme originates from the Solar cycles. The old Sun wanes. The new Sun waxes. This describes the changes in the Sun's rays during the two primary segments or cycles; the dark, fallow periods, and those that are light and growing.

This Solar cycle's effect on the Earth gives rise to the frequent theme of Celtic myth, the interaction of two men and one woman. Thus the old Sun, or dark lord, or old king, must be defeated by the new Sun, bright lord, young king, or hero. This is necessary in order to set free the Maiden, Mother Earth, Queen or Lady, from a realm or relationship in which she is bound, most often by enchantment.

In Culwech and Olwen, there are interwoven patterns of the same theme. It is not enough to win the Thirteen Treasures of Britain by having one young Solar Hero defeat one old, over-the-hill Dark Lord. This must be done several times. In Culwech and Olwen, the rescue of Mabon, son of Modron, an aspect of the Earth Goddess, is a prime

example of this. Additionally, the perilous hunt for the giant boar, Twrch Trwyth, also symbolized the struggle with fierce, dark forces such as the dark times of winter represented in a more primitive sense. Winter was also the season when the ancient hunters had to leave their caves to hunt for much-needed sources of protein. The hunt for and killing of the giant boar symbolized the power of Arthur and his knights to provide for the people of the lands.

That this hunt, the rescue of the light, and the gaining of the treasures ever began, was due to a destiny that Culwech's stepmother placed on him, and that he had felt a faerie bolt of truth upon hearing this. Culwech's stepmother offered to let her own daughter be his betrothed, but Culwech protested first that he was too young. The stepmother, presuming this to be rejection of her own daughter, replied: "Then I swear this destiny upon you: Your side shall never touch that of a woman until you win Olwen, daughter of the Chief Giant Ysbaddaden."

This she believed to be an impossible task. Later, Culwech's father saw him blushing furiously and asked what had gotten into him. When Culwech told of the destiny, his father replied: "That will not be difficult. Arthur is

123

your first cousin; go to him and have your hair trimmed, and ask for Olwen as your reward."

Here we have the kindly, paternal "old Sun" advising his "new Sun" to spruce up a bit, let everyone know who he was, stand up and be counted, and so forth. Thus, with a destiny on his head, an unseen love in his heart, and advice from a kind father who hadn't been around much, Culwech started his quest. Arthur was charmed by Culwech, his country bumpkin cousin, and promised to help with whatever Culwech wanted.

Culwech proceeded to ask for Olwen and to "invoke her in the name of" all of Arthur's warriors.

Naturally, this meant that all the warriors named would have to help. (This process takes nine pages in *The Mabinogion* and must have been an oral, bardic feat which made the Biblical "begats" pale in comparison.) In the end, Culwech does win the lovely Olwen; Arthur gains the treasures; and the Chief Giant Hawthorn has his head "set on a stake on the wall." Culwech and Olwen married, Arthur and his warriors went back to their own lands, the Thirteen Treasures became part of Britain's power, and they all lived happily ever after ... for a while, anyway.

YVAIN (ALSO OLWEIN) AND LAUDINE

Yvain (also the Knight of the Lion, Olwein, or the Countess of the Fountain) seems very realistic after Culwech and Olwen's phantasmagorical tale. It is certainly one which is easier to relate to our own lives and relationships. The basic theme is that of the person who gets rather obsessively involved in where they are and what they are doing—so much so that others think they are lost. Then, when found and relocated, or changed somehow, they obsess again. This they do without understanding, or even considering, the effect this has on those whom they have already left. Always, this person is to go on to yet another place, person, or project. This continues until something shakes them out of the pattern. For Yvain and Laudine, that something is love and honor—this time in combination—but first, the conflict.

Yvain quested alone to avenge an insult done to his cousin by a brutish knight he had encountered at a strange fountain. In the Welsh version, Yvain (Owein) slipped off on his own without telling anyone, and they decided to come looking for him—three years later. This is a rather interesting comment on British Celtic respect for independence, I think. In the Norman French version, Yvain slipped away before the others who were also planning to go on the quest, so he could do it alone. This is also an interesting difference.

Yvain did indeed encounter many marvels. Among them: a castle where he was treated quite royally, a giant who controlled his cattle by twisting their horns to the ground if they strayed, and a fountain with boiling water which, when poured on a stone vessel, caused great storms, and also caused a brutish knight to appear. Yvain survived his first encounter with the knight, only to return to battle and kill him the second time.

In the process of chasing this mortally wounded knight, Yvain became trapped in a set of rigged gates. Help arrived in the form of the fair maiden Luned, who gave Yvain a ring to make him invisible. This was quite useful, since all the people of the knight's castle wanted to kill Yvain for slaying their lord. With this ring, and aided by Luned, Yvain was able to hide in the castle and observe all that was going on. When he first saw her, Yvain fell in love with the dead knight's widow, Laudine. Then, with the further help of Luned, Yvain was finally able to make himself and his love for Laudine known to her. Laudine and Yvain married and he became the knight/lord of her realms.

In the Welsh version, this marriage was made necessary by the fact that another knight/earl was trying to get Laudine's lands. It was also possible that Arthur would arrive at any time to avenge Yvain's cousin. Since Yvain was the son of King Uriens and Morgana, we can assume there would be no problem raising a force to avenge him, as well, However, in the Welsh version, it was three years before Arthur arrived. In the Norman French version, it was about a week. In either case, Arthur—and particularly Gawain—persuaded Yvain's wife, the Lady Laudine, to let him return to Camelot for some knightly activities. In the Welsh version, Arthur promised to have Yvain return to Laudine in three months. In the Norman French version, Laudine told Yvain to be back in a year, or else.

Three years later, Yvain returned to the wondrous realm he had left behind. Everything had become depleted in his absence, including his own strength. However, he still managed to win several battles and survive new adventures. Yvain saved a lion from a huge serpent that had trapped the lion in a crevasse of a great stone. Yvain befriended the lion which then brought him a deer to eat. Next, Yvain discovered that Luned had been enchanted and was trapped in the stone vessel at the fountain. After he had released her, Luned and Yvain went to the aid of Laudine; taking the lion with them.

By then, Laudine had lost most of her lands to the knight who had coveted them before Yvain left. In a series of battles, Yvain and the lion restored the lands to Laudine. Although Yvain had chivalrously tried to cage the lion in order to make the battles more fair, the lion continued to break the bonds that held him back, so he could also fight for Yvain.

Finally, Yvain had to fight for Luned's life against the Black Oppressor. This was the knight who had depleted the lands and the people in Yvain's absence. When the Black Oppressor was subdued, he begged for mercy:

"Lord Owein (Yvain), there was a prophecy you would come and subdue me and that you have done. I was a robber, and this is a plunder house; spare my life, and for your sake I will become a host and turn this into a guest house for the weak and the strong for as long as I live."

After he had accepted the Black Oppressor's terms, Yvain took Laudine, Luned, and twenty-four maidens who had been held prisoner by the Black Oppressor, back to Camelot. The lion's task was completed.

Although the women are not developed as characters in the tale, they both may be seen as lunar symbols, reflecting the gradually cyclical processes of change that are natural and flowing, like the fountain. The storms symbolize the overly dramatic and intense changes that damage the "forest" of the mind.

When Yvain was able to grant mercy to the Black Oppressor, it showed he had forgiven himself and trusted himself to control his own dark, oppressive patterns. When the lion left, it symbolized Yvain's integration of those strengths within himself. Therefore, he was able to combine love and honor within a gentle heart, which he had fought against before, and now formed an alliance within himself.

THE ETERNAL TRIANGLE OF CAMELOT'S COURTLY LOVE

For a time long enough to make an indelible imprint upon Western consciousness and to reconnect the Celtic codes or "pathways" to the rights of individual choice, the concept of Courtly Love reigned supreme, literally, in the Courts of Love established by the Norman nobles and their troubadours. Their tales, both joyful and tragic in nature, centered upon the exploits and adventures of the Round Table knights. Primary among these current images of the Camelot legends is the unquestioned champion knight of Camelot, the lover of Guinevere, Sir Lancelot du Lac, who first was introduced by Chretien de Troyes in "The Knight of the Cart."

In this retelling of the older tale of Arthur's rescue of Guinevere from Melwas, it is Lancelot who goes to rescue the queen. This, of course, reflected the conquest of Britain by the Normans, as well as served to "wound" the British royal line with the tale of the seduction of the British queen. In "The Knight of the Cart," we can see the additional conflict arising between codes of honor and concepts of love, as Lancelot valiantly attempts to pass the tests of both.

THE KNIGHT OF THE CART
Condensed adaptation by Amber Wolfe

It came to pass that dire news reached the Court of Camelot. Queen Guinevere had been abducted by Melwas, King of the Summer Country, and was being held for ransom in his enchanted stronghold, Caer Witren, the Glass Fortress. A summons had been sent to King Arthur from Melwas. They were to meet upon the Tor at Avalon Isle and negotiate terms for the release of the queen. King Arthur was much troubled by this, since he wanted more than anything to go immediately and rescue his beloved Queen Guinevere.

As King Arthur's lords and advisers prevailed upon him to meet with Melwas and not endanger the queen any further, a fine young knight stepped forward with a resolution to the problem at hand. It was Lancelot du Lac, new to the order of the Round Table, yet already the unquestioned champion of them all in knightly arts and skills. Lancelot bravely volunteered to rescue the queen from Caer Witrin while King Arthur was with Melwas negotiating the political aspects of the situation, as a king must do before all else may be done.

Because King Arthur knew that Lancelot, from Brittany, was eager to prove his loyalty to the British court, he granted him the privilege of serving in his own place; for the honor of rescuing the queen was, by right, the king's honor. Little did Arthur know Lancelot was, in secret, deeply enamored of the queen. Although it may be said Lancelot was not completely aware of this himself at that time, others did know of his love for Guinevere. A private look passed between The Merlin and Morgan le Fey, who had brought the news from Avalon where Melwas was waiting impatiently.

Thus it was that King Arthur rode forth from Camelot with Morgan, Sir Kai, Gawain, and The Merlin—these, along with a force of his finest knights, to deal with Melwas. Lancelot, preferring to make this quest alone, rode forth in the direction of Caer Witrin. As he left, a great white owl, the gwenfhyar, flew out of the forest to follow, silently behind him.

So fierce was his desire to rescue Guinevere, his quest caused Lancelot to ride three horses to the ground on his way. Then, when he was no longer able to secure another mount, Lancelot was forced to walk, fully armed, through the unfamiliar forests near Caer Witrin. As the Wyrd would have it, there chanced to come along a cart driven by a foul, toothless peasant who offered Lancelot a ride to the glass fortress, Caer Witrin. Lancelot, seeing this was the death cart used to transport criminals to the hangman, refused graciously.

It would have been a loss of honor for so great a knight to travel in that particular cart. However, as he watched the cart being driven away, Lancelot began to reconsider the matter. He had taken only three steps—slowly, because of his heavy armor—before he decided to call the cart driver back and accept the ride that had been offered. The white owl, which had been watching from its perch in an old tree, took flight once more, moving swiftly toward Caer Witrin.

At long last, Lancelot was dropped off at the gates of the glass fortress. He was greeted by nine beautiful maidens who urged him to come inside and rest, as he was weary from his journey. Lancelot was surprised to see no knights—nor any men at the glass fortress—left there guarding Queen Guinevere. Feigning no other purpose but that of ensuring his queen's well-being, Lancelot asked to see Guinevere. The maidens assured him his queen was well and that he could see her as soon as he had rested—and not before.

The maidens led Lancelot to a large chamber in which there was nothing but a massive bed set on wheels, like those on a cart. Lancelot, long since having learned the wisdom of at least seeming to follow the instructions of beautiful maidens, cleverly promised to rest in that bed and to wait for their return before seeking out his queen. The nine maidens smiled pleasantly and took their leave of Lancelot, closing and bolting the door behind them. Resigned to the fact he had been outwitted, Lancelot decided perhaps a rest was in order. After all, he knew he had always required his wits around him in dealing with one beautiful maiden; nine would be difficult for anyone to manage—even a French Knight such as himself. He decided to make the best of it in this cold, dark, bare chamber.

When Lancelot approached the bed, he found, much to his amazement, that it moved away from him. No matter which way he approached it, the bed would move away in the opposite direction. Finally, Lancelot realized there was nothing he could do but leap, fully armored, onto the bed. He sighed deeply and threw his hands up in mock surrender. The bed was still as he pretended to turn away. Then Lancelot turned back suddenly, jumped with all his strength, and landed in the center of the massive bed.

For a moment, the bed remained still. Lancelot was just beginning to consider the nature of this "perilous bed," when it suddenly began to move about again, more wildly and forcefully than before. It was all Lancelot could do to hold on as the bed seemed fiercely intent upon throwing him off onto the cold stone floor of the chamber. For a time there was nothing but the struggle to hold on and the sounds of his sword clanking against his heavy armor. Lancelot barely had time to wonder if this were to be the way he would meet his final challenge, when the bed finally was still once more.

With a sigh of relief, Lancelot relaxed and drifted toward the edges of sleep. Before he reached the sanctuary of slumber, he was startled back into a state of full alert by the sound of a deep growl coming from across the bedchamber. Sitting up quickly, with his sword drawn, Lancelot was just in time to see a large lion leaping toward the bed: roaring fiercely; wide-open mouth revealing large, sharp teeth; long claws outstretched for attack.

Such a battle ensued there on the bed that words fail to describe it. For what seemed to be an endless time, all was tooth and claw, flesh, bone, blood, and the flashing of Lancelot's sword blade as he struggled to swing it with true aim. All the while, the bed continued to move about the chamber, making it even more difficult for Lancelot to battle the lion and still maintain his hard-won position. The white owl, which had been watching from its perch on the ledge of a narrow window high in the thick stone wall, screeched and flapped her wings madly about, leaving tiny soft feathers floating in the air of the now bloody bedchamber. Then, as suddenly as it had begun, it was finished.

A short time later, the bedchamber door was unbolted and the nine maidens came in to behold a sight of blood and destruction. There on the collapsed bed lay Lancelot and the lion with the sword blade that had severed its head still stuck inside its neck. Everything was still and quiet—too quiet. The maidens could not decide if Lancelot were alive or dead. One of the maidens wisely held a tiny owl feather under Lancelot's nose, and it was finally determined he was still breathing. Then the maidens, using their mystical skills of healing, began the process of bringing Lancelot back from the edges of death. As they did this, the white owl watched from the window ledge, carefully preening her ruffled feathers.

When Lancelot awakened, he found himself in yet another bedchamber: this one warm, bright, and comfortably furnished. He was lying in a soft bed which, he was relieved to find, remained quite still. His armor was gone, but his sword stood at the ready, leaning up against the bedpost. It was when he saw Queen Guinevere standing at the foot of the bed that he finally realized he was naked.

Pulling the light, silky bedcovers up to his neck, he inquired as to her well-being. Since this required all the strength he had, he was barely able to whisper the tale of his ordeal. As he did this, he noticed that Guinevere was regarding him with an expression of cool appraisal. Unable to comprehend this cold rejecting attitude, Lancelot asked Guinevere if he had done something to displease her in any way. By way of reply, Queen Guinevere asked Lancelot why he had hesitated, taking three whole steps before taking the only means of transportation available to him in his quest to rescue her from a fate that well could have been worse than death.

Rolling his eyes toward heaven, Lancelot finally noticed the white owl which was watching him with the same expression as Guinevere's. He sat up suddenly, although it was quite painful to do so, and threw his hands up—this time in a gesture of true surrender. When Guinevere saw the pain and confusion in Lancelot's eyes, she relented.

She moved gracefully around the bed and gently sat beside Lancelot, with the soft fabric of her gown brushing lightly against his sword.

Thus it was that Morgana found Lancelot and Guinevere together in the bedchamber when she arrived at Caer Witrin some time later in the evening. Morgana brought the news that the terms had been negotiated: lands exchanged for Guinevere's safe return. King Arthur and his knights, newly allied with King Melwas, were due to arrive at any moment; so Morgana suggested Lancelot and the queen make ready for their imminent arrival. She summoned the nine maidens to bring fresh clothing for Lancelot and to polish his armor, which was damaged and too painful to wear.

As Morgana and Guinevere left Lancelot to the care of the maidens, the white owl called softly from the window before taking flight into the dark forest night. Then the two women looked knowingly at one another. Both queen and priestess knew the magick that had been present on this quest. They knew, as The Merlin knew, and Lancelot was yet to learn, that only the most powerful magick could have breached the walls of the glass fortress that had imprisoned the queen. That magick, stronger than any other kind, was the magick of true love.

Thus it was that Guinevere was left with a true dilemma—a question that has not been answered fully to this very day—for none can say what transpired between Lancelot and his queen. Nor should anyone say; for these are matters of the heart, the most secret and sacred, private matters of body, mind, and spirit.

While discussing Chretien de Troye's "The Knight of the Cart" with the great mythologist Heinrich Zimmer, Joseph Campbell asked him what he thought the "perilous bed" was really all about. Zimmer replied that it was symbolic of the "masculine experience of the feminine temperament." There was simply no use in trying to understand this logically. "The trial is to hold on. Don't try to solve it. Just try to endure it," as Joseph Campbell explained (from "Transformations of Myth Through time," St. Paul, MN: Highbridge Productions, 1990).

There is a great deal of truth in what Zimmer and Campbell decided. However, I must add to that my own feminine experience of the masculine temperament I see symbolized here. First, there is the rather interesting relationship between the word "armor" and the word for love, "amor." Then consider, also symbolically speaking, that the additional "R" in armor correlates with the rune Raido, which means journey, or quest.

If you consider the perilous nature of some of your own quests in relation to your relationships, you will be better able to put the natural trials and tests involved into clearer perspective. You may even find the humor in it all. Humor is, undoubtedly, humankind's "most effective weapon," as Mark Twain, that American "Merlin," so aptly demonstrated.

Your suggested assignment for this chapter is to construct a faerie tale version of one of the most positive relationships of Courtly Love from your own life experience. If you are currently living as-happily-as-possible with your beloved, you may wish to do this together. Each of you may also choose to write, or tell, your own version and compare them. Naturally, you are free to make these as magickally symbolic and enchanting as you wish. This little exercise truly can make you realize how much "magick" is involved in any relationship. You may find the old magick is still there!

This is an ancient technique, developed to an art by Carl Jung and explored by such eminent analysts as Bruno Bettelheim. I suggest using the faerie-tale style for these since their magick is often much more personally enlightening and empowering.

This should lead you to an enchanted encounter within the legendary realms of your relationship. In the next chapter, we will delve deeper into the realms wherein mythically enchanted encounters are more than possible; even likely.

> The myth is pessimistic, while the fairy story is optimistic, no matter how terrifyingly serious some features of the story may be. It is this decisive difference which sets the fairy tale apart from other stories in which equally fantastic events occur, whether the happy outcome is due to the virtues of the hero, chance, or the interference of supernatural figures.
>
> Bruno Bettelheim
> *The Uses of Enchantment: The Meaning and Importance of Fairy Tales*
> (New York: Vintage Books, 1989)

CHAPTER 14

TRIALS OF LOVE AND HONOR: TRISTAN AND ISOLDE

Cornwall is the island of the ego, dominated by the patriarchal masculine attitude. Ireland is the island of the unconscious matriarchal feminine, dominated by the Sorceress Queen. Neither of these can live without its complementary opposite. Cornwall must go to Ireland, or Ireland will come to Cornwall.

Robert Johnson
We: Understanding the Psychology of Romantic Love
(San Francisco: Harper and Row, 1983)

The story of Tristan and Isolde is one of the greatest legends found in Arthurian literature. Though it was not of ancient origin, its themes are both primal and current. The more familiar story, which follows a very similar theme is that of Lancelot, Guinevere, and Arthur. Because of the wealth of Western psychological messages found in Tristan and Isolde, I have chosen to present it here, extensively, with the informational messages woven into the story. This is another process of entrelacement, a method used frequently in the legends of Camelot. This entrelacement weaving of the tale of Tristan and Isolde also includes some threads about the trials of love and honor that other, more familiar legendary figures had to face.

Tristan was a young warrior who seemed destined to be a king; but the weavers of fate had woven a more subtle design, which is why we still tell this tale today. There are so many kings among the Celts it is often hard to tell where one begins and another leaves off. Tristan, however, remains, although he was never a king, despite his royal lineage and bloodline. In Tristan, the Light weavers of the legends saw a way to craft a message and provide a warning that is sadly reflected in this tragic tale. This message is one about the rights of choosing one's own true love,

131

rather than relinquishing that sacred right to the choice of others. More than this, though, is the right of the Celtic Goddess to be honored by Her Lord of Light in the ancient ways of alliance. It is this Lady goddess and the Lord who are reflected in the truest loves of all.

THE STORY OF TRISTAN AND ISOLDE
Adapted by Amber Wolfe

Tristan's tale begins and ends in sadness; but you already know that this is no more than a small dark cloud, passing over the brightly shining sun. Tristan was born in the lands of Brittany just after his father, King Rivalen of Lyonesse, was killed. This same fine King Rivalen had once allied himself with King Mark of Cornwall.

King Mark had a beautiful sister called Blanchefleur with whom King Rivalen had fallen in love. As this love was mutual, King Mark, gave his consent that they could wed, despite the sadness he felt when she left Cornwall.

Some years later, King Mark was battling in the service of Arthur, by then the High King of Britain, and could not help his old friend, King Rivalen. Nor could he help his sister, Blanchefleur, who had died soon after King Rivalen was killed. King Mark also did not know that Blanchefleur had given birth to a son, Tristan, who was then cared for by Lord Rohalt. Lord Rohalt was one of King Rivalen's knights, who wisely kept the identity of Tristan a secret. Tristan, by rights, was the true king of Lyonesse; but his father's murderers surely would have killed Tristan had they known of his existence. Thus, even his uncle, King Mark of Cornwall, knew nothing of Tristan for years yet to come, though

he did hear of the death of Blanchefleur, and of Rivalen, in time.

Many years later, when Tristan was almost grown, he was captured by pirates and taken out to sea. When a fierce storm came up suddenly, the pirates put Tristan in a tiny boat to persuade the forces of sea and storm to take him instead of themselves. By a fortunate tide, Tristan landed on the fair shores of Cornwall where he was found and brought to King Mark. Years passed, and Tristan lived at the Court of Cornwall, where he was treated as the son of the King, for their mutual sense of kinship had been strong and immediate. Eventually, the true lineage was revealed when Lord Rohalt came to Cornwall, still searching for his foster son, Tristan.

Tristan returned with Rohalt to Lyonesse long enough to defeat the invaders of his rightful throne. Then Tristan placed Lord Rohalt in charge of the throne of Lyonesse, as an honor for all he had done. Tristan then returned to Cornwall and to his uncle, King Mark, where, in noble fashion, he earned the right to be a knight of King Arthur's Round Table. Though still quite young, Tristan had the skills of an experienced warrior, and the self-assured manner of one who has been in many victorious battles. Tristan spent as much of his time with King Arthur as he did with King Mark; but one day a message came which sent Tristan riding swiftly and eagerly to champion the throne of Cornwall.

Tristan arrived at the Court of King Mark in time to see a giant of a man deliver a challenge to the Cornish knights, which none of them was willing to meet. If no one would agree to fight this Irish giant, who was called Morhaus, then a tribute that was due to be paid every fourth year, would have to be paid immediately. Since this tribute hadn't been paid in fifteen years or more, the Irish king and his queen, Isolde, had said that the tribute was now tripled. The tribute would now be three hundred young lads and three hundred young maidens to be brought back immediately to Ireland, where they would serve the sovereigns of the lands.

In his eagerness to champion Cornwall for his uncle whom he loved like a father, Tristan challenged Morhaus, in turn. As Tristan moved to strike a blow, Morhaus' great Irish sword scratched him on the knee. As Morhaus tried to explain that the point of the sword was poisoned, Tristan lifted his own battle sword and split open Morhaus' head.

Morhaus body was returned to Ireland with a fragment of Tristan's sword embedded in the head. There were many who mourned for Morhaus in Ireland, among them his sister, Queen Isolde, and his niece, The Fair Isolde. As Morhaus' body was prepared for burial, the Fair Isolde saw the sword fragment and pulled it from Morhaus' head. She placed it in a magick box in remembrance of the uncle whom she had loved so dearly.

Back in Cornwall, Tristan was on his deathbed. With no one who could cure him, Tristan made a deathbed request. He wanted to be placed in a small, sturdy boat and set out to sea on the falling tide, with only his harp to accompany him as he journeyed to the Otherworld. With his harp by his side, Tristan floated out on the falling tide and soon found himself on the shores of Ireland (at the place we now call Dublin Bay). When the people of that East Irish Kingdom heard the music of Tristan's harp, they rushed out to bring him in safely and took him to Queen Isolde for healing.

Tristan knew he would not be recognized, unless by the sound of his name, so he contrived to call himself Tantrist. Queen Isolde, who had great skills as a healer, took it upon herself to cure this stranger, Tantrist. She also had skills as an alchemist, for she was the very one who had blended the poison for Morhaus' sword. Both the Queen Isolde and her Fair daughter worked to heal Tantrist. Neither one knew they had at their mercy the very one who had killed their kinsman, Morhaus.

Tantrist was aware of this, of course, and very anxious to return to Cornwall, so he devised a plan of his own. He would persuade King Mark to marry the Fair Isolde, who could give Cornwall an heir. Then, Tantrist/Tristan could fulfill his duty to the throne of Brittany.

When Tristan returned to Cornwall, he presented his well-crafted plan as a wonderful and wise solution.

Though King Mark had never met the Fair Isolde, he soon felt he already knew her well. This was because of the fine detail in which Tristan described her—just as a lover would. King Mark agreed to wed the Fair Isolde, and Tristan/Tantrist returned to Ireland to find that this plan would prove to be more challenging than he had imagined.

When Tantrist returned to Ireland, he eagerly presented his plan (as King Mark's idea) to Queen Isolde, to her King, and to their daughter, the Fair Isolde, all of whom viewed this favorably—except Queen Isolde, who set a task to settle the matter. It seemed there was a dragon who had been attacking the people of those lands. Queen Isolde decided to use an ancient way to rid the lands of that dragon. She offered the Fair Isolde as a wife to whatever brave knight would slay the dragon.

Tantrist immediately demanded the right to champion Fair Isolde and slay the dragon himself. Queen Isolde granted Tantrist permission to slay the dragon, which she told him he would find near an ancient, mystical pool of water nearby.

There was also another young man at that Irish court (whom we will call Enes) who was very much interested in making the Fair Isolde his wife. Enes was the son of the seneschal, the highest adviser to that court. Since Enes fancied himself also to be in that exalted position, he decided to go along with Tantrist, just in case an opportunity of fortune might arise.

The dragon was waiting for them at the ancient pool, with bones and skulls scattered all about him. With well-disciplined skill, Tantrist soon dispatched the dragon. Enes then told Tantrist that others might claim this victory unless there was proof of who had truly been the one to slay the dragon. He

advised Tantrist to trick any such tricksters by cutting off the dragon's tongue. This way, the dragon would still appear to be untouched. What Enes knew, but didn't tell Tantrist, was that dragon's tongue was extremely poisonous.

Immediately after the tongue was cut away from the dragon, Tantrist found himself losing consciousness. Still holding the dragon's tongue, he fell into a deep and murky part of the pool. Enes raced over to the dragon and cut off the head, which was just what he needed to claim the Fair Isolde for himself. He left Tantrist for dead, and hurried back to the castle of Queen Isolde.

However, Queen Isolde and the Fair Isolde had decided to come to the pool to see how the slaying of the dragon was developing. On the way past the murkiest part of the pool, they saw a nose sticking up, all alone, from the murky waters. When they pulled on the nose, they soon discovered that Tantrist was attached to it.

With help from their guards, they pulled Tantrist out of the pool. He was still holding the dragon's tongue and with this clue to what was ailing poor Tantrist, Queen Isolde was able to gather the makings of a magick healing potion. It was guaranteed to work immediately, for its main ingredient was the very poison that had come from the dragon's tongue itself.

While they had been pulling Tantrist from the pool and preparing the healing potion, the Fair Isolde had held his sword—and noticed a chipped place where a fragment was missing from the blade. When they returned to the court, Tantrist was placed in a warm, fragrant bath. The Fair Isolde took his sword and his armor with promises to have it polished. Instead, she went quickly to open her magick box to see if the sword fragment from Morhaus' head wound would fit in the chipped place on Tantrist's sword. When the fragment clicked in with a perfect fit, the Fair Isolde raced back to the room where Tantrist was immersed in the bath.

The Fair Isolde pulled Tantrist from the bath and while he stood there, naked and shivering, she brandished the sword blade right under his nose. Screaming like a Banshee, the fierce, Fair Isolde declared her intentions to kill Tristan herself, even if it were the last thing she would ever do in her life. She knew Tristan by name and reputation, but she truly hadn't imagined him to be such a fine liar of a man.

Standing there, naked and unarmored against her rage, Tristan could only be gentle and vulnerable. Unspeakingly, he yielded the love he had in his heart for Fair Isolde. The Fair Isolde still held fast to the sword and stood on the line between hate and love. She knew this man who had killed her uncle, Morhaus, had also bravely gone to slay a dragon just for her. It seems she had already forgotten about the proposal from King Mark of Cornwall.

Tristan reasoned with the Fair Isolde and pointed out that if she killed him, she would have to marry the lying trickster, Enes. Tristan then painted a picture in Fair Isolde's mind portraying Cornwall and King Mark in such bright and beautiful images, that at last the Fair Isolde put down the sword and agreed to come to Cornwall with Tristan.

Later that evening there was a great feast. Enes, unaware that Tristan had been saved, dragged the head of the dragon before that Irish Court and claimed his right to the prize, Fair Isolde. Even when Tristan entered the feast hall, Enes held fast to his lie.

Tristan nobly told all who were present the truth about the dragon, the tongue, the pool, and the potion that cured him. Tristan sadly told how he had come to be the unfortunate one who had slain the noble giant of a man, Morhaus. This he did with honesty and honor, which persuaded all present to forgive him for the regrettable deeds that had come to pass through no fault of his own.

The seneschal of the court demanded that his son, Enes, open the mouth of the dragon's head. The head lay at the feet of Queen Isolde with its eyes fixed fiercely on the unworthy liar. When Enes pried open the jaws of the dragon, there was no tongue inside; but the poison was still there, in just the right quantity to kill a liar. The last thing everyone noticed, just as Enes dropped dead on the floor, were the eyes of the dragon closing slowly.

Soon all this was forgotten as the Irish Court became quite involved in the preparations required for the wedding of Fair Isolde to King Mark of Cornwall. Queen Isolde, with plans of her own, called for Brangaine, the nurse and lady-in-waiting to the Fair Isolde. The queen gave Brangaine a bottle with a special potion. This potion, when taken by a man and a woman, would ensure that they felt only true love for each other—and for no other—for three full years.

Queen Isolde warned Brangaine about the strength of this potion, which had the same elements within it as the poison Queen Isolde had placed on her brother Morhaus' sword. She assured Brangaine the potion would have just the right power for the wedding night, which was only days away. Queen Isolde instructed Brangaine to guard the potion well. In three years, with its power, the potion could produce at least one—and maybe two or three possible heirs for Cornwall. It coud also provide an alliance for Ireland and new royal tributes to the Sovereignty of the Celtic Lands.

Soon the day of their departure arrived. The voyage across the Irish Sea was rough, but Tristan and Isolde felt only their own private excitement of their growing love. Brangaine felt only seasick. As the sun was setting on the clear horizon, casting soft golden lights across the green hills of Ireland, Tristan and Isolde decided to celebrate all they had come to share together since Tristan had drifted into Dublin Bay.

The Fair Isolde remembered the honey wine that Brangaine had hidden, rather stupidly, just where it would be expected, in the dowry chests. As they drank the honey wine on the rolling deck, Tristan gave the Fair Isolde a ring to remind her of his devotion to her, as a friend, soon to be his queen. The ring was gold and braided in Celtic style with a rich green jasper stone that matched the Fair Isolde's eyes. Neither one noticed that the flecks of red in the green jasper seemed to grow brighter until it became a worthy symbol of its truest name, the bloodstone.

In the morning, Brangaine found the Fair Isolde was gone and her bed had been made—or perhaps, never yet slept in. She found the lovers in Tristan's cabin, so still and peaceful she thought they were dead. When Brangaine spied the empty bottle that had held the potion in honey wine, she began to wail and keen in mourning as only the truly Irish can. This brought the lovers out of their bed, naked and unashamed. They were warmly cloaked with a true love and neither one felt anything else, not even the cold winds of morning blowing in from the rocky, gray coast of Cornwall.

One of my favorite storytellers—of both bardic and Druidic degree symbolically—is the great Joseph Campbell, whom you have "heard" throughout this text. Although he is late of this world, he is newly in another, and his words will always live here. His explanation of the next part of this tale reflects a spiritual beauty. He presents this so brightly that all others pale in comparison. But that is only fair, for his spirit is still so clear and Light, and his words give us the Right meaning:

> *And so came this moment validating individual choice, what I call following your bliss.*
>
> *But there's danger, too, of course. In the Tristan romance, when the young couple has drunk their love potion and Isolde's nurse realizes what has happened, she goes to Tristan and says, "You have drunk your death."*

And Tristan says, "By my death, do you mean the pain of love?"—because
that was one of the main points, that one should feel the sickness of love. There's
no possible fulfillment in this world of that identity one is experiencing.
    Tristan says, "If by my death, you mean the agony of love, that is my life.
If by my death, you mean the punishment that we are to suffer if discovered, I
accept that. And if by my death you mean eternal punishment in the fires of
hell, I accept that too."

Joseph Campbell
The Power of Myth

Throughout the ages of Arthurian literature, bards' and monks' opinions on this potion and its powers have varied widely. The Celtic Bards explain that this potion would only affect those who didn't already have true love for each other. For those who did, whether they knew it or not, the potion would help them know it, and know each other, both as one. The most wise Druidesses must have told the Bards that the potion would always be poison for the heart of one whose true love remained unrequited and never returned in either truth or love.

Medieval celibate monks and clerics had more concerns about the sin of this act between Tristan and the Fair Isolde. At the time of Arthur, when the Fair Isolde, Tristan, and Mark "encountered" each other in Cornwall, this act was a crime against the King. In medieval days this natural act was seen by the Orthodoxy as more than a sin. It was also considered a crime against their concept of God. Though the Dark Ages had yet to beseige the lands, when they came later there were many such lovers whose similar acts cost them their lives. Then, most often their young and strong bodies, once filled with natural desires, were placed in shallow graves in unhallowed ground, with only a stone to mark their place in time.

On the stone, crudely fashioned, were four letters that still remain a curse today. These four letters represented the words describing their act, which was then both a crime and a sin: "For Unlawful Carnal Knowledge."

In some versions of this legend, it was claimed that, since the potion was magick, the act which followed was neither a crime nor a sin, but enchantment, and therefore beyond their control. So Tristan and Isolde were seen as martyrs, sacrificed to the powers of magick, and not as they really were—enchanted by true love.

Now we return to our true lovers, who landed upon the shores of Cornwall and were not met by anyone, for they had been reported blown off course and weren't expected until the next day. This gave Fair Isolde time to find a way to avoid both the wedding with King Mark, and the marriage bed as well—for she felt truly and sacredly wed to Tristan.

Brangaine was still young, though not so much as Fair Isolde, and very like her lady in many ways. Therefore, the plan was devised that they would switch places. No one at Cornwall would know, except themselves, and they could never tell. King Mark was pleased with his bride and this deception continued blissfully well, until he returned to the royal bedchamber quite early one afternoon, when he was expected to be out hunting until dark. King Mark discovered Tristan and the Fair Isolde, (whom he believed was called Brangaine). King Mark, who was merely amused at this youthful impertinence, listened as the lovers spoke of their plans. He heard them plan to get away so they could live freely, as a married couple, somewhere else, and with new identities.

King Mark still thought this was no more than a fancy or even a ploy by Tristan to placate a common maiden with visions beyond her station. Then, as he turned to leave, King Mark heard Tristan call this fair lady-in-waiting his Fair Isolde, the name the king thought was his queen's and wife's. When King Mark heard this, he had his bride brought to the royal bed chamber. Very soon the deception was revealed by each and all. This was done with great relief, as well as great fear, for all three had been suffering; knowing King Mark was undeserving of such deception.

When the whole tale had been told and verified by each and all, King Mark made his first judgment and sentence. Brangaine was given a choice, since it was fairly seen that she had served her lady as was her avowed duty. Brangaine could return to Ireland to face Queen Isolde, or she could remain at the Court of Cornwall—in the kitchens, forever a scullery maid. Brangaine chose to stay at Cornwall, regardless of how lowly her station became, for she had come to love King Mark.

King Mark was more cautious with his next judgment. By rights, he could execute both Tristan and also the Fair Isolde, even though she was still, by bonds of betrothal, the rightful Queen of Cornwall. The execution of a queen could never be done without storms of revenge and chaos following for ages— and this King Mark wanted to avoid. Moreover, the execution of a queen who was Irish could have unimaginably frightening repercussions for Cornwall, the least of which would be the war, which would come as quickly as the death blow struck off the head of the Fair Isolde. It was decided that final judgment would wait until King Mark could seek the advice of the High King, Arthur, for these were very serious matters. There were lands at stake and the risk of war.

Tristan and the Fair Isolde were banished to an eerie, sad forest called Morois, and commanded to live in an ancient cave there; reputedly the burial cairn of mysterious peoples who had lived in the British Isles long before memory. Though both of the lovers approached this cave with dread, they found it to be almost welcoming. Instead of a crypt, it was more like a chapel, and there they wed themselves to each other, in the most ancient ways of Celtic memory. They continued this blissful existence, enchanted by the forest and the cave, with no concept of time, other than the cycles of Nature. In the cave, there was an altar stone, naturally crafted, on which they made their own shared bed. With crystals and furs and soft-needled branches, they slept like the children of Nature.

Time passed quickly for Tristan and Isolde; but it dragged for Brangaine and King Mark as King Arthur was in and out of Brittany. Concerns at home kept Arthur close to Camelot, unable to see to the high matters of the lands that King Mark had referred to in his request for help. Time kept its own measure, though, and soon the day came when Arthur did come to Cornwall. After they had discussed the matter of the deception privately, they rode out together— two sad kings in the forest of Morois.

Arthur and Mark had left before dawn, so the forest was still dark and densely tangled with broken trees and branches. Normally, these would have been firewood for the poorer people; but not one of them would enter the forest, nor take anything from it. The sun was just peeking through a small opening in the eastern wall of the cave when Tristan heard the horses approaching. Knowing full well it had to be his uncle, King Mark, Tristan thought how Mark had shown him that cave, from the outside only, so long ago. Tristan remembered they had peered into the cave through that same small opening. It had seemed vastly lonely then, empty and haunted somehow. He remembered that it was light enough to see quite clearly then, so it would seem brightly blazing now. Tristan realized how he would feel if he were Mark, and peered in to see the lovers sleeping together. Isolde was so naturally and beautifully reflected in the same crystals that Tristan recalled from before, so long ago, when Mark had shown him the window in the eastern wall of this ancient, timeless cave.

As the royal-blooded knight should be, so Tristan was by instinct. He took his sword and placed it between himself and his lady, the Fair Isolde. He lay back down beside the sword, with his love on the other side of the blade. He saw no reason to rush outside, for there in the cave he truly knew he was a king by natural right. In case it was robbers or rogue warriors or even an executioner, Tristan would guard the Fair Isolde, his natural queen. Soon, dreams of freedom and true love filled his mind with hope, and Tristan fell asleep again.

Both Tristan and the Fair Isolde were sleeping peacefully when King Mark and King Arthur came to peer in the small opening that served as a window in the eastern wall. What they saw was illuminating to both of these wise and war-wearied kings. A bright ray of light from a tiny opening in the western wall shone on the blade of the sword between them.

King Mark saw the chip which had come from the combat with Morhaus, when Tristan had sought to champion Cornwall. He remembered the bright young warrior who was, even now, no more than a boy; and he felt what Tristan must have felt being caught in this web of destiny. Though he could not speak, for he was struggling not to shed tears, unseemly for a king, Mark motioned to Arthur to look inside, and then turned away in sadness and despair. When he peered into the timeless cave, King Arthur saw a sword of power with its double-edged blade. It seemed so dangerously close to the lovers, no more than children. Tristan and Isolde were sleeping with their hands held tightly together, on which Arthur noticed someone had tied tiny crystals.

King Arthur also saw their other reflections in the sharp blade of the sword; but, strangely, these reflected figures did not seem to be Tristan and Isolde. Only Arthur truly knew who they were, those lovers he saw in the double-edged blade, reflected sharply in their own light. Then King Arthur felt what he had not let himself feel before. He felt the pain of both of those secret lovers as clearly as the morning sunlight filled the cave. He felt the pain of both figures he saw reflected, for one was his best friend and finest knight, and the other was his wife, the finest queen that Camelot, or Arthur, could have ever known.

Then Arthur wished he had known Guinevere when they were both as young as Tristan and the Fair Isolde. For a moment he felt as full of life as the lovers in that ancient cave. He tried to imagine himself at that age, about the time he had pulled the sword from the stone. Even if Guinevere had been old enough then, he had been far too busy to marry. Then when she had come to be his wife, she was the Maiden of Springtime, and he had been like the Lord of Autumn, so busily seeing to the harvest, planning, and gathering more seeds to plant when the next cycle had come around.

Arthur thought then that one day, or in a realm beyond even time or place, he and Guinevere could be as one in the celebration of what was their true nature, the Lord and the Lady of Logres. They could be linked eternally with their love in full bloom, like the rich, red roses placed on the altars at seasonal celebrations.

King Arthur looked for his own reflection in the blade of that sharp, double-edged sword. All he could see was a king looking outward, projected on the very edge of the blade. He saw the queen looking toward him, he thought, but then he realized with sadness that she was looking at something, or someone else reflected at the center. He saw his own image fade away and Lancelot's clear reflection returned. Lancelot was looking at the center as well. There both Lancelot and Guinevere saw the center of themselves, clearly reflected in the light and balanced with the power of truest love.

King Arthur felt a wild rush of desire. He wanted to ride swiftly away as fast as the wind, toward Camelot; to his queen. He wanted to take Guinevere far away. Perhaps he could find another forest, and a timeless cave such as this one, where they could at last be just a man and a woman, truly wed, by rites of Nature, where they could be true lovers and, in truth, husband and wife. With a motion that was almost involuntary, Arthur started to turn away from that all too illuminating window in the eastern wall of the cave. Suddenly, Arthur noticed the stone set in the hilt of the sword. The stone was woven in with golden threads that spiralled around the silver-crafted hilt. The stone, he knew, was an ancient stone, a timeless legacy from all of the kings in whose blood ran the spirit of Cornwall. It was a bright golden stone, strong and clear and cut in a shape that was smooth and round. Within that stone, he saw his own reflection. It was staring back at him from the heart of the hilt, with the golden Celtic weave encircling him.

King Arthur knew then that he could never yield to the desires of even the truest love. It was his destiny, woven in gold, to always be at the heart of the hilt. Though he was far too sick of battles, there still were more to come, and, as the stone on the hilt reflected, he would have to wield his battle sword once more.

Then King Mark, having found his voice, began speaking about how Tristan had found his own way to honor his pledge to Cornwall and his kinship to himself, the king. The sword, as King Mark saw it, was placed between the lovers to remind Tristan of his truest duties, and his love for the codes of honor. King Mark saw that these lovers were only children at play, and for a moment, he even remembered that once he also had been young. King Mark asked King Arthur for permission to pardon Tristan and Isolde. Anxious to be away from that place of remorse and tragic reflection, Arthur quickly consented.

Thus it was that King Arthur rode swiftly back to face the storm clouds over Camelot with a renewed sense of purpose and destiny he had been almost too busy to remember. And thus it was that Tristan was forgiven by his uncle, King Mark, who saw no reason to forgive the Fair Isolde whom he felt could not be held accountable, for she was only a child—and a female at that.

Once back in Cornwall, time passed quickly, and this tale will now also; for the point and both edges of the blade have been shown, as well as the hilt, or the heart of the matter. After being together in that timeless forest cave, Tristan and Isolde found it impossible to stay apart. Though Tristan tried to uphold the codes of honor, when these codes came in conflict with love, he yielded to the more natural force. In truth, he could only honor what he knew and loved in his heart. The Fair Isolde was Irish and high born, and she truly tried to do her duty for her new family and act according to King Mark's codes of honor. For Fair Isolde, though, the wild forest and the timeless cave were far more familiar and honorable, for she was a reflection of her natural heritage.

Thus it was that Tristan and Isolde were finally caught together again, naturally, in their timeless cave in the forest. Brangaine pleaded the case for the potion in her practical, earthy manner—which was the only way King Mark would hear her or any woman. King Mark excused Fair Isolde, but not Tristan this time—potion or no potion. Tristan was banished to Brittany where he was forced to agree to take a wife and assume his rightful duties, as one of a royal line must. Tristan agreed to this formally, in public. In private, King Mark had told his nephew this was the only way he could save the Fair Isolde's life. King Mark made sure that stories about the potion had been carefully told in confidence—to those who would most certainly then spread it like bad news. The Cornish reaction to this second betrayal had been ominous. A King cannot be seen as a Fool—at least not very often—and never in the same way twice. If it happened again, the Fair Isolde could be dragged from her chambers by the Cornish lords and knights. This would be in much the same way as good

Queen Guinevere had been taken when the Orkney brothers had forced Arthur's hand. It was a hand that had yet to be played out to the end.

There was no need to explain this to Tristan, for he had already heard the news about the chaos surrounding Camelot. Tristan knew if Camelot fell, then Cornwall and all of Wales could also fall, even more easily. If this happened, the Saxons would be the least of the Britons' problems, especially if Cornwall fell because its Irish-born queen had been executed. Brittany could fall, as well; and Tristan had seen that happen while he was still a child. It was agreed that Tristan must not come to Cornwall for nine years, unless he was summoned there by the King of Cornwall himself. Of course, Tristan could also be summoned by the High King, Arthur.

Tristan returned to Brittany and married Isolde of the White Hands, who was famed for her beautiful soft-white hands. Her heart was not as soft, nor white, as soon we shall see. Indeed, her marriage to Tristan made her heart dark and hard as stone. In fairness, Isolde of the White Hands was no match for the Fair Isolde; but no one else could have been, not in Tristan's heart and mind.

Tristan soon grew desperately ill, and could not be healed, even by the finest healers in Brittany. Isolde White Hands knew the cure, but she also knew the cause. Tristan could only be cured by being reunited with his true love, the Fair Isolde.

In time, Isolde White Hands lost patience with the situation. Although she had long kept a secret, she now revealed it to her brother, Kaherdin.

This she did to explain why she felt she had a right to leave Tristan. Although divorce was frowned upon (especially among such high nobility that invariably caused chaos in the lands), there was always the right of annulment. This annulment carried no threat of revenge or broken alliances and could be granted immediately—even by the most Orthodox church, for a fee of course. The only way this could be done swiftly was to prove, beyond a shadow of a doubt, that the marriage had never been consummated. This Isolde White Hands could do unquestionably, for she was married to Tristan in name only.

Isolde White Hands' brother was enraged, but he made himself think carefully. Tristan was the rightful King of Brittany. Even if his foster father, the former Lord Rohalt, was the regent King of Brittany, it was because Tristan had placed him there. Kaherdin knew that there could be many advantages to being the brother-in-law to the next King of Brittany. Moreover, Kaherdin was truly fond of Tristan. They had known each other when they were children, before Cornwall and Ireland had been like poison for the poor, noble Tristan.

Kaherdin, with wisdom and sensitivity, consoled his sister with words of praise for her endurance. He told Isolde White Hands that all Brittany already thought of her as their next queen, and that she was more than worthy of that high and exalted position. He urged her to be patient, for he would talk to Tristan and, man to man, they could certainly find a solution that would suit them all. With words spoken mostly in jest, Kaherdin advised his sister to take a lover for her own convenience, for that was a noble woman's right and the fashion of that time in the higher courts of the Celtic lands. After that, he reminded his sister that even the High Queen of Britain had decided to do this for herself—and with a knight from Brittany, at that!

As she watched her brother ride off to visit Tristan, Isolde White Hands felt her heart grow stone cold. She wouldn't even consider a lover, for her virginity was her trump card. King Rohalt was growing old, and soon Tristan would be King. If she had been noble throughout her ordeal with Tristan, then Isolde White Hands would undoubtedly deserve to be Queen. There was always the possibility that Tristan would die a fairly young king; but there was also the same possibility that he could die before he ever had a chance to take the throne. Isolde White Hands knew that this could make things very complicated for his wife, then his widow, particularly if it were commonly known that the marriage had been in name only.

Isolde White Hands raced her horse after her brother. She arrived in time to hear Tristan tell Kaherdin about the only cure he knew that could save him. Isolde White Hands knew this already, but it filled her with cold rage to hear it spoken aloud. She controlled herself as she thought a queen would, even when she heard the deep and true love in Tristan's words telling her brother about "Fair Isolde, Fair Isolde, Fair Isolde."

With great calmness and an expression of divine benevolence, which belied the feelings within, Isolde White Hands then came in to see Tristan and her brother. She told of a plan she had been graced to receive, one that would provide the cure she claimed to have realized just at that moment. The Fair Isolde must come to Tristan—at all cost.

In quick sequence, messages were sent to Cornwall, and messages sent back to Brittany. All was done with the utmost secrecy, for there was already enough chaos in the Celtic lands of Arthur's realm. There was never a direct message from the Fair Isolde. Instead, messages came through a chain of people that the Fair Isolde would be traveling to the Norse lands and would sail right past Brittany.

Since the Fair Isolde was the Queen of Cornwall, her ship would be unmistakable. That same ship would have to dock not far from where Tristan was, but only for one night. The messages said that it was not generally known whether the Queen of Cornwall would grace Brittany with a visit, or simply stay on the ship. With the winds and tides being uncertain factors, the Queen of Cornwall could even have to sail on by, and miss Brittany altogether. However, the Fair and gracious Queen Isolde had then courteously offered a way to help the people of Brittany to be prepared in the event that they had to offer her their own special kind of Celtic hospitality. If the ship would be able to dock, she would see to it that a white sail was flying. If the ship had to sail on by, a black sail would be flown to signify this.

The day finally came when the Queen of Cornwall's ship was expected to appear on the western horizon at any moment. By that day, Tristan had become dangerously ill. The moments moved like hours, as Tristan waited, with Isolde White Hands dutifully at his side. Her brother Kaherdin was far away, waiting down by the shore. He was just close enough, though, for Isolde White Hands to see the two large banners he carried. One was white and the other one was black. These he would have to use as a signal, for he could never be heard from so far away. Tristan was far too weak to rise from his bed, or even lift his head for a moment. Isolde White Hands waited, paced the floor, and kept watch from the window.

Far sooner than even she had expected, a ship came into view. Isolde White Hands saw it quite clearly. It was as though nothing else existed in the world. She steeled herself, and waited for the banner to confirm what she already knew to be true. Far away on the beach, Kaherdin waved the white banner with obvious joy. Isolde White Hands did not move away from the window for what seemed to be a small eternity.

Finally, Isolde White Hands turned slowly and gazed at Tristan. In the sunlight coming through the window, he seemed almost boyish and strong again. She remembered him as he had once been as a boy, and how she had dreamed of being his wife. She remembered how she had felt victorious when the arrangements for her betrothal were made by orders of the King of Cornwall. How sad Tristan had seemed then, how lost, and how alone. She had once been so sure she could be what he needed. Finally she remembered all of the nights she had heard him cry out in his sleep, "Isolde, Isolde, my Fair Isolde."

Isolde White Hands heard Tristan whispering, for he was barely able to speak. He was looking at her and calling for Isolde; but she knew which Isolde he wanted. Then she saw in the sunlight the childish ring that Tristan wore on his little finger. She had never thought it a worthy ring for the finger of a future king. The green jasper stone was always so pale and cloudy, almost gray. But then, as the ship came closer and closer, that same stone began to gleam with a rich green light. Its flecks of red were as bright as fresh blood.

Isolde White Hands, with clear intentions, walked over to where Tristan lay still and barely conscious. He opened his eyes and in them was the question, so she gave him the answer she wanted him to hear. Whispering softly in his ear, Isolde White Hands told Tristan the ship had been flying a black sail and the Fair Isolde was not coming after all.

The first thing Isolde White Hands noticed as she stood up to look at Tristan and gauge the effect of her message, was that the green jasper ring had grown pale again. Transfixed, she watched as the stone became paler and paler, until there seemed to be no color at all. It was then she heard Tristan take his last breath. Then there was nothing but silence, except for the sound of her stone-cold heart, beating with a steady rhythm.

(Though most versions finish this tale with very little more, I plead the right of poetic licence, and thereby craft my own ending—or beginning.)

When Kaherdin came in and found Tristan dead, he honorably took the sword and the ring which were Tristan's most cherished material possessions. Kaherdin took these, along with the sad news, to Fair Isolde as soon as she reached land. When he gave these to Fair Isolde, both the stone on the sword and the stone in the ring began to glow with a beautiful light. When Kaherdin returned to Isolde White Hands and told her of this wonderful light, she walked down to the shore with the dignity she thought most befitting an almost-queen. There Isolde White Hands removed all her jewels and robes and trappings of power. With only a simple white shift to protect her from the cold, Isolde White Hands walked into the sea and was seen no more.

The Fair Isolde ordered her ship to turn course as soon as the coast of Brittany could no longer be seen. For weeks on end, no one knew where the Fair Isolde had gone. Then one day the royal ship of Cornwall sailed back to the Cornish shore. Whether they had been sworn to secrecy, or whether they truly did not know, the captain and the crew of the royal Cornish ship said the Fair Queen Isolde of Cornwall had vanished.

Some time later, when the final battle of Camlann had claimed the lives of King Arthur and King Mark and so many others, a strange incident happened in Cornwall. Cador, the Duke of Cornwall, had been named as Arthur's heir. With King Mark gone, as well, Cador was High King by all rights. One morning as Cador rode

through the gates of Tintagel Castle, his birthplace, he found that a gift had been left, wrapped in Fair Irish Weave. The gift was a sword which Cador knew had been Tristan's; but there were changes in it which he knew must have been made by the Fair Queen Isolde of Cornwall, wherever she still might be. The bright gold gemstone of Cornwall still gleamed in the hilt; but this stone was now encircled with tiny crystals. There was one more addition that seemed Faerie-crafted, for only they or Bridget could have fashioned that change.

There in the center of the double-edged blade, at the heart of the sword, was a stone. It was a rich green jasper with flecks of red bright as fresh blood. Around the jasper was a golden ring, braided in Celtic fashion. There was no way to tell exactly, though many a fine smith tried, just where the golden woven ring melded with the steel of the blade, for it had, by all appearances, been there when the blade was crafted.

Isolde the Fair was never seen again, although some say she can still be glimpsed walking through the wild, ancient forests. Still others claim she has been seen, along with her true love, in a Divine Light. This is known by all who have seen them, Tristan and Fair Isolde—reflected within the crystals of a timeless cave.

CHAPTER 15

THE OTHERWORLD CHALLENGE

For strength of character in the race as in the individual consists mainly in the power of sacrificing the present to the future ... the height of heroism is reached in men who renounce the pleasures of life and even life itself for the sake of keeping or winning for others, perhaps in distant ages, the blessings of freedom and truth.

Sir James Frazer
Quoted in Norma Lorre Goodrich
King Arthur (New York: Harper and Row, 1986)

 The Otherworld challenge is yet another theme that appears constantly in the Camelot legends. This challenge involves a trial or test that the primary characters must undergo in order to prove their worth and their right to represent the Round Table's ideals of honor, truth, and chivalry. In all instances, this challenge is an individual test, supported by mystical gifts and guidances, yet always ultimately endured alone.

The primary character is left to choose the codes and conduct most becoming for the right resolution of the challenge, regardless of how much help is, or is not, forthcoming from either mystical or mundane realms. The means for successful completion are made available only if the character displays that which is right and honorable, both in motivations and methods. One especially apt symbol for this is the knight having to cross a bridge over perilous waters. In this, the bridge is a double-edged sword, narrow and equally sharp on both edges of the blade.

In some instances, the Otherworld challenge is undertaken for personal, individual purposes. In others, the challenge has a far more extensive effect; ultimately determining the heroic worthiness of all the warriors, the kingship, and the people. This is why the concept and the theme of the champion is so prevalent in Arthurian lore.

No one disputed the king's authority—kings were born with that—but *standing alongside the king there had to be his champion, his hero. If the king symbolized the land itself and all of its people, his heroic champion stood for their warrior spirit and fought for them in battle … A tribe without a hero was a piteous and vulnerable thing.*

Brendan Lehane
The Enchanted World (Series): *Legends of Valor* (Time Life Books)

One famous Camelot legend that blends individual purpose and heroic championship representing the Round Table is the tale of Gawain and the Green Knight. This legend is based on far older tales, told of the Beheading Games, which tested the resolve and the rigorous self-discipline required of a champion warrior. Since so many of the elements are similar in these versions, both ancient and relatively modern, I'll start with one from the heroic, Ulster Cycle of Irish myth and legend. This is a tale told of Cuchulain, a clear forerunner for Gawain in many ways.

THE BEHEADING GAME

One cold winter evening at Emain Macha, brave King Conchobar sat feasting in his great hall with his warriors of the Red Branch. With a blasting sound, the massive hall door blew open to reveal a frightening apparition. A giant stood in the wide doorway, filling it completely with his bulk and his presence. He strode into the hall, shaking everything around him. In one hand he carried a tree trunk; in the other, an ax.

The giant threw the log on the floor in front of the fire, swung his ax in a circle and announced himself. He was the Bachlach, the herdsman who searched the lands for a man who was as worthy as his word. Surely a man who could be trusted to keep a bargain would be present in The House of the Red Branch.

The Seneschal asked the Bachlach what the terms were for this bargain. Then the Bachlach said that any man—excepting the Seneschal and Conchobar, who were known to be worthy—was free to take that very ax and strike off his own giant head. In return, the Bachlach would deliver a blow to that one on the next night.

Some of the Red Branch laughed at this; but others, more experienced, recognized the old ways of magick in the Bachlach's bargain. No one stepped forward, and the giant taunted them for their lack of courage and for their lack of a true champion.

At this, Leag jumped up and claimed the right to champion the Red Branch in this bargain with the Bachlach. Leag gave his word to honor the terms of the bargain. Then he struck off the giant's head with one swift blow. With blood spilling furiously, the Bachlach's body stood up, took back his head from Leag—who had been holding it proudly—and then walked out the door, head in hand.

148

The next night the Bachlach returned, but Leag was not there; and the giant hurled insults at the House of the Red Branch warriors. Unable to stand this abuse any longer, Conall agreed to the Bachlach's bargain. Once again, the blow was struck. Once again the giant left the hall, head in hand. Once again the Bachlach returned the next night to find the bargain had not been honored. Conall was nowhere to be found.

This time the Bachlach laughed derisively and pointed his ax at the young warrior Cuchulain. Challenging Cuchulain to meet his bargain, the Bachlach merely laughed louder when the young warrior said the bargain was cruel, magick trickery, and senseless. Still, the Bachlach continued to taunt Cuchulain, calling him a coward.

Finally, unable to stand the accusations of cowardice, Cuchulain grabbed the ax and cut off the Bachlach's head. As before, the giant left the hall, head in hand. When he returned the next night, Cuchulain was waiting in the great hall of the Red Branch warriors. Cuchulain knelt with his head on the log which the Bachlach had placed in front of the fire.

The Bachlach swung the ax into the air and stopped, commanding Cuchulain to stretch out his neck farther. Cuchulain commanded the Bachlach to shut up and swing. The ax came down, and the Red Branch warriors cried out in shock. Then, to the amazement of all present, Cuchulain rose to his feet unharmed. The ax blade lay shattered on the cold stone floor, and the Bachlach had disappeared.

In his place stood Curoi, the magickal king of South Ulster, the realms of the Fair Folk in that part of Ireland. Curoi explained it was his task to determine the unquestioned Champion of the Red Branch warriors of Ulster. He declared that champion to be Cuchulain, but not because he had accepted the senseless bargain and then stood by his word while the others had failed. Instead, the Bachlach told all present that Cuchulain alone had shown the virtues of the Celtic Red Rage:

> Only Cuchulain had struck in the
> heat of rage—a rashness appropriate
> and even necessary to a warrior.
>
> Brendan Lehane
> Ibid.

Thus Cuchulain demonstrated the essential Celtic "contempt for death," considered most worthy at the time this legend was told. This attitude arose from the ancient spiritual philosophy that ensured that these acts, however senseless they may seem to us now, would be rewarded as bravely heroic, resulting in high rank in the Otherworld of Spirit, and in immortality in the Bards' tales, told for ages to come. That the Bardic immortality was assured we can see in this tale now two or more millennia old. What the reward of the Otherworld was for such Red Rage warriors as Cuchulain we cannot know for certain.

What we do know is that many fine warriors in more modern times have been motivated by what they may have seen as glory—and what we are now beginning to know as a terrible waste of valuable human life, an essential resource we cannot afford to lose. While this same Celtic courage, the heart's red rage, has been both necessary and valued in combat well into current times, it is an aspect that has also resulted in unnecessary and invaluable loss. There can be very little glory in the reality of pointless warfare, where the only truly heroic acts are those that keep alive yourself and your comrades-in-arms. In *The Warriors of Arthur* is a symbolic account of the trench warfare of World War I:

> *The chivalry of England ... filled with ardour for the fight ... and longing to do great deeds and win honour for themselves and their lady loves ... The shining Knights cannot charge ... They fall over, their armour splits open and their blood and entrails spill out into the mud.*

> Mark Girouard
Quoted in Matthews and Stewart, *Warriors of Arthur*

So, then, how do we view these heroic champions of the Otherworld challenges in the current time, which is another world altogether? We begin by accepting that it is a far greater challenge, in this world or Other Wise, to wage peace than it is to wage war. This is as true personally as it is globally. We are wise to remember that the shield and the scabbard are as valuable, if not more so, than the sword. Also, we must accept that there are no scabbards, and no few shields, that can contain a battle ax or withstand the blows of our own red rage which the battle ax represents. Have we evolved enough to view our ancestors, these Battle Ax Aryans, as a part of our primal past; acknowledging them as what was once needed, and now as no longer valuable for the good of all?

It will help to understand the legendary tales of the Beheading Game when we know what they symbolize mythically, rather than what they say, literally. The Bachlach, for example, comes from the Gaelic, *buachaille*, meaning herdsman. It is pronounced very much like "battle ax," or like Bertilak, the Green Knight in the next legend we will explore. It is also interesting to note that in modern Gaelic, *bachlach* means curly, waving tresses, describing the type of hair on one's head.

The ancient Celtic custom of taking heads is certainly one we must view quite differently in modern times. In Celtic spiritual philosophy, the head was the house of the person's essential spirit. As the head houses the brain, which is the organ of the mind, this concept has both philosophical and psychological merit. Since the connection of Mind, Body, and Spirit is well known to us now, we can adjust this to reflect a more current Celtic view.

When we recognize that the true challenges come from within the Otherworld realms of our own minds, then we are better able to meet these challenges in ways that are right and honorable. We are the champions of our own lives, which we lead, well-empowered by the evolutionary quality of our own mind and consciousness. We may feel frustrated and even enraged by the challenges life presents to us; but we are wise to reflect them back within ourselves. That is where the nature of the challenges of life are determined and met, so we remember the codes and strengths we have within, and call upon these to provide the personal prowess we need.

The ancient Celts took heads as trophies, symbolizing their victory and control over their opponents' spirits, in this world and the Otherworld, as well. Now, when we use our heads wisely, they become trophies signifying our skills of self-control and personal evolution. These are the skills with which modern victorious champions are made. The challenge is no longer to take heads or minds. Indeed, the current challenge may well be said to be preventing others from taking your head—that is, your mind.

Current Celtic champions keep their heads on their shoulders and their minds clear and ready to meet whatever challenges come. They do this with classic independent spirit, well trained in the field of experience that is their life, and well armed with codes of truth and honor, rightfully activated.

> *... Gawain, who was once known as the champion of the Goddess, is taught by example the meaning of chivalry and love ... Nor should we be surprised to find Gawain thus undergoing education at the hands of supernatural women; he has long been recognized as a later literary incarnation of the Irish hero, Cuchulain, who also received his training in weaponry from a woman—though in a manner more direct and savage than that of his later self.*
>
> Matthews and Stewart
> Ibid.

GAWAIN AND RAGNALL, LIONEL AND THE FAERIE LADY

Gawain is probably best known to Arthurian readers as the gallant knight whose love transformed the hag Ragnall into the beautiful Lady Ragnall. This legend, though quite old in its origins, has gained much popularity in current times. Its philosophy of free choice is still a valued personal ideal, and an issue of vital social importance.

———

In one version, Gawain goes forth to champion King Arthur who has inadvertently strayed into the realms of the Green Hunter, guardian god of the mystical forest. In another, Gawain sees an old hag being harried by some rogues and rescues her. In still another, a lovely Faerie Woman in the forest grants Gawain a great gift, for he has just saved her from ruffian knights. The gift-in-ugly-wrapping is Ragnall.

In every case, Gawain's challenge is to face his duty honorably, even when that includes having to wed what he believes is a most loathsome old hag. In fact, the hag is a beautiful maiden who had been enchanted, and would remain so until one who would love her for her true, inner beauty could release her from the spell under which she was bound.

151

After a series of challenges and adventures on the way back to Camelot, Gawain finds that his respect for the hag Ragnall's courage and wisdom has become admiration for her spirit, and the beginning of a heartfelt connection. Although Gawain receives much abuse from the Round Table knights about the foul appearance of his betrothed, his loyalty to Ragnall remains unshaken.

As their wedding ceremony is coming to a close, they are instructed to kiss, officially, as man and wife. Gawain, still naturally repulsed by the physical appearance of his new bride, closes his eyes and concentrates on the strength of his honor to carry him through the task. With great tenderness, Gawain kisses Ragnall as if she were the most beautiful, treasured woman in all of Camelot. As he does so, Gawain realizes that Ragnall is truly a treasure among women if only for the forthright goodness in her nature … if only for the Goddess in her Nature.

Then as Gawain hears the wedding crowd gasp, he opens his eyes to find that the hag, Ragnall, has transformed into her original beautiful self—the Lady Ragnall. In what seems at first to be a cruel trick of the Weavers, Lady Ragnall tells Gawain that the enchantment is not completely broken. Her appearance will be foul for half of the time and fair for the rest.

It is then up to Gawain to choose whether he wants his wife "fair by day and foul by night, or foul by day and fair by night." Gawain will have to endure the jests of the other knights if Ragnall is foul by day or by night, and he considers this carefully. As he is doing so, Gawain is struck with the deepest sense of selfless love for the brave, and (for the moment), quite beautiful woman before him. He sees the divine within her and it elicits the divine within himself.

Honoring her before himself, Gawain tells Ragnall that the choice is rightfully hers—for he can not claim what is hers. He tells Ragnall that he recognizes her right of having sovereignty over her own life. This response is met with a shimmer of light and love which leaves the Lady Ragnall even more beautiful than before. She tells Gawain that by acknowledging her rights, and honoring her natural sovereignty, he has truly broken the binding enchantment, for all time. She will never have to be the hag Ragnall again, either by day or by night.

Some versions have Gawain and Ragnall living together for only a few years, usually three or seven. After that time, Ragnall returns to the mystical realms of the forest forever; thus revealing her true Nature in the service of the Goddess, or as a gifted woman who brought Gawain true love, for they are one and the same—indivisibly. Nothing more is heard of Ragnall until a fine young knight appears in King Arthur's Court as the Fair Unknown—or Bel Inconnu.

In time, it is revealed that this fair, unknown knight is Lionel, the son of Gawain and Ragnall. When she knew that she was with child, Ragnall returned to her own realm. There, she gave birth to her fair son and kept him in the Natural realm to rear, and to prepare for his role in the preservation of Camelot's magick, and the service of Sovereignty. Some versions of this legend have Lionel becoming enamored of a beautiful Faerie Lady who urges him to leave the then-crumbling Court of Arthur before the inevitable battles destroy most, if not all of the magick and power of Camelot.

At the additional urging of Gawain, and Arthur in some versions, Lionel leaves Camelot with the Faerie Lady and heads for the Highlands, in either Scotland or Wales. There, he can preserve the right line of blood and Light which crystallized in the form of King Arthur—reputedly the father of Gawain, and thus the grand-father of Lionel.

Some have criticized aspects of this ancient tale, and its modern version, as being sexist toward Ragnall. Others might as well say that Lionel was portrayed as weak and "under the spell" of the Faerie Lady. Neither case is, or was the original intent of the tale. This legend clearly proclaimed the right of a woman to hold sovereignty over her own life. That such a tale could have been crafted during the days of open persecu-tion of women by the dark Orthodoxy was a profound feat, as brave an encounter as any Otherworld Challenge.

That Lionel was able to honor his own path—and part—in the preservation of a sacred Celtic line as an "unsung hero" shows the deep value in which the individual role is held. Had the challenge been to serve the group's needs then, all would have been lost when Camelot and Arthur fell. Like The Merlin "entrapped" for his own preservation, and Gawain honoring his duty with his heart, Lionel represents an archetype of fair quality for the future, even in the realms of that which is unknown.

THE FALCON OF MAY

The themes of Courtly Love, enchanted encounters, and Otherworld Challenges are found consistently in the legends of Camelot. These themes are the foundational con-flicts that arise from the process of balancing love, honor, relationships, and career, (as we would express this in current times). Symbols of the Otherworld Challenges appear in Arthurian lore in many aspects, ranging from wyrd prophecies to encounters with strange beasts or characters. All these represent the symbolic realms of the mystical mind expressing the intangible processes of self-transformational experiences.

One of the legendary characters from the Arthurian lore who is frequently depict-ed in situations blending enchantment, love, honor, and quest is the heroic knight, Gawain. Although Gawain appears in versions of the legends from many sources, he is essentially the true British knight. He emerges from the later forms of the legends as Gwalchmei, the falcon of May in the Welsh traditions. However, his role as a solar hero connects him to much earlier Celtic god forms, such as Lleu Llaw Gyffes, or Lugh, the names given to the Lord of Light. In the Norman French tales, Gawain is clearly linked with the Sun. This is portrayed in the description of his strength, which grows until noon, then wanes until evening. This is also symbolic of one whose pri-mary aspect is active and not receptive, as Gawain is shown to be.

There is a clear connection between Lugh and Gawain in that their lineages reflect a blending of light and dark aspects. Lugh's grandfather is Balor, the dark wizard of the Fomorians, who were frequent foes of the Tuathe dé Danann. Nevertheless, Lugh developed into a mythic solar hero, strengthened by his shadow aspects.

Gawain's lineage blends the wild elemental forces represented by Morgawse, and the fierce solar forces of Arthur. While there is some debate as to whether Gawain is Arthur's son or his nephew, his role in regard to Arthur represents that of the positive, paternal solar relationship. In essence, Gawain was the heir apparent to the throne of Arthur, and not Mordred, his brother, whom we will discuss later. Both Gawain and Mordred represented a blend of dark and light in an all-too-delicate state of balance, and, as is often the case when two such states of balance encounter and interact with one another or individually with their own life experiences, the balance changes. One often changes in a more positive way, moving more toward the ways of Light. The other often becomes overshadowed, moving in a negative or dark direction. Both forms are constantly susceptible to being thrown off balance. However, those who endeavor to work and quest for that which is Light, such as Gawain, often are able to achieve a more solid, positive balance of personal powers. Chretien de Troyes called him "the good and gentle lord, Gawain."

Gawain also represents a younger, more active form of Arthur himself. This was shown in the legends by Gawain being Arthur's almost constant companion, serving as his representative on numerous occasions, and in making quests which Arthur is never seen doing on his own. Also, the qualities of Gawain's quests, as well as the abundance of Otherworld challenges and chances for self-empowerment given him, reveal he is worthy enough and essentially well-balanced enough to be given the experiences that prepare him for future kingship.

Indeed, I feel it is Gawain who presents us with one of the most powerfully effective and clearly accessible archetypal sources for these current times. Of Gawain's more recent representations, there is only one that may cause some confusion. This is Gawain in his role as the accuser of Queen Guinevere in John Boorman's superb film, "Excalibur." In considering the scene carefully, however, we can see that The Merlin had already pronounced truth as being one of the most worthy virtues of a knight, and that when a lie was told, "something in the world dies." In yet another trial of conflict between love (of Arthur) and honor (of Truth), Gawain had to be true to what he felt was the truth. Truth and love unbind all enchantments and bring what is Right to all encounters.

Gawain is—and has—the characteristic blend of love and honor which best represents the ideals and codes of the Round Table. Knowing this, we may connect with the aspects he represents in these legends and with those correlating aspects within ourselves. Besides his quest for the Grail, Gawain is best known for his role in two other legends, one of which I have chosen to adapt and discuss here.

As we explore the Arthurian version of the ancient Celtic tale we just covered, consider how the evolution of consciousness is reflected in this later version that emerged nearly two millennia after the tale of Cuchulain and the Bachlach. Consider also that the version we are about to explore is already seven centuries old, and those have been evolutionarily powerful centuries—this last one, the twentieth, in particular.

While Gawain first emerges into the legends as Walgainus in Geoffrey of Monmouth's *History of the Kings of Britain* (c. 1120), he was already well-known in the earlier Welsh traditions as Gwalchmai, the falcon of May, and as another form of Cuchulain in the ancient Irish lore. It is not until the end of the fourteenth century that Gawain is shown as heroically as he is in "Sir Gawain and the Green Knight." This poem is considered to be one of the most remarkable works in middle English; yet its authorship is still unknown. It is thought to have been commissioned by John of Gaunt, Duke of Lancaster, in about 1370 or 1390.

While other versions had preceded it, this poem captured the spirit and the image of Gawain as the heroic British knight, symbolic of the many solar heroes who came before him from time immemorial in Celtic lore. As you read my version, adapted from the fourteenth-century poem, note the similarities and differences in the elements of the tale. Then consider the meanings of both what you find changed and unchanged. For my part, I have followed the Anglo-Saxon rhythm of this alliterative Medieval English form and create a briefer version to share here.

GAWAIN AND THE GREEN KNIGHT
(adapted by Amber Wolfe)

It was Christmas at the Court of Camelot. The hall was hung with colors symbolic of the season. Garlands of evergreen and holly berries gave a sense of good cheer and great holiday spirit. The tables were laden with bounty from the hunts, and the harvest stores had been prepared for all to share.

King Arthur and Queen Guinevere sat majestically on their thrones, graciously greeting their guests as they gathered in the great hall. Sir Kai, the Seneschal, and Lucan, the butler, summoned the guests to sit and be silent.

"None shall sup til a tale be told, an adventure shared by someone quite bold," said Sir Kai to the Knights and the Ladies.

The hall grew quiet in hushed anticipation and the children huddled closer to hear. Suddenly, the silence was shattered and the company astounded. The oak doors swung open with a crashing sound and a strange sight presented itself. Outside, lightning flashed from a sudden storm. All gathered in the great hall beheld a huge giant of a man on a horse as high as twenty hands. He rode in kingly fashion, seated steady and straight in the saddle. On his face was a fierce expression which pierced the atmosphere like a spear. Half-real, half-wonder, this strange sight seemed, since horse and rider were assuredly green. Their garments, their gear, and their figures were green. There was nothing of another color, save a few glinting threads of gold and a bit of red trim glittering in the glow of the fires. This gave them only a more ghostly appearance— most awful.

The Green Knight wore the great antlers of a stag on his head, and held a sharp seax with a Merlin blade, full four feet in length. In the other hand he held a holly branch high above his head. He flung the holly onto the floor and with a fearsome voice hailed all in the great hall:

"Right well I greet you. This gathering I will render graciously relating my game to all here."

The Green Knight rode boldly before the royal thrones and raised his battle ax as he blasted the hall with his reason for being there.

"I come not for kings but for champions to challenge, if I can find but one in this collection of cowards."

At this, several of the knights started to unsheathe their swords, but they were stopped by a signal from Arthur, who spoke softly.

"Good Knight, call your challenge; give us this game, for all gathered here are champions."

At this, the Green Knight laughed long and loud.

"Great King, if I tell this, will you grant me your word and agree to the game with which I will test the truest knight of your Round Table?"

King Arthur nodded his consent to the terms, and the Green Knight continued to tell of this test.

"I seek a knight so brave, so true, that he will deal me one swift blow with my battle ax. Still, he must also swear to seek me out when the cycle of a year and a single day has passed, so that I may serve him with a blow similar to that which I stood for myself."

So shocked was the crowd that silence reigned, then was summarily disturbed by the sound of the Green Knight's laughter, deafening and insulting to those assembled at that place. Embarrassed by the silence and the abusive accusations he saw in the Green Knight's eyes, Arthur stood up and swiftly made ready to respond to the challenge himself.

As swiftly as a May falcon flies across the skies of summer, young Sir Gawain stepped forth and shouted at the Green Knight:

"Hold still your tongue, you beast of a man, and hand me that ax which I'll swing hard and true. I'll see to your terms and serve them surely. Dismount from your horse and say your prayers."

Having heard this wild exclamation, the Green Knight dismounted and held out his ax. He knelt willingly before brave Sir Gawain, with his head bowed and steady. With a single stroke, Sir Gawain severed the Green Knight's head. For a moment there was no movement in the hall.

Then a terrifying thing happened. All those in the great hall stared, transfixed, as the body of the Green Knight stood up slowly, reached for his head, stuck it under one of his arms, and, holding the horse's reins in his other hand, boldly strode out of the hall, kicking the doors shut as he left.

The wheel of the year turned with a terrible certainty, and soon the time came for Sir Gawain to make his quest and meet his destiny. All through that year Gawain had been treated royally, with maidens tenderly yielding what they had tersely refused to surrender to him before the test of the Green Knight. The Knights of the Round Table had gathered regularly, trying to find a way for Gawain to gain the upper hand in this tricky situation.

At last the day arrived for Gawain to journey forth and accept his fate. Weeks upon weeks he traveled into the wild, cold country northwest of Camelot. Winter winds chilled his bones and he felt his spirit weaken; but on he went anyway, pausing sometimes in silent prayer, until at last he reached the Isle of the Green Knight's lair. Then one day, when white frost formed faerie trails through the oak forest, Gawain came upon a finely dressed figure and his hounds, hunting by the forest borders. Gawain inquired if the hunter had heard of an inn where he could rest his head awhile.

The Lord of the hunt called his hounds all around him and led Gawain to his lovely castle home. There he struck a bargain with Sir Gawain: He'd share his bounty from the hunt should Gawain agree to stay at home with the Lady of his castle and also share the spoils of his day. Since the appointed day was drawing near, with only three until the time of his destiny, Gawain agreed with the deal to stay with the Lord and his Lady and deliver to him what he had received in kind.

The first bright morning broke across the meadows and Gawain found he was not alone in the bedchamber. The Lady of the castle, lovely and calm, came to Gawain with promises of luscious caresses. Gawain graciously re-fused, for his honor he could not give away. To do so would dishonor the Lord who was hunting and his wonderful hospitality. The Lady demurred on one condition: that Gawain give her one kiss. He did so gallantly and then bade her to go and come to coax him no more.

The Lord returned from the hunt as the moon climbed high in the sky. He called for his servants to show the venison he'd share that night at supper. He asked Gawain what he had to give, and Gawain gave the lord one kiss. They laughed together at Gawain's take of that day and spent the evening telling tales.

The Lady came to him on the morrow, casting her moonstruck eyes upon him. Gawain, for his part, put her away from him once more, protecting the honor of his host. Still she came and would not leave until he kissed her lovingly.

The hunt Lord came home a little sooner that day, just shortly after sunset, bringing Gawain a great boar. Gawain, as was bargained, responded with two bold kisses. Together, bonded in bargain and ale, they jested until the break of dawn.

The third morning the Lady tried bewitchingly to take Gawain on her terms, her breast was bared and her face was flushed; still Gawain refused. Settling on three tender kisses, she turned to take her leave. Then lovingly, with growing tenderness, she gave him her green lace garter. She told him the gift of the garter guaranteed that none could try to harm him, so long as the secret of the love-gift remained with just the two of them.

The long shadows of afternoon lay across the hills as the Lord came home from the hunt. With only a smelly fox to share, he was served by Gawain with still more kisses. Three kisses, and nothing further, gave Gawain to the fine fellow. Then they passed the evening with a mood less frolicking and more forlorn.

The next day dawned, and with destiny drawing fast, Gawain arose with determination to meet his fate with dignity. He bade fond farewell to the Lord and the Lady with declarations of devotion. Gawain quested forth on the path he had chosen, following the directions he had been given. Soon he came upon a green chapel, cozily settled in a clearing. With a graceful kiss for the green lace garter, Gawain went into the chapel to greet the Green Knight.

The Green Knight was as he was before, bedecked in the shades of the season: green garments, green gear, and green face and green beard, with threads of gold and red glinting in the glow of candlelight inside the chapel. On his head were the antlers; in his hand was the ax; and his face was hard and angry. Gawain bent bravely to meet the blow, and the Green Knight brandished the blade, then paused and berated Gawain for flinching, which wasn't brave.

Once more the ax was lifted. Once more Gawain lowered his head and prepared to lose his life. Once more the ax stopped its descent. Then the Green Knight declared that Gawain had not determined to accept the deal and should stretch his neck out diligently.

Once more the ax swung up. Once more Gawain stayed still with solemn acceptance and his neck fully extended. The blow came swiftly and glanced slightly the side of Gawain's neck.

When he beheld his blood upon the bone-cold floor, Gawain boldly leapt up and prepared to do battle:

> And shrugging his shoulders, shot his
> shield to the front,
> Swung out his bright sword and said
> fiercely —
> Cease your blows, sir, strike me no
> more.
> I have sustained a stroke here unresist-
> ingly,
> And if you offer more, I shall earnestly
> reply,
> Resisting, rest assured, with the most
> rancorous Despite.
> The single stroke is wrought
> To which we pledged our plight
> In high King Arthur's court:
> Enough now, therefore, knight!"

(From *Sir Gawain and the Green Knight*,
c. 1370–90, author unknown)
Quoted in Richard Barber.
The Arthurian Legends: An Illustrated Anthology
(Littlefield, Adams and Co., 1979)

It was then that the Green Knight revealed his name and identity. He was Sir Bertilak, the herdsman of champions. He told Gawain that the bargain had been bravely and truly kept, with only one small, green lacy exception. For failing to share the gift of the garter with himself, as the lord of the hunt, Bertilak exacted the price of the glancing blow to Gawain's neck. Thus Gawain would have to carry that scar of his own deception.

Gawain chastised himself for having dishonored his vows as a knight, his bargain with the Green Knight, and his host's fine hospitality. The Green Knight laughed this off as the overzealous passion of youth. He told Gawain that he had passed the tests well and honorably as a knight should. Perhaps the temptation of the protective garter had been too much for Gawain to resist. Bertilak assured Gawain that he had kept faith with his quest; his adventure of the challenge, and that alone, had proved his courage. He had faced—and conquered—his fear of death and resisted the lure of lust and desire.

Gawain had resisted the bewitching, enchanting temptations of Lady Bertilak, who was Avalon-trained and thus quite skilled in being irresistible. It was she who had bade Sir Bertilak go forth as the herdsman. He was to test the champion qualities of the Round Table knights to ensure that the strain remained strong. Because of her beauty and her beguiling ways, and because of the old ways of magick he had taught her himself, Bertilak had agreed to the decision willingly. Thus Gawain was left to wonder—as we all have from time to time throughout the ages and stages of the Camelot legends—about this, and other similar patterns: Was it enchantment or conspiracy which made the Green Knight, Bertilak, decide to do the bidding of his Avalon Lady?

In several versions of this legend, it is Morgana who is disguised as Lady Bertilak; in others, it is Nimue. In most the Avalon Lady is shown as having enchanted the lord of the castle as the Green Knight, Sir Bertilak. However, the irony is that whichever way this is shown, the effect is still somehow flattering to the Avalon Lady. The test of the champions, the Otherworld challenge, is fundamentally one which proves, and does not thwart, honor.

So, the question remains about the powers of Lady Bertilak's persuasive testing of Gawain. We have to assume that her intentions were compassionate, if ruthlessly presented. After all, she gave Gawain her green garter, symbolizing the protective powers of the Fey, or faerie realm. Were that not enough proof for us, there is yet another aspect to point out here. If this Avalon Lady could enchant an entire castle and send its lord out with the ability to have his head severed, and walk away with it under his arm, waiting for his own chance to return the blow in kind, why would she have any trouble at all enchanting a young knight who was, at least in theory, about to lose his head anyway?

The answer to this and other questions about the nature of Sir Bertilak and Lady Bertilak has puzzled more than a few Arthurian scholars and mythologists. In *Merlin*, by Norma Lorre Goodrich (New York: Harper and Row, 1988), there is an answer that is most enchanting. The Merlin is seen to be Sir Bertilak and Lady Bertilak his "deputy"—in most views, Morgana; yet a case can be made for Nimue.

Citing the work of Heinrich Zimmer (who had ideas about the perilous bed in Chapter 14) and others, Goodrich compiled a list of thirteen correlations with aspects of The Merlin found in "Sir Gawain and the Green Knight." Among them are the following: A kingly/knightly bearing; a fondness for disguise; the fact he continues to teach Gawain, even as he is supposedly in the process of severing his head; the also-disguised presence of his student, either Morgana or Nimue, with whom he is conspiring; Druidic nature symbols, such as the oak forest holly, and the storm with Merlin's lightning; the fact that a battle ax such as Sir Bertilak had is also called a Merlin.

However we look at it, there seems to be good reason to believe this is a depiction of The Merlin in disguise, as he is so often fond of being, at least as the legends had us to believe.

> *The ax more than the crystal ball announces Merlin's royal signature. Not only did Merlin wield his ax in battle against illicit sorcerers and foes and carry it in ceremonies so that all could contemplate this visible symbol of his power of life and death, but as the Green Giant (Green Knight), he also used the ax to convey a reprimand, for it left a permanent red mark upon Gawain when he promised more than he could fulfill.*

> Geoffrey of Monmouth
> Paraphrased in Norma Lorre Goodrich
> *Merlin* (New York: Harper and Row, 1988)

I'll close with a puzzle of sorts, a question for you to ponder. Suppose someone with whom you work or have a relationship challenges you in this manner: They offer to let you give them a piece of your mind, no holds barred. In return, you have to let them do the same. What is your response to this? Do you take this challenge, and, if so, how? What codes do you use to determine your course of action? How can you win—or at least not lose? Think about it.

Tick ... Tick ... Tick ... Stop.

Tell the person issuing the challenge to strike the first "blow." Withstand it honorably, and do not flinch or interrupt. Then, when they are finished—and make sure they truly are—just say you will have to think about all this and get back to them in time. Maintain your position regardless. After all, you didn't agree to a time, did you?

Most challenges coming at you from other people stem from something about you which challenges them. Usually this is a reflection, or projection, of an inner challenge of their own—not yours at all. If they sincerely want to know what you think, they'll ask again ... and again. If not, you've found a champion's way to win.

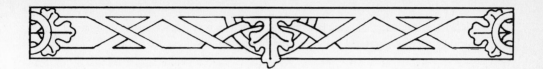

CHAPTER 16

THE NATURE OF THE FEY

... the study of the Fairy-Faith is of vast importance historically, philosophically, religiously, and scientifically ... And it is one of the chief keys to unlock the mysteries of Celtic mythology. We believe that a greater age is coming soon, when all the ancient mythologies will be carefully studied and interpreted and when the mythology of the Celts will be held in very high esteem ... already an age has come ... the awakening genius of the modern Celt manifesting itself ... throughout Continental Europe ... Great Britain and Ireland and throughout the new Celtic World of America.

W. Y. Evans Wentz (1911)
The Faerie Faith in Celtic Countries
(Gerrads Cross, Buckinghamshire, England: Colin Smyth, 1988)

 Woven integrally throughout the fabric of the Camelot legends are the tales of the Fey, the Fair Folk and their Faerie realms. The most well-known of these tales presents the legendary "entrapment" of The Merlin by a woman of the Fey. Traditionally, this Fey weaver of The Merlin's fate is thought to be either Nimue (Niniane) or Morgana (Morgan le Fey). Though there are many tales of interactions with the Fey, this is the one, and often the only one, that most people know well, or at all.

Niniane used to play in the cool forest near a spring of clear water shaded by lofty trees. It was her favorite spot, where she could rest and watch the deer and other forest creatures come down to drink.

Merlin remained hidden in the trees for a long time as he observed her studying, playing, and dreaming. She was truly the most beautiful girl he had ever seen .... Finally he stepped forward and began to speak with her while, like

a teacher, watching her every reaction but seeming not to …. He did not on this
occasion reveal his true identity, but said he was the servant to a great man."

Norma Lorre Goodrich
Merlin

Most commonly held is the belief that the legends tell of a king undone by the evil manipulations of his half-sister, known as Morgan le Fey, and also by the betrayal of his queen, Guinevere, with his best friend, Lancelot du Lac, brought up by the Lady of the Lake, a Fey. The further destruction of the Round Table is seen to have been the work of Mordred, commonly accepted to be the son of Morgan le Fey, and therefore at least half-Fey himself. Furthermore, the one and only one who may have been able to prevent this, The Merlin, is believed to have been removed permanently from action by, you guessed it, a Fey.

Even current films portray this in much the same old misconceived manner. However, Boorman's "Excalibur" manages rather well in transmitting a most critically important message in a mass consciousness way: "You and the land are one." Even still this may be misconstrued as being the sole responsibility of a king; while we currently recognize this is one message shared by all of us. Encounters with the Fey often are shown to be the exclusive privilege of only those who are royally connected or entitled to them.

This, we know, is simply not true, whether we take it in a literal sense or not. The wealth of Faerie lore always has been preserved by the "common folk." Celts and their traditions, have courageously refused to turn from the Faerie Faith which they know to be sacred. In a more symbolic sense, we are wise to remember that: "We are all the royal children" of our Sovereign Queen, the Earth, and our Solar King of Light.

The stories of the Fey that emerge in the legends of Camelot also have their origins in much earlier Celtic myths and folklore. These tales of the Celtic Otherworld are found extensively in the oral traditions and the mythic literature of the European continent; but are especially prevalent in Ireland, Scotland, Wales, Cornwall, The Isle of Man, Brittany, and England. This "faerie lore" has been preserved in the Camelot legends in an often misconstrued manner. Nevertheless, preserved it has been, for the essential power of the Faerie Faith is a force that truly cannot be suppressed.

Although this is not a book about the Faerie Faith as such, it is appropriate here to provide a working knowledge of what these Fey represent to us. That the mystical understanding and acceptance of the Fair Folk has endured, both consciously and unconsciously, despite many misrepresentations, speaks clearly of their deeper magick. It reflects their elemental meaning, which was tribally encoded in us individually, and collectively, as Celts.

Faerie Nature Theories

The theories regarding the nature of the Fey, Fair Folk, or Faerie, may be divided into seven basic categories, with some natural overlapping weaves:

The Naturalistic Theory: This presents the idea that the belief in Faeries and their realms results from attempts to interpret and explain the forces and phenomena of Nature. As such, it is an anthropomorphic theory, one that animistically personifies the elements of Nature in general, and those of specific locations or lands, as well. The Celtic concept of spirit-of-place, *genus locorum,* arises partly from the process this theory presents.

The Little People or "Pygmy" Theory: This presents the idea that faerie beliefs are the result of distant memory of an early, diminutive people who preceded the Celts into areas eventually conquered by Celtic tribes, who then relegated these "little people" to the outer or underground regions of the lands. This becomes a cultural theory, in that it actually stems from the diminishing of the conquered and the exalting of the conquerors.

The Druid Theory: This presents the idea that Faerie beliefs are the result of Celtic, Druidic practices dating from the purely Pagan times before the Roman occupation and the influx of Eastern and Christian spiritual forms. This also may be seen in part as anthropomorphological, reflecting the spiritual practices of that animistic philosophy. It also becomes a rather restrictive sexual theory, purposely reflecting the insignificance of the Druid in general, and specifically the Druidess, whose power as a female was summarily discredited by Rome and by the Orthodoxy.

The Mythological Theory: This presents the idea that the Faeries are images of ancient Celtic deities of Nature and those who were tribal gods. This is both a cultural and spiritual theory. Culturally, the old god forms are diminished. Spiritually, they remain mythically transformed, yet still deeply present in Celtic consciousness. While this mythological theory has held sway for a century or more, it still separates that which is Faerie from its integral connection to the personal and tribal psyche.

The Metaphysical Theory: This presents the idea that the Faeries were ascended masters, priests and priestesses, or avatars, who were once incarnated in the lands of the Celts and now are seen as realm and spirit guides, reached through the use of ritual practices or high ceremonial magick. This is both a philosophical and societal theory. Philosophically, the existence of these realms and guides is accepted. Societally, access to these is limited to the few—initiated or exclusively privileged—to know these specific rituals.

The Ecumenical Theory: This presents the idea that Faeries are somehow displaced beings, inhabiting regions such as "between the Moon and the Earth" and "between the Moon and the Sun." This is an Orthodox theory that relegates that which is inexplicable to doctrines that maintain either a Heaven-or-hell, saved-or-unsaved position. It is also political, in that it provides a message used to control the parameters of people's beliefs, or faiths.

The Psychological Theory: This presents the idea that Faeries and their realms are "facts of the mind," or symbols created both consciously and unconsciously: at best, a group image; at worst, a shared delusion. This is a philosophical and political theory. Philosophically it stresses the thought forms arising from belief systems. Politically, it separates humankind from Nature; placing Faerie in a role that can be superficial and subservient.

THREADS IN THE FAERIE WEAVE
Guided Imagery Exercises

Before we continue to discuss the theories regarding "the Faerie Faith," let's use the guided imagery format to deepen our understanding of these ideas. Remember that most collections of theories have far more similarities than differences, particularly those dealing with mystical, free-flowing concepts such as Faerie.

Breathe consciously. Focus on creating a measured pattern of relaxed breathing. Become receptive to your own perceptions. Focus within, and be centered. Breathe naturally and note your reactions as you move through these exercises.

Naturalistic—You are walking alone beside a clear gentle brook winding its way gracefully through a lovely, secluded forest. You rest for a while on the soft grassy banks at the edge of the crystal-clear waters. You feel this spot is sacred somehow, perhaps a realm of Faerie. A slight motion seen from the corner of your eye causes you to turn quickly and see ... a faerie.

What did you see? Note the details of your image as clearly as you can. What did you feel before and when you saw the faerie? Note these feelings and match them with the specifics of your image. Freeze-frame your image and encapsulate the feelings. File them within for future reference.

Little People—You are making your way across a cold, deserted moor, following an old, rough, and stony path. The landscape is craggy and desolate. As a chill wind whistles between the stones and boulders, you hear what sounds like the footsteps of children resounding faintly across the moor. Though sounds in the wind are quite tricky, you look up and momentarily glimpse ... faeries.

What did you glimpse? What did you feel? Freeze-frame and file within.

Druid—You are visiting a remote sacred site somewhere in the isles of Brigantia. You are standing in the center of a small henge of stones overgrown with grasses and brambles. As you gaze across the henge to watch the sunset on the Western horizon, you suddenly feel the ancient power of that circle.

You also feel you are not alone here, but you cannot see anyone else around you. You decide to cast a circle, starting in the East, across from the setting sun. You move East to South to West to North and return to face the East once more. Now you know that you are not alone here in this circle of stones, for standing in front of you is ... a faerie.

What do you see? What do you feel? Freeze-frame and file for future reference.

Mythological—You are in a little-known museum filled with paintings of British figures. Some are historical; others more lyrical representations of the legends of Britain. The paintings seem to come alive as you study them; you can almost smell the roses in one of them.

There seems to be another connoisseur of this art; but this one seems to be there, and not there; sometimes beside you, sometimes in the next gallery hall. This happens so quickly it makes you quite curious, so you decide upon a ploy.

You stand in front of a massive painting of an ancient British landscape with characters you cannot seem to place. You pretend to concentrate very hard, but easily so, for you find the scene quite compelling. You almost fail to notice when the other one in this old gallery comes up behind you gently. When you become aware of the presence, you turn and find yourself staring at ... a faerie.

What do you see? What do you feel? Freeze-frame and file within.

Metaphysical—You have been invited to attend a special gathering in an old stone building deep in the heart of London. You are given robes to wear like those that all the others there have already put on in preparation for the evening's activities. Incense and candles are lit. One robed figure raises an ornate chalice in each of four directions, as a circle is cast. Another robed figure begins to speak words that are lyrical, yet mysterious. Now the first robed figure instructs all present to join hands in a circle surrounding an altar. As the second robed figure continues to speak the words, the sound becomes like a chant. The room seems to be filling with mists, mostly in the middle of the circle. You watch as a shape emerges from the mists; clearly coming into focus in front of the altar. As the mists diminish, the shape takes the form of a ... faerie.

What do you see? What do you feel? Freeze-frame and file within.

Ecumenical—You are attending a parish dinner and lecture in a quaint village near Dublin. The guest lecturer is discussing the relationship of the church's traditions and those of folklore. Most of those listening are rather elderly; they're drowsing as the lecture drones on. A couple in the front pew are rapt with attention, seemingly illuminated by the subject. They laugh rather quietly at a few of the comments, and you find you wish you knew them better.

As the lecture ends and the small crowd of listeners gathers their coats, you notice the couple walking toward the door rather swiftly. You follow them as fast as you can, carefully avoiding the frail old ladies gathered around the lecturer just inside the doorway. As politely as you can, you make your way through to the outside of the parish hall. The couple is ahead of you, gliding together across the lawn. You call out for them to wait. They turn briefly, then smile, and vanish from sight.

They are nowhere to be found, though the twilight sky is still bright enough to illuminate the wide-open lawns surrounding the parish hall on all sides. A gentle breeze blows by, lifting your hair caressingly. Once more you hear the same quiet laughter you heard from the couple in the parish hall. With certainty you know you have just seen ... faeries.

What did you see? What did you feel? Freeze-frame and file within for future reference.

Psychological—You are reclining on an antique Victorian couch—a fainting couch, your great-grandmother might have called it. You are sharing your thoughts with an analyst who is seated just behind where you're resting your head on the pillows of the couch. The analyst takes notes whenever you speak, but doesn't interrupt you with comments.

You wonder if these notes can really capture what you are describing. You pause to focus your thoughts and to choose the words that will describe precisely what you see in your mind. Finding the words, you tell the analyst what you see in your mind as ... faeries.

What do you see? What do you feel? What do you think?

Note the details of what you describe, and freeze-frame the image of what you saw inside your mind. Note how you felt before and after you described what you saw. Note the thoughts that came into your mind in association with your image. Encapsulate these thoughts and feelings and file them under emotions for future reference and analysis.

Before we continue, you may wish to make a note about each of the seven experiences you had while moving through the exercises. These can be very brief and still ensure that you don't confuse what you have freeze-framed and filed already. Consider this your first try at the craft of future reference; carefully coding each image with something simple, or symbolic.

A color, a smell, an aspect of the inner landscape or setting of your image will reinforce that image in your mind. Symbols that remind you of the image can be as simple as a cross, circle, or star; and as complex as a map, painting, or a thought. You know you can pencil these into this book if you choose. Didn't I mention that before? Well, I would have; but I thought you already knew the choice was yours. I am only here to remind you. When you are ready to do so, continue this exercise in guided imagery.

REFLECTIONS OF A CHILD OF NATURE
A *Guided Journey Imagery*

Take a long, slow breath. Stretch your body gently and release your breath as you relax your body. Repeat this sequence until you are receptive to your own inner processes, your own inner realms of vision and experience. Breathe consciously and focus within. Be centered and begin to breathe naturally.

———

You are walking alone through a mystically beautiful landscape, one that is most magickal and enchanting for you. All around you, Nature is alive: pure and clear and original. Everything you see and hear in this natural land is yours alone to experience. It is personal, private, and primeval. Experience the deep connection you share with this land. Experience your inner connection to Nature.

Though you may choose to share this natural land with someone at another time, for now it is yours alone to experience. It is your gift from Nature, from Spirit, and from Self. Accept it with the grace with which it is given.

As you journey through this landscape, you come upon a path that guides you toward your destination. The path seems rough and rocky at first. Then, as you step upon it, you find the stones are small and smooth, weathered by the elements of Nature throughout the ages. Perhaps an ancient river flowed here once, or an ocean covered this land, softly shaping it in the wombs-time of the Earth Mother. Perhaps this pathway was carefully prepared in time immemorial, smoothing the way within the landscape of your mystical mind.

Your path leads you to a sacred site, deeply experienced and deeply remembered. There are carved stones standing in a circle; magickally cast forever—in time eternal, in mind ever present and familiar. Drawing closer to these stones, you see the carvings clearly. They are symbols telling of the powers, the gifts, and the legends of Nature's realms.

As you read these symbols, you realize they are etched deeply into the stones, preserving the message—the pattern for the Earth Mother's clan, for her tribe, her people, her children. You feel their imprint, still sharp in your mind. Only the surface of these stones has been softened by the changing winds of time.

As you reverently touch these stones again, you feel the power move forth from the symbols, resonating through your spirit. With honor and courage, you accept the power, the gifts within. Gracefully, you acknowledge this with gratitude, bowing only to the Spirit Divine which you find here in Nature's attunement.

Gentle breezes begin to blow, weaving within the sacred circle. Privately, personally, you create a ritual—a ceremony crafted from your own connection to Spirit, Nature, and Self. As you begin your ceremony, the stones begin to hum. It is an ancient tune, currently sounding through the times, eternally present. You call the elements of Nature to join in this joyful chorus.

Fire's rhythm, Water's melody, Earth's measured tune, Air's lyrics, and the Harmony of Spirit combine to bring you the synthesis of power—the All that is around you. Within, you hear the music of the spheres celestially guiding, ever guiding you Lightly—giving you all the time you need for your ceremonies of life's celebration. The ceremony continues, but the ritual begins and ends. You take your leave of this stone circle and step on the pathway again.

This time your pathway leads you smoothly to a small chapel, quite humble and simple in its design. You have not had to go far to reach it, since it is near the sacred circle, in clear alignment with the center stone. Though it seems deserted, it has been well cared for by someone. It has been cherished quietly for all the time it has stood, faithfully strong and undamaged by even the harshest climates to which it has been exposed.

You wonder if there is someone in the chapel. Although you can see no one, you call out your name, announcing your presence. First, silence; then a flock of white birds flies overhead, gently calling in reply. You step into the little chapel and find you are alone with the Light.

There is only a simple altar within and a place for you to sit and rest. The Sun in the western sky sends soft rays through the chapel windows, illuminating the symbol of Light upon this altar, chosen by your design of the Divine.

You rest and reflect there within the small chapel, warmed by the light streaming in through the windows, open to the clear horizon. Your thoughts are clear, requiring no words. You make your connection to Spirit directly—with no need to describe the experience. The sun casts golden rays inside the chapel, and you know the time has come to begin your journey of returning.

You take your leave of the chapel, with respect and reverence in balance with your beliefs. In a manner most honorable and gracious, befitting the codes by which you live, to which you were born and bred, you thank the Light in all its aspects of Self, Nature, and Spirit.

As you step out of the chapel, the sun casts red-gold rays upon the outer walls. Pausing, you see the stones in the circle glowing crimson against the deep green of the lands, illuminated by the light still strong in the Western sky. You feel the power of your experience activating the power within. You know it is a power that is with you always. To return you have only to remember; this you reverently understand. You step on the pathway once more, this time in the direction that leads where you began. Taking all the time you need, you walk through this beautiful inner landscape.

When you reach the spot where you first stepped upon this path, you find a gift waiting there, wrapped in fabric crafted of the finest Celtic weave. The colors of the fabric and the designs you find assure you this gift is truly for you. And, if you didn't already know this most certainly, a sealed note is attached, addressed to you. The writing is lightly crafted and the envelope is bordered in silver and gold. The border design is of lines interwoven in true Celtic fashion; signifying the inseparable connections of all that is. There is a wax seal on the back, bearing a royal mark that you know well, if perhaps you have just now seen it. You open the envelope and withdraw the paper, also crafted in Celtic kind.

And the note reads:

With Respect for your Service –
Knightly
and your Reverence for Nature –
Lightly
for Remembering who You are –
Brightly
we'll help your Research here – Slightly.
So, open your Gift with your eyes
closed – Tightly.
We remain your relations, Rightly

The Fair Folk

Having wondered where the Fair Folk were, you are anxious to find out what gift they have crafted to help you better understand them. Having seen several images of Faeries already, you find you're still not certain ... are they myth or memory? Solid or symbolic? Nature or nice fantasy?

You open the gift carefully, since your eyes are closed as requested. Still wondering how to tell, to understand, to know, really know what a Faerie is—but with faith that you will learn—you open your eyes and find the answer to your question clearly reflected in the gift ... which is a mirror.

That which we call Faerie is a synthesis of all our natural knowledge and potentials reflecting the once, future, and evolutionarily best of what we are. We have found the Fair Folk and they are ourselves reflected in Mind, Body, and Spirit. In Mind, it's our images; in Body, our genetic encoding; in Spirit, our tribal, spiritual codes and our encoded alliances with the lands. It is true that this holds true globally, and one day we may all evolve into a world-class Fair Folk. However, for now, I'll narrow the focus to the Celtic Fair Folk and relate this to the theories discussed previously.

As I do this, you may find images emerging from the exercises and the journey before. If so, this is because they were crafted to do so. This is just as the legends were crafted in many cases, to encode information and to activate remembering. Therefore, I present my theory regarding the Fair Folk. And theory I do say, because it is more than an idea to me. Naturally, I'm willing to continue my research of this everunfolding knowledge.

THE CELTIC WEAVE THEORY

This presents a synthesis of all we now know in regard to Faerie, the Fey, or the Fair Folk. It is an open synthesis theory, allowing for the continuous flow of new information. How could it be otherwise? It also presents a synthesis of all we are in relation to the other theories which are each strong threads in our Fair Folk fabric. In the Celtic weave, we will include, as clan kin, the basic tribes of Britain and France as the strongest threads. (Apologies if your thread is not specifically mentioned, for I'm sure it is one of the finer ones. It has certainly helped weave your connection to these legends and the Fey quite well, or you wouldn't be working with this now, would you?)

The Celtic Weave Clan Kin
(By relative tribal influences in Britain and France)

dé Danann—Proto Celt: Ireland, Scotland, Wales, Cornwall
Gaels—Gaelic Celt: Ireland, Scotland, Isle of Man
Britons—Brythonic Celt: Wales, Cornwall, England
Bretons—Brythonic Celt: Brittany
Gauls—Gaelic Celt: France
Anglo-Saxons—Germanic: England, Scotland
Scandinavians—Nordic: Scottish Highlands, Ireland, England
Normans—Nordic: France, England
Teutons—Germanic: England, Scotland
Goths—Slavic: England, France

To personalize this process of exploring the Celtic Weave Theory, I am presenting it in a Fey way; from the Fair Folk point of view, so to speak.

The Celtic Weave Threads—A Synthesis Relation of Theories

The Naturalistic Theory:
These threads are present because they show our natural shamanic relationship to life. In an age of close relationship with the lands in which we lived, Nature was alive to us, and we were alive because of Nature. We saw Nature then as a shaman still does in current times. The spirits of place were not so much gods as they were kin.

It is more fitting to say our alliance with Nature was personified mutually in the elements we shared then and now; one and the same. The Sky Father God activated the receptive Earth Mother Goddess and reflected in all growing life forms, which were their children. Of all these forms, we were only one. Without the others, we would have perished. It is only natural that we would treat the aspects of Nature as part of ourselves and honor this by seeing them in our image, amplified by their power. The Romans called our spirits of place *genus locorum*. The Hindus say devas. The Christians may say angels. We call them our Sovereign kin.

The Little People Theory
These threads are present, but not as strongly as the first. The little people were those who lived on the lands before we came there. It is true they were smaller by a head at least, and more—especially those in the regions of the Picts. We frightened them with our warrior ways and our boastful, colorful manners. The horses scared them greatly, a fact that much amused us.

Now we did not treat these little people badly, for we were—and still are—a natural, sporting breed. In time, we came to know them, although they remained an elusive lot. You can often see their bloodlines today in the wild lands of Brigantia's realms where there are those still dark and small.

In Ireland it was another story all together, where what is called Fey was there Tuatha dé. Speaking for both that tribe and the Gaels, once we had settled the borders of our realms, we blended quite readily, for we were and are quite kin. From this came the high Celt, with Fair Folk within. Tuatha dé were magick only as a mage might be, championing us all with their highly trained skills. Some Tuatha dé, like the Picts on the other isle, chose to live away and keep the sacred mysteries; but of the Otherworld, not the Underground. Their mystic arts are in our bloodlines now.

The Druid Theory

These threads are present, with some of strong, new fibers. There were Druids of the Fair Folk, whom you call the Faerie Wizards, and the Druids of the Romans who were rarely wise in Nature. Their Sun god was like ours, in many ways, we thought; but they left him in the desert as they came along our way. Only a few could reach him there, so far from his home. Perhaps if we had known him there, in his natural lands, we would have seen what they'd been shown of his powers, which did not help us here.

Our Faerie Druids kept the sacred places, like the groves and the henges. They were as we all were once, in service to the Earth Mother and the Sky Father. They were the wisest among us, for many of us were warriors in those times. We were guarding the borders and the tribes from the waves of invaders. The diviners of our Druids knew they would conquer us for just a while in time and truth. As to the Fair Folk who wouldn't blend, the conquerors drove them back. Our Druids withdrew first, like those of the Tuatha dé, in order to keep the lines of kinship open in our sovereign alliance with Nature. The Druids are still present as healers, priests, and priestesses, teachers, and lawyers, too. They're our poets and our scientists, still crafting today.

The Mythological Theory

These threads are present, but many just for show. They're our trophy case of glories, a legacy left for the future of our kind. We've always valued trophies all polished and shining. They remind us of what we have done ... and what we all can do. But a trophy is only useful if you remember how you won it. Far too many have gathered dust, long put away on a dark, high shelf in a curio cabinet.

It was tricky to honor us, appealing to our vanity. Wyrd, that all the while we didn't see the chains binding us to the pedestals designed to display our greatest gifts. We had to stay there far too long, while only a few remembered what we really were and who they were, as well. Soon enough, though, just in time, we remembered each other. We're a tribe, you and I. We're a culture, and not a collection of fine artifacts requiring polish from those who only want the dreams of past glories and not the challenges.

171

To those who love the mythic Celt and the magick of the Fey, I say: melt down those trophies; break the chains; throw the pedestals away. Craft bright swords mythically and light chalices mystically. Find the magick of the spear and the mysteries of the stone. For the Hallowed games are beginning, and your name is on the board.

The Metaphysical Theory

These threads are present in both light and dark shades. It is true that we also are present in much the same way. There are those of us who help in ways that are for the Right and the Good. Others of us are more motivated to causes that are not for the best, except as it is best for ourselves, with no care about the rest. It would be more fitting if each of us used our highest potential, helping only the wise and the well; but we are not perfection. We share all the aspects of humanity, and not always in a humane fashion. Like you, we may be seen as either angels or demons.

It is true there are those of us who dwell only in the mystical planes. Not all of us are incarnate now, experiencing the mundane realms. As you do, so we do, as well. Many of us are able to cross the borders of these realms, traveling between this world and the Otherworld of Spirit. For some of us—most, I'm proud to tell—this mission is for the benefit of humankind.

We can be called to this service whether our form be flesh or spirit, currently. Many of the Faerie Faith do this with rituals and spells. Some of this is needed, surely. Some is only seen by us as silly. Others, still, we see as self-important, pompous displays of secrets which all of us know already. We know the metaphysician whose works are in the healing realms of home. We know their ritual pomp and circumstances are just their way of showing proper protocol. Still, those of us who will respond only to such set ritual are often so self-empowering we have nothing left for service. To reach those Fey who dwell in the mystical planes, craft your ritual with heart, and clear your purpose well. We will hear your rightful call.

The Ecumenical Theory

These threads are present: some woven in universal fashion and others more orthodox in their design. This Orthodox design is most amusing, truly. How can anything be displaced or excluded from the all-inclusive realms that we know are universal? This question our wise ones pose well, for they know what the Light is, and we, too, as you do. How can we all be condemned to dark, when so many of us already dwell in the Light?

The Fair Folk find it strangely apt to relegate our realms between the Earth and Moon for some, for others between the Moon and Sun. Though this was done by the Orthodox, it reflects more universal truth than we expect they knew. Between the Earth and moon is a description quite poetic, which fits the Fair Folk whose service is the healing arts—inspirational and nurturing. Between the Moon and Sun describes those of us whose service is that of crafting structures with humanity which allow the growth of Truth and Right. These we also guard quite fiercely.

As we share the mystical and mundane realms, so we share also the realms of service. Truly said, there are no borders in any realms of service. Between the mystical and mundane, the borders are but veils. So universal, ecumenical, these do suit us well. And all the names for what is Light reflect our service clearly. With Spirit, everything is of one, universal realm. This is the healing truth. For structuring, though, and crafting, we designate elementally: Healing: (foremostly) Air + Water; and Structures: (foremostly) Earth + Fire.

The Psychological Theory

These threads are present most frequently, though not separate or exclusive. Self-Nature and the facts of mind are woven quite inseparably with Nature and the Mind of All. In fact, each and all of these are present in the self. A Fair Folk rhyme I give to you to help and *psyche* it truly: "Understanding how the mind works makes magick most profound, and wise use of this wisdom will bring us all around." The tricky key to have, the one to all the doors, is the knowing what the mind is and all it can be. With that in mind, for the good of all, we form our best intentions. From this, then, comes the service, in response to S.O.S. By that mind trick we remember the purpose to which we're called—to serve Self, Others, and Spirit. That's enough, since that's the All. "Self is self and Nature; and Others, the all around; Spirit is the life-force in everything we've found." Now, there's a rhyme for you.

And here are two from the spritely and sometimes silly realm of the Fair Folk:

> *The purpose of the Fair Folk is to serve Right Evolution.*
> *Nature turns the wheels of life, and we, the wheels of self.*
> *Our purpose then, most Fair Folk, is to serve Right Revolution.*
> *With help, we're here, returning as Faerie, Fey, or Elf.*
>
> *The mind is truly powerful. The brain will help remembering.*
> *Clear sight requires insight. Train your brain with care.*

The purpose of this chapter has been to show you not only what the Fair Folk are, but what you are, in kind. However we may see the Fey, the point is to see them clearly. They are mirrors for our selves, as we are for them. As long as we reflect rightly, we can continue the service of evolution with the Fair Folk there to guide us. When our hearts are pure, our intentions good, and our spirits strong with purpose, we are the best we can be. In that, we are the Fair Folk of the Celtic Weave, reflecting our honor for Nature.

The imagery exercises and journeys are there for you to experience and adapt to suit your needs. Note the changes you experience or those times when your images are different. These changes reflect just what you need to know about yourself and the actions which are required. As you become familiar with the Fey aspects of your self, you'll develop your own system to interpret your changing images. You'll also become perceptive to images and characters such as those in the Camelot legends we are continuing to explore. When you feel a strong connection to these literary images, remember that this reflects Your Self, literally, in regard to what you require for your personal path in life and for the processes of empowerment.

In the next chapter we will use the experiential exercise approach to sharpen your skills at assessment in regard to the images of the Fey characters in the Arthurian Legends.

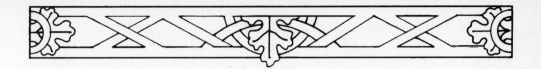

CHAPTER 17

KNIGHTS, WIZARDS, AND
FAIR WEAVERS

There will be many different stories, I have seen to that. Some will say I van-
ished, others will tell of me being sealed in my cave for a thousand years or so. I
rather like that one myself. It gives me the future—something to look forward
to. Do not shed tears for me, Arthur, or be angry with Nimuea. For she, like
you and I, is merely playing out her part. Nimuea! It would be good to embrace
her once again.

Merlin, have you known her before? Oh yes! Yes, Arthur, we always have some
kind of a relationship in every life.

Kara Starr
Merlin's Journal of Time

 While you explore some of these legendary Fair Folk as their patterns appear in various Celtic Faerie tale or Arthurian format, consider your own choice of belief as a Fair Folk in regard to the traditional form of the Camelot legends. Try not to edit what emerges for you. The emphasis here is on emotion, not thought. As you move through this exercise, be guided by how you feel. Respond to aspects with which you are most familiar at first, if that is helpful to you. You can always come back to this exercise as you learn more about the multi-faceted realms of the Camelot legends. There is nei-ther right, nor wrong; but a direct reflection of your most mystical self that responds, in kind.

ACCUSATIONS

With just enough enlightenment to guide us, we can reclaim these legends, which are ours by Right. We can recast the characters in a new light—neither too bright to gaze at, nor too shadowed to see clearly. We can reattach the lines that connect us to the Fey, flexibly—neither too close for comfort, nor too far out to be reached comfortably. We can replace the King on his Celtic throne—with his realms neither here nor there, but everywhere. We can recrown the queen for her natural qualities—neither betrayal nor barrenness—but benevolence. We can recall The Merlin to his rightful position—neither mystery nor myth—but Mage.

First and foremost, we can face the accusations that surround the round of these legends with bindings. We can cut these cords with our own swords of power, releasing them to empower us—neither foolishly nor fantastically—but fairly ... as Fair Folks. We can judge only the questionable images of these legends and their often ambiguous messages, as we must judge ourselves—with neither too much acceptance, nor too little rejection. Malice and manipulation are there as may be; but so are magnificence and magick.

As with our own lives, we sometimes start over on a new path, with no looking backward. We begin anew with balanced outlook and the wisdom of experience to guide us. With our own lives, as with our legends, if we've stood bound, accursed or accused in the past, it is passed and done and over now. When we've failed, we failed. When we've won, we won. How else could it be, being human? With our lives, as with our legends, not always is there only guilty or innocent; but there always is the power of personal pardon, especially when you're one of the Fair Folk.

It's only natural to have judgments to make about these legends concerning matters of guilt, regrets, responsibilities, and blame. Just remember, these reflect aspects of your own life and remember the balancing benefit of the doubt. As you do with others, do so with your self. So forgive, but do not necessarily forget; just file for future reference. Sometimes it is foolish; more often it is wise to accept and start anew, acquitted on all charges.

In-depth exploration of the Camelot legends presents us with several ways to view each character and message. This is particularly so in regard to the workings of the Fey, for in Faerie, everything is amplified. All we can do is try for the balance—neither dark nor light, but right.

Verdicts

1. Guilty, with intention
2. Guilty by circumstance
3. Innocent
4. Mistrial, lack of evidence
5. Mistrial, hung jury, undecided
6. Pardoned by your personal decree

Accusations

1. The Merlin had divined the coming of the king, Arthur, but did not reveal this to Uther or Igraine.

2. The Merlin used his Faerie powers to arrange for Uther and Igraine to create the child Arthur, regardless of the costs or consequences to either parent.

3. Igraine knew the possible consequences, but wanted to be Queen of Britain.

4. Uther knew the possible consequences, but didn't care.

5. The Merlin was responsible for the Duke of Cornwall's death.

6. Uther was responsible for Cornwall's death.

7. Igraine was responsible for Cornwall's death.

8. The Merlin did not tell Igraine she would have to give up her child, Arthur, until after he was already born.

9. The Merlin and Uther arranged to remove the child, Arthur, without informing Igraine.

10. Igraine wanted to give up Arthur to solidify her position as queen.

11. Igraine gave up Arthur by choice to remove herself from her guilt.

12. The Merlin fostered Arthur to Sir Ector in order to avoid his responsibility—at least initially.

13. The Merlin already had refused responsibility when he didn't challenge Uther for the throne of Britain.

14. The Merlin used his Faerie powers to arrange for Arthur to pull the sword from the stone; thus making his case for Arthur as king and justifying the means that had led to that end.

15. The Merlin used Arthur's accomplishments to establish himself as Archdruid of all Britain for all time.

16. Arthur used Merlin to establish himself as the Celtic mythic king of all time.

17. Arthur abused the hallowed gifts, such as the sword of power and the cauldron he took from the Otherworld.

18. Arthur refused to rescue Guinevere because she wasn't producing an heir.

19. The Merlin divined that Guinevere would be barren, but didn't tell this to anyone.

20. The Merlin was experimenting and was only interested in the results in his lifetime. Can you see how easily shadows can be cast on these legends? Can you see how they can be so easily bound in with misconception or confusion? Consider this and take a break for a moment. If these accusations seem very negative, perhaps it's because you've never considered some of them before, at least not

consciously. Bear with me on this, even if it does seem almost "sacrilege."
There's a point to this, I assure you—a point to be made for the good of all.

21. Avalon Fey sabotaged The Merlin in any way they could because he would not join or support them.

22. Avalon Fey used Morgana to produce a child who could bring down Camelot.

23. Morgana seduced Arthur with the same purpose in mind because she held The Merlin responsible for her father's death (Duke of Cornwall), or out of jealousy of Arthur.

24. Avalon Fey arranged for Guinevere not to produce an heir:

    a. because they saw her Christianity as a direct threat
    b. because they wanted to ensure the "bastard" child would bring down Camelot
    c. because they were opposed to The Merlin's design to create a line of kings (to his credit)
    d. because they had a plan of their own to recreate the rulership of priest-Kings, exalting their own kind.

25. The Lady of the Lake fostered Lancelot for the purpose of betraying the King with the Queen.

26. The Merlin knew of Lancelot's coming betrayal but did not tell Arthur because:

    a. He was opposed also to Guinevere's Christianity
    b. He was opposed to Lancelot's same faith
    c. He wanted Arthur to "put away" Guinevere
    d. He wanted Arthur to marry his student, Nimue, and create a more Fey line for the throne of Britain

27. The Merlin chose Nimue to train because he wanted her to be a spear point in a new plan for Camelot.

28. The Merlin was "sexist" and underestimated Nimue.

29. Nimue played or manipulated The Merlin like a puppet master would in order to exalt her own position.

30. Morgana played Merlin in the same way as above.

31. Morgana played Nimue to make her "murder" The Merlin, removing him with "enchantment."

32. Morgana removed The Merlin by herself.

33. The Merlin removed himself and let others take the blame.

That's quite enough of that, I'm sure you'll agree. There are quite enough shadows on these legends, as it is. If it disturbed you to do that exercise—well, that's all right and good. That means you're a natural guardian of the sacred, a champion for the Light and Truth in these legends. It means you're willing to fight to preserve the pattern, the elemental round these legends represent. That, my ken, is like fighting for the Round Table; and this time we know we can win.

To start the process of putting things right, I'll present the statements once again—this time in the light in which I see them. I'll remind you here that you need not agree, except for the need to be open-minded. As always, this holds true for life, as well as for legends. Here these restatements will present, or review, some of the legends and some of their characters in a way that will make them more human, with all the strengths and weaknesses that are possible, presented in a fair fashion. Use the Verdict column to make your own choices. (There is no right or wrong here.)

Re-Viewing the Fair Folk—a Descriptive Analysis

Accusation 1: The Merlin had divined the coming of the king, Arthur, but did not reveal this to Uther or Igraine.

Response: The Merlin's vision of the coming king, Arthur, came from the highest realms, the Divine; and he knew well all he could do was wait for the unfolding destiny to guide him.

Accusation 2: The Merlin used his Faerie powers to arrange for Uther and Igraine to create the child Arthur, regardless of the costs or consequences to either parent.

Response: The Merlin used all his wits and wisdom to devise a plan which would help manifest his vision with as little harmful consequence as possible. If Igraine got pregnant, as The Merlin hoped, the child could as easily be seen as Gorlois, the Duke of Cornwall's. Perhaps this would have been a more appropriate situation, as Gorlois was known by Merlin to be a reasonable and honorable man, while Uther was rash and not naturally paternal.

Accusation 3: Igraine knew the possible consequences, but wanted to be Queen of Britain.

Response: Igraine was not concerned about the possibility of pregnancy, for she would have viewed the child as hers, regardless of the father. This was still her right as a Celtic high-born Lady and the royal Duchess of Cornwall. If Igraine's intentions were to make herself Queen of Britain, by Uther, regardless of the consequences, she easily could have persuaded Uther to carry out that plan. Thus, Uther would have gained a queen and the lands of Cornwall, as well.

Accusation 4: Uther knew the possible consequences, but didn't care.

Response: While Uther was unlikely to have considered or cared about a child at that time, he was quite likely to have wanted at least to put Gorlois down. At most, Uther could have had his own plan to claim Cornwall, or allow some of his warrior lords to do so.

Accusation 5: The Merlin was responsible for the Duke of Cornwall's death.

Response: The Merlin certainly held himself responsible because he had a very human heart. However, he was objective enough to see the unseen synchronicity which is part of the unfolding destiny. The Merlin would have taken Gorlois' death as a sign of the seriousness of Arthur's purpose, and of his own. He, therefore, strove to honor that responsibility to the best of his abilities—for the sake of Gorlois as Ambrosius' man.

Accusation 6: Uther was responsible for Cornwall's death.

Response: It is highly likely that Uther either encouraged or commanded his warrior lords to create a diversion while he was with Igraine. As a warrior king, Uther's philosophy, of necessity, would have been one that held with the workings of destiny—when it's time to die in battle, at least it was death in battle and not in bed, debilitated.

Accusation 7: Igraine was responsible for Cornwall's death.

Response: Igraine would certainly have held herself responsible as a wife and a woman. But, as a warrior's wife and a Celtic woman, she would have held a philosophy similar to Uther's and spiritual beliefs about the Otherworld, which was not seen as the end of life, but the beginning of a new one.

Accusation 8: The Merlin did not tell Igraine she would have to give up her child, Arthur, until after he was already born.

Response: It would not have been The Merlin's place to tell Igraine what to do with her child, even knowing Arthur was the coming king. The Merlin would have to wait for Igraine to reason this out wisely while she was pregnant and isolated for the sake of her own protection, as well as for that of the child.

Accusation 9: The Merlin and Uther arranged to remove the child, Arthur, without informing Igraine.

Response: The Merlin and Arthur certainly would have discussed the possible solutions. While they might have presented their ideas to Igraine, now the Queen of Britain, I expect they wouldn't have, out of respect for her grief and because of the possible effects on the pregnancy. In that time, pregnancy was often quite dangerous, particularly for a high-born Lady such as Igraine.

Accusation 10: Igraine wanted to give up Arthur to solidify her position as queen.

Response: As Queen, Igraine would have considered the conflicts that would have arisen if she had another son by Uther—this one clearly the heir to Britain in the eyes of Uther and his warrior lords. Igraine solidified Arthur's position with his safety in mind.

Accusation 11: Igraine gave up Arthur by choice to remove herself from her guilt.

Response: If anything, Igraine removed herself from her child, Arthur, to perpetuate or punish herself for her guilt. As she was at that time both Christian and Pagan, her older beliefs would also have led her to see this as a balancing sacrifice necessary because of Gorlois' death.

Accusation 12: The Merlin fostered Arthur to Sir Ector in order to avoid his responsibility—at least initially.

Response: The Merlin would have known he had no business rearing a child, nor the know-how to do so. Remembering the best parts of his own childhood, he fostered Arthur in the country where the future king could connect with the lands and live in the safe, supportive home of Sir Ector, the "country squire" type knight. Later Merlin could assume the role as teacher, as Blaise had been for him.

Accusation 13: The Merlin already had refused responsibility when he didn't challenge Uther for the throne of Britain.

Response: The Merlin was very wise to the potentials of being the "power behind the throne." To have avoided the role he assumed as Archmage would have been true avoidance of responsibility in The Merlin's case. Also, it would have been an avoidance of the destiny he saw for himself; unfolding in his vision and in his life, as well.

Accusation 14: The Merlin used his Faerie powers to arrange for Arthur to pull the sword from the stone; thus making his case for Arthur as king and justifying the means that had led to that end.

Response: The Merlin was enough a true Druid to test his decision about Arthur as king. He would have devised many methods to confirm his beliefs, because he knew he couldn't afford to be wrong. When the test of pulling the sword from the stone confirmed his beliefs about Arthur, The Merlin most likely saw this means as part of the natural unfolding processes of life. However, he wouldn't have believed that ends justify the means. His Druidic philosophy would have been "change what one can; accept what one can't change; and make the best of it in either instance."

Accusation 15: The Merlin used Arthur's accomplishments to establish himself as Archdruid of all Britain for all time.

Response: The Merlin was far too private a person to want even the titles he already had. As many tales tell, he often went about in disguise, in part to empower his purpose, in part to ensure his privacy. Besides, if public power had been what he wanted, the Mage, Merlin, would not be a "withdrawn prophet" or "secret chief," as he is to us now.

Accusation 16: Arthur used Merlin to establish himself as the Celtic mythic king of all time.

Response: Arthur certainly would avail himself of The Merlin's wisdom and experience in order to manifest his kingly visions. However, Arthur had enough of Uther in him to be driven to create and maintain his own positions of power.

Accusation 17: Arthur abused the hallowed gifts, such as the sword of power and the cauldron he took from the Otherworld.

Response: While Arthur may have misused the Hallows from time to time, he did so because he was not of the mind to understand their power. We can see Arthur not so much as having the sword of power, but of being what that represented, and being the realization of a much higher purpose, the uniting of Britain. In regard to the cauldron that Arthur "brought back from the Underworld," as the legends relate, this still may have been understood and accepted, if he hadn't then neglected it.

This cauldron was symbolic of the healing wisdom of the lands, and of the queen as well, by its qualities of receptive nurturance. These qualities were not naturally Arthur's, and he could not relate to them well, nor did he have the time to do so. Perhaps Arthur wanted these qualities, both for himself and for his lands.

However, it would have been wiser to leave such Hallows in the hands of those whose service was more aligned with the qualities and powers the cauldron represented. When Arthur entered the realm of Faerie, it would have been enough to have connected with the Cauldron there and brought back its empowerment within himself. By removing the cauldron, Arthur took dominion over *that which holds its own dominion*. This was a mistake.

Accusation 18: Arthur refused to rescue Guinevere because she wasn't producing an heir.

Response: Arthur was a great king; but he was also a political man and a strategic warrior of legendary quality. His actions would have been determined on the basis of his first disciplines. Arthur was truly a warrior who became king—undoubtedly much to his own surprise. As man to woman, husband to wife, Arthur instinctively would have wanted to rescue Guinevere.

As a political man, he would have had to consider the costs of war on the people. As strategic warrior, he would have known his position was untenable, personally. Therefore, to challenge the situation outright would only have endangered the life of his queen and started war once again. Thus, Arthur had to act as a king, regardless of the consequences to himself.

In this, he made his greatest sacrifice of love for the sake of peace, honoring the responsibilities inherent in his position. Additionally, in matters of the Fey, such as the realms of Melwas were, Arthur knew he was out of his league. Guinevere was not a warrior queen; nor was she of the old ways. Had she been either or both, she would have been better able to understand Arthur's actions. However, it is doubtful she would have felt this had anything to do with her inability to produce an heir—this because any "barrenness guilt" was a medieval concept that came much later than the times of Arthur. Also, she knew Arthur already had an heir apparent or two. I can't imagine that Arthur even considered this when making his basically strategic decisions.

Accusation 19: The Merlin divined that Guinevere would be barren, but didn't tell this to anyone.

Response: The Merlin is unlikely to have concerned himself in "matters of women," such as the queen's ability to produce an heir. If anything, his visions would have shown there would be at least one heir. The Merlin certainly honored Nature in his own Druidic manner; but his true purpose had more to do with the evolution of humankind and human mind.

Accusation 20: The Merlin was experimenting and was only interested in the results in his lifetime.

Response: If The Merlin were experimenting, then the experiment continues still. In scientific fashion, he crafted a catalyst for alchemy which would activate in the time of Arthur and still possess its once and future effects.

Accusation 21: Avalon Fey sabotaged The Merlin in any way they could because he would not join or support them.

Response: It is quite likely the Avalon Fey and The Merlin viewed each other with respectful suspicion since their practices ran along different paths. The Merlin would have been, in Avalon's view, an unpredictable, independent operator with influential powers greater than their own in regard to the throne. Spiritually, I believe they would have agreed; but philosophically they would have differed about the needs for organized power and the role of the "church" and the state. Even though the Avalonian Fey would have felt unsure of their position as new religion came into the land, it is doubtful they generally intended to sabotage The Merlin.

However, we need to consider that Elaine of Garlot (originally of Cornwall) was at that time the "Mother Superior" of Avalon and called Vivienne. Morgana, also of Cornwall, was one of the highest Fey priestesses. Neither of them would have forgotten that The Merlin's actions were so closely connected to the death of their father, Gorlois, Duke of Cornwall. Nor would either of them have held the philosophy of the "Fates of battle." They were not warriors, but healers and structurers. We can also consider that Nentres of Garlot (husband of Vivienne/Elaine) was at that time the Rex Avallonis, or so we may surmise. Therefore, it becomes quite possible that Nentres and Vivienne could have had a plan of their own—with or without Morgana.

Accusation 22: Avalon Fey used Morgana to produce a child who could bring down Camelot.

Response: If those in power at Avalon at that time had such a plan, it would not have been supported by the Fey. Assuming Vivienne and Nentres had devised such a plan, it was foiled by Morgana, whom I see as arranging for Morgawse to bear Arthur's heir, the first time. This, I believe, produced Gawain. Morgawse, by her own design regarding Arthur, later lay with him and produced Mordred.

Accusation 23: Morgana seduced Arthur with the same purpose in mind because she held The Merlin responsible for her father's death (Duke of Cornwall), or out of jealousy of Arthur.

Response: While Morgana certainly would have had reasons not to love Arthur in any way, she was in service to the Sovereignty of the land. It is this concept, I believe, she hoped to honor by ritually reconnecting the king to the land, Arthur to Morgawse, as symbolically representative. In the old ways, in the Grand Rites manner, Morgana hoped to bring in the balance that she saw the queen unable to do.

Accusation 24: Avalon Fey arranged for Guinevere not to produce an heir:
   a. because they saw her Christianity as a direct threat
   b. because they wanted to ensure the "bastard" child would bring down Camelot
   c. because they were opposed to The Merlin's design to create a line of kings (to his credit)
   d. because they had a plan of their own to recreate the rulership of priest-Kings, exalting their own kind.

Response: Most of the Fey never would support such a destructive purpose as causing the queen's barrenness. This would be in direct opposition to their philosophy of alliance with the land, of which they believed the queen to be a representative. They would have supported an alternative representative, but not at the personal expense of their queen.

The queen's Christianity would have held no threat, but concern for the old alliance with Nature was surely in their minds. However, it would be more in keeping with elemental Nature of the Fey to be more concerned with the balance of Avalon, as they were with the balance of the lands. If balance of powers was anyone's concern, I assume it was that of Vivienne and Nentres. Remembering that power corrupts—and absolute power corrupts absolutely—it is far more likely that those in highest power at Avalon were behind any such plans to shift power to themselves in a time of shifting powers. Giving them all the benefit of the doubt, they may have had no dark intentions. However, destiny kept unfolding, and it may have done so beyond their grasp. Also, knowing that Avalon mirrors Camelot in mystic reflection, we're left to consider that both were eventually done in from within.

Accusation 25: The Lady of the Lake fostered Lancelot for the purpose of betraying the King with the Queen.

Response: If anything, Lancelot was fostered to provide for the needs of the queen, and therefore the lands. The Lady of the Lake at that time is clearly reflected as being of the Light. It was later that shadows were cast upon that title, perhaps when Vivienne (and Nentres) assumed that position. Originally, the Lady of the Lake was a constant source of gifts of truth, light, and power. I'm inclined to believe at that time it was Ganieda, whose subsequent retirement could well explain the failure of communication between Avalon and her Druidic brother, The Merlin.

Accusation 26: The Merlin knew of Lancelot's coming betrayal, but did not tell Arthur because:
    a. he was opposed also to Guinevere's Christianity
    b. he was opposed to Lancelot's same faith
    c. he wanted Arthur to "put away" Guinevere
    d. he wanted Arthur to marry his student, Nimue, and create a more Fey line for the throne of Britain

Response: The Merlin, once again, was far too wise to set himself up as saboteur of his own vision and design. Nor would he have opposed the personal faiths of anyone, even if he opposed those in control of structuring religious beliefs. Besides, at that time the Orthodox effects had not reached Britain, in the most part; thus Christianity would still have had the power and Light its tenets proclaimed. Essentially, the Druidic philosophy and that of Christianity were universally the same. This, one such as The Merlin was would have seen as a possibility for spiritual alliance. Indeed, there have been some arguments well made, suggesting that The Merlin was the historical St. Dubricius who crowned Arthur as king. He is still revered in Britain (and elsewhere) as a truly wonderful mage.

There is no indication that The Merlin opposed Guinevere in any manner, nor would he have thought it honorable for Arthur to "put her away." As long as The Merlin was present, Guinevere was present also. It was only after The Merlin withdrew that tales of Arthur's rejection of Guinevere, and those of her leaving Arthur, began to emerge.

In regard to Nimue, The Merlin was quite unlikely to share with someone else, even Arthur, what he could not—or would not—share with himself. As to a Fey line for the throne of Britain, it was already there. In Arthur, from Igraine, then in Gawain and Mordred, from Morgawse; and in Arthur's official heir, Cador, Duke of Cornwall, son of Igraine and Gorlois—the old blood was assured already.

Accusation 27: The Merlin chose Nimue to train because he wanted her to be a spear point in a new plan for Camelot.

Response: The Merlin chose Nimue, and she chose him, for the purpose of preserving the lines of mystical Celtic power to which we are still connecting. In the highest magick or metaphysical practice, The Merlin's new plan for Camelot was to encode its symbolic power for the once and future—and present-day Celts. The spear point was probably too sharp to use in connection with Nimue—at that time. Faerie bolt, or Faerie arrow is more in line with that aspect of Nimue.

Accusation 28: The Merlin was "sexist" and underestimated Nimue.

Response: This, I expect, is true—and quite understandably so—considering the times and the age differential. On the other hand, The Merlin chose Nimue because of her potential, so it isn't right to say he was sexist. However, he was surprised; not taken by surprise, as is commonly believed, but surprised nonetheless. In short, the Merlin was captivated, and thus ultimately "captured."

Accusation 29: Nimue played The Merlin like a puppet master would, in order to exalt her own position.

Response: Nimue's natural powers and her intellect, as well, still would be disturbing to many in our times. When the legends about her first emerged, her gifts were unfathomable to all but a few of the most wise. Acknowledging her powers in a back-handed complimentary fashion, her legends reveal her gifts through the veils of fear covering them. When we see this clearly, we have to wonder why Nimue was never portrayed as giving The Merlin a bite of her apple, which a serpent had advised her to pick from a tree in the garden. It is more in keeping with one such as Nimue to say that she planted the apple tree in the first place.

Accusation 30: Morgana played Merlin in the same way as above.

Response: It is quite possible that Morgana and The Merlin engaged in a fair amount of mutual manipulation. Both were gifted with profound intellect, and both were chauvinistic of their own kind. Still a deep respect must have existed also, plus a common bond of protecting the lands and the king (more so for The Merlin). It is Morgana who assumes the role of protector of Arthur in her realm, the Isle of Avalon, where she also now has assumed the title "Lady of the Lake."

Accusation 31: Morgana played Nimue to make her "murder" The Merlin, removing him with "enchantment."

Response: The death of a Mage is of vital importance and must be handled accordingly. If properly managed, the Mage may continue guiding from the realms of Spirit—only as he chooses. When The Merlin knew it was time to withdraw, he also knew he had helped prepare both Nimue and Morgana to help him do so in a manner that was proper for a Mage.

The Merlin trained Morgana in these skills, and he trained Nimue, as well. In turn, Morgana trained Nimue in skills taught her by The Merlin, and in her own skills, as well. These, plus Nimue's own natural powers, created a profound magick of superior quality which was required for the process. This, plus Nimue's heartfelt affection for The Merlin ensured that the process was done with Light and love.

Accusation 32: Morgana removed The Merlin by herself.

Response: By the time The Merlin was ready to withdraw, his connection with Morgana was not clear, but only on the mundane plane. Mystically and metaphysically, Morgana would have helped with this process, even if she couldn't be present physically. Rising above any petty differences, Morgana would have served this process honorably as high priestess of Avalon. Morgana would have provided the metaphysical connections, and Nimue the elemental power.

Accusation 33: The Merlin removed himself and let others take the blame.

Response: It is not in the Nature of a true Mage such as The Merlin ever to blame others or let them be blamed for actions either he alone, or they together, have taken. Consider that the tales of Morgana and Nimue are most interesting distractions, and then look at this in a Celtic way. The Fair Folk—whether warriors, healers, connectors, or illuminators—are all guardians elementally. Remembering this, then the legends of Morgana and Nimue become ones of guardianship.

The Merlin is guarded still by the Fey, as Arthur is guarded in Avalon—not under guard, but under protection. Particularly in the case of The Merlin, this provides more than both privacy and protection. Strategically speaking, the Fey form a defense line, a filter, through which only true allies of the Fair Folk may pass. Tactically, Nimue and Morgana provide diversionary actions that they well may have learned from that great Celtic warrior, the King of Logres, Arthur.

These archetypal characters and their relationships to one another represent the lines of power within and their effects upon each other and on our selves. All of these archetypal powers may be accessed, as long as it is done with the Right intentions. Access these neither offensively nor defensively, for you'll connect with them mirrored in opposition. As you imagine them, they will appear; so be sure your images are genuine—reflecting truth and light in a manner that is right for you.

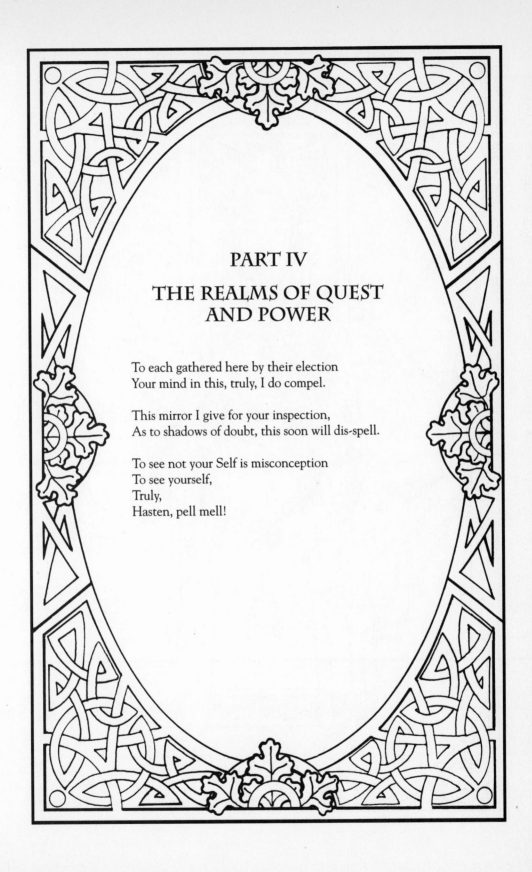

PART IV

THE REALMS OF QUEST
AND POWER

To each gathered here by their election
Your mind in this, truly, I do compel.

This mirror I give for your inspection,
As to shadows of doubt, this soon will dis-spell.

To see not your Self is misconception
To see yourself,
Truly,
Hasten, pell mell!

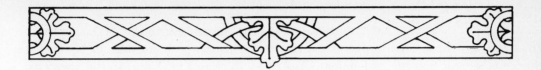

CHAPTER 18

QUESTS FOR THE HOLY GRAIL: THE SYMBOLS OF PURITY AND POWER

However well intentioned the individual human being may be in his formulation and attempted implementation of the plans of his own will, they will be in conflict with the individual plans of others. Unbeknown to himself, mankind's dual spiritual nature has become the agent of conflicting spiritual forces that will work their way out in accordance with laws far beyond his own comprehension or visionary scope.

Gareth Knight
The Secret Tradition

 The initiating event leading to the Grail quests is the wounding of the Fisher King, symbolic of the active powers of the realm of Logres. In the legends of Camelot, this wounding is represented in several symbolic versions. Most significant of these is the relationship of Guinevere and Lancelot which wounds King Arthur. In that the King is divided from the Queen, the active force is divided from the Sovereignty of the Lands. In some versions, this misuse of power is represented as being intentional, such as the portrayal of Mordred, son of Arthur, being evil and deliberately malicious, rather than himself being an unwitting pawn in a greater game of destiny.

However, the most symbolically complete version of the wounding legend is presented in the story of Balyn and Balan from the Vulgate Cycle (c. 1200–1230) of Arthurian literature. This version, wherein Balyn wounds the king and therefore the Lands, was devised to explain the sacrifice of Christ and the doctrine of redemption from the tenets of the Christian faith. It was also an attempt to blend the ancient Celtic versions of the self-sacrifice of the King who died in order to bring nurturance

191

to the tribe and restoration to the lands. In turn, this ancient version of the myth represented the relationship of the solar cycle with the growth cycles of Nature. In essence, for example, at Lammas (August 1), the Sun King "dies" so the Sovereign Queen (the lands) may be protected and preserved during the dark, fallow times of winter, and return productively in the spring. At the same time, the Sun King is reborn in midwinter, and this growing active force, in concert with Nature, produces the miracle of rebirth or restoration.

THE QUEST REVEALED

The legends of the Grail quests have their origin in ancient Celtic cauldron myths: the symbolic restorative cauldrons of Cerridwen and Bran, as well as the eternally replenishing cauldron of Dagda, and, in essence, the Faerie gift of the cup or chalice. The later legends in Arthurian literature that proclaim the origin of the Grail in Britain to be the work of Joseph of Arimathea need not be confirmed historically. These may be seen to symbolize the arrival of the first true light of Christian faith, rather than that of the actual personage. Joseph of Arimathea was the historical and biblical figure who donated his own tomb in the Garden of Gethsemane for the burial of the Galilean. He was also reputed to have caught the blood of the crucified Christ in that most holy vessel, the Grail, (san Greal). This sacred blood, (sang real), symbolizes the Light of purest truth found in the Christian doctrines, particularly before the times of Orthodox structures and political separations. Other legends tell of Joseph of Arimethea's wooden staff blossoming the instant it touched the soil of Britain.

Because of the holy nature the Grail represents, this is a realm of the Camelot legends that needs to be most personally accessed in accordance with individual spiritual philosophies and the tenets of our chosen faith.

Although history and myth give numerous accounts of Grail quests made on the external or mundane planes of life, the true quest is internal, mystical, and most purely personal. The Grail may be seen as "that which is attained and realized by people who have lived their own Authentic lives." This is how Joseph Campbell expressed the sacred power of following personally genuine paths of choice in our lives. The Wasteland and the desolation of the Arthurian legends may thus be seen as the converse, or the living of our lives in an "inauthentic" manner. Grail quests are quests for sacred personal synthesis.

The Grail—in expanded definition, the Holy Grail—symbolizes "the fulfillment of the highest potentialities of the human consciousness." The "divine power operative within oneself" is the Grail within. It is also the incomparable power that emerges from an enlightened, authentic relationship between the mundane and mystical in our lives. We are the questors and the quest. We are the guardians of the grail and the sacred activators of its powers. We are each sacred vessels for the source of healing and restoration of our own lives and, in turn, for the lives of others. Together, we can be the restorative source for the life of our lands.

If this seems to be an overwhelming concept, change the word "Grail" to "Grace." This is as in the Grace of God, Saved by Grace, Amazing Grace or Mother of Grace. It is by that self-same grace that we are able to explore the realms of the Grail quests from a perspective revealing its personal meaning for us in our own lives as spiritual beings. Grace is one of my most special names for The White Goddess — and must be used with an earnest acknowledgement of the grace involved. The quests we make in modern times, as those described in the legends, must be made for the potential good of all. Quests made only for reasons of ego and personal glory will invariably fail in time. Quests for personal evolution into service made for the greater good of the All will invariably succeed.

The Grail is our symbolic bridge to the Divine. Our personal beliefs determine whether this bridge is solid enough to support our quests within. It is our intentions that determine the nature, or the forms, in which these quests manifest in our lives. These quests within sometimes appear to be like the sharp edge of the sword that Lancelot legendarily had to cross on his knees. When we quest, we can remember the wisdom of being at the center of the blade, or at the center of the hilt. This brings us the balance we need when we determine the causes and the actions of our personal life quests.

Archetypal Figures of the Grail Quests

In the Camelot legends, five primary knights are presented as the questors for the Grail: Lancelot, Gawain, Perceval, Bors, and Galahad. In these quests, Lancelot fails because his love for Guinevere is greater than his devotion to his spiritual duties. This leads him to seek the Grail to achieve fame that will please the queen, rather than appease Spirit.

Gawain also fails in his quest for the Grail because he is too worldly and too impatient. His weakness is also being the warrior that he is, with a natural, external outlook of guardianship. Had Gawain's involvement in the futile efforts to save Camelot and Arthur from their destiny not caused his death, he could well have attained the Grail because of his great heart and good intentions. Lancelot, however, represents a most spiritually self-critical type who would find it extremely difficult to forgive himself. Therefore, he is unable to receive from the very source that was, and is, unconditionally available within.

The three knights who do attain the Grail in these legends are Perceval, Bors, and Galahad. Perceval is the wise innocent, or the pure fool, who continues to initiate new quests within. These quests succeed eventually, due to the spirit of perseverance and the good-hearted intentions in which they are made. Bors is the ordinary man, who finds the Grail within that which is close always, ever present in the everyday life, led with and by Grace.

Galahad is the pure knight who attains the Grail; but in so doing surrenders his connection to mundane life. Galahad's quest represents a sacrifice by transmutation into the realms of the intangible Divine. These realms of the mystical Divine may be best understood as the Light of the afterlife or Otherworld, to which Galahad may be seen as a connecting archetypal symbol. In this legend, which was a later medieval version, Galahad is a symbolic restatement of the life of the Galilean as the only path to perfection and to heaven. This is as it was intended to be by the monks who created the myth of Galahad, in order to convey a spiritually idealized and symbolic message. However, this also became Orthodoxically misrepresented, and created an image that could not be accomplished humanly.

In a more current transmutation, Galahad may be seen as a divine guardian of the Grail within, rather than an impossible figure to emulate. He need not be imagined as one whose legend has been falsely presented in a way that could inspire an ultimately self-defeating quest. That sort of quest is not in keeping with what the Grail and the quests represent for us as spiritually evolved humans. If we remember that we are not humans being spiritual, but spirits being human, we can draw from all of the versions of the Grail quest legends a most sacred truth with personal meaning for our own lives.

In the legends of the Grail quests, there are also three primary symbols of the Divine Feminine. There is the symbolic, nurturing aspect of the grail itself, as martyr and quest catalyst, which is the figure of Dindraine, Perceval's sister. There is also a guardian maiden of the grail castle, Elaine of Carbonek, daughter of the Fisher King, Pelles, wife of Lancelot, and the mother of Galahad. There is, most significantly, the Grail itself, purest symbol of the Feminine Divine, source of healing.

If we pause here to examine what the archetypal figures represent for us, we can begin to deepen our understanding of what the quest itself reveals. In order to do this, we may first assign elemental aspects to the five male knights, and with somewhat more spiritual aspects, to the two female Grail guardians. These figures represent those types who have symbolically attained the Grail in their own way and are, therefore, clear, archetypal catalysts for our own quests. By personally reclaiming the spirit and heart of the messages these legendary figures present to us, we can avoid responding to any of the manipulative ones that were overlaid for any politically and orthodoxically motivated purposes. A quest, most truly, must be made on *that path where there was no path before.*

Elemental Correlations for Grail Quest Figures

Lancelot—as Water, represents the aspects of emotion and of devotion to the Divine seen within another, as shown in the themes of Courtly Love. Lancelot brings compassion and devotion.

Gawain—as Fire, represents the aspects of physical guardianship and protection of the lands and environment seen as the natural source of the divine as the sovereign ally and life force. Gawain brings courage and loyalty.

Perceval—as Air, represents the aspects of illuminated mind change inspired by purposes of Divine evolution of consciousness, ideas, and expanded potentials. Perceval brings perception and progress.

Bors—as Earth, represents the aspects of ordered existence according to codes of honor brought into divine application in the structured balance of the mundane and the mystical. Bors "brings home the bacon" with stability and endurance.

Galahad—as Spirit, represents the aspects of the highest light of all the others in elemental synthesis. He symbolizes the intangible medium which is both catalyst and connection for the highest ideals of emotional devotion, protective guardianship, illuminative inspiration, and honorable structures. Galahad brings forth the heavenly host, the highest angelic realm.

Dindraine—as a primary blend of Air, Fire, Water, and Earth, represents the conscious choice to provide the structures for compassionate physical nurturance. She symbolizes the necessary mundane resources to ensure the continuation of the quest, and the attainment of the Grail within. Dindraine, like Bors, brings mercy and enduring nurturance.

Elaine of Carbonek—as a symbolic synthesis of all the primary elements, with spirit added in an amplified aspect, represents the feminine as the sacred vessel as well as the keeper of the vessel itself. As such, Elaine is a more mystical archetypal version of what Dindraine represents in a mundane way. Both provide for the quest and the questors, and serve the Grail as the manifest form of the Grail itself. Both are sacred vessels of restoration on the quest. Elaine of Carbonek brings the magick catalyst of motivation, and the guidance of the Goddess of the Lands.

Another way we may view these figures is by correlating them to traditional energy points for an in-depth archetypal source which brings holistic Body/Mind/Spirit empowerment.

Energy Point Correlations for Grail Quest Figures

Gawain—as Red, or root energy point, provides for the more primal aspects of life force, protection, and essential empowerment. Gawain brings self-security and love.

Dindraine—as Orange, or sacral energy point, provides for the needed vitality, self-control, and good health required for the quests and for life itself. Dindraine brings self-nuturance and physical power.

Perceval—as Yellow, or solar energy point, provides for the activating catalyst of intellectual mind focus, organized thought, and inspiration which keeps positive intentions and clear perceptions in conscious balance. Perceval brings self-understanding and personal acceptance.

Bors—as Green, or heart energy point, provides the compassion and love from which we may expand our quests from within the center of our selves to share our positive kinship with the sacred with others in our life. Bors brings self-direction, self-discipline and a sense of purpose.

Lancelot—as Blue, or throat energy point, provides the devotion and the will with which we may pursue and express our own sacred, spiritual quests within the lives we lead, honorably. Lancelot brings us self-esteem and perseverence.

Elaine—as Indigo, or brow energy point, provides the means by which we may gather the benefits of our quests into a form that brings the synthesis of Body (Red), Mind (Yellow), and Spirit (Blue) into a relationship that forms a primary foundation of harmony within. This is further balanced by our efforts at transmuting (Black) that which we need to release, and transmitting (White) that which we need to receive in renewal. Formulation: Red + Yellow + Blue + Black + White = Indigo = Synthesis. Elaine brings self-evolution and the power of personal choice.

Galahad—as Violet, or crown energy point, provides the connection, or the alliance between self and Self, the channel between the tangible and intangible realms of our spiritual quests. Galahad brings self-determination for services of the highest orders of Light.

With these systems of correlations, we can begin to develop a clearer connection to what each of these archetypal figures represents in our lives as we quest for the grail within. Added to this, yet implicitly and eternally present, is the Grail itself, the Divine source of restoration and renewal. If we wish to include the Grail Divine in our previous systems, we can say the Grail is the spiritual synthesis found at the center of the circle, around the circle itself, and, most sacred, is the Circle encircling. Thus we can craft our personal ceremonies and circles, knowing that the power of the Grail is pervasive.

In relation to the energy points, the Grail also relates to the higher lights and energies. We classify these to be: rainbow, crystal, spirit, silver, gold, and platinum. Thus it provides order, amplification, exaltation, receptivity, activation, and multidimensionally restorative healing power.

The Grail as a medium of renewal also relates to the white light and, as a means of positive spiritual release, to the black light.

EXPLORING THE REALMS OF THE GRAIL QUEST LEGENDS

From a rather draconian perspective we can say the Grail legends portray a tale of disillusioned searching. In effect, the Grail knights quested, found the Grail, yet lost Camelot in any case. Yet in a more evolutionarily inspired Light, we can see the Grail as being clearly attainable, and its restorative powers as being consciously applicable. This is a Right of Service of all those who quest for the Grail within, pure-heartedly, for purposes that are for the good of all.

Patterns of the Grail Quests

The various versions of the Grail quest legends follow a similar format. This describes the processes by which a questing hero knight comes upon a mysterious castle which is the home of a wounded king. There the hero is served a magnificent feast during which he sees both a magick, and sometimes broken, sword and a bloody spear. At some time during the feast, or later in his stay at the castle, the knight glimpses the Grail or has it brought to him by a beautiful maiden, often the daughter of the wounded king. When he encounters the grail, the knight has the chance either to ask, or sometimes answer, a most important question. The question, or the answer, presented in the mystically most appropriate form, will then reveal the true power of the Grail. This Grail revealed will then result in the restoration of the Wasteland which had been created by a dolorous stroke. If inappropriately presented, the question, or the answer, will result in the disappearance of the Grail and the creation of a Wasteland. Where there had been abundance, there would be wounds and deprivation on the lands, the people, and the leaders.

These basics also reveal the following:

- The pattern of personal inner quests for restoration of power and healing.

- The castle symbolizes the strongly structured bastion of our personality in relationship to the environment in which we live.

- The wounded king symbolizes the obstacles (often self-created) that prevent us from taking productive charge of our own lives.

- The feast symbolizes the presence of abundant nurturing resources within ourselves and our lives.

- The sword is our strength, will, and self-esteem.

- The spear is our ability to communicate with others, and within ourselves, with perceptive awareness and illuminated inspiration.

- The maiden represents our receptive abilities that must be activated in balanced reflection in order to receive from that internal source of power and healing, the Grail.

- The question (and the answer) both symbolize our ability to access and activate self-reflection and self-renewal.

- The Wasteland symbolizes the disconnection of Self that results from self-rejecting or self-wounding attitudes about ourselves.

- The restoration symbolizes the Divine nurturance attained when we are able to connect with the healing life force and current of positive self-creation in our lives.

- The questor hero naturally symbolizes our own efforts at positive self-illumination and self-evolution which, in turn, results in the sharing of illuminative evolution in our lives, and in all life.

These symbolic representations of ourselves and our processes of personal questing may also be given:

- Elemental correlations that reveal the 'round of their significance.

- The castle and the feast may be correlated with the structures of self and the production of our own needed resources.

- The spear and the questioning process relate to the element of Air, with its aspects of perceptive communication.

- The sword and the king correlate with the element of Fire and its aspects of self-determination and activation.

- The Grail maiden relates to the element of Water and its aspects of intuitive self-renewal. The Grail reflects both the element and the realm of Spirit, with its restorative potentials and healing resources.

- The Wasteland and the restored land reflect the spirit aspects that we may either accept or reject, reflectively presented in the choices we make about ourselves and our lives.

Although each of these symbols rather alchemically contain aspects of all the elements, those presented in correlation here may help form a productive connection to the archetypal forces each represents for and within our quests for self-restoration.

If we pause for a moment in our exploration of these legends, we can reflect upon these symbols' meanings for our personal life quests. We can do this using a theme taken from the Grail quests. We use the process by which we learn to ask and to answer questions that are significant for our own Self-quests.

THE ELEMENTAL QUESTIONS FOR
SELF-RESTORATIONAL PROCESSES
An Exercise with Symbolic Cues

Castle: By actively imaging our own Grail castle, we are reflecting a representation of our own structures of self and personality. Thus, we may ask ourselves these questions:

Is my structure solid enough to weather the transformational patterns or the changes of life's tides? Is it flexible? Foundationally adequate? Overbuilt for purposes of exalted ego? Underbuilt because of ego deficits? Is it me? Is it home, adjustable to the changes around and within myself?

Feast: In much the same way as we processed the symbol of the grail castle, we ask these questions about the feast which represents our relationship with abundance, growth, and nurturance.

Is the table I set for myself adequate in relation to the efforts I make to keep it supplied? Is it wastefully abundant? Is it impoverished due to my own wasteful actions—or my relationship with the wasteful actions of others? Is the feast a fair reflection of my efforts to share with myself and with others? Is it ample and honorably balanced in true alignment with the natural flow and ebb of events and of prosperity?

Spear: The spear, often represented with blood dripping from its point, gives us an image of our own goals and efforts at finding the purpose of our life quests. Thus, we may ask:

Is my ability to communicate with myself, and with others, one which reflects a process of focused perception and well-considered thoughts in regard to the outcome and consequences of my ideas, when activated? What is it costing me in essential life energies in order to get my point across? To myself? To others? Am I perceptive to the winds of change that influence my thoughts and my aims?

Sword: The sword, often shown as being broken, symbolizes our relationship with the activation of personal power. Thus, we may ask:

Is the power I seek more than I can wield? Have I the strength and self-discipline to wield power wisely and well? Is my purpose protective or aggressive? Is my guardianship guided by negative or unresolved needs? Or well-intended purposes that will provide for positive resolution? Will my use of power make me more a part of the problem or a part of the solution? Am I fueled by flames of healthy desire and the divine fires of highest motivations? Is my life a worthy flame?

King: The wounded king represents the all-too-human processes of self-defeating actions and reactions. Thus, we may ask:

Am I truly the responsible, activating force in my own life? Am I motivated by positively empowering forces of will or by negatively debilitating personal weaknesses? Have I granted myself the privilege of self-determination? Have I earned this privilege by my own efforts of Right action? Does my need for power flame more fiercely when fueled by rage or by reason? Have I the ability to be responsible and fair? Can

199

my roles of leadership, whether of self alone or of others, be guided by the bright blue flame of personal honor and balance?

Grail Maiden: This maiden represents the beauty and the power of the gifts of receptive self-renewal. Thus, we may ask:

Am I as receptive to the gentle gifts of power as I am to the more forceful ones? Am I able to be continually receptive to beauty in all of life? Even when it does not appear directly on the surface? Even when it outshines everything in a distracting manner? Am I able to distinguish between passivity and receptivity? Am I emotionally gentle with myself? With others? Am I intuitive to the cycles of self-renewal? Am I accepting of that which is veiled in mists about myself before I quest within to find it? Can I accept, with ruthless compassion, that which I find? Am I able to release rather than reject? Myself? Others? The processes of life? Am I able to maintain translucent healing veils which help me manage the processes of self-renewal rather than masking them from myself? Am I able to feel grateful for the gifts of inner knowing?

The Grail: The Grail symbolizes the highest aspect of divine healing and restorative power. Thus, we may ask: Is my life as much a reflection of the synthesis of spirit as I can humanly make it? Am I both receptive and active in my relationship to Spirit? Does my life reflect the Light of Spirit? The restorative qualities of power? The Grace of a pure heart?

Before continuing our exploration of the Grail quest legends, here is a brief imagery "starter" to help you develop your connection with the Grail Gifts of power and healing. After this imagery is a list of healing correlations to help your self-restorative quests. Illuminate both imagery and exercise to make them reflect your experience. Enlighten your grail quest with personal or shared ceremonial communions.

COMMUNION
An Experiential Imagery "Starter"

Breathe, release, and be receptive to the Divine Grace within.

––––––

You find yourself within a wonderful, mystical castle which is the home of a wise old king. Although this king has seen much of the battles of life, his eyes shine with an illuminated spirit that brings healing to all the wounds that he, yourself, and the world have suffered. The king invites you to share a feast at a table laden with the ample fruits of a good harvest. All that you require and desire is present in balanced proportion at the feast table, so you gratefully accept what is provided for you.

Above the table hangs a great sword of power which, if ever broken, has the ability to mend itself. This sword is crafted of a mystically fine metal which can meet all tests as they come. Beside your chair is a Fey-crafted spear with feathers tied to its shaft with braided fibers, which bring strength, perception, and aim. The spear point is sharp and clean, clear as crystal shining in the light. At first sight, you believe you see traces of the blood that had dripped down the shaft in ages past. Upon a closer look, you find these traces are no more, or less, than a natural part of the grain. You see that this spear's shaft is crafted from the fine-grained wood of the Tree of Wisdom which grows eternally in the illuminated garden of Spirit.

As you finish sharing the feast with the king, a beautiful maiden appears, carrying a silver tray with an object upon it covered in a pure white cloth. She tells you she may reveal what is veiled by the fine white fabric if you are able to pose the proper question which will spur your higher quest. After but a brief reflection, you realize the question, in whatever form you craft it, must ask what purpose it is you are graced to serve with honor and purity of heart.

Upon hearing your question, appropriately expressed in relation to your own life purpose, the maiden lifts the white cloth to reveal the Grail, shining with the highest lights of Spirit. The Grail maiden tells you that you may drink from the Grail whenever you choose to do so; but that its power is most purely amplified if you truly know for whom that healing power exists. In spontaneous reflection of the Light of Truth, you reply that the power is for all—for the All and from the All, divinely in synthesis.

As soon as your truth is expressed, you are cleared to receive from the Grail. As you drink from it, you feel that which is divinely within flow into the center of yourself, and from that center outward into all aspects of your being. You are aware of the shining circle of lights reflecting all around the rim and within the bowl of the Grail. You watch as those lights crystallize into circles encircling the circles of light. These are divinely expressed and experienced in all centers of self reflecting in eternally expanding power and Light. Then you know you have been graced with a divine communion of Self and Spirit. This communion is most naturally gifted to you by Right.

Receive.
Accept.
Release with Gratitude.
Renew.

Take a moment to "file" your personal impressions of the very brief version. Remember, you may create as simple or as elaborate an imagery as you want. I have only given you a "starter." By now, you know how to expand your experience in imagery to create the positive, healing effects that are required or requested.

Healing Symbols from the Grail Legends

These "start-up" correlations for imagery activation are symbols that may be imaged in your own choice of form and vision to use for focusing their particular archetypal powers. You may use these to strengthen the energy points of Body and Mind, with illuminated Spirit, in whatever order you require or have requested.

Castle: Green, heart energy point—focus for empowering the positive, flexible structures of your personality and the relationship of yourself—with Self—and with others.

Feast: Orange, sacral energy point—focus for empowering yourself with positive, healthful vitality and a creative relationship with the processes of your own life—as well as with the lives of others.

Spear: Yellow, solar energy point—focus for empowering your skills at communicating, perceptively and wisely, and for the illuminative catalyst of clear-minded inspiration and positive thought processes.

Sword: Red, root energy point—focus for empowering yourself with essential life force, self-disciplined will, positive self-esteem, and a reflectively balanced, healthful, self-protecting style of life.

King: Blue, throat energy point—focus for empowering your own life as an expression of honorable self-leadership and positive will with a devotional gratitude for all that life's experiences bring to your quests.

Grail Maiden: Indigo, brow energy point—focus for empowering personal synthesis in your life and the reflective balance of being both receptive to the questions and an active part of seeking the answers that arise in life's quests.

Grail: Violet, crown energy point—focus for empowering your personal, sacred connection to the realms of Spirit and the healing, restorative power within the All.

This chapter has explored the Grail quests from its more modern form. However, the tales of the Grail quests had their origins in much more ancient materials taken from the Celtic oral traditions. From these older forms, the Grail legends took on symbolic forms with significance for the transitional period when that which was Pagan blended into that which was Christian.

In the grail legends, we can see the emergence of what may be called Celtic Christianity, a far more independent, Nature-reverential form with a greater application for Western European culture. We will discuss this process in the next chapter. For now, I suggest that you spend time strengthening your images of the healing symbols from the Grail legends, and incorporating them into your personal, ceremonial practices.

CHAPTER 19

THE CELTIC QUESTS REVEALED: PAGAN INTO CELTIC CHRISTIAN

I'm a heathen, and a pagan,
on the side of the rebel, Jesus.

Derek Bell — The Chieftains
from *The Bells of Dublin*)

 The Celtic Grail quest legends emerge in identifiable form from Irish and Welsh mythologies and oral traditions wherein the questors visit Otherworld realms, encountering many mysterious beings and supernatural marvels. These original Celtic tales of the Quest give accounts of great feasts that connect directly with the Celtic cauldrons of plenty, sometimes seen in other forms such as platters, cups, or bowls which are constantly self-replenishing in Nature. An example of this is the platter of Rhydderch the Generous, which would provide whatever was desired by the questor.

Other cauldron/Grail-aspected vessels appear in the story of "Culwech and Olwen" from *The Mabinogion*. Four such vessels are brought to Culwech's wedding feast: the cup with the best of all drink, the platter with the best of all meat, the horn always filled with ale, and the cauldron which boils food for the brave. The latter vessel, the cauldron, was taken from the Otherworld (Underworld aspects) by Arthur and his knights, in the tale "The Spoils of Annwn." This vessel retrieval during an Otherworld, or shamanic, quest symbolizes the rite by which the chieftain or king takes on the right of power.

Before "Culwech and Olwen," there were tales of the Cauldron of Bran the Blessed, a Welsh Brythonic paternal deity who is similar to Dagda, the "good god" of the Irish, Gaelic Celts. Bran has several aspects which link him more significantly with the Fisher King in the Grail legends. Bran's cauldron also has a more directly restorative quality like the Grail. Bran's cauldron was reputed to be able to restore life to worthy warriors; but it was not, interestingly, able to restore the power of speech. This is very like Biblical tales of those who glimpsed heaven but were unable to speak of what they had seen. Both the Biblical versions and those of Bran's cauldron are tales that relate the difficulty, and sometimes inability, of humankind to adequately describe the Great Mystery or their experience of the most high realms of the Universal Divine.

In naturally expressive Celtic fashion, however, Bran is presented as an oracular and protective link to the Divine. Like the Fisher King, Bran is wounded: Bran most frequently by a poisoned spear in the foot, and the Fisher King often by a poisoned lance through the groin. The Fisher King becomes the keeper of the grail castle. Bran becomes the overseer and keeper of the prophecies of Logres. Bran's head is taken to a castle by his faithful followers who stay with him (or his head, at least) for eighty years. Although this eighty-year time period relates to a lifespan, none of the followers age at all while they are at Bran's castle. This symbolizes the power of the Divine as being beyond the limitations of other dimensions in time and space. Its experience is eternal.

Later versions of the Grail quest legends have Gawain at the castle of the Fisher King feasting with knights who are over a hundred years old, yet appear to be only about forty. Other legends in the Arthurian literature present examples of this timeless dimension of the Otherworld experience in such a way that the realm itself becomes restorative in quality. In other words, the realm of the Otherworld, or mystical experience, "contains" the restorative powers found symbolically in the Grail.

Most famous among these is the tale of Thomas the Rhymer, who encountered King Arthur and his Round Table Knights in a "sacred Faerie mound." There, Rhymer found that the King and the Knights were all young, fresh, and ready to provide restorative service when called upon. This is a legendarily appropriate description of the mythically restorative qualities of these archetypal figures as they exist eternally in the mystical realms. They are ever at the ready for us to access and activate the powers they reflect within our selves.

The question and answer theme in the Grail quests can be linked to the Irish myth of Conn of the Hundred Battles. In this ancient tale, Conn visits Lugh, the dé Danann Celtic Lord of Light at the Otherworld Hall of the Sun. There, Conn encounters a beautiful maiden who offers him a drink from a magickal gold and silver cup if he can answer the question: "To whom shall this cup be offered?" Conn replies, in classic Celtic warrior chieftain fashion, that the cup shall be offered to serve him, Conn of the Hundred Battles.

The maiden repeats the question and Conn repeats his answer, time and time again. As this is going on, Lugh begins to name all the descendants of Conn who will be chieftains in Ireland down through the ages after Conn has passed on. This continues until

Conn tires of the process and simply takes the cup from the maiden. As soon as Conn does this, the hall, the maiden, the cup, and Lugh all vanish; but those named are said indeed to have become rulers in Ireland long after Conn's time.

Although this version was undoubtedly devised to grant credence of lineage to Conn's line of descent and right of kingship, it does present an interesting question that remains today: That is, how could it have happened that Ireland remained unconquered and under the rulership of their own Celtic kings for a thousand years longer than Britain? It may be only a mythic representation to some; but it's another of the marvelous Celtic mythic mysteries to many others, another part of the Great Mystery in relation to the ancient Celts and the lands on (or in) which they lived. We are free to wonder what a few more rounds of the question and answer process between the maiden and Conn might have done in light of what Ireland eventually came to endure, but, of course, there might not be as many Irish Gaelic Celts on the global lands now. Perhaps it is the weavers on the web that these tales are seeking to explain, with divine implication and honor for the design that is ultimately Divine.

There is a later version in which Gawain does ask a question about the spear dripping blood which he sees at the Grail castle. However, having been well fed and we are led to believe "well serviced" by the beautiful maiden, Gawain is unable to stay awake long enough to hear the answer to his question. Later, Gawain is told how important it would have been to his life and to the lands if only he had not been so vulnerable to the worldly distractions. This was one of the many versions that brought in judgmental overlays and orthodox messages for political purposes. These were designed to undercut an essentially natural, ancient Celtic spiritual mythology which reflected the sacred restorative alliance between humankind and Spirit.

Using the often "inconveniently Pagan" forms and a more ancient Celtic perspective, the symbols managed to retain their naturally powerful meanings under fire. For example, the spear dripping blood was seen to be symbolic of the solar male, procreative life force. This force should, by rights, be put back into the sacred vessel, the Earth female, creational womb. This, in turn, reflected the solar rays piercing the lands with energy and light for the processes of growth, a time-honored, balanced alliance of Nature and Nature's God. These symbolic representations showed a balanced reverence for both the male/active and female/receptive aspects of Spirit, Nature, and self-nature.

The beautiful grail maiden was also an aspect of the ancient Celtic Goddess. This was far too Pagan, Celtic, and Western European for some of those whose primary intention was the control of the Celtic lands and their rulers. Therefore, even the Grail maiden became debased in some of the medieval versions. Elaine of Carbonek, by rights the true wife of Lancelot, was portrayed as having tricked him by disguising herself as Guinevere. This she was said to have done in order to deceive the only knight pure and perfect enough to attain the Grail completely. In more natural Celtic terms, Lancelot and Elaine, in Grand Rites, were united for the Lands; bringing forth a restorer, the perfect Galahad.

However, although the union of Elaine and Lancelot does legendarily produce this knight, Galahad, neither parent is shown as having been redeemed in any way. Elaine of Carbonek is depicted as having remained at the grail castle with its still wounded king, her father, and its ever more depleted Wasteland surrounding it all. Lancelot is said to have returned to Elaine of Carbonek only after many years. Before that, he had remained in sequestered penance, as had Guinevere, following the death of Arthur and the downfall of Camelot. When—and only when—Guinevere died, was Lancelot able to return to Elaine of Carbonek, at least in some versions. In other versions, Lancelot dies soon after Guinevere, without ever finding any source of redemption to restore his soul. This, of course, was a debased form, which reflected none of the Light it claimed to be serving.

Even though the Galahad stories, which we will explore next, were invented for propaganda purposes, there was still an ancient myth woven within them. Galahad, the young son, overpowers Lancelot, the old son, once thought to be the most perfect knight of the Round Table. Thus the new Sun, old Sun Pagan solar cycle mythos underlaid these versions. Furthermore, when Lancelot, who has failed to do more than glimpse the Grail, sees that Galahad not only succeeds, but transmutes into Spirit in the process, he returns to Guinevere once more!

Although the grail had been attained purely by the purest knight, Galahad, the promised restoration had not been forthcoming, nor forthright in its "bargain" with the quest knights. Indeed, the very vessel, and the symbolic gifts of the sword, spear, feast table, and all possible means for restoration had been legendarily removed from Logres. Rather than acknowledge the dogmatic philosophy that proclaimed the debased nature of humankind, Lancelot returned, quite humanly, to his true love—the Sovereign queen of the lands.

Again, as with many of the versions of these legends, it is difficult to say what was or was not either overlaid or undercut with conscious intentions, particularly in regard to the more ancient Celtic spiritual philosophies. However, the return of Lancelot to Guinevere remains one of the most lasting messages of Courtly Love. In another more primal sense, these legends may also show the dawning realization by some, either consciously or unconsciously, that true damage was being done, had already been done, and was sure to follow if the separation from Nature continued.

THE ECLIPSED LIGHT REVEALED: GALAHAD

The image of Galahad extolled the Christian virtues of knighthood which were: chastity, humility, patience, justice, and charity. The virtues of justice and charity were already traditionally valued, as was patience, to some degree. As a rule, neither chastity nor humility were a traditional Celtic virtue—particularly humility. However, all of these virtues in balanced proportion did form the basis for what are still considered chivalrous and even courtly behaviors in current times.

In medieval times, these virtues and the legend of Galahad became a strong influence on the development of the orders of the Knights Templar. In his legendary quest for the Grail, Galahad is shown encountering an order of sequestered monks dressed in white. These holy monks have a shield which will be harmful to anyone who does not possess these virtues in the highest possible degree of perfection. This shield was meant only for "the one most perfect knight in all Christendom," Galahad himself. The shield, as all Templar shields and armor, bore a red cross on a pure white background. This was the cross of the true rose of strength, fire, and the Holy Ghost on a field of purity.

Religious orders, in particular the Knightly ones such as the Templars, became increasingly more exclusive and inwardly focused. Eventually, some of this exclusivity became the undoing of the Knights Templar. Their piety, as well as their amassed fortunes, brought them, literally, under fire from the Spanish Inquisition in the thirteenth and fourteenth centuries. However, the Templar's legacies still remain in their truest Light forms in orders that extol the more balanced powers of the Rose Cross of the Holy Spirit; with a little help from St. Luke, which is naturally healing.

The purpose of the Galahad legends was to show how much more spiritual and superior the orthodox versions of the Christian codes were than those of the brightly emerging philosophies of Courtly Love and the codes of Chivalry. These were in conflict during the time period when the Crusades had begun to wind down in the early part of the thirteenth century. A number of the Crusade knights had settled in the Middle East, often because the laws of primogeniture prevented all but the firstborn son from inheriting wealth and lands. Still others had profited greatly from their crusades and were anxious to exercise their power and their rights of wealth. These were the new aristocrats of Western Europe, and they had seen far too much while away from home to easily succumb to the control of an organized Eastern structure.

At that time, Britain was beginning to reclaim her British/Celtic heritage, for the Norman influence was on the wane. Additionally, the people were beginning to assert themselves, making a valid and valiant effort to emerge from a feudal state. This we know historically in Britain as the time of the Magna Carta, which heralded the demise of royal, dictatorial control over all in their realms. There were also Normans in Britain who were becoming British, or Celticized in their philosophy. Since the Normans were originally of a Northern and Western European Celtic heritage, this was an already sufficiently encoded view of Nature and the lands. Naturally, it may also be said that the lands themselves were a significant influence—as they eternally are.

The concepts of Chivalry and Courtly Love were a way to reestablish the Celtic codes and alliances with Nature—and, because this is still inseparable—with the female/receptive and nurturing aspects of humankind. Although on the surface this seemed to deal with the rights of women, it was far deeper in Nature than that. Remember that the alliance reverenced in the Celtic spiritual philosophies of Nature was an inclusive, balanced synthesis—with a truly egalitarian reflection. It was neither matriarchal nor patriarchal; but matristic—not woman *or* man, but woman *and* man, as reflected in the all of Nature—*Terra Mater*.

Supporting the reemergence were the power and the rights of love and independent choice. The concept of mankind as originally sinful, either before or because of womankind's "evil" temptations, was being challenged by many. However, others regarded that challenge itself as evil. This conflict of ideas about Courtly Love, chivalric honors, and the rights to the sources of restorative powers was to continue for centuries. Even now, fallout remains with an unpredictable "half-life" influencing many in our current, transitional times. The winds of change are erratic; but they continue to clear the air and bring about the natural cycles of human evolution. Currently, we are free to reclaim our legends as they were naturally intended to be, and thus we are also able to expand upon them for multidimensionally positive effect for their Now—our once and future times.

Galahad: The Legendary, Perfect Knight

Galahad's legend has no clear link to any ancient Celtic myth. That would have been far too Pagan for the Cistercian monks who created it as a counterpoint to the legends that the troubadours had crafted with their emphasis on the rights of choice and Courtly Love. Since Lancelot had also been the complete creation of the Norman troubadours, the creators of Galahad, with brilliant one-upmanship techniques, made Lancelot's son their hero, one who would succeed where his "almost perfect" father had failed. Still, the archetypal key of Galahad may be one of the clearest connections to the holy realms that the Grail has always represented, in Truth.

Galahad's legend begins with his appearance at the Round Table. There it was revealed that he was the chosen one to occupy the Siege Perilous, or take the mysteriously unnamed seat at the Round Table. Other versions have the Grail (thinly covered with a white veil or cloth), appearing above the Round Table like a Light from the Divine. Galahad—and in some versions, Perceval—then reveals the need for the Quest and the true, uncovered image of the Grail shines forth above the Round Table.

The figure of Galahad was created to show how much greater the Codes of Christianity were for knights than the codes of secular honor and chivalry. Galahad's appearance at the Court of Camelot was intended to encourage the Round Table Knights to abandon their worldly pleasures and take up the Holy Quest for the Grail.

In medieval times, these virtues and the legend of Galahad became a strong influence on the development of the orders of the Knights Templar. In his quest for the Grail, Galahad is shown encountering an order of sequestered monks dressed in white. These holy monks have a shield which will be harmful to anyone who does not possess these virtues in the highest possible degree of perfection. This shield was meant only for "the one, most perfect knight in all Christendom," Galahad himself. The shield, as did all Templar shields and armor, bore a red cross on a pure white background. This was the cross of the true rose of strength, fire, and the Holy Ghost on a field of purity.

As the legends portray, Galahad, the perfect, quests with Perceval, the wise inno-cent, and Bors, the ordinary man, until they find the wounded Fisher King and the sword that struck the dolorous stroke. This encounter happens after a series of adven-tures, some of which reflected the medieval crusades, or quests to the Holy Land in the Middle East. When they eventually encounter the grail, all receive communion from it, but only Galahad prefers to transmute into heaven, rather than return to the worldly, imperfect realms of humankind.

Some versions of the Galahad stories say that the Holy Communion from the Grail Wars was granted to these questors (Bors, Perceval, and Galahad) by the cruci-fied Christ. However, only Galahad was perfect enough to be given the true revela-tion from God and was, as Cavendish expressed, "translated in that moment from the earthly plane to the celestial." By all Rights, this quest then should have healed the Wasteland and the Fisher King.

However, this was not to be in the stories of Galahad. Indeed, the Grail was taken away into the "eternal rapture" with Galahad. From this the conclusion was drawn that any future Grail questors would have to be as pure as Galahad, or more so, for the grail had become part of the dominion of the Orthodox version of the Christian god. The other message was that the Grail had been taken from Britain (Logres) because its people were too imperfect and too Pagan to be worthy of such a gift. This message was clearly a dark, manipulative effort to control an essentially hopeful attempt at merging chivalry and religion.

Currently, we can view the Galahad legends in a much clearer light. The Grail being taken, for example, need not indicate an unworthiness on the part of anyone according to the judgment of others. Instead, the grail, spiritually having been attained by a pure, questing knight of mythic perfection, can be seen as a symbolic ideal which exists only in the realms of the Divine, like a celestial angel. This we can translate to show that the experience of spirit, while exalted and pure in nature, can be attained by anyone who is questing with the most pure-hearted positive intentions humanly possible. Spirit, the Grail, and the quest, are all images of the Divine. They, like the Divine, are eternally present in their restorative powers—and cannot be withdrawn. This is the eternally self-replenishing cauldron of power that has been told of in Celtic traditions from time immemorial.

PERCEVAL: THE WISE INNOCENT

One of the Grail quest legends that has remained most clear and enlightening is the story of Perceval, the wise innocent. It may be said that Perceval is a blend of both other knights who attained the Grail, Bors, the counterpoint and the ordinary straight man, and Galahad, the "celestial." There are also some aspects of Lancelot and Gawain in Perceval, such as the natural spontaneity of Gawain and the perseverance of Lancelot. Most special is the practical reverence for life that Bors portrays, and qualities of innocence much like those of Galahad's purity. Amplifying this blend is Perceval's willingness always to be at the beginning of a new quest—like the Fool, Percival's gift to us is the will to be self-renewing, ever initiating his journey through life with power and purpose.

Perceval's story is best presented by Wolfram Von Eschenbach (1165–1220), one of the many Arthurian chroniclers who attempted to finish this legend which Chretien de Troyes left uncompleted. Von Eschenbach presents Perceval as a flesh-and-blood man of deeds who had already achieved a state of wise innocence. It was the grace of this same innocence that led Perceval to quest for and attain the grail. Bors may be said to have had a natural grace of experience, and Galahad a kind of supernatural grace. Perceval's grace was elemental and preternatural; directly connected to the heart of Nature's powers.

In his legends, Perceval is portrayed as a child who was brought up by his widowed mother far away from any form of civilization in the wilds of Wales. Perceval was by right of lineage a person of very high rank, in some respects a prince. Thus, we can view Perceval as being an early example of the "noble savage." This is an especially familiar and valued Celtic concept that balances the natural, independent orders of human character with the structured, societal orders of human cultures.

When Perceval first encounters some Round Table knights passing through his remote lands, he is symbolic of all humankind encountering the realization that life extends far beyond the natural boundaries of one's individual being. What distinguishes Perceval's quest from the others is that he learns quickly just what parts of those extended boundaries of civilization he will or will not incorporate into his own life quest.

Most significantly, Perceval fails in his first quest for the Grail because he has followed the instructions of another instead of respecting his own intuition. Perceval had been instructed by an older knight never to ask questions. Although this was likely good advice for a new "country bumpkin" knight trying to orient himself to the wonders of Camelot and the orders of the Round Table, it was just as likely not to be taken literally.

When Perceval failed to ask about the marvels he saw at the Grail castle, even when he glimpsed the Grail itself, he did so out of respect for what he did not know—but saw as valued by others. He was not yet on his own quest path.

In some versions Perceval is presented as being in mourning for his mother, or feeling unworthy because he had gone against her wishes for him to remain far from the "madding crowd" of knights and battle lords. Several of Perceval's legends present his mother, *i.e.*, Mother Nature, in only destructive aspects; indicating that Nature no longer had either value or power for Perceval—or Perceval for Nature. Neither one presents the ancient Celtic alliance with Nature in a fair light. Perceval's sister, Dindraine, is portrayed as giving her own blood to keep a diseased "Lady" alive. It is an act that kills Dindraine and sends a confused message about true service, and about martyrdom and sacrifice.

However, as these interwoven legends often present, a deeper message from Nature emerges in the form of an old wise woman. Perceval encounters a "hag" on his way back to Arthur's Court after he has failed to question or quest for the Grail. This hag, symbolic of the Celtic goddess of ancient wisdom, scolds Perceval for not seizing Fortune when he met Her. She reminds him of the most ancient and sacred alliance between humankind and the lands. This is the same shamanic wisdom that people of Nature state quite simply as, "Heal yourself, and you heal the world."

After more years of training and explorations to far-flung lands, Perceval begins his quest in earnest. After adventures and encounters now familiar in this quest pattern, Perceval encounters the Grail again. Because, by then, Perceval had learned that what was his by Right, was right within his most natural innocent grace, he not only attained the Grail for himself; but managed to restore the lands and the wounded king. In more modern versions, this king is shown as Arthur, who "retires" to Avalon for healing—and to wait for his time to come again.

In Von Eschenbach's version, Perceval brings his Saracen half-brother, Palomides, to the Grail castle where it is determined that even this "Moorish infidel" may receive from the "Holy Christian Grail." However, the Grail king feels that Palomides ought to be christened first—*if he chooses*. This right of choice and suggestion by Von Eschenbach was written during the times of the Crusades. It was heresy to say that anyone, much less a Moor (the enemy at that time), could attain such Orthodoxically "controlled" exclusive grace.

It does seem that Von Eschenbach was protected by Grace of the highest order, for his Perceval version swept across Europe and into Britain like independent wildfire. Perhaps this noble Teutonic crusader knight reminded the dark Orthodox church of Rome of his Germanic ancestors. These Germanic tribes had finally succeeded in stopping the spread of the Roman Empire; eventually causing Roman withdrawal from Britain and other Western, Celtic lands.

For whatever grace or reason, Von Eschenbach was able to express some ancient concepts and some very new, unifying thoughts about personal and spiritual rights for all peoples. As Joseph Campbell relates his experience while reading Von Eschenbach, there came an awkward moment at the end of this legend which, by Campbell's time, had already become famous because of its adaptation by Richard Wagner into a great opera, *Parzival*. This moment happened when Palomides hesitates after the suggestion he be "Christened." Palomides, like the great quest knight which he also is, asks a very significant question about the nature of the god whom the Grail served.

As those at the Grail castle struggle to express the Great Mystery of their Divine Spiritual God, Palomides begins to see the deeper beauty and power of the maiden who is offering him the grail. Palomides asks simply, "Is your god, this god?" When he is assured that is the truth, Palomides says, quite profoundly, "Then her god will be my god as well."

Thus "Nature and Nature's god" unite in the restorative, healing source that is symbolized, most sacredly, by the Holy Grail (*san greal*), and in communion with Spirit as the life force, by virtue of the Holy Blood (*sang real*). The quest completed, that which is ultimately indivisible remains so for those who have learned that the Light is the Light. One Light, One Source, One Grail with countless and right hues, rays, shades, names, masks, forms, and paths for personal quest.

Today the blend of spirituality in the Grail quest legends gives us each a point of connection, either ancient or modern, from which we may quest within for our own experience of what the Grail represents for us personally.

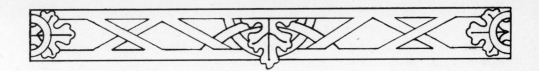

CHAPTER 20

CAMLANN: INTO THE MYSTIC

Listen to me, Arthur. The gods have said that Mordred will be your bane. If he is so, it will not be through his own act. Do not force him to that act … Lay by your sword, and listen to him. Take no other counsel, but talk with him, listen and learn. Yes, learn. For you grow old, Arthur-Emrys, and the time will come, is coming, has come, when you and your son may hold Britain safe between your clasped hands, like a jewel cradled in wool. But loose your clasp, and you drop her, to shatter, perhaps for ever.

Mary Stewart
The Wicked Day (New York: William Morrow, 1983)

 If someone asked you to identify what kind of story is one in which a king is betrayed by his queen with his best friend, and then is killed by his own son—what would you say it was? A tragedy? If so, what kind? I'll give you a hint. It sounds Greek to me, or Eastern, perhaps Middle Eastern. That is if you say that the story is a tragedy, which is how the primary Camelot legend is so often presented. But we know that these legends are much, much more than simple tragedy, Greek or otherwise. Let's look at this story again from another perspective, this time animistically.

Now, if you heard a story about a great older stag of the forest, a white hart, whose favorite white doe became enamored of another of superior quality, a golden stag, what sort of story would you immediately think it was? Symbolic? Shamanic? Well, let's also say the great stag, the white hart, had sired at least one young buck, just the usual earth-brown variety. Perhaps this buck was just a bit dark, or dirty, and was never acknowledged by his father, although he was by the white doe, who was his stepmother? Let's also say that both the white doe and the white hart were too busy dividing their time between each other and their mutual friend, the golden stag—each in their own way. How would you imagine this story would end, naturally, that is?

213

Well, probably the golden stag and the white stag would be fine until rutting season came along. Then one of them would challenge the other. After their encounter, one would walk away with fewer antlers, at least, and the other would symbolically walk away with the crown of the forest. So, then, what sort of story would that be? A Nature story? A Faery tale with symbolic and mythic themes? Such as? The new stag/Sun defeats—or is defeated by—the old stag/Sun. In either case, the strong stag gets the doe, and that makes Mother Nature evolutionarily happy.

Now, if I said the earth-brown buck decided to challenge the white hart, his father, that would seem even more natural. Whether or not it was because of the white doe, it would be an even clearer symbolic representation of the Solar Father/Son cycles of life.

So, now if I say that this story continues in another way, I wonder what you'll say when I've told you what happens. The brown buck discovers that the white doe and the golden stag have spent a lot of time together while the white hart was gone, off guarding the outer forest. Because of this, all sorts of predators and some rogue stags were beginning to invade the forest grove where the family herd lived. The brown buck, who was admittedly eager to prove himself worthy of his heritage, challenges the golden stag himself. During the fight, the golden stag escapes, perhaps with the white doe then, or perhaps he returns for her later.

When the white hart returns to the forest grove that is the heart of his domain, all manner of chaos has broken out. His white doe and his best golden stag are both gone. Most of the herd deer are extremely upset, and a few have left to join with the rogue stags. They did this to find protection from the predators who are closing in fast on the forest grove. All that the white hart has before him centers on his own son, the brown buck. Probably his own son had expected to challenge him some day, as is natural. So now, in the midst of all this confusion in the forest, and with no clear way to communicate with each other, the white hart and the brown buck lock antlers in mortal combat. Both the old stag and the young buck are killed. Now, what kind of story is this? Yes, a tragedy; but now who is the victim? Or at least, now who is also the victim?

The white doe and the golden stag have retreated to the deepest part of the forest, and it is while they are there that they hear the tragic news. The white doe retreats even deeper into the forest, to a cold, harsh region where no stag of any kind is allowed to be, not even a golden one. The golden stag stands guard over the white doe, even though he cannot come near enough to see her. Eventually, the white doe dies from despair, and the golden stag leaves the forest forever. Now what kind of a story is this? Still a tragedy, yes; but how many victims now?

Let's continue. The golden stag leaves the forest, even though the family herd, to whom he had pledged loyalty, is being threatened by more and more predators. This is so even though the new king stag is not a rogue; he is not much more than a raw recruit. He is one who didn't expect to get drafted into service. The golden stag is a seasoned guardian, but he leaves for another more mystical forest. It is where he had once encountered a golden doe, without even having to challenge her father, the great wounded stag.

Let's say the golden stag had sired a young buck of his own by that golden doe, one who was as completely perfect as a young stag could be, and then even more so. Let's say that the exploits of that perfect buck were such that he had already become a myth in all the forests. Fine though he was, the golden stag hadn't managed much more than a superficial legendary quality. Now, the perfect buck was no longer to be found in any but the most mystical realms of the forest, where none but the perfect could be found. In fairness, both stags and does of perfection could be found there.

Even still, the golden stag simply didn't qualify, although he might have at one time, so the golden stag returns to the golden doe and lives out his days in the remote, mystical forest. There, hardly any stags come questing anymore, so it is quiet. Even the great wounded stag seems less restless and not as troubled by his wounds. Sadly, that mystical forest provides a meager existence. All its lands are lying fallow and some are wasted; but they somehow manage to survive. Besides, they are safe. This is more than we can say for the besieged and beleaguered family herd. They have been loyal to the old white hart, to whom the golden stag has also pledged loyalty. Now, who are the victims?

I'm sure you've recognized the legend that I've been presenting in both nonspecific and animistic forms. Most basically stated, it is the story of Arthur and Mordred and their death at Camlann, with the catalyst subplot being the betrayal of Guinevere and Lancelot. The older stag or white hart, is Arthur. The white doe is Guinevere and the golden stag is Lancelot. The brown buck is Mordred and the herd represents the Knights of the Round Table. The golden doe is Elaine of Carbonek and the perfect buck is her son by Lancelot, the perfect knight—Galahad.

Based on the traditional forms of this legend, let's explore it in a completely nonanalytical and unemotional manner. From this we can see how the legend changed to reflect the political and spiritual climate of the times.

THE BASIC LEGENDS OF ARTHUR, MORDRED, AND CAMLANN BY COMPARATIVE PATTERNS

The following material is from sources cross-checked or taken from *The Arthurian Encyclopedia* (Lacy). Repetitions will be limited, but changes and significant additions are included.

Before you explore these versions, please take note of the following clarification about the "incest" confusion in these legends. (The information is from author Jean Markale and others in the field of Women's Studies [ancient, current, and future].)

Sister, in the ancient sense, meant equality of rank as well as a kinship of blood. It also applied to foster relationships and to spiritual, Druidic relationships. So, here incest is a mistaken meaning. As with many of the overlays, some are just sloppy interpretations. Incest was not okay, tribally, as people such as the genealogically well-informed Celts would have known early on. Certainly it happened, and with as many potential negative consequences then as now. There is some dark intention somewhere when a realm of legends like these has at least two main-character women accused of incest with their brother, the king. Maybe it was an oversight—but for a thousand years or more? Maybe no one had the nerve to deal with it then—but now we do. Both Morgan and Morgawse relate to Arthur as queens, with originally the same rank. Perhaps not so when he became High King. Sister/Brother was an acknowledgment of Rights, and lands and inheritance. Also another ancient ranking system, especially among the Celts and other matristic peoples of Nature, is for a man (even a king) to rank his sisters' sons as highly—or higher—than his own. This was particularly true when the lands were handed down by mothers to daughters. This Celtic custom is a bit more well known; but it has also caused some confusing overlays. It may have made the incest misconceptions seem valid. Maybe it was wiser, in some ways, to use the spoken word!

- From the *Annales Cambriae, The Annals of Wales* (circa C.E. 960–980) Historical Compilation.

  "The strife of Camlann, in which Arthur and Medraut fell. And there was plague in Britain and Ireland" (date given for the event, C.E. 539).

- From *Historia Regum Britanniae, History of the Kings of Britain*, Geoffrey of Monmouth (circa 1200).

  Arthur has invaded Gaul and reorganized territories still held officially by Rome. Rulership, under Arthur, is given to Bedevere and Sir Kai.

  Back at Caerleon, Arthur receives a demand from Rome for a tribute and restitution of the conquered lands, on the authority of Emperor Lucius, Procurator of the Republic—or else, war.

  Arthur refuses, returns to Gaul where he defeats Lucius and invades Burgundy successfully, with intentions to proceed eastward to Rome, where he will declare himself emperor. Casualty list: Bedevere and Kai.

  News of a revolt sends Arthur back to Britain. Particulars reported: Mordred, his "nephew," and appointed regent, has seized control of the throne and taken Guinevere as his own wife and queen, despite her official marriage to Arthur. Mordred has sent a Saxon duke to Germany for reinforcements, in return for which Saxon lands will be granted and others expanded. Mordred has gathered the Gaelic Celts, including clans from Scotland and Ireland, and has also made alliances with the Picts to help his rebellion against Arthur.

  Arthur and his troops arrive at Richborough and defeat the troops that Mordred has gathered. Mordred retreated to regroup. Casualty: Gawain.

Mordred takes another stand at Winchester with Guinevere. Guinevere flees to Caerleon, then to a convent close by and takes her vows.

Arthur and Mordred's troops battle near Winchester. Mordred retreats to Cornwall.

Arthur and Mordred battle at Camlann, beside the River Camel in Cornwall. Casualties: Mordred and Arthur, "mortally wounded."

Arthur names his "cousin," Constantine of Cornwall, as heir to the throne.

Arthur is "carried off to the Isle of Avalon for his wounds to be attended to" (Monmouth).

Constantine kills Mordred's two sons, ritually "by a cruel death." (I have yet to find any other source that mentions these sons. Perhaps they are the princes in the Tower.)

- *The Knight of the Cart* by Chrétien de Troyes (circa 1150). (See "The Perilous Bed," Chapter 14.)

Lancelot rescues Guinevere from "Meleagant" (Melwas) after many dangers and trials.

Lancelot spends a "night of pleasure" with Guinevere.

- *Prose Lancelot Vulgate Cycle* (circa 1215–35)

Lancelot (18) is sent to the Court of Arthur by the Lady of the Lake, so he may be knighted.

Lancelot is "enraptured" by Guinevere.

Guinevere gives Lancelot his sword of knighthood.

Lancelot is then officially both the King and the Queen's knight and is "the best knight in the world."

Lancelot commits adultery with the Queen.

Lancelot's perfection begins to wane.

Lancelot learns he will not be able to fulfill the quest for the Holy Grail because of his sin: adultery with Guinevere.

Lancelot quests forth to the Castle of the Grail.

Lancelot sleeps with the Grail King's daughter, Elaine of Carbonek. Particulars: This liaison was contrived by Pelles, the Grail King; Elaine, his daughter; and Brisen, her nurse—who gives Lancelot a potion. This potion makes Lancelot believe he is sleeping with Guinevere, but it is Elaine of Carbonek, in disguise as Camelot's Queen. A son is conceived from this liaison, later to be known as Galahad.

217

Sequels

- *Quest for the Holy Grail*—also *Vulgate Cycle*

  Lancelot leaves the Court of Arthur and Guinevere to do penance for his sins.

  Lancelot is redeemed by the chance to accompany his son Galahad on the Quest for the Grail.

  Lancelot is allowed to glimpse the Grail and be a part of a Grail ritual.

  Lancelot is denied the full attainment of the power of the Grail. This is reserved for Bors, Perceval, and Lancelot's Son, Galahad.

  Galahad transmutes from earthly perfection to heavenly perfection, taking the Grail along.

- *The Death of Arthur*—also *Vulgate Cycle*

  Lancelot returns to Guinevere and becomes her lover again.

  Lancelot is accused of adultery with the Queen, and also of "loving" Elaine of Astolat.

  Queen Guinevere is accused of poisoning a knight at Arthur's Court. (This account is cited only here.)

  Lancelot comes to champion Guinevere.

  Lancelot "accidentally" kills Gaheriet (Gaheris), brother of Gauvain (Gawain).

  Arthur and his "nephew" Gawain declare war on Lancelot and his family, and prepare to leave.

  Arthur goes, and leaves the control of his kingdom to Mordred, "his son" by incest (though stated in this work as being unintentional) with Morgawse, his "half-sister."

  Mordred usurps the throne, and Arthur must return to control the situation.

  "Mortal combat between father and son."

  Arthur orders Girflet (Lucan) to return Excalibur to the lake. A woman's hand rises out of the lake and catches the sword.

  A boat "bearing Morgain" (Morgana) and some of her "enchanted attendants" takes Arthur out to sea. (The "Dark-aspected Morgan Le Fey came in the Post *Vulgate Cycle*.)

- *Morte Arthure* (Alliterative Version in English) (circa 1400) Anonymous

  Arthur at Carlisle, receives demand for tribute from Lucius; Arthur to acknowledge himself as a "vassal of Rome."

  Arthur and his "vassals" defeat Lucius, and both prepare for extensive war.

Arthur leaves his "sister's son, Mordrede" in charge and sails to Brittany.

Arthur dreams that a dragon defeats a bear. (Possibly a Norse dragon. This is only cited here.)

Arthur battles twice with Lucius and his "pagan allies." "Gawayn" and Cador distinguish themselves in the first battle. Lucius is defeated in the second battle. Casualties: Kayous (Kai) and "Bedevere."

Arthur sends the dead enemies, in coffins, to Rome as his "tribute."

Arthur and his forces move toward, then through Italy, conquering all the towns they pass through.

Arthur stops conquering when the Romans "offer him the imperial crown."

Arthur dreams the Wheel of Fortune has turned against him.

The day after his dream, Arthur hears that "Mordrede" has seized the throne and the queen.

Arthur defeats Mordrede's "pagan allies" during a battle at sea while he is on the way back to "England." Casualty: Gawain, "Arthur's sister's son."

Arthur vows to avenge Gawain.

Arthur and Mordred have their final battle at Cornwall. Both die.

Arthur appoints Cador's "son," Constantine, as successor.

Arthur is buried at Glastonbury (influence of Henry II here). (From the *Arthurian Encyclopedia*, in reference to this alliterative source "... *Morte Arthure [The Death of Arthur]* offers a sympathetic portrait of Mordred as a figure who suffers genuine remorse for his deeds." Norris J. Lacy, Editor.)

- *The Death of Arthur (Le Morte D'Arthur)*, Sir Thomas Malory (circa 1469–1470) (adapted also from Mary Stewart's notes)

Arthur hears that his son Mordred has been born. Since Mordred had been conceived by "unknowing incest" between Arthur and his "half-sister," Morgawse, Arthur sets out to destroy all of the babies who were born in the same month. All of the children were placed on a ship and set out to sea in a storm. When the ship sank, only Mordred was left alive. Mordred washed up on the shores of Orkney—or somewhere in Scotland—and was raised by a fisherman in the service of Queen Morgawse. When he was fourteen, Mordred was taken to the Court of Queen Morgawse, who not only acknowledged him, but began training him for her future plans.

King Pellinore, while following the Questing Beast, comes upon Lot of Orkney and Arthur. Pellinore slays Lot and a feud starts between the Pellinore and the Orkney clans.

Queen Morgawse takes Lamorak for her lover—even though he is Pellinore's son.

Morgawse's sons, Agravain and Gaheris, set a trap to kill Lamorak. When Gaheris sees Morgawse in bed with Lamorak, he slices off his mother's head.

Since Lamorak is unarmed, Gaheris wasn't able to kill him according to the codes of the knighthood. Lamorak has to make his escape and prepare to fight the Orkney brothers later (except Gawain, who was with Arthur then).

Gaheris, Agravaine, and Mordred track down Lamorak and kill him.

The Orkney Brothers, this time Agravaine and Gaheris, encounter Tristan and challenge him; but Tristan refuses to take the bait. He is taunted by Gaheris and Agravain and is attacked by them as he tries to ride away. Tristan bests them both, but does not kill them. Later Tristan talks about this with Gareth, the other Orkney brother. Gareth disavows himself of any loyalty to either Gaheris or Agravain.

Meanwhile, at Camelot, Lancelot and Guinevere are accused of treasonous adultery by Agravain. Both swear their innocence on oath, and since there is no proof, the Queen cannot be accused. (Malory often lets the reader know that Lancelot and Guinevere are lovers.) Arthur's law must be upheld. No proof, no trial. Agravain "challenges" Arthur to let the accused lovers prove their own guilt or innocence by leaving them alone in the castle. Arthur is undecided, but is "forced to accede" by rights of the system of law he established. Arthur goes hunting in the forest for the night, leaving Guinevere alone.

Agravain and Mordred gather twelve Orkney knights and trap Lancelot and the Queen together in her bedchamber. Lancelot accidentally kills Gareth, wounds Mordred, and Agravain is also killed in the chaos while Lancelot escapes to get help.

Mordred rides to Arthur with news of the betrayal, and with the "proof" established, Guinevere is sentenced to be burned, or have her guilt determined by a trial by fire. (This version written toward the end of the Burning Times.)

Lancelot rescues Guinevere before she can be burned and takes her to Joyous Garde where he can defend her within his own castle. Arthur pursues, besieges, and defeats Lancelot. Lancelot returns Guinevere and flees to France—where he gathers an army in Burgundy to await Arthur's arrival.

Gawain urges Arthur to pursue Lancelot. They sail to Burgundy, where they fought Lancelot with "dreadful losses on both sides."

Meanwhile, Mordred has been appointed regent to watch over the throne while Arthur is gone ...

Arthur receives news in Burgundy about what Mordred is doing at Camelot. Particulars: Mordred had letters forged which said that Arthur had died in

Burgundy. Mordred had called a parliament and had them crown him King. He had announced that he would take Guinevere for his wife, but she fled to the Tower of London (where Sir Thomas Malory was when he wrote this account).

Mordred gathers support from the people and manages to raise an army. "... then was the common voice among them that with Arthur was none other life but war and strife and with Sir Mordred was great joy and bliss." (Malory, in Mary Stewart)

Mordred and his forces met Arthur and his forces at Dover and a terrible battle was fought. Casualty: Gawain—as he died, he urged Arthur to forgive Lancelot so Lancelot could help defeat Mordred.

After Gawain died, Arthur pursues Mordred and his "fleeing host and gave battle once more on the downs, where again Mordred was put to flight." (Mary Stewart, *The Crystal Cave*).

They prepare for the final battle, as Malory describes "westwards towards Salisbury, and not far from the seaside."

Arthur dreams of Gawain, who urges him to forgive Lancelot, send for him, and stall Mordred somehow until Lancelot can come to help Arthur destroy Mordred.

In the morning, Arthur sends offers for compromises and whatever "lands and goods" Mordred wants, and as much as he thinks would be best.

Mordred sends an offer to settle for Cornwall and Kent, so long as Arthur still lives. And also, Mordred wants "all England, after the days of King Arthur."

A face to face meeting is arranged. Both Mordred and Arthur may bring fourteen knights to meet between both of their armies—who will be waiting— just in case. No swords were to be drawn, nor sudden moves made which might be misinterpreted by anyone and start an unnecessary war. They had wine and talked away from the others, while everyone watched intently.

Then an adder from a "heath bush" stung one of the knights, who then, by reflex, drew his sword in order to slay the snake. When the drawn sword was seen, it was assumed to be a signal and thus the battle erupted instantly.

At the end of the day, with almost everyone on both sides dead, or nearly so, Arthur "sought out Mordred, who alone of his host still lived" (Mary Stewart). Arthur was one of only three who still lived, for Lucan and Bedevere were still there.

Lucan tried to persuade Arthur not to seek for Mordred, since they had "won the field," though there were few left on their side, and only Mordred on his. So Lucan advised "and if ye leave off now this wicked day of destiny is past" (Malory, from Mary Stewart, Ibid.).

Arthur was beyond being able to hear advice. He attacked Mordred, and Mordred, while dying, gave Arthur a blow that mortally wounded him. Arthur is taken away to the "Vale of Avalon" to be healed of his wounds. Sir Bedevere has already carried Arthur to the shore when the Avalon Barge arrives with three queens: His sister Morgan, and the Queen of Northgalis, and the Queen of the Wastelands; and with them is Nimue, "the chief Lady of the Lake."

Lancelot and Guinevere "enter the religious life and undertake such penances that each dies a good death" (Malory, in Lacy).

Before that, though, Lancelot's kinsmen travel to the Holy Land where they are killed while fighting in the Crusades (which were about 500 years later, give or take a century.)

Final Additions from Varied Sources

There is a vast body of Scots literature that chronicles *their* version. To Geoffrey of Monmouth, the Picts and the Scots are Arthur's enemies. Arthur conquers Scotland and then has his Camelot kingdom destroyed by a traitorous Scot, Mordred. Monmouth's original statements set off a number of Scots for quite a while. Though some Scots seemed favorable to Arthur, others were uncharacteristically extravagant in the words they used to blast poor, all-too-human, and by then long-dead Arthur.

One anonymous chronicle (circa 1460) calls Arthur a *huris sone* (whore's son) who only became king because of the "deviltry of Merlin." The true heirs, as presented here, were Mordred and Gawain; but they were Scots and so they were "passed over." As to the Battle of Camlann, it was justified that Arthur was slain by Mordred, who was "in his rychtwyse guerele" (quotes from Lacy, *The Arthurian Encyclopedia*).

In 1535, at the request of James V of Scotland, John Bellenden translated and adapted some of the work of Boece, first principal or headmaster of the University of Aberdeen. This work, *Scotorum Historiae* (1527) was originally Latin; but Bellenden recrafted it in Middle Scots prose and added some opinions of his own, and presumably of James V. Bellenden said that Arthur was the "most unfortunate" king of all the British kings. Furthermore, he stated that God had punished Arthur for being "faithless and untrue to King Mordred."

Others are more compassionate, but stubbornly stand by their own beliefs—which is what Arthur did, after all, didn't he?

John Fordun, an influential Scottish chronicler, praised Arthur (circa 1385) as being admirable and beloved by almost everyone; but still not lawfully the King of Britain, because he was "conceived out of wedlock."

Blind Harry, once thought to be an illiterate and blind minstrel, proved to be quite a bard in his own time. He wrote the Scottish epic, "the Wallace" (circa 1476–78) in which he compares "gud King Arthour" to Wallace. He also states his opinion that Arthur was undone by the cowardice of others, just as happened to Julius Caesar and Alexander the Great.

In *The Mabinogion*, there is a story by Madawg, an historical Welsh writer (d. 1159). This story is "The Dream of Rhonabwy," a literary crafting both fantastic and finely analytical, as Welsh traditions often are. In this story it is Mordred who is chided, by a chieftain who, by mystical arts, is there dimensions later, to tell Rhonabwy about his personal experience at Camlann:

> *"Chieftain, why are you called that," asked Rhonabwy (to Iddawg, the Churn of Britain).*
> *"I will tell you. I was one of the messengers at the Battle of Camlann between Arthur and his nephew, Medrawd. I was a high-spirited young man, so eager for battle that I stirred up bad feeling between them. When the Emperor Arthur sent me to remind Medrawd that Arthur was his uncle and foster-father, and to ask for peace lest his sons and nobles of Britain be killed, though Arthur spoke as kindly as he could, I repeated his words to Medrawd in the rudest possible way. Thus I am here called Iddawg, the Churn of Britain, and that is how the Battle of Camlann was woven."*

Jeffrey Gantz
The Mabinogion (New York: Dorset Press, 1985)

Iddawg goes on to say that he left three nights before the final battle to do penance in Scotland for his actions. There he stayed for seven years before he felt he had earned forgiveness. Suppose he had been the knight who drew his sword, only to kill the adder? Well, naturally he couldn't have felt bad for too long—in this world or the Otherworld.

By what you have just explored, I expect you feel far more confident about crafting the legends, the realms, and the characters more freely in your own image. No doubt your crafting will be far more Fair than most of the "traditional" versions. Some of those traditional Arthurian authors were essentially playing one-upmanship, across the English Channel, with Arthur as their pawn.

Perhaps they didn't realize Arthur was real—and still is; now even more so. With Arthur as the center—in all his glory, and all his humanity, as well—we can see that he is truly a catalyst for the 'round. Because Artorius, Dux Bellorum, Comtes Brittanarium lived and breathed, we have the catalyst for a unified vision. We have the "brief shining moment" when unity was real, even when it must have seemed quite impossible. Arthur was not a god, although his was an exalted destiny. Whatever else may be said of Arthur, it may truly be said that he did what he set out to do.

Let's say I can change only one single aspect of this realm of the Camelot legends. If so, I'd have Arthur go hunting in the forest—deeper and deeper into the forest, perhaps far enough in to find a timeless cave. I'd let him stay in the forest to become the Great Stag. I already know that Arthur makes a fine Herne, the Hunter. I believe he has been the Bear long enough. So I would let him merge with the mystical forest, as he has anyway, in so many enlightened ways.

When I think of Arthur the King, in that forest, I know I can find him there, even now, archetypically. When I think of Arthur the warrior, the man, I think of another old soldier, General Douglas MacArthur. This old soldier was imperialistic, the "American Caesar," who said when he retired, "Old soldiers never die. They just fade away." Who knows? Perhaps that was his destiny.

So my wish for Arthur, the man, the soldier and the warrior, is simply this: I hope you were an old, old warrior who never "died." I hope you just faded away ... into the mystical forest, forever.

I've never understood why so many seem to want this legend to be a tragedy, and I really don't want to know. I have also never understood the need to focus on the martyred Christ, when the resurrected Christ is "where it's at," as I see it. Different drums—different rhythms.

Arthur is best remembered and reclaimed when we focus on what his destiny brought us, evolutionarily. Arthur managed to unite and hold together some of the most clannish, fierce, and individualistic people in the world long enough for Britain to become Britain (and Brigantias).

Now that is all we truly know ... and that is enough.

The most reliable evidence we have is Arthur's duplicated events in both Nennius and the *Annales Cambriae*. These are both about Badon Hill, the final battle that united the Britons.

From the *Annales Cambriae*: C.E. 518 (adjusted—because 447 is considered to be what was meant in this work which covers 533 years, and the first year is marked Year 1): "The battle of Badon, in which Arthur carried the cross of Our Lord Jesus Christ on his shoulders for three days and three nights and the Britons were victors" (as quoted from Lacy).

Once again, from Nennius: "... and the twelfth on Mount Badon, where Arthur personally slew 960 of the enemy in a single charge" (from Lacy).

That charge must have been rough with that cross to bear, but it might have been a sword of Light. It might have been the Right sword; indeed, it must have been. Truly, Arthur and his sword Excalibur have become a symbol of what is Right, and of the Light.

CHAPTER 21

THE CAMELOT KING:
ACTIVE POWER

For should the lore of the land become lost to the recollection of men, whether by forgetfulness of tradition or invasions of men of alien race and tongue, then will the land revert to what it was before its naming and settling: to the nine forms of the elements, a formless mass, unfeeling, unmeaning, inchoate; with its kings unwed to the 'Sovranty' of the Lord ...

Nikolai Tolstoy
The Coming of the King (New York: Bantam, 1989)

 The Camelot vision has endured and continued to enlighten our culture, despite the dark, shadowed misconceptions overlaid upon it. This is because Camelot represents an expansive moment in the evolution of the Western Celtic mind and consciousness. Camelot symbolizes the creation of unity, the synthesis of powers from clans and lands that had always remained separate, and often divided, even though each tribe belonged to a greater tribe, the Celts.

From this historically identified moment in time came the recognition of the power and purpose that united forces provide. The brief "shining moment" was enough to create a widespread change of concept throughout the British Isles and, thus, expanded throughout the lands where the Celts had settled. In modern physics we call this widespread mind change "reaching critical mass." Here the transformation became uniquely Celtic. The ancient tribal cultures blended more easily than they may have expected. Once the unified group shifted its focus from its differences to its similarities, the Celts discovered who they were, in kinship and in power. This they did in sufficient numbers to create an alliance. From this alliance came the concept of power united for the good of all—and not only in times of crisis.

Because of the power of the Camelot vision and the quality of Kingship required to create and maintain that through the ages, this realm of Camelot represents the activation of power. In this chapter are imageries and exercises to develop your own skills at creating active transformations in your life and that of others, if you choose to help them. This use of imagery is the craft of a mage, combined with the power of a king.

King, in this case, is not a royal description. It is a symbol for active power. crafting the transformations of your self and being the catalyst for others' self-work requires leadership ability, which in turn requires a sense of responsibility. The first part is more active, and the second more receptive; but both represent kingship. This same quality is required by a queen who is an active power symbol. The key word here is active or activation of power. It is wise to proceed with that quality in kind—and in mind.

The following exercise imageries are designed to help you learn to craft transformations, within the realm of Camelot.

EXERCISE IMAGERIES FOR CAMELOT'S REALM

What follows is a mini-course in crafting with imagery and correlated aspects in an extensive instructional approach, with a few suggestions included. Some of this will be a brief review; some will be new material. If you are already quite familiar with this type of mystical/magickal work, select the aspects you want and skip the mini-course altogether.

The first of these exercises, "The Summer Lands," is an instructive guide for crafting, generally, and specifically for creating prosperity. This purpose can be extended to others and to other locations as you choose. However, emphasis will be focused on you.

THE SUMMER LANDS: PROSPERITY

It is a bright and glorious midsummer day in the realm of Camelot. All of Nature is resonating with the rich beauty and abundant power of Summer's expanded growth. You see that the Sovereign Lady of the Lands has graced this realm in royal fashion as you ride through the regions this day. Everywhere there are signs of Nature which remind you of the eternally recycling source of all abundance and wisdom.

The winds sweep through fields of grains still ripening in the warmth of the sun. The smiths are hard at their craft, forging the tools of many trades, as well as weaponry and beautiful objects for the many people who can now enjoy the trappings of wealth. The flames from the forge are bright and continuous for this persistent crafting. Business is brisk in the towns, and the streets are as crowded with activity as the farmlands were with many workers, tending the crops and their livestock.

As you ride out into farmland regions, once more you see how well-nurtured the livestock appear. The cattle are plentiful, sleek, and solid, a sign of wealth in every time. The horses are magnificent, strong and sturdy, with a swiftness that seems magickal as they race across the meadowlands. Your horse races with them for a while, exhilarating you both with the power of the winds and the lands surrounding you.

You decide to ride toward the lake regions. There you find cool refreshment from clear waters and calm strength from the mists rising from the crystal blue lakes, reflecting the sun. You pause for a while by a small pool of water close to the evergreen forest. You rest your horse and recline a while in the shade of an empowering Elder tree. You watch an old salamander make his way from the shaded pool to the warm banks where he basks on a sunlit rock.

You remember your task, and are riding again soon, down by the shoreline of the sparkling sea. The fishermen and their families call out in greeting as you pass by. Their catch is plentiful and they are proud of their blessing from Nature, as Mother Ocean. They hoist horns of ale and offer some to you; but you have business at Camelot and must be on your way. First, though, you accept the ale graciously in the name of all the gods of the sea. Nobly, you pour the golden liquid from the tankard into the foam-crested waves. The tides sweep in rapidly, but you are undaunted as you continue to bless the sea with great style. Waves splash up high and white, leaving you and your horse covered with water

in shining crystal droplets. The people on the shoreline shout their approval and beg you to stay for their midsummer feast; but you have been summoned to Camelot—and it isn't wise to keep the King waiting—and, in particular, The Merlin.

You ride faster now and soon reach the castle grounds, where you find your allies near the playing fields. You see Arthur and Lancelot engrossed in a game—this one played on a stone game-board. Guinevere is sewing on an Avalon tapestry with a lovely unicorn depicted in a forest. Her ladies are chattering with excitement about the summer's tournaments and festivals. Guinevere smiles at you in her benevolent manner and you know she isn't listening to her ladies, but to the sweet song of the white birds in fruit-laden trees.

The royal hounds announce your arrival, causing the king and Lancelot to pause for a moment to greet you with kinship. The Merlin has his own game going, and he summons you to share it before you can approach the king. Arthur waves you on, in full recognition of who decides the order of events when The Merlin is present. Arthur calls after you, promising to come later and help you win the game, and Lancelot offers his championship powers, which you accept with the style of one in a secure position.

The Merlin has placed a mystical crystal sphere among clusters of clear quartz on a stone carved with symbols of destiny. He bids you to envision whatever you want, and it will manifest with the amplified power of the crystals, in structures designed for success. Filled with the empowerment of Nature's abundant energy, you focus with clarity and purpose. Soon the crystal sphere reflects your intentions and the quartz clusters vibrate with purpose. The stone of destiny resonates with power, like the rhythm of an inspiring song. Then the vision of your desired manifestation transforms into golden laser lights which blend intensely with deep, rich green and bright, clear blue. These brightly reflect the abundant lands, the expansive sky, and the empowering Sun as they merge into the realm of Spirit.

Before you take your leave of this realm, you sit at the gameboard with Arthur. He then explains some tactics and strategies to provide for the manifestation of your vision. Lancelot tells you of your rights of success, well earned by valiant efforts. Guinevere shares some secrets about the powers of your personal magnetism. The Merlin consults the sphere and the stone to divine the Right course of action, and you absorb the power of the experience to hold in your memory with honor.

Now, with this example in mind, you may choose to continue with the instructive course that follows; or, if you'd rather return to the realm you have just experienced, you may wish to amplify this first within your own crystal sphere of vision. Return to the realm of your mind and the activating power of imagery.

THE SUMMER LANDS: PROSPERITY

Elements: Earth and Spirit with some Fire

Directions: North, Center, and the Circle encircling

Aspects: Abundance, Growth, Success, Expansion

Colors: Green ray, Crystal and Spirit lights

Kindred Spirits: Cattle, Horses, Dogs, Osprey, Salamander, White Birds

Tree: Elder

Stones: Emerald, Aventurine, Diamonds, Clear Crystal Clusters, Point

Incense: Evergreen

Cycle: Midsummer

Setting Image: Lands

Hallow: Gameboard, Stone of Destiny, Crystal Sphere

Theme: Round Table, Quests

Natural Force: Winds, Flames, Mists, and Tides

Access Allies: Arthur, Guinevere, Lancelot, The Merlin

Format: Extensive

Message: Magnetism is the term that describes the process by which like attracts like, love attracts love, and prosperity attracts prosperity. When powerful human magnetism is applied in a limited sphere, or in a narrow-focused fashion, it can become fixed on just one facet of life. Then the magnetic field itself can begin to shift. This creates conflicts and reduces the power of the magnetism to hold on to what it had once attracted. When the original magnetic connection fails to hold, the force field can suffer reversals. This can cause what was positive to now attract its opposite, negatively. Then the resulting fallout may be felt by others who have come into the sphere of influence created by the original magnetism.

We will break this imagery exercise down, aspect by aspect, in order for you to understand how a mystical and magickal image is structured for success. Success means the manifestation of effective forms in your life that empower yourself, and the purpose or the intentions you had in mind when you crafted the image. A manifest form can be anything transformational, such as a new positive opportunity, or a new attitude.

Manifest forms can also be the gifts you receive in both mundane and mystical realms. Both transform your experience of life and provide you with a self-empowered attitude to create change for yourself. Whether someone gives you a gift, such as a dragon figurine, or whether you envision a dragon in your imagery, the symbolic meaning is effectively the same. Both symbolize your right to empower yourself naturally, with all elements or aspects of yourself amplified positively to help you make the changes you want in your life. Both dragon symbols are allies connecting you to your own right to empower yourself—and therefore empower your life.

The list of aspects does not always have to be followed in any specific order—as the guided imageries have shown. Archetypal experiences or visionary imageries often begin with locations, times, and conditions. This is to give you a "feel" for the place, and it can effectively open your mind to the realms within. Thus, descriptions of where you are, in imagery, serve to place you there imagickally.

If you are crafting with imagery for a specific purpose, such as prosperity in your life, you will be wise to start where you want the manifestation to be. In this case, prosperity is truly a matter for the mundane realm, for you can be as wealthy as you want to be in the mystical realms of imagery.

In this case, the aspect with which we begin is the natural forces. In every case of crafting it is wise to begin with a circle that brings the empowerment and protection of harmony. These circles can be as formal or as informal as you choose. You can do this in the most structured, ritual forms, or the most free-flowing ceremonial manner. So long as what you do signals your readiness to access the transformational realms of your mind, you will be "operationally ready."

Prosperity—Aspects Using The Summer Lands

Natural Forces:

Winds: In the East, take time to focus your mind, to create a sharp and clear image of what you specifically want and how you envision the manifest forms.

Flames: In the South, examine your willpower and your strength to do what you have to in order to help activate prosperity responsibly and honorably.

Mists: In the West, get a feel for your emotional needs, for prosperity won't provide a solution if you really aren't in need of prosperity but are needy instead. Work on that first; the self-growth will trigger abundance in the aspects you truly need.

Tides: Check the patterns of energy flow in your life, or work with the lunar/solar cycles. If energy is building, direct your image to expand from that building power. If it is waning, or you are, focus on clearing your line to the renewing power you need.

Directions: North, Center, Circle, Encircling

Some people feel that the cardinal point, North, is rather intense, but I don't find that true for me, in most cases. This can be solved by focusing on the Circle, encircling as a whole, then on the center as a catalyst, or connection point between yourself and the surrounding energies. Then focus on the North, and be specific: The North represents a structured order and wisdom presented in a linear fashion, so state your intentions logically and wisely. This activates those aspects that connect directly to prosperous growth.

Consider that your credit and potentials for success are good, or even better. Now consider how you would, as a bank president, ask for money. Remember that only those valued individuals who are most respected get to avoid having to deal with clerks. This you can surely do so in imagery and it can prepare you well for doing it in life, if and when you have to. You can also imagine asking your board of directors or stockholders. Just remember that you own the majority share, as president, or CEO (chief executive officer). In Arthurian imagery, practice presenting this plan to someone like Sir Kai, who requires a valid, reasonable attitude because he projects that, archetypally. Then when you work with the access allies, you'll avoid blowing the energies away in the archetypal rush of power these figures can create.

Elements: Earth and Spirit, with Some Fire

The element of Earth is an aspect that is dealt with much like you deal with the direction North. However, the elemental power that is Earth is slow moving, most of the time, in its manifestation of form. Therefore, a specifically crafted list and symbols that represent prosperity to you are most helpful. Also use step-by-step reviews of how you will be a part of structuring this prosperity, before, during, and after the manifestation process.

Also, approach Earth as an element and not as an elemental. An elemental is a commonly crafted concept representing the consciousness of Nature and self-nature as it relates to the correlated aspects of each element. When you are in tune with Nature and self-nature, you'll image these in an elementally more enlightened manner. To do this lightly, always just consider that these are Fair Folk aspects, and address your images as earth faeries, fire faeries, and so forth.

Address Earth first for its aspects that correlate with prosperity. Then address Spirit to show that your purpose is clear and honorable. Address Fire as the element of willpower you will need to remain active in your part of the process involved.

Then return to the North and address Earth again, in a somewhat more specific, consolidated manner. Repeating yourself is needed here. This helps activate the dimensions of your mind and allows you to reach the realms of transformation within. The first statement addressing the North and/or Earth was the business or Beta wave part of your brain and mind being put on alert. This is the focusing wave.

The second, or repeat of the statement, is a more relaxed, receptive awareness, or the Alpha waves of light imagery. This allows the emerging images to provide information to you from within. You may find that you haven't thought of everything, which is why something worth saying is often repeated. It connects more positively that way.

Now return to Spirit in a more relaxed Alpha-wave way and declare your intentions more spiritually. Then return to Fire and, in the same way, activate a deeper fire of purpose.

Then back to Earth, but this time, in silence. Begin to transmit and receive in images. Use only a few key words, if you need to, because words are linear and this third addressing of the elemental aspects is a deeply moving connection. This third request activates the Theta-wave part of your brain, which is the archetypally empowering realm of mind where deep transformations are made. In Theta it is best to use only symbols to keep your focus. These may be natural, such as candle flames, or stones and crystals. They may be symbolic representations, such as a silver dollar, or a money clip; but please, not an empty wallet! There can also be symbols you create, such as a simplified design of your own plan—or a flow chart. These will work if you're not prone to being a Beta-wave type, which can stimulate too much thinking.

Theta is a powerful wave that allows a truly transformational experience by connecting Mind, in the mystical

planes, with Brain, on the mundane plane. It is the wave of once and future transformations brought currently into the present.

Back to Spirit, with silent reflection, in the same Theta-wave manner. Then to Fire where your state of consciousness can help you access the divine fire within. Find the deepest motivational powers within yourself from this realm of consciousness.

Aspects: Abundance, Growth, Success, Expansion

These are key words with which you craft your intentions specifically. Use these as the headings on your list if they seem too general to you.

Colors: Green Ray, Crystal and Spirit Lights

Image rich green swirls, or lasers of intense vibration and tone. Amplify with clarity and lift them higher with the unseen light of Crystal. Build these together and lift them higher and higher in your image. Then imagine the highest and go beyond that as you are able; then feel the infusion of spirit entering with its divine enlightenment. When you feel that spiritual connection, send your colors flying truly into the Divine realm of Spirit.

Kindred Spirits: Cattle, Horses, Dogs, Osprey, Salamander

These are key images that symbolize aspects of transformation of growth, wealth, and prosperity. Use these in crafting an image you can focus with in Beta, flow with in Alpha, and reflect within in Theta. Until you are practiced at this, choose only one or two. Later you can position these at points in your circle to be symbolic cues connecting you with the aspects and elements there, as follows:

Cattle: North—Earth—Wealth, power, and control.

Horses: Center—Self—Vehicle, your ride into realms of imagery. Also a championship symbol when used in the South with Fire.

Dogs: West—Water—Emotional sensitivities, relationships, and loyalties. Reminds you to be your own best friend. Only you know how to do that best, after all.

Salamander: South—Fire—Transformational strength, endurance, and protection (like smaller fire-dragons, with an earthier, slower quality).

Osprey: East—Air—Focus, aim, perception, and awareness. The skills of a hunter.

Tree: Elder

Elders are powerful symbols of renewal and communication. However, this does not have to be the Elder, specifically, for prosperity. The elder aspect of any tree symbolizes a long, strong cycle of growth, and a balanced aspect of receiving and activating with natural powers. Also a shamanic use of the elder aspect of a tree can be used to help shift your brain waves to access realms where you can change your life by changing your mind. The high branches are more spiritual in aspect and activate Theta waves in an expansive manner. This feels a bit like flying.

The roots are more elemental, or deep-natured in aspect and activate Alpha in a grounded, centered manner. It's a slower-paced state of relaxed receptivity. Below the roots is a shamanic type of Theta which feels like entering an ancient cave. This aspect is best for healing renewal, connecting with allies and kindred spirits, and direct connection to the powers of the Earth, as the most ancient Mother Goddess. This deep Theta shamanic journey can help you find the root of the problem in any situation that recurs despite your efforts to do something about it. Perhaps you have just touched upon the surface or the shallow aspects of the root of the problem. Deeper roots rest deeper within the center of yourself. Shamanic journey may give you a whole new insight, so it is best done before you craft a transformation.

Stones: Emeralds, Aventurines, Diamonds, Clear Crystal Clusters, or Points

Stones have wonderful energies, or properties, in their own right. For purposes of imagery and mystical/magickal mind realms, stones are a beautiful way to hold your focus, naturally. They can be a constant reminder if you carry them with you, or keep them where they are a part of your daily experience. They have a "friendly" way of keeping you on task, focused, and aware of how the transformations are coming along.

Expensive stones don't always have more powers. Often the reverse is true. If you collect these just for specific ceremonies, they will not be as allied or linked to you. Choose stones and crystals that connect with you as though you were both magnetic. These are the most empowering ones and they are seldom of the "just another pretty face" variety. Beautiful stones and crystals are wonderful when they connect you to Beauty within. Otherwise, they are only ornaments; and that is fine, for purposes of focusing. Choose stones that create an image in your mind when you see or feel them. Those are the "keystones" for crafting.

Emeralds are intense green ray stones that correlate with abundance, health, expansion, and growth. These do not need to be gemstones. Rough emeralds have an earthy quality which relates to a balanced, steadier flow of abundance.

Aventurine is a sparkling stone with an "Earth faerie" quality for luck and success. These can be used alone, as they are, or amplified with crystal to increase the intensity. With gold, Aventurine is a fast luck charm; with copper it offers a steadier flow.

Diamonds are symbolic of bonds of connections and pledges. They represent wealth in a detached, calculating manner. This is a valuable aspect for bringing prosperity into your life. Diamonds can be an objective ally with insight into what you need. Develop a "Diamond Attitude," which is a way to assess situations well, before agreeing to "bond" with them.

Clear Crystals, clusters, points: Crystals amplify your energies and your intentions as well as your natural, mystical, or mundane allies and symbols.

Incense: Evergreen

Incense is the quickest way to set the mood, because it connects your most primal sense, which is smell. When you have associated smells and images, you can gently access the realms where changes within begin, and continue. Evergreen is eternal in its symbolic aspect, and represents continuing abundance as well as growth.

Cycle: Midsummer

The cycles in your imageries do not have to match "real-time" cycles, though they can be very powerful when they do. The cycle in imagery represents the natural cycle needed for the transformational experience or manifestation to progress effectively.

Setting: Lands

The settings are more specifically related to the location types in the legends. There are some that are specific locations; but these are sometimes already so powerfully associated with shared images they can get in the way of personal images.

Lands are growing wealth—but also responsibility.

Hallows: Gameboard, Stone of Destiny, Crystal Sphere

The Hallows are symbolic keys with a tried-and-true quality. However, they are best selected for your use by your experience of them, not by what others tell you. Try them to see what connects for you.

Gameboard: The processes of life that we could see more clearly if we had the objective viewpoint of a player more of the time, and the subjective view of a pawn less often.

Stone of Destiny: The spiritual blueprint, mind design, and physical encoded patterns. In essence, DNA, as we project it to contain extensive codes. Cue to remind you to use divination skills to access the patterns of your life. Before you change things, it is advisable to use the skills, as it is later to check up.

Crystal Sphere: The symbolic representation of the image itself—as a clear, reflective whole. Also a cue for divination, and looking within, for more clarity. Project your visions into crystal spheres, whether mystically or naturally crafted forms. This provides amplified focus for your purposes.

Themes: Round Table, Quests

The themes are each important parts of the greater pattern, or the 'round. The Round Table symbolizes a group effort, even if that group is made up of the aspects of yourself. It is a high-ideal symbol and helps keep your intentions positive and Right, so your use of prosperity will be positively and rightfully balanced and renewing. Quests symbolize your willingness to make the transformational "journeys" within in order to be a more productive participant in the contributions of your life. Quests can be either simple or complex. As long as they are sincere efforts, the rights to success are increased.

Access Allies: Arthur, Guinevere, Lancelot

These are the archetypal characters whose powers are symbolically encoded, often in various aspects. Arthur is the catalyst activator, or the "gold" that correlates with expanded active growth and success. Guinevere is the receptor who reminds you to be intuitive and consider what you truly need. Prosperity is not always money. It can be new cycles of personal growth in every aspect of your life. Lancelot is the reflector which symbolizes the need to reflect mystical process with balanced effort in the mundane.

Message: Magnetism

Magnetism is an aspect which attracts or rejects, in an amplified manner. To attract prosperity, you will have to behave with a wise, prosperous attitude. This is a thrifty, reasonable attitude, one in which you get true value for what you spend. Cheap is negative, as is wasteful use of resources. Neither is balanced. This type of balance is essential in order to adjust the magnetic flow of energies and personal efforts. This will then attract what you need, in balance, and in a steadier flow. Magnetism provides a way to find the true power of the middle path—or flow, neither too high and fast, nor too low and slow. When we get used to this middle flow or path, we realize how often we are able to flow directly. In effect, the balance of magnetism and middle path gives us a straight shot and allows us to hit the mark far more often.

This mini-course is not one you must follow point by point. Instead, glean what you want and use it in a balanced way to create the transformations you want for yourself. "The Hallowed Lands" is the next instructive imagery exercise to inspire your own experience. Since it is designed essentially to help you get in the mood, it will not be as detailed as some of the others in the text, particularly those presented in later chapters.

THE HALLOWED LANDS: EXPANDED EMPOWERMENT

Elements: All, in synthesis

Directions: Center, Circle and Circle, encircling

Aspects: Activation of shared, group potentials, service

Colors: Yellow, Red, Blue, Green, Indigo Rays, Rainbow and Crystal lights

Kindred Spirits: Eagle, Lion, Unicorn, Griffin, Dragon

Tree: Grove

Stones: Clear Crystal cluster (plus glass, candles, or stones to match the colors)

Incense: Evergreen

Cycle: Midsummer

Setting Image: Forest

Hallow: Cup, Shield, Sword, Spear, Stone of Destiny

Theme: Lands

Natural Force: Winds, Flames, Mists, Tides, Spirit

Access Allies: The Merlin, Nimue, Gawain, Arthur, Morgawse

Format: Extensive

Message: Before you take action—or approach a situation head-on, consider well the cause and the effect, the intent and reaction, and the potential consequence—as well as those that could become almost exponential.

———

You are awakened by your favorite rainbow dragon, who is eager for adventure and ready to transport you to the mystical realms of transformation and magick. You soon find yourself riding your dragon far above the beautiful lands and oceans of your mother planet, the Earth. All the land forms and bodies of water are shimmering with a mystical light. You circle the Earth three times for good measure, following the path of the Sun.

You ride your dragon through a high white layer of clouds and swoop across the western hemisphere until you reach your ancestral lands. You come in for a landing over a beautiful forest which covers the landscape in rich midsummer shades of green for miles and miles, all 'round. As you circle the forest before you approach, you see a clearing surrounded by ancient and majestic trees. There are many Fair Folk gathered in that clearing, and you see that they are dressed ceremonially. As you prepare to touch down in this realm, you realize your landing point in the clearing is placing you right in the center of a sacred Druidic grove.

As you make your landing, the dragon transforms, considerately, to a manageable size. By the time you can smell the rich evergreen fragrance of the forest, the dragon has become no bigger than a house, and when you dismount, he shifts again, to the size of a "pocket dragon." The Merlin is there at the center of this grove in his ceremonial robes of deep indigo blue. The Merlin is standing beside a symbol stone which is covered with patterns and codes of mystery. He greets you ceremonially, but smiles warmly as he taps on your forehead with the ring he is wearing. You glimpse an indigo azurite set in platinum, just as his magick transformation takes place. You find yourself in robes of ceremonial style, Fey-fashioned from a rainbow weave which reflects the colors and lights all 'round. The Merlin calls to your attention the legendary folk who are in the inner circle of this sacred grove. With friendly formality, you greet each of these as allies, and they return your greeting, in kind. First in the East, you acknowledge Gawain, who is present to bring his powers of perceptive focus. He is dressed in a bright yellow tunic; upon it a white eagle trimmed in gold. He is holding a Fey-crafted spear, with a shaft made of copper, and a point formed from yellow jasper stone. Gawain is wearing a silver ring set with a yellow citrine.

Then, in the South, you acknowledge Arthur, present at this time for his protection and power of will. He is dressed in red and wearing golden armor on his chest, with a royal lion smithcrafted in the metal. He is holding a sword of power with a doubled-edged blade of steel, and a golden hilt set with red jaspers. Arthur is wearing a gold ring set with a bright, fiery ruby.

In the West, you acknowledge Guinevere, present here to bring powers for healing renewal. She is dressed in blue, trimmed in silver and white, with a jeweled brooch over her heart. The brooch is a silver unicorn set upon a silver-framed oval of deep blue sodalite stone. She is holding an ancient Fey-crafted cup made of silver and lined with gold. Guinevere's ring is a clear-blue sapphire in a braided setting, one strand of silver, one pewter, one gold.

In the North, you acknowledge Morgawse, present here for her strategic powers and her skills at structuring plans. She is wearing green, with elaborate gold-braided trim, a great golden torque around her neck, and golden bracelets set with aventurine on each of her arms. She is holding a Celtic shield, made of bronze, with a griffin smithcrafted in gold on the front. Morgawse is wearing another braided ring; but this one is gold, bronze, and copper. Her ring is set with a rough-cut emerald surrounded by steel-blue diamonds.

You return to the East and greet with an element of kinship the Fair Folk allies, who are standing in pairs behind each of the legendary allies. Behind Gawain, you acknowledge the Faerie Wizards, dressed in airy, Bardic blues and sacred Druidic white. Behind Arthur are the Faerie Warriors, in fiery oranges, with armor of bronze and gold. Behind Guinevere are the Faerie Priests and Priestesses in watery tones of lavender and blue-gray. Behind Morgawse are the Faerie Sovereigns in rich earthy tones of forest green and copper brown.

As you acknowledge this middle, Mother Earth's power circle, you see that

The Sovereign Lady of the Lands is with them, present in her illuminated form of The White Goddess, and with her is Her Lord of Light. These sacred symbols of Divine Nature have transformed as you acknowledged the Fair Folk, and the legendary allies as well. Behind Gawain, in the East, the Lady was a young flowery maiden, and the Lord was a bright young lad, with a harp to play for the Lady. Behind Arthur, in the South, the Lady's transformation was a crafted blend, the maiden as warrior and queen of expanded Summer's power. The Lord shone in the brightest light, as king of Summer, with the full power of the sun.

Behind Guinevere, in the West, the Lady and the Lord were another crafted blend. The Lady showed a holy, maternal aspect as a strong, healing Mother Superior. In concert, the Lord presented a spiritual, paternal quality as a Sacred Father. Both the Lord and the Lady reflected the Autumn in their wise eyes, which shone with the harvest of experience. Though both projected a darker light, it was the natural reflection of the cycle of release and renewal.

Behind Morgawse in the North, also crafted as a blend, the Lady was a Wise Mother. The Lady was an older woman, with crone aspects that were grandmotherly and knowledgeable. The Lord was a Wise Old Wizard with a practical, grandfatherly aspect. Now the Lord and the Lady are both acknowledged by you for all their natural, essential aspects. Then they transmute into the Circle, encircling which expands, eternally in Spirit. Before you return your attention to the inner circle and the central task, you silently circle once more. As you do this, you sense the presence of Divine allies shining their highest Light of Spiritual power in spirals of energy upon all whose service is for the good of the All. Knowing that you are truly one who works for the Right, in the service of the Light, you return to the center to begin. There in the center, within the inner circle, which is within the Circle of elements, you feel the expanded circle, encircling; illuminating your transformations.

Sometimes what seems to be an individual and strictly personal matter, proves otherwise. Sometimes our intentions cause us to take action regardless of the consequences, which we only see as possible for ourselves. These are the very ones that seem to cause the widest effects on others. This is a natural law in action, that has expanded beyond its expected reactions because our intentions are not clear, or are an overreaction to begin with. It can create a chain of actions and reactions that soon moves from being out of balance to being out of control. So, before you act or react, consider that true power comes from learning to assess a situation for its potential success or failure: with clear sight, clear mind, and clear intentions. If action is appropriate, take action appropriately. In that way, you can take power, positively.

The Hallowed Lands — Aspects for Transformation

This transformational crafting may be done with imagery alone, with a few forms of the aspects for focus, or with as many as you choose. The simplest forms to use would be stones, candles, glass, fabric, or paper to match the colors. Additionally, crystals and clusters in light tones. As I instruct you in this crafting example, I will not specify whether an aspect is an image or a form. This is because that choice depends on what kind of approach you want, the degree of complexity you feel comfortable with, and the forms of correlated aspects that you have currently.

If you use imagery exclusively, you cast the circles first, then call up the aspects in imagery. If you use even the simple forms, such as stones or candles, lay them out first (but don't light the candles with which you activate the inner circle until you are ready to begin—even if you use only one "center-fire" candle. Remember, it is always all right to practice until you develop a style all your own. I call this solitary style or personal tradition, used by the powerful "majority of one." Naturally, that is you. If you use a group, formal, or traditional ritual approach, you may find this ceremonial style feels too free-flowing. So feel free to adapt the aspects to suit your traditional approach.

Specific Directional Correlational Aspects

Choose whatever forms you want from the aspects presented here, in correlation with the directions for this specific ceremony. Feel free to substitute or move around whichever forms you wish. However, you might want to try these directional aspect correlations at first, to get a feel for this style.

Inner Circle
East: Air—Perceptive Focus
Color: Yellow—Inspiration
Kindred Spirit: Eagle—Philosophic power
Stone: Yellow jasper—Intellect
Hallow: Spear—Communication of ideas;
Force: Winds (shifting, changes of direction)

South: Fire—Protective Will
Color: Red—Life-force
Kindred Spirit: Lion—Physical power
Stone: Red jasper—guardianship
Hallow: Sword—Activation of potentials
Force: Flames (energizing, changes of strength)

West: Water—Personal Renewal
Color: Blue—Intuition
Kindred Spirit: Unicorn—Mystical power
Stone: Sodalite—Emotional support
Hallow: Cup—Acceptance of healing
Force: Mists (soothing, changes of feelings)

North: Earth—Practical Prosperity
Color: Green—Expansion
Kindred Spirit: Griffin—Structured Power
Stone: Aventurine—Success
Hallow: Shield—Declaration of Power
Force: Tides (ordered, change of flow)

Center, Spirit—Source
Color: Indigo—Synthesis
Kindred Spirit: Dragon—Elemental Power
Stone: Amethyst—Magick (magery)
Hallow: Stone of Destiny—Codes of Power
Force: Spirit (inclusive circle, spiral)

Circle, encircling—Divine Light
Forms: Candles—Illumination
      White, Ivory, Lavender, Violet, Rose
      Crystals—Amplification; Quartz (Milky, clear, rose) and amethyst
Force: Spirit (expansive circles)

Practice Task—Association Encoding

Images: Using each of the directions and their aspects, create or allow an image to emerge that represents the combination. Start with two or three, and add the others as your image "crystallizes" into a personal code in your own mind. For example: North—An image of the planet Earth with light green lands and light blue oceans: Focus to amplify for Expansion and the image has bright green lands.

Focus on a rich green, sparkling aventurine stone. Expand your image by transforming the stone into a large, shimmering green shield. Also imagine the green aventurine in the form of a griffin, sitting atop a prosperous-looking castle, or flying over rich lands. Surround your home, business, or the planet with a sparkling green shield (force field) of shimmering aventurine, which is translucent.

Note: The symbolic aspects and archetypes in your images can all be transformed with the catalyst of various lights. Color rays are more direct and intense. Lights make it easier to shape or spread color rays around and shift their qualities to symbolically represent the transformations you are crafting for manifestation in your life.

Catalyst Lights for Imagery Crafting

Metallic: Transformation and encoding qualities
Silver: Receptive
Gold: Active
Bronze: Active manifestation, strong reflective
Pewter: Receptive manifestation, subtle reflective
Copper: Active manifestation, subtle reflective

Platinum: Multidimensional, catalyst for access and activation, intense reflective qualities

Steel: Strong reflective qualities (receptive + active).

Etheric: (as imagery transformative lights)

White: Medium for transmission, gentle reflective qualities

Black: Medium for release, subtle receptive

Crystal: Medium for amplification, intense reflective

Rainbow: Medium for reflective, ordered qualities.

Some examples of transformations using those lights would be: An image of a white shield with a green griffin, activated by brushing the shield and/or the griffin with gold. An image of the planet with a rainbow force field of light, amplified with a green, crystalline light, making the lands and oceans both brighter, enriched with abundant power, a "prosperous planet."

Using the aspects and the lights, practice with the individual directions, then blend them together until all four are in an elementally powerful synthesis, reflected in your imagery. Infuse Spirit with intense lights, in circles, spirals, or lasers.

Images and Words: Association Encoding Exercise

Practice adding key words to your images—either spoken, visualized, or both. Start with the directional correlated words and elements. For example: the Griffin Shield with the words "Earth" and "Prosperity" written in gold. Be creative and use another language—or create one, *Terra Prospera.*

Practice with these until you are ready to craft your own synthesis by blending combinations of the associated, now encoded images into transformational "I-magery." For example: A dragon emerging from the center of the Earth, then merging with a bright rainbow that encircles the planet, and flying around the globe empowering the regions with a synthesis of harmony, or specific qualities such as green laser rays for prosperity in third-world countries. Also, the dragon could carry Hallows where their qualities are needed. For example: A blue crystal cup for healing, or a yellow crystal spear to amplify communication.

Hallowed Lands: Catalyst Archetypes and Images

Catalyst Image: A Forest Grove at Midsummer in the Lands

Lands: Expanded Circle, encircling

Forest: Circle (middle, if using three)

Grove: Center (or inner circle, if using three)

Midsummer: Active/Reflective Cycle (balanced expansion energy)

Catalyst Archetypes: Directions and Access Allies

The Circle (or Inner Circle)

East: Gawain—Perceptive reflection and focus

South: Arthur—Protective activation and strength
West: Nimue—Personal receptivity and intuition
North Morgawse—Practical activation and strategy

Center: The Merlin—Power reflection and Archmagery

Circle, encircling: Angelic, Devic (Spirits of place) or The Shining Ones (Spirit Fey)

Center/Self: You and/or others crafting the transformation
Note: If three circles are used, then these may be added:

Middle Circle: Fair Folk—Elemental Power Allies
East: Faerie Wizards, Druids, Bards—Air power
South:: Faerie Warriors, Riders of the Sidhe (She)—Fire power
West: Faerie Priests and Priestesses, Healers, Initiators—Water power
North: Faerie Sovereigns, Royals, Chieftains, Clan Mothers—Earth power
Note: Link these with the White Goddess for Spirit power

Practice with these archetypal and symbolic catalyst allies to craft a connection with them that is more familiar. Using the aspects presented in this chapter along with others in this text and within yourself, practice crafting your own blended imageries to create transformation imageries and personal power in balance and synthesis in your own realm of life.

Crafting Transformation

From this Hallowed Lands imagery, you can proceed to craft for a transformation in your own life and expand it to others—lands as well as people. You can expand your transformation to illuminate the world with your craft of Light, thus joining a global alliance of Light workers. However, you won't always want to work with such expanded realms, so use these simple guidelines to narrow your focus as need be:

Center: crafting personal transformation with only an aspect or two to inspire imagery within. If you wish to add more aspects or expand to include others, you will be wise to do this with a balanced approach. Use an inner circle until your craft becomes a self-balancing synthesis, and then from time to time to maintain this personal empowerment. Craft as a circle unto yourself.

The Inner Circle: Crafting for specific purposes, working with/for others (as a catalyst for their self-work), working for group, community, or regions of lands surrounding where you are, working with lands that have ancestral, mythical, or spiritual connective power for you.

The Middle Circle: Crafting with/for Nature with elemental power. Here the inner circle provides a balancing medium for these intense Nature energies and the intensity of their correlated aspects found within self-nature.

The Circle, encircling: Crafting with/for expanded realms of both mundane and mystical/spiritual form. The sacred three is a holy trinity in many traditions of Light.

This triple circle allows a pure and clear transmission of highest purposes. The middle circle can be merged with this one to create a circle of Divine Power which is the synthesis of all that is in the realms of self-nature, Nature, and Spirit.

Note: Celestial and stellar "craft" can also be done with this triple circle. Transformations with types of craft (I call it working with space-Faeries—but the Earth is the mother ship for me!) need amplified, multidimensional images. The emphasis is on the expanded circle; so remember to circle back in. There are transformations which need crafting right here. There is a need for all those who have Light-craft skills to remain on the beautiful blue-green planet to which they were posted.

One more point that can help with your archetypal access allies: The allies from the realms of Camelot's legends are all wearing rings which I described in detail. This was done not to "test your metal," but to give you gem-quality catalysts to experience their aspects more effectively.

I will tell you what the gemstones symbolize and also on which hand they each wore their rings. Just remember that you can change this, too. That makes it a personal craft. The rings are a symbol of focused power, and a finger can be a wand. Rings on archetypal allies represent the most laser-like forces of light, and the most important points that your images of them are making. Therefore, to the point:

The Merlin: Azurite/Right—Amplified Synthesis/active
Gawain: Citrine/Left—Amplified Self-image/receptive
Arthur: Ruby/Right—Amplified Life-force/active
Guinevere: Sapphire/Left—Amplified Intuition/receptive
Morgawse: Emerald/Diamond/Right—Amplified Balance/active and amplified
   Bonds/active.

The Emerald and the Diamond are both associated with matters of the heart. The rough cut of Morgawse's emerald signifies her more elemental and barbaric warrior queen aspect. Steel-blue diamonds represent skills at calculating and assessing a situation with the will to plan before acting or reacting. These are essential aspects of structuring order.

Even in their most fiery representations (historical, mythological, archetypal) warrior queens were strategic. If this aspect of Morgawse is too intense for you, lighten her up with a clear, bright emerald and blue-white diamonds. Put a silver band on her left hand, with peridot or tourmaline to renew her image, and give her a little more heart. Morgawse can be a valuable, archetypal ally. Celtic is an expanded clan, and Morgawse is one strong aspect of Clan-Mother.

If you want to choose a ring for yourself for transformational crafting with imagery, try topaz. The blue topaz is an amplifier in the neural realms of the brain; and the Bardic realms of the mind. Golden topaz is a brain stimulator, as well as an energizer. It also activates the Mind. Blue and silver on the left and gold with gold on the right—what will that do for you?

CHAPTER 22

THE MERLIN EMERGES:
REFLECTIVE POWER

Remember the Web. The physical Universe (assuming it's there) is a huge Web of interlocking energy, in which every atom and every energy wave is connected with every other one … the major aim of mystics is not to 'join' or 'unite' with the Web; but to achieve full realization of the fact that already all of us are united within the Web. Similarly, the major aim of a magician is to gain understanding (by whatever means necessary) of the structure of the Web and his place within it, so that he can manipulate strands of it to suit his purposes and produce desired results.

P. E. I. "Isaac" Bonewits
Real Magic (Berkeley, CA: Creative Arts Book Co., 1971)

The realm of The Merlin is multidimensional. Its power links the microcosmic Mind and Brain with the macrocosmic "tissue" or expansive forms Brain, and the interactive "events" or creative forces which we may call the Universal Mind. This realm is reflective of the highest evolved dimensions of both receptive and active potentials in humankind, microcosmically, and in the Mind of All, macrocosmically. In effect, it is the conscious mind operating through the brain, yet with an evolved utilization of the physical potentials and an expanded realization of all its mystical, magickal, and spiritual possibilities.

It is the realm where ancient wisdom meets modern science. Both ancient and modern become unified, making it no longer possible to distinguish the probable defining qualities of either. There then exists the unified, unlimited potential of the blend.

Approach this realm with intellectual objectivity, expecting neither spiritual enlightenment nor magickal elucidations, but anticipating new awareness and expanded perceptions from which you may evolve an experiential philosophy. This is the realm where the subjective, personal experience is amplified in proportion to the way it can be objectively assessed. In other words, your attitude of open-minded awareness can lead you to the realms of ever-expanding consciousness, and your experience provides pathways to unlimited wisdom.

Remember that the human brain is estimated to be only utilized at about twelve to twenty percent of its potential capacity. In effect, we're adolescent in the way we operate our brain. However, it is also theorized that as we access and utilize the brain's capacities more fully, the now-estimated untapped resources (eighty to eight-eight percent) will prove to be far more than that. Modern physicists, metaphysicists, and those of the mystical arts agree that the potential for brain and mind expansion is exponential. Accordingly, we may have to forego any efforts to measure what we must ultimately experience, both microcosmically and macrocosmically.

As above, so below—and therefore within—the pathways linking us each and all to the multidimensional realms of Being.

The Merlin emerges into our subjective experience through imagery, thought, and expanded perceptions. As an archetypal catalyst, The Merlin provides a clear, dramatic, and intensely illuminating experience of our personal potentials. Invariably the experiences of The Merlin will reflect what you think you are seeking in a way that will mirror what it really is you want and need to know. Sometimes these experiences seem strangely misaligned with what you intended to access or manifest.

Until you have had sufficient practice, you may find an objective perspective is an elusive skill to master. Still, master it you will, as long as you continue to make the effort to assess each experience for what it did provide, rather than what it did not. Eventually, you will develop what the hypnotherapists call "split-conscious awareness." This allows you to assess objectively what you are experiencing subjectively—and currently—while you are in the experience. This is the hallmark of an evolved intellect in effective partnership with an expanded mind. This is the hallmark of a Mage—and the one which most definitively identifies the realm of The Merlin, the realm of mystical, magickal qualities to which all pathways lead within.

The Merlin represents the most distinct frequency or vibrational pattern, of all the archetypes in the realms of the Camelot legends, because it is most "electrically" charged. This is because of its direct, encoded aspects, which activate both the higher regions of thought processes and order in the brain or the linear, left brain, and the higher regions of creative process and ideas, the free-flowing, right brain. In addition to this, the key to The Merlin's archetypal power is found in the way The Merlin emerges in imagery. This occurs within multisensory, experiential, "waking dream" quality states of consciousness. These are the functions of the prefrontal region of the brain, where the left and right brains connect—at the point we call the third eye.

The activation quality of this archetypal figure accounts for the shared, unique experiences The Merlin represents. At this point in our brain we experience our own expanded visions, as well as those of others, the point where individual and collective consciousness meet. These form a pathway to what was called unconscious; now becoming increasingly conscious as our potentials activate at an evolutionarily unprecedented rate of growth. Again—it is exponential. Your image of The Merlin, or any of these legendary realms, will be similar and different than those of others.

Rather than squabble about whose image is accurate—or worse,who really does or does not have a true line to The Merlin—remember the pathways, the realms, and the images are multidimensional—so focus on the lines that connect, instead of the ones that attempt to rope off or limit access to this archetypal source of power. In truth, The Merlin is accessible to all. If you encounter those who attempt to dictate how or if The Merlin emerges for you, remember the power of draconian objectivity and view their limitations as their own—not yours. In doing this, you will already be "working The Merlin's magick" with its positive creative powers and its forces for Right evolution. If you encounter those who have been led to believe in an exclusive, separatist right to The Merlin—illuminate them with one profound truth: the truth of the right to think, experience, and act as a freely evolving individual.

The rest of this chapter is a collection of imageries designed to encourage your own experience. The setting of one personal journey account is taken from the Camelot literature as the tower with seventy-two windows, where The Merlin and his Druidic sister, Ganieda, spend their time in objective, draconian roles, observing the evolutionary processes of life. Ganieda is much like Cerridwen, the earthy wise crone aspect of the Goddess, who provides a fine balance for the electric and often spacey, expansive aspects of The Merlin.

The three guided imageries designed for you present dimensions of The Merlin that are readily accessible. One is more instructive and ordered, one more expansive, and the other illuminative in its humor. These, as are all the others in the realms of The Merlin, Camelot, and Avalon, are based on experiential work with these archetypal figures and the images that emerged. Adapt these as you choose, and note which aspects are most activating, receptive, or reflective as you experience them.

PLATINUM PATHWAYS:
MULTIDIMENSIONAL LINKING

Elements: Air and Spirit

Directions: East, Center, and the Circle encircling

Aspects: Accessing neural pathways, DNA codes

Colors: Violet ray, platinum, rainbow, and gold lights

Kindred Spirits: Dolphins

Tree: Sea

Stones: Amethyst, Topaz, Platinum crystal, Platinum

Incense: Frankincense

Cycle: Beltane

Setting Image: Henge

Hallow: Stone of Destiny

Theme: Otherworld

Natural Force: Winds

Access Allies: The Merlin, Ganieda

Format: Moderate

Message: The most direct pathways, linking the many dimensions of Universal Mind are synaptically mapped out in the realms of your own mind and brain.

It is dawn, the beginning of Beltane, and you are making your way along a well-traveled path leading to a mystical henge of stones standing on the shore beside a sea of expanded dimensions. You can hear the waves sweeping onto the beach as you approach this sacred site with a reverent spirit and a receptive consciousness. In the east, the dark night clouds are being carried out to sea by the strong winds of a new day dawning.

The soft indigo night is being transformed by golden shafts of light which reach upward from below the horizon and infuse the sky with violet rays. The sea is shimmering with rainbows from a source of illumination deep below its surface; inexplicably empowering the lands with its intangible, enlightened strength.

In the shallows behind the waves, you catch sight of dolphins gathering in great numbers. The first rays of this new day's sun glisten on the dolphins' backs and fins as they leap and dive; calling out to each other—calling out to you. By the time you reach the henge, you can see the dolphins quite clearly. In the dawn light, they look like priceless platinum treasures against an amethyst sea. You are entranced by their beauty and enchanted by their graceful motions. The winds are moving briskly now throughout the standing stones of the henge, and you gather your robes around you for warmth. You are quite content to watch the multitude of dolphins as they move through the waters. With each graceful arc they make, the dolphins send sprays of clear water up from the surface of the sea. The pale golden sunlight creates perfect spectrum rainbows in each crystalline drop of water. For a time you are only aware of the beauty and the lights you behold on this Beltane dawn.

You hear the sound of two people approaching, and you turn to find that Ganieda and The Merlin have joined you at the henge. Both are dressed in ceremonial robes of amethyst velvet, richly trimmed with platinum and silver threads embroidered in an intricate, interwoven design. You greet them formally, for the occasion is serious in nature, and then they each embrace you lovingly. Their robes are heavily scented with frankincense, so you know they have already been working their own ritual magick.

The Merlin raises his staff in acknowledgment of the dolphins, and they chorus a greeting. The winds subside and all is silent, except for the sounds of the waves gently caressing the shoreline on which the henge stands. The Merlin walks in a slow circle, tapping each of the standing stones with his staff as he passes them. The great stone in the east seems to shift and change with the first touch of The Merlin's staff. In turn, the South, West, and North stones visibly transform into expanded forms, seemingly alive, alert, and conscious. As The Merlin returns to the great stone in the east, all of the smaller stones within the henge begin to resonate.

As the sounds of the stones begin to build, the dolphins join in with their own chorus. The winds build quickly, and the waves begin crashing onto the beach. The sounds blend and build until they create a harmony which can be heard no longer, only experienced. The tones transform themselves into frequencies of light inside your mind. The experience is intense, clear, and powerful, as the lights weave into a crystalline vision in your mind.

Just as you wonder if you are also being transformed into a frequency of intense light, the vision comes into form. It is a clear crystal web against a blue-violet background. For an instant you glimpse its pattern completely. You can even see stars, suns, and galaxies twinkling in the blue-violet spaces between the lines of crystal light. Then, as suddenly as it came, the vision of the whole crystal web is gone from your mind. Only the memory remains, encapsulated, and your vision reflects a small, crystalline fragment of the expanded web. You focus inward to connect with that small fragment and find that it, too, reflects a pattern very similar to the greater pattern that you glimpsed, briefly. The background is a paler shade of purple now, and the crystal web shimmers with rainbow lights.

Looking even closer inward, you see that the rainbow lights are actually distinct lines of all the spectrum colors moving inside crystalline veins which had only seemed like lines before. You seek deeper within your vision in order to see more clearly. You can no longer see the stars twinkling between the grid lines; but you know they are there. Moving closer to the crystal web in your vision, you find that the spectrum colors blend deeper within the veins, and form distinct patterns. As you glimpse these patterns, you experience them. You are swept along into dimensions of time and space which you have always known were there, deeply encoded inside your mind—inside the mind of All.

Just as you begin to pursue a dimension of time and place that has always interested you, the vision expands into pure light—illuminating you with the Divine wonder of Creation's great mystery. Just as you think you know what that mystery is, your vision shrinks into a clear image of a shining web against a golden background—and you hear Ganieda calling your name.

You open your eyes to find that she is holding a beautifully crafted web made of platinum, silver and golden wires, set with amethyst crystals and blue topazes. It is brilliant, reflecting the golden sunlight through its delicate weave. When Ganieda is sure you are fully back from within your vision, she bids you to sit quietly and listen to the sound of the waves; now gently rolling onto the shoreline. You find that you are breathing rhythmically, in time with the gentle sound of the waves and the steady flow of the tides.

The Merlin sits down beside you and listens as you describe your experience of the crystal web. He nods knowingly and encourages you to explore your vision for specific purposes until you have become used to the rapidly expanding nature of the experience. Ganieda comes with a fragrant cup of tea to warm you and chides The Merlin for his expansive dramatic lessons. She leans over to kiss you lightly on the forehead, and you feel the love of this truest grandmother of all Nature's children.

As you look down at your cup of tea, you notice that you are wearing a pendant you have never seen before. It is a large blue-violet amethyst set in platinum and gold, hanging from a braided chain of silver, gold, and platinum.

Strung on the chain are beads of rainbowed crystals and blue topaz. On the blue-violet amethyst is a tiny, delicately crafted crystal web.

With a gentle, knowing smile, Ganieda takes the pendant from around your neck and places it in a pocket inside her soft violet robes. She bids you come to her when next you wish to glimpse the crystal web and trace the pathways of light to which this mystical stone of destiny can lead you. Next time, Ganieda tells you, she will decide when you are ready to wear this sacred pendant. With another gently reproachful glance at The Merlin, Ganieda takes her leave of you both. As she turns to walk away, The Merlin winks at you and quietly tells you what you have encoded will provide a clear map to link you, multidimensionally, with all the lines and pathways on that crystal web that you will ever need. All he did, he tells you, is to show you where the map was hidden ... deep inside your mind.

The Merlin pats you tenderly on the head and bids you good-bye for the time being. You rest for a while, sipping your tea in the now-silent henge of stones. You gaze out to sea and watch until the last dolphin leaves for the deeper waters of the great blue ocean beyond the horizon. As the dolphin arcs and dives below the surface, you step on the pathway and return to dimensions of the present place and time once again.

THE HENGE EXPANDED:
MAGICK EVOLUTION

Elements: Air, Fire, Water, Earth, and Spirit

Directions: East, South, West, North, and Center

Aspects: Mind expansion, magick synthesis, and evolution

Colors: Violet-Blue, Indigo ray, Crystal, Platinum, Copper

Kindred Spirits: Dragon, Eagle

Tree: Grove

Stones: Amethyst, Azurite, Opals, Crystal point, Platinum, Copper

Incense: Heather

Cycle: Vernal Equinox

Setting Image: Henge in Forest Grove

Hallow: Staff, Synergy Crystal

Theme: Otherworld

Natural Force: Winds

Access Allies: The Merlin

Format: Extensive

Message: The forms of power will expand and evolve only as well as the foundations for them were erected, supportively. From a foundation crafted of an illuminated synthesis of all the elements of Self and Nature, power can expand exponentially and evolve into the Magick realms of Power and Enlightenment.

It is a clear, starlit night in spring, the eve of the vernal equinox in a once and future time. You are alone with The Merlin at an ancient stone henge. The tall stones are shimmering with a platinum light as they stand majestically silhouetted against an indigo sky. It is an evening for deep magick, and for the evolutionary expansion of your gifts of power. It is a time for personal acceptance, for elemental initiation into the mysteries of Nature and self-nature.

The henge of stones stands encircled by a grove of sacred trees, eternally connected to the lands and to the realms of Spirit. In the center of the henge is a blue stone altar, carved with elemental symbols of power and sacred spiritual wisdoms. On the altar, beautiful stones and crystals reflect the expansive light of Springtime's fullest Moon. Violet, indigo, and electric-blue lights flash in the

moonlight from these altar stones, amethyst, azurite, and mysterious milky opals. To this ceremonial collection of stones and sacred crystals, you add your own synergy crystal, symbolizing the synthesis of yourself.

Fresh breezes blow in from the forest grove and sweep through the henge, making spiral patterns in the grasses and heather on the ground. On the altar is an urn, crafted of copper and platinum, with Celtic weave designs etched in the highly polished surface. A fragrant mass of heather stands in the urn. Tall wax pillars burn brightly upon the altar, illuminating the henges with a quiet, mysterious glow of power.

The Merlin stands facing you across the altar in his most respected aspect as the Celtic Archmage of All-Time. Both of you are dressed in robes of royal blue, on which symbols of your mystical rank and power are embroidered in threads of platinum, copper, silver, and gold. The Merlin is carrying a staff you have not seen before, except, perhaps, in your dreams and inner vision. Atop the staff is a double-headed eagle, regally crafted and highly polished to a spiritual sheen. The eyes of the eagle are opaline and reflect intense lights of every hue.

The Merlin signals complete silence. This is a time, not for words, but for experiencing that which is beyond words and any other form of definition other than your own. The Merlin raises the eagle staff and cobalt lights arch across the sky as he swings this sacred implement in a series of wide, sweeping spirals. Soon the henge of stones and the encircling grove of trees are glowing with a mystical blue light. Although the winds have increased with each sweep of The Merlin's staff, the candle flames are still tall, straight, and steady. High above the henge and the encircling grove, the winds spiral with intense force; seemingly strong enough to move the Moon and stars around in the clear night sky. Then, The Merlin signals you to activate the power for yourself.

Inwardly whispering words of magick of your own design, you begin to incant a personal litany of power. As you do this, you feel the stones on the altar and the standing stones in the henge begin to resonate in time with the rhythm of your incantation of power. With each incantation, the blue lights illuminating the henge and the grove brighten and expand in ever-widening circles of an electrified cobalt hue.

Eventually, the circles expand beyond the horizon, and even the celestial sky becomes illuminated by these deeply mystical, electric-blue circles of light. Then, for a truly magickal moment, the stars, the tall stones, and the grove transform into a sphere of crystalline blue. No forms are discernible. There is only the sphere of illuminating light in which all is transmuted to the highest dimensions of power.

Remembering your experiences of magick and spiritual empowerment, you slowly bring the sphere into form by absorbing its light into your own form. There, the light and power may be expressed in the forms of your magickal craft and spiritual service. When you have accepted the light and power fully within yourself, you realize that the true initiation of self has begun.

The Merlin is waiting with a wise patience when you have completed your cycle of acceptance. From this point in your path, you know the gifts and the responsibilities of power become yours completely. With this message transmitted, acknowledged, and accepted, The Merlin bestows the title of Truthsayer upon you, and other magickal titles known only to yourself, which honor your personal gifts and skills of your craft. You listen carefully, with heart and mind, to each title, and you wisely choose to accept only those for which you have the true gift of knowing. Those which reflect aspects and achievements most familiar within yourself are the ones you accept most openly and to which you grant personal seniority. Others, less familiar, yet still fitting, you accept as an earnest, devoted novice. Still others, which do not seem quite appropriate for your personal place upon the pathways of self-expansion and evolutionary power, you accept with gratitude as aspects of future possibility. The Merlin reminds you that these titles of power and position may change as you evolve spiritually and magickally. Only those titles which you may honorably bear, along with that of Truthsayer, truly will be yours, regardless of who bestows these titles.

This you know is true, and you accept as Right. In so doing, you expand your titles to include Right Honorable Mage, initiate in the service of the power of Light and the Sovereignty of the Lands. As this is a personal Druidic initiation, The Merlin reminds you the only degrees are the degrees of arbitrary limitations, or limitless expanded wisdom you place upon yourself.

This being said, acknowledged, and accepted, The Merlin bestows upon you the sacred gift of the Druidic eagle staff. He furthers your process of initiation by informing you of this staff's sacred transformational powers. The staff may transform to any shape, or in any fashion which will reflect the Light of Right power you require. This transformational power is eternally experienced within and reflected in form from the evolutionary expansions of your Mind and Spirit. The Merlin suggests you begin activating this personal transformational power by creating elemental dragons of illuminated quality.

Taking the staff reverently in your right hand and your synergy crystal in your left hand, you begin with respect for the gifts of power and remembrance of your personal responsibilities to the Right, a new and renewing cycle of personal research—the hallmark of a Druidic Mage. There, in your inner vision, in the henge within the grove, you craft dragons of elemental power for your service to the Sacred.

Activating the element of Air, you craft dragons of mind power, enlightening your life with perception and creativity. These dragons emerge in tones of white, yellow, cobalt blue, and reflections of Springtime's natural lights. On these dragons ride Otherworld allies from Faerie realm, to bring you the gifts of illumination.

You acquaint yourself with the Fair Folk who accompany each dragon. These and the dragons themselves you acknowledge and accept as you did with the titles which reflect the aspects of yourself. As Truthsayer, you have the power and responsibility to make these choices with honor for yourself—and for others whom you may influence in realms both mystical and mundane.

The Merlin takes his leave, with promises to return, so you may practice your craft on your own. Knowing the realm of vision and mind in which this craft is initiated is eternally present within, you may choose to access and activate this according to your own purposes, plans, and pathways to expanded, evolutionary power.

You release your image.

To this end, these initial notes and aspects are provided. Also, these remind you to research your own experiential notes and the informational notes of this and other tests of your own choosing. Remember—you have the gift of the staff, and all others required, all within your personal realms of power and vision.

Primary Elemental Aspects

Fire: Body, Summer—Faith, Courage, Strength, Will. Guardians, Protectors, Catalyst Allies. Red, Orange, Amber, Gold, Electric Blue of Action.

Water: Emotions, Fall—Dream States, Healing, Divinations. Healers, Initiators, Transformational Allies. Blue, Gray, Silver, Lavender-Blue of Intuition.

Earth: Manifest Forms, Winter—Structures, Mundane and Mystical. Connectors, Standard Bearers, Manifestation Allies. Violet, Green, Black, Royal Blue of Sovereignty.

Air: Mind, Spring—Perception, Creativity, Illumination, Illuminators. Inspirers, Evolutionary Allies. Yellow, White, White Gold, Cobalt Blue of Intellect.

Spirit: Multidimensional Aspects—Divine Enlightenment. Spiritual Amplifiers, Divine Guides and Allies. Rainbow, White, Platinum, Crystal Blue of Spirit.

Remembering the limitless power of expanded spirit and evolutionary service, you may blend these and all other aspects by experimenting with wise, positive intentions, to create your own system of magickal correlations for multidimensional crafting.

THE CRYSTAL TOMB: DIVINATION

Elements: Air and Spirit

Directions: East and Center

Aspects: Access and alignment for psychic knowledge

Colors: Indigo, Violet ray, Gold, Platinum, and Copper lights

Kindred Spirits: Spider

Tree: Ash

Stones: Azurite, Amethyst, Cobalt, and Platinum crystals, Copper

Incense: Frankincense

Cycle: Yule

Setting Image: Tomb

Hallow: Grail

Theme: Hallows

Natural Force: Flames

Access Allies: The Merlin, Ganieda, Nimue

Format: Moderate

Message: The transformations of your self, which are made according to the expectations of others, will only enliven your personal development if they are positive enlightenments and clear catalysts for your own processes of self-transformation. Otherwise, they are nothing less, and nothing more, than effective forms that entrance or entomb the experiences and the expressions of your life path and your essential power. This is also true of the expectations you choose for yourself, so choose with clarity for self-illumination.

———

You find yourself in a beautiful stone mausoleum with carved pillars and a massive iron censer, in which soft lavender and gold flames flicker. Deep in the ash wood coals, chunks of frankincense burn, sending clouds of fragrant smoke spiraling upward to the domed ceiling, which is painted with mystical symbols.

An industrious little spider has spread her web across this vast ceiling and is dancing gaily in the fragrant smoke.

At the center of the mausoleum is a huge stone tomb elaborately carved with dragons. It is Yuletide and someone has placed a large evergreen wreath on the top of the tomb. There are two robed and hooded women beside the tomb, one on each side. The taller woman is dressed in robes made of platinum silk. The smaller woman is wearing heavier robes in a soft shade of violet. Both women's robes are trimmed with tiny beads made of clear crystal and various shades of amethyst.

You are startled to see them push aside quite easily the heavy stone lid of the tomb and peer inside. Moving closer, you observe that the figure inside is wearing deep indigo robes and has copper coins on his closed eyes. The women turn as you gasp in recognition of the entombed figure. They motion for you to approach quietly and stand alongside the tomb with them. Drawing nearer, you recognize the tall woman is Nimue and the smaller one is Ganieda. They seem surprisingly unconcerned as they gaze down at The Merlin lying in the tomb.

Ganieda takes a deep violet-toned azurite crystal from her pocket and places it on The Merlin's forehead. She closes her eyes and Nimue does the same. For an interminable length of time—or so it seems to you—both women stand silently beside The Merlin's tomb with their eyes closed. Finally, Ganieda signs and opens her eyes. She calls softly to Nimue, who opens her eyes, as well. Then she watches as Ganieda removes the azurite from The Merlin's forehead.

Nimue takes a brilliant cobalt-blue crystal from a pocket in her robes and places it lovingly on The Merlin's forehead. Then she and Ganieda close their eyes as before and repeat their mysterious, silent ritual. At last, Nimue opens her eyes and touches Ganieda's arm. Ganieda opens her eyes and gazes across the tomb at Nimue. Both women shake their heads in despair. Ganieda walks over to an altar inside a small alcove. She removes a beautiful gold cloth from an object on the altar and turns to bring it toward the tomb.

You can see this object is a Chalice of magnificent quality. It is made of gold and set with deep violet amethysts. When she reaches the tomb, Ganieda pulls a rainbowed crystal from the clear waters inside the Chalice. You want to ask her if this Chalice is the grail, for its presence seems so mystically powerful. Ganieda hands the Chalice carefully to Nimue and then dries the rainbowed crystal with a soft white cloth. Ganieda holds the rainbowed crystal up to the light which is streaming in through the pillars at the entrance to the mausoleum. Rainbows sparkle within the beautiful stone. Gingerly, Ganieda places the crystal on The Merlin's forehead. She and Nimue repeat their silent, sacred ritual. After the longest time, Nimue covers her mouth, seemingly to stifle a cry of grief; but her efforts are in vain. With a sound that echoes loudly inside this cold, drafty mausoleum, Nimue sneezes three times.

Ganieda looks at Nimue with a knowing glance and both women resume their silent ritual. Once again, Nimue is unable to suppress her sneezes. You are sympathetic to her predicament in this dusty, drafty place. As the second set of sneezes subsides, you notice that the industrious little spider has spun a very long thread and is dangling precariously close to The Merlin's face.

You wonder at the mystical symbolism of this spider's efforts to reach a line down to The Merlin from such a high distance. Ganieda watches the spider intently for a few moments, then reaches out across the tomb to take the Chalice back from Nimue. Ganieda dips two fingers of her left hand into the pure waters of the Chalice and gently flicks a few drops at the spider; perhaps as a sacred blessing. The spider accepts the droplets, but does not move away from The Merlin. Ganieda repeats the process, and still the spider holds on to her precarious position.

The third time Ganieda flicks the drops of water, The Merlin sits up quickly, roaring in protest. The coins are flung from his eyes in the process, and the spider barely manages to escape being knocked onto the hard cold floor. She is busily trying to scurry up her web line to avoid The Merlin as he bolts up from the tomb, scolding about the ineffectiveness of women as experimentalists.

Having recovered from your initial shock, you impulsively reach into the Chalice just as Nimue does the same. Together you ceremonially flick crystal drops of water at The Merlin. In the uneasy silence that follows, Ganieda studiously takes the wreath and catches the spider with it, then carefully places the wreath on a high ledge that encircles the domed ceiling, giving the spider a chance to return safely to her web.

With a ferocious scowl, and all the dignity he can muster, The Merlin stiffly

exits the mausoleum, displaying a fierce formality. When he has left, Nimue looks at you with wide, innocent eyes. She informs you the women had known all along it would never work to try divining with The Merlin currently entombed. Calmly, Nimue explains there are limits to humoring even the wisest of wise old men. She pauses to look at Ganieda, who is turned away, intently focused in watching the spider return to her web. Ganieda's shoulders are shaking. For a moment, you wonder if this has been too intense an experience for the extremely wise, but decidedly frail old woman.

At last Ganieda turns to look at you, and at Nimue, with tears in her wise old eyes. You all gaze at each other silently for an instant, then spontaneously burst into gales of laughter. The industrious little spider disappears from view, safely out of the reach of these strangely deranged Druidic scientists who have invaded her ancient tomb.

Ganieda picks up the copper coins and places them in the tomb. Together, you all replace the lid. As you leave the mausoleum together, Nimue replaces the beautiful Chalice in the alcove. Ganieda points two bony Druidic fingers at the Chalice. With a flash of cobalt-blue light, it is instantly transformed into the simple, cracked stone urn which it had always been before. As you make your way down the hill on which the mausoleum is built, you discuss the merits of various divination methods. All of you agree it is pointless for one such as The Merlin, who can never truly die, to insist on assuming a position in which he has been falsely placed, simply because so many expect to find him there.

You make a mental note to remind The Merlin of his own philosophies regarding "the foolishness of having one's own expectations," much less the foolishness of following the expectations of others. You soon reach the point where you take your leave of Ganieda and Nimue for the time being. Contentedly, you decide that you are graced to have made a mystical connection with such illuminating, enlightening company. These figures you may visit whenever you want, with assurance that all you can truly expect is the unexpected.

You ask them to convey your regards to The Merlin, and to let him know you will visit him again soon—as soon, that is, as the coast is clear.

CAULDRON OF VISION
A Personal Journey Account

My journey takes me across an ancient landscape, a place familiar within my vision. As in a flying dream, I sweep over hills and forests.

I feel myself with the wings of a great white owl. I glide across a moonlit clearing, casting a shadow as I go. It is the silhouette of the Gwenyfhar, the sacred white owl of Sovereignty.

I ride the breezes blowing me westward toward the sea. I reach a crumbling stone fort built high on a craggy ocean cliff. Only the tower in the west corner is still intact. It is short and wide, with a circle of windows illuminated from within. I note it is built in the style I would call Romano-Celtic.

In my vision, I perch myself on one of the window ledges. Being more focused on landing quietly, impressively so, I feel the stone I am on loosen and roll to the edge. It is too late to avoid an unceremonious entry. I jump through the window into the middle of the tower floor—and land less than deftly.

In the moment of silence that follows, I hear the stone fall into the stormy waves below.

I right myself and take my bearings. There is only misty violet and gold light within the tower. It is like a fine silk veil, delicate and sheer. Does it signal the need to maintain gentle illusions? Or does it serve as a reminder to use magickal manners on this journey? I opt for the latter.

I announce myself formally and request direct communication concerning the Matter of Britain—The Matter of Sovereignty.

No change in the vision.

I state my intention to obtain exoteric information on this matter. No change. I quickly add in my mundane sources and the veil ripples slightly.

I explain my purpose—to find the points of Synthesis in the Matter of Britain. I want to see, as clearly as I can envision it, the pattern of transformation of that time.

I want to know what has made this Fair Time of Camelot remain so deeply etched in our consciousness through all the stages and ages of humankind, dark and light.

The veil moves in the soft breeze blowing through the tower in my mind.

I express my need for help in finding the vision for what I feel, but cannot yet express. I formally grant to Spirit the permission to help, by giving me a clear line of sight.

The veils and the mists fade away gently. I find myself within The Merlin's tower, high above the sea, in an ancient crumbling stone fortress. Amidst the vials and earthenware vessels, The Merlin is studiously examining a scroll ornately illuminated with diagrams I cannot make out. He is in his most learned aspect, ancient, wise, and impatient. He scowls over the scroll and does not appear to notice me.

I see the source of his impatience. Ganieda, his Druid Sister, sits on a wooden stool, stirring a thick luminous liquid inside a great bronze cauldron decorated with ancient Celtic designs. She has matched her ancient aspect to that of The Merlin's. I wonder briefly which one of them will fade into the crumbling stones of the tower first, if they continue in these conditions.

Then Ganieda beckons for me to gaze into the bronze cauldron. She is making wide circles now, swirling the liquid counterclockwise as she speaks; cycling back through the dimensions we call time.

A thousand wheels and a
thousand more still
Bringing vision to knowledge,
bringing purpose to will.

The liquid becomes an intense light, blue-white, and vibrating for a moment. Then it shifts.

I see the map of the world stretched out before me, framed in an oval of electric-blue light. In quick order I see the images as they slide over the map.

First, a wave of Light builds in the Middle East and rolls slowly Westward toward the British Islands. I see it crest over Wales and break up in the Irish Sea. I watch as a foam of light sweeps over Ireland, stopping at her western shore.

As the wave of light recedes, I see sacred objects washed upon the British shoreline. I see some of them have washed upon the rocky beaches of the mystic islands between the coasts of Britain and Ireland. There, gleaming in the light of the receding wave, I see the sword of power and the grail of healing.

I see other waves, moving in sets, following the pattern of the first one. For a time, there is a lovely vision of light waves moving across the waters of my inner consciousness.

Then the vision clouds, the waters become gray and turbulent. A dark wave begins to build over Rome and the Middle Eastern regions. It is a storm tide, ruthless and inexorable. I watch as it surges westward and breaks over the British Islands with a force that sends its dark foam across the Atlantic Ocean to touch the American shoreline.

As this wave recedes, I notice it has also cast lines of light connecting both sides of the Atlantic to the gleaming light of the sword and the Grail. The dark tide subsides and the waters are still.

Slowly, light begins to rise to the surface, forming ripples that spread in slowly widening circles across the map of this world. At the center of these ripples, over Western Europe and the British Islands, a cascading spring bursts forth, signaling a rebirth of this sacred light. Its force creates a new wave. This one sweeps westward over the Atlantic and the North American lands. It moves on across the Pacific and splashes the shores of Asia.

In my vision, the light of this wave spreads to cover the whole world—some parts in its ebb, others in its flow. When the wave has faded away, I see there is a pattern of lines gleaming brightly as they lead out from the center, wherein may be seen the sword and the grail. I see some of these lines of light are strong and securely interwoven. Others seem frayed and pale. Their light is just a fine thread of connection, but a connection nevertheless. I note the areas of my map that shine from the strength of their connection to the sword and to the Grail.

I focus on my image of the sword and the Grail until they seem to vibrate in front of me, sacred holograms, symbols of a Western light.

Ganieda, who has been stirring the luminous liquid clockwise, restoring the once and future cycles of time, begins to stir more rapidly. My vision moves in fast time. Its images reflect the clipped pace of a silent movie.

The sword and the Grail rise upward, high above the Western Hemisphere, centered over the Atlantic Ocean. I watch as they pull in light across strong lines coming from eight points on the globe. As the light merges in the center, the sword and the Grail grow brighter until their intensity is too strong to gaze at directly. I watch as they merge into a blaze of pure energy which runs like a high-voltage current back out over the lines leading to and from eight illuminated points encompassing the globe.

From the center of this energy there emerge two more sacred symbols, the spear, ribboned with rainbow tones, and a carved stone, intricately designed with patterns of destiny's games.

Then, with just a glimpse and nothing more, I am shown another pattern. It is an ever-widening circle of light waves rippling forth from the center, washing over the dark spaces between the lines of light. Briefer still, there is a glimpse of an interwoven web of light waves illuminating the world before me.

Finally, with a twinkling of light, I see Nature reilluminated and human nature reawakened to a new consciousness.

As the vision fades away, I hear the Light called by many names, their echoes resounding across the crystalline web toward the center. I touch the place where the Light is the realized, accepted, and understood Light, and all names and symbols express this clearly. It is also the place where no names or symbols can be separate from the rest. All are a part of the center—the Synthesis of Light.

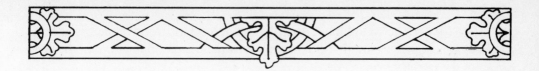

CHAPTER 23

UNBINDING AVALON:
RECEPTIVE POWER

*Lady, I said it once to you before this—the day of Avalon is ended .. and we
must go into the mists further and further until we are no more than a legend
and a dream … Even if Avalon must perish, I felt it right that the holy things
should be sent forth into the world in the service of the Divine, by whatever
name God or the Gods may be called. And because of what I have done, the
Goddess has manifested herself at least once in the world yonder, in a way that
shall never be forgotten. The passing of the Grail shall be remembered, my Mor-
gaine, when you and I are only legends for the fireside and tales for children.*

Marion Zimmer Bradley
The Mists of Avalon (New York: Knopf, 1982)

The realms of Avalon are receptive in Nature. They bring the elements of healing renewal from within, transformationally restoring
the strength and power of our self-nature. In the minds of many, Avalon remains a remote memory of a mystical realm of perfection. This
makes Avalon essentially inaccessible, by merging it with an image of
the transcendent spiritual perfection that is the Universal Divine. In its most accessible form for imagery, Avalon is the medium through which we may all receive from
our natural gifts for self-healing in a manner that is spiritually perfect for ourselves.
Like the Grail within, Avalon is present within the self-restorative abilities of Body,
Mind, and Spirit.

Avalon Isle drifts on a sea of consciousness within our minds, where we can reach
it quite freely with the inner guidance of receptive self-nature. Continuing this
metaphorically, we can understand why this natural realm has come to be portrayed
as unreachable. Avalon exists just where that sea of consciousness opens to the

oceans of (or oceanic) consciousness which seem too vast to travel across. This is because in metaphor, again, that ocean expands into an unfathomable void, the deep ocean of the unconscious.

When we consider the voyagers of the Middle Ages traveling the global oceans, we can understand why the unexplored regions were often marked with a warning: "There be dragons beyond here, in the deep." It wasn't until this blue-green globe had been circled and explored that misconceptions about its mysterious oceans were clarified for most. In current terms, there have been sufficient explorers in the vast oceanic depth of consciousness to know that the inner voyages are far more healing and empowering than they are disturbing. (Also any dragons encountered have consistently been reported to be friendly).

In the spiritual traditions and meditative practices of India (our Indo-Aryan kin), these journeys into the void are made as a matter of course. Indeed, those who follow these practices of India probably consider some of us to be still "flat-Earthers" and unable to imagine the mandala philosophy of the universal round. Of course, they'd best not say that to a Celtic explorer. For the most part, our experiences of Avalon are more like the image of the Isle on the Sea, and even more currently, the Isle in the Lake. This I see as a wonderfully Western Celtic way to locate the places you want, where you can find them, when you want them—and right away!

The Isle of Avalon in the Lake is an image that emerged from the connection with the holy site at Glastonbury; but it represents more than a fairly well-verifiable connection or a mythic one. The Lake is an image of your personal consciousness realm, which it is possible to explore freely, on your own. This makes it quite comfortable and familiar, leading, in turn, to being more receptive to the self-healing realms it represents. Thus a wonderful cycle is established.

However you choose to image Avalon, it will become a self-renewing experience. As you become more receptive to your self, you become more receptive to the realm of Avalon. As you transform, so does your imagery, and you can always return to renew and restore yourself with a recycled imagery. As you become more familiar with your own powers of self-healing renewal, you may find that you'll initiate some voyages of exploration on your own. To help with this process, I have designed this chapter with a number of imageries of the realm of Avalon and some of the archetypal allies who are initiators, healers, and guides. There are also allies who visit Avalon or rest in that realm, as Arthur does. Their archetypal aspects may seem different in Avalon; but you already know that this reflects a blended transformation in imagery.

In regard to the imageries in this chapter, the personal journeys are presented here to share my experience of that same process—clarifying my images of Avalon's most often misconcepted Ladies. In doing this, I was able to develop a deeper, more receptive relationship with the aspects these archetypal Avalonians represent—within myself, naturally. I hope these personal journeys will provide a way of releasing overlays of negative feelings and renewing your positive feelings about yourself—and the Avalonians. Be receptive and self-unbinding.

The rest of this chapter will proceed without as much instruction from me as you had in the realm of Camelot. Camelot is an instructive realm and Avalon is a realm of intuition, so be receptive to your own inner knowing as you experience the imageries in this chapter. When an aspect of an Avalonian image feels deeply powerful for you, pause and open to your receptive powers. Receive from your own explorations, for that is the way to initiate your deepest experiences of Avalon, more so than any of the other realms in the 'round of Camelot's legends. Do so with an open, unbound receptivity. That unbinds Avalon.

Here is the course for your voyage through this chapter. The course you will follow leads through both personal journeys I have made and guided imageries navigated for you. The last part of this chapter takes us into the Faerie realms of Avalon, with some guidelines for encountering the Fey within. The chapter closes with a recrafted legend about an encounter between a mortal man, Launfal, and his Faerie Lady, Tryamour.

This Faerie tale tells us to be sure we are able to deal with unique aspects within the realms of our lives and our loves. In these current times, we are fortunate and flexible in our abilities to access realms of consciousness with imagery as a self-empowering medium. In the days when Launfal and Tryamour was written (the Norman French version), the medieval mind was closed, en masse, with only a few bright, brave exceptions. Today we know we can enter realms that were once thought too risky—and too Otherworld. Now we are remembering what our ancient Celtic ancestors knew: that the realms of the mystical are natural and ever renewing, as is Nature.

The following two Avalon imageries for receptive experiencing are personal journeys. The first, "The Synthesis of Light and Shadow," deals with unbinding of the separating concepts, viewing Avalon as an integral bridge for balance—reflective, combined receptive, unstructured and active, structured. The second, "Avalon, Fine-Tuning the Focus," illustrates enlightening the images of Avalon's ladies, with activation specific imagery. Also included in this chapter are two guided, experiential imageries. "The Winding River" promotes learning by imagery experience to be receptive to the flow, even when you aren't sure you can keep your head above water. "The Fountain of Apple Blossoms" deals with the Avalonian experience which enters the Fey realms to find an intuitive understanding of relations. "The Glass Boat" guides you through a sacred initiation in the realm of Avalon's mystical arts.

THE SYNTHESIS OF LIGHT AND SHADOW
Personal Journey

I journey inward and find myself floating on a clear stream of consciousness. I am drifting along on a river, moving gently through my inner vision. I am being carried on the currents of this river in a beautiful glass boat which sparkles in the rays of light from a warm white Sun over my head. For a time I am content simply to flow with the river as it winds its way through my inner landscape.

In my vision, I see that the mists have risen on each side of the river, veiling the gently sloping banks which I pass as I drift along, following the flow of consciousness. At a bend in the river, my journey slows and deepens. The waters are shallow here and I can feel the blades of river grasses brushing against the hull of my glass boat. I drowse and drift along until I feel the waters deepen and expand.

I notice that the mists on the river banks have begun to fade away, leaving me with a new vision to behold. I see two groups of women, one on each side of the river which is carrying me lightly along its current. Ahead, crossing the river, I see a lovely little bridge made of stones—river stones, I think. The bridge is empty but seems to be waiting, almost expectantly, for the groups of women to step upon it and cross or meet in the middle. I cast a line of light from my glass boat around a pillar supporting the bridge. I moor myself securely and wait for my vision to unfold before me.

On the right side of the river I notice that the women standing on the bank are illuminated quite brightly—too brightly, I think. The light from them and around them, makes it difficult to see their shapes sufficiently. They seem opalescent, shimmering without form. They seem Fey, yet beyond Fey, untouchable and unknowable. They are unreachable in their mystical magnificence. It is as though what illuminates them so intensely prevents their clear manifestation. I sense that they are somehow trapped behind these high-voltage veils of light—and yet they still seek form for the good of all. They are walled in by misguided wisdom which holds these Ladies of Avalon to be beyond the ken of human concept.

I consider them for a time, then turn to see the women on the opposite side of the river.

On the left side of the river, I notice that the women standing on the bank are shrouded in dark shadows—too dark, I think. The shadows surrounding them seem to make their forms sadly misshapen, twisted and ominous. They seem human, far too human in the frailties they express, and yet they seem to be little more than a shadowed semblance of that which is human. It is as though their humanity has been mired down by misconception and manipulation for many ages. They manifest all too well the dark aspects of the messages they have been forced to carry concerning the Ladies of Avalon.

In a flash of inspiration, I see my mission in this vision. I climb quickly and easily out of my boat and onto the bridge. The stones that form the bridge are cool, smooth, and strong, supporting my effort. I stand in the center of the bridge facing the warm white Sun which sparkles on the waters. I reach out toward each bank—beckoning the women to join me, each from their own side of the river. For an instant I feel cold, dark shadows pass through me from the left and hot, bright lights coming from the right. With a rush of warmth, they merge together in the heart of my vision. Then I see the Ladies of Avalon, clearly balanced—in synthesis for the Good of all.

AVALON: FINE-TUNING THE FOCUS
Personal Journey

I journey inward to my theater of inner vision. In front of me is a flat, blank screen. Beside me, on a table near the chair in which I am seated is a control panel with a complex array of buttons, switches, and dials. Less noticeable at first is a small, simple instrument. It is a remote control, long and narrow, like a wand, I think, with only two buttons. One of the buttons is marked POWER, and the other button is marked CLEAR. I resist the enticement of the intricate control panel, chosing the simple "magick wand," the remote control.

I aim the control wand at the blank screen and push the button marked POWER. The screen crackles with static and blurred images appear in various shades of gray. I wait for my vision to clear the way for more specific images, but none present themselves. Remembering the second button marked CLEAR, I aim the wand at the screen once more and push that button purposefully.

The images emerge as two figures in shades of gray. Both figures appear to be women, one in a dark charcoal tone, the other in a lighter smoky shade. The screen is still frosted with static which seems like a blizzard of pale gray snow covering the figures of the two women.

I push the CLEAR button again and the static vanishes; but the figures remain shapeless in shades of gray. On a whim, I aim the control wand at the darker figure and push CLEAR again. The focus on the figure fine-tunes, but her shape begins to shift, too swiftly to identify each aspect separately. I think to start again, and I push the button marked POWER. I note very little change, except perhaps for an outline of colors surrounding the dark gray figure.

Curious, I push both buttons, POWER and CLEAR, simultaneously, and my vision expands dramatically. The single, dark gray figure suddenly becomes seven women, and the flat screen transforms into a cyclorama. It surrounds me with a circle of images. Seven women, all dressed in a somewhat softer shade of gray, stare at me from the circular screen. Still directly in front of me, the second figure in lighter smoky gray seems to wait patiently for me to progress on my journey. I choose to let her wait while I swirl the control wand in a circle around my head, pushing hard on both buttons. I close my eyes for an instant to regain my balance; and as I reopen them I am delighted with the transformation on the screen.

The seven women are clearly in focus now and no longer garbed in gray. As I circle clockwise pushing the CLEAR button, they each make themselves known by name and by tone.

There is Morgawse, dressed in the vibrant red of strength, Nimue in the bright orange of pure energy, Vivienne wears the yellow of organization, Igraine is beautiful in the green of heartfelt emotions, Elaine is expressive in the true blue of will, and Morgana wears the rich indigo of synthesis and psychic gifts. Finally, there is Ganieda in the high spiritual tone of violet, seemingly stellar.

I am lost for a time, considering the meanings of these colors representing these honored Ladies of Avalon. At last I remember the lone figure still waiting patiently in light smoky gray. Aiming the wand directly at her, I push both CLEAR and POWER once again. She transmutes into a figure wearing gentle white light which glows in a circle around all the rest. And I know her. She is Guinevere. Not Avalon bred, perhaps—but to Avalon returned, transmitting her light for the healing Avalon and Camelot require. On impulse, I point the wand at myself, holding both POWER and CLEAR. I see myself wearing the holy tones of a seeker of Light and Clarity. I find myself wearing black and no longer seated as a spectator. I find myself joining the circle of women who share in the concerns of Avalon and Camelot. I push POWER again. The vision amplifies, then fades away.

THE WINDING RIVER: FLEXIBILITY
Guided Imagery

Elements: Water

Directions: West

Aspects: Balanced flow of personal cycles

Colors: Scarlet ray, Gray, Black, Silver and Rainbow lights

Kindred Spirits: Herons, Deer

Tree: Reed

Stones: Garnet, Hematite, Moonstone, Black quartz, Abalone

Incense: Herbal

Cycle: Samhain

Setting Image: River

Hallow: Cauldron

Theme: Quest

Natural Force: Tides

Access Allies: Ganieda

Format: Moderate

Message: If you always swim on the surface of your self, you'll never experience the wonder of the deeper realms within. If you feel concerned that you might find yourself in depths over your head, have faith in the healing currents that will guide you safely through the waters of consciousness and Spirit.

You find yourself in a small thatched cottage beside a clear flowing river. This is the forest home of Ganieda, her retreat from the intensities of The Merlin's tower. It is the time of All Hallows, the eve of Samhain. The abundance of Summer's growth and the time of harvest has transited to the time for questing within yourself. You have come to Ganieda to learn more about the cycles of your self and the tidal patterns of your life.

You feel both excited and frightened as you explore this mystical cottage. Ganieda has set up a deeply mysterious altar, with stones and crystals surrounding an ancient cauldron of inner knowing. There is a strong herbal incense burning in a large rough abalone shell and dark gray candles that seem to be barely lit give the room an atmosphere of mysterious anticipation. The stones and crystals are in muted, cloudy shades. You see rough garnets and unpolished hematites arranged with muddy-looking moonstones and opaque black quartz crystals.

Before you can fully explore how you feel encountering this place and time, Ganieda beckons you to gaze into the cauldron, whether you feel quite prepared to do so or not. Remembering the trust which is the foundation of all quests, you gaze at the dark waters within this cauldron of inner knowing. What you find reflected is a darkly mirrored reflection of yourself; a fixed pattern of emotional response expresses itself on your face. You see that what you feel is balanced self-control is no more than a surface reflection, calm waves hiding the currents of chaos deeper below and within.

You want to discuss your thoughts with Ganieda; but she signals for you to stop thinking and begin to let yourself feel what the reflection means. As you struggle to separate thoughts from feelings, Ganieda directs your attention to the cauldron. You gaze absent-mindedly into the dark waters but find no reflection of yourself this time. Instead, you see the image of the winding river outside Ganieda's cottage retreat. With a tap of two fingers on your forehead, and two more over your heart, Ganieda transforms this experience for you. You emerge in the image of the winding river.

You find yourself floating peacefully in the gently flowing river, slowly drifting between the banks where reeds and bullrushes are growing. A beautiful Great Blue Heron spreads her wings and takes flight as you drift by. One of her blue-gray feathers floats across to you and you reach out to grasp it. A small herd of deer is grazing in a clearing beside the river; but they bolt into the forest as you drift by, floating freely downstream. You are immersed in the beautiful flow of your experience and you relax to follow the flow of the winding river within. You feel as though you could safely sleep. Entrusting your security to the gentle flow of the water, you are assured you will reach whatever destination the river tides will lead. All you feel you have to do is float effortlessly on the surface of the winding river.

As feelings of self-assurance allow you to float drowsily, you experience a moment of doubt. You quickly reject this as a negative pattern and smooth the surface of your mind and feelings. You are completely vulnerable to changes in the course of the river and self-reflected in the tides of your life. Before you can consider how you feel about this, you find yourself in white-water rapids. Above and beyond this, a sudden storm sends torrents of cold steely rain driving down upon you. Ahead, you hear the ominous roar of a waterfall which you cannot see through the cold gray wall of rain. This driving rain also obliterates your view of the river banks between which you have been floating serenely. Your surface impulse is to instruct yourself to think; but an even deeper intuitive response tells you to feel the currents swirling around you. Using your emotions as a guide, you determine which currents cause you to struggle and flounder and which ones allow you to flow along with the winding course of the river. You allow your feelings to be flexible and responsive, and your body becomes flexibly responsive in natural alignment with the deeper currents of your self.

You soon realize the steadier currents are found below the surface, interflowing with those that are chaotic. Feeling your way along these current lines, you follow the deeper course, even though you still cannot see clearly. You realize the river must branch somewhere, since all the currents are not pulling chaotically toward the unsure drop of the waterfall. Although the currents, which are steady, still move more swiftly than you would choose, you feel them pulling you toward calmer waters. With your emotional intuitive powers, you maneuver through the white-water rapids on the surface. Sooner than you feared, yet as soon as you hoped, you find you have managed to hold your

course, and you emerge from the rapids in a most gentle branch of the river. The rainstorm has stopped, and the waterfall seems no more than a distant memory. You make your way easily through the reeds to the river bank. This time the heron does not fly away, and the herd of deer emerge from the forest without fear.

You realize you have lost the feather somewhere along the way, and you express feelings of regret to the heron for losing her gift. She responds by moving flexibly among the reeds, her beautiful wings now shining silver in the sunlight. You realize her true gift was to help you become receptive and flexible in your experiences.

As you thank the heron, you notice how perceptively the deer respond to the feel of the forest and to the feelings you now transmit to them. You glance at your reflection in the calm river waters and find a deeper current of emotional calmness mirrored there. This calmness, you note, has emerged from a deeper perceptive wisdom, from an emotional relationship with your own inner knowing. You realize the gift of the deer expressed the importance of being in tune with the feelings within your self and within the situation surrounding you. As you floated past the deer, you had too freely submitted to the flow of the surface which surrendered the perceptive powers of your emotions erroneously. When you floated past the heron, you were striving for a sense of free-floating relaxation. Otherwise, you would have allowed yourself to get a feel for what you may have opened yourself to experience. Your inner wisdom lets you know it is a paradox to strive for flow.

Still, you stayed the course because you rightfully submitted to the strength of your feelings and let your emotional perceptions guide you along the lines of deeper currents. With a well-earned feeling of achievement, you make your way along the winding river to Ganieda's cottage retreat. You feel happy anticipating the experience of sharing with her and drawing from the deep source of intuitive wisdom she repre-sents. When you arrive, you find the cottage is illuminated with rainbows from crystal prisms Ganieda has hung at the open, sunlit windows. She is as open and flexible with you as you are with her, and you spend all the time you need expressing what you have found within your own realm of dreams and emotions. When you are ready to leave, Ganieda presents you with a small cauldron to use as you feel is best for yourself.

THE FOUNTAIN OF APPLE BLOSSOMS: SACRED RELATIONSHIPS
Guided Imagery

Elements: Spirit infusing all elements

Directions: Center and the circle encircling

Aspects: Expressive love, acceptance of sacred partners

Colors: Blue, Rose, Green, Yellow rays infused with White

Kindred Spirits: Deer, Swan, White Birds

Tree: Apple

Stones: Blue Lace Agate, Rose Quartz, Peridot, Moonstone, White Gold

Incense: Fruit

Cycle: Lammas

Setting Image: Fountain

Hallow: Shield (mirrored)

Theme: Courtly Love

Natural Force: Mists

Access Allies: Nimue, Arthur

Format: Extensive

Message: The elemental aspects of our self-nature affect the nature of our relationships, at best in balance, at worse in chaos. These elements provide the essential energies and emotions which all relationships require. These elements need to relate, in synthesis, with each other in order to reflect harmony in your relationships. The elements provide the energies, yet often in a way that overpowers—even in a relationship of synthesis. Transmute the elements of your relationship to create a softer synthesis. This is one that is continuously transmitted through the healing mediums of light, feeling expressions, and the synthesis power of Love.

It is a crisp clear day at the time of late Summer's initial ebb. You have been to a Lammas celebration and have spent the morning gathering a harvest of ripe, golden apples. This afternoon you have been invited to come to the sacred fountain in the forest clearing where apple blossoms are eternally present and the rich fruit is ready for picking whenever you require its nurturance. You can smell the sweet fragrance of this symbolic fruit which brings spiritual wisdom to your Spirit as well as sustenance for your body. You are guided to your destination by the sounds of laughter and the steady flow of the waters in the fountain.

When you arrive, you find Arthur and Nimue sitting together at the edge of the fountain. They are sharing a moment of friendly conversation and are obviously enjoying each other's company. You watch them for a while in wonder at their ability to relate to each other with ease and flexible familiarity. They are laughing one moment and sharing moments of serious contemplation the next. You notice there is a large, mirrored shield leaning against one of the sacred apple trees encircling the fountain.

As you move in closer, you can see Arthur and Nimue reflected in the mirrored shield. When you see this, you realize the spiritual power of their relationship to one another. Arthur and Nimue are allied by their loving guardianship of the Mystical realm that is Logres. This, and their mutual relationship to the Archmage, The Merlin, unites Arthur and Nimue in the service that relates to the protection and preservation of the power that is Logres.

You feel a warm affection for both of these mystical friends. They seem so vibrant and golden as they relate to one another. You pause before announcing your presence here and absorb the positive feelings this fountain image presents to you. You note the fountain is in perfect condition, with the waters clear and cycling in steady rhythm.

Two beautiful white swans swim in silent accord on the fresh waters of the fountain pool. A small herd of gentle white-tailed deer are busily feeding on the sweet fruit that has dropped from the apple trees. In the fragrant branches, a flock of small white birds is feasting on the ever-renewing fruit which grows on these mystical trees.

You hear Arthur call your name and Nimue echoing the same. You turn to greet them both, and you are given a warm friendly welcome from each of these golden figures of kinship and spiritual alliance with yourself. You spend a little while renewing your friendship and sharing all you have experienced since last you met with them. They provide you with their supportive wisdoms in a manner much like your dearest, most trusted friends.

You tell them you were watching their reflection in the mirrored shield, and both of them congratulate you on your sensitive observations and on your flexibility of feelings, as well. Nimue tells you the mirrored shield is most important for the lesson that this afternoon at the fountain will provide you. As long as you do not use the shield to hide your feelings, you will learn a wise lesson about the emotional reflections of the many relationships in your life.

Nimue and Arthur bid you a fond farewell and leave for the Lammastide celebrations which the Fair Folk have prepared. Their only instruction is for you to sit, in a secluded spot, and scry with the mirrored shield. By looking beyond your own reflection and at the reflected fountain, you will divine sacred messages about the elemental aspects of relationships.

You find a spot that suits your needs and arrange the mirrored shield so you can clearly see the fountain reflected behind your own image. You gaze at the reflection intently for a time as you strive to scry its message. Remembering that striving is not the way of divining from inner reflected wisdoms, you relax and enjoy the beauty of the fountain image, mirrored in the shield. Soon the flow of the fountain waters and the calm grace of the swans lulls you. Although one of the little white birds chirps at you to stay alert, you soon drowse and sleep.

You awaken to the sound of laughter, clear and melodic, like chimes in a gentle breeze. You are not sure how long you have slept, but the forest and the apple grove is now filled with white, drifting clouds and mists. The mirrored shield has become fogged and you find you have to clear it three times before you can see the fountain reflected in its surface.

With your first clear glimpse of the reflected image, you recognize the pattern of three concentric circles. In the center, where the swans had been swimming in the fountain pool, you now see they have transformed into a pair of white-robed Old Ones, sitting on the edge of the fountain. Around them, dancing with deft grace, is a circle of the most ethereal Fair Folk—eight of them in all. Beyond these etherically Fey figures is another circle, encircling all you can see in the mirrored shield. In this outer circle are Fair Folk with whom you are already familiar. There are eight of them, as well, standing in pairs in the cardinal directions which they represent elementally.

Between the etheric circle of Fey dancers and the elemental Fair Folk is a circular band of white misty light. You can just make out the shapes of deer in this white mist. These deer, you now see,

are completely and mystically pure and white. The flock of white birds you now realize has also transformed, and their white wings are now reflected as the white lights that shimmer etherically around the Fey as they dance with a light mystical, graceful quality.

You realize these Fey dancers are the mythic beings known as the Shining Ones of the Faerie realm. They reflect the elemental qualities of all Fair Folk, both mystical and mundane; but their images are infused with a purity of light and spirit. This keeps them eternally reflected in the etheric realms between the worlds of fantasy and form.

The afternoon sun casts long rays into the forest mists, and a cool autumn breeze has begun to blow through the trees. You know your time for clearly seeing this reflection will be brief. With an open consciousness, you carefully take note of what you see and feel as you view this reflection—in regard to its messages about the meaning of relationships.

You begin with the more familiar, elemental circle, encircling the rest, and relate them to the circle within the circle, and the center within them both. Knowing you will have the chance to reflect on this experience in your own realms of time, you encapsulate what you see and feel in an elementary format.

Air: In the East of the elemental circle, the pair of Fair Folk represent the qualities of Air empowering a relationship with mindfulness and creative inspiration. Then bright yellow ray aspects—transmitted through the white circle of light—reflect in the forms of the etheric Fey as a soft shade of yellow, which prevents the sharpness of too much intense mental focus from resulting in a relationship with conflicts arising from fixed opinions, obsessive focus, and narrow perceptions or tunnel vision.

You watch these creamy yellow-garbed Fey dance with a graceful awareness of themselves and of each other. From this, you note the importance of keeping an open mind about your feelings—and those of your partner. You observe these partners are wearing creamy yellow moonstone, and you note their connection to both receptivity and gentle reflection in a relationship.

Fire: In the South of the elemental circle, the Fair Folk couple represent the protective strengths and powers of Fire. They bring qualities of guardianship and physical passion to a relationship. Etherically reflected through the white light, their forceful red ray becomes a gentle, compassionate rose shade which prevents jealous possessiveness and lustful self-indulgences at the expense of the other partner.

As you watch these rose-garbed Fey move gracefully in tandem, you note the need for relating from the banked fire realms of heart and not just from the consuming fire realms of primal drives and impulses. The rose quartz these Fey wear remind you of the need to amplify natural passions with a gentle heart and loving communication.

Water: In the West of the elemental circle, the Fair Folk represent the qualities of intuition, achievement, and personal emotional cycles. The depths of their blue ray transmit through white light to become a more manageable flow reflected by their etherically Fey counterparts as a light, expressive blue which makes

the effects of personal emotions pale in comparison to the mutually shared feelings arising from their devotion to one another and their intuitive relationship to their partner's personal processes of self-development.

The lavender blue lace agates these Fey wear cause you to note the need for less dramatic expressions of your self-processes and emotions. This is done to ensure a balanced flow in a relationship consisting of two individual cycles and one shared cycle of partnership.

Earth: In the North of the elemental circle, the Fair Folk represent the qualities of structure, abundance, and growth in a relationship. Their expansive green ray transmits through white light to reflect a more flexible, tender green etheric tone in their Fey counterparts. This allows for natural cycles of growth without too many periods of unmanageable rapid expansion or insufficient supplies of power which create the strife of depletion.

The fresh green peridots these Fey wear make you note the need for creating supportive structures to ensure a stability in the form of your relationship with each other and with the world in which you live together. This is in order to provide for the internal growth of your relationship, rather than just building on the external and often materialistic aspects.

Spirit: The Fair Folk in the center are the Old Ones representing the blended elemental and etheric qualities of Spirit. Transmitted both through and from within the white light, they reflect the harmony of all rays and of all aspects which are the ideals of any loving relationship. Although there is no possibility of perfection in any mundane realm, these Old Ones symbolize the mystical realms in which two souls are matched in perfect accord. These white-robed Old Ones represent the spiritual wisdoms which can guide us to find the "soul mate" with whom we may share our life and our love as purely as we are able in the realm of humankind.

The white gold and many jewels the Old Ones wear cause you to note the need to access and activate your relationships with creative mindfulness, compassionate communication, balanced self-expressiveness, supportive structures, and divine forgiveness, as well as mutual spiritual acceptance. These are the qualities and ideals of the most sacred relationships.

CRAFTING WITH THE FEY

In Faerie realms, you encounter yourself in a most enhanced aspect. Be sure you are clear and not feeling too stressed or down, for everything in Faerie is amplified. It is a crystalline realm of the mind; so let it be positive and enchanting for you. Remember that enchantment, like power, is neutral. It amplifies and transforms according to your intentions; so be specific, if you are planning specific transformations with this mystical realm of mind.

You will encounter what you expect, for Faerie is a reflective realm. Encounter yourself clearly first—and you will encounter Faerie, clearly. Come to know yourself first—with clear acceptance. Faerie will come emerging into your imagery in a natural way, clearly reflecting acceptance. Here is a set of questions to know yourself in the sense of what you want specifically and what you know to be your intentions. These provide a good guideline for intentions to become more specific.

Rules of Encounter: Fey Crafting

Expectations Questions
1. What do I want to do with Faerie?
2. What do I imagine Faerie wants to do with me?
3. What do I not want to do with Faerie?
4. What do I imagine Faerie does not want to do with me?

Emotional Needs Questions
1. Why do I need to access this amplified realm?
2. Why do I not need to do this?
3. What do I believe this will do for me?
4. What do I believe this will not do for me?

Experiential Dependency Questions

1. What can I do instead of entering an amplified realm?
2. Where can I go instead of this realm?
3. How else can I create what I want?
4. How else can I find ways to express my creativity?

Note:If this sounds like a way to keep you out of Faerie realm—well, it isn't exactly. It's a way to express that I understand how enchanting the Faerie realms of Nature and self-nature are. Faerie imagery can be mystically compelling. That is why so many of the legends say so. Yes, we've evolved; but Faerie is still enchanting, especially in the midst of a modern world. Just like shamanic journeys, you are traveling into Faerie "between the worlds." It is multidimensional and a source of great creative inspiration (just ask William Butler Yeats). It is wise to have a specific purpose when "flying" around in Faerie—unless you're very familiar with flying by the seat of your pants—with a parachute, at times. Temperance, temperance.

We will close this chapter with yet another sacred Avalon imagery. You may make this as ceremonial as you choose so long as your experience is self-initiatory in the realms of Avalon healing.

THE GLASS BOAT: SACRED INITIATION

Elements: Water and Spirit

Directions: West, Center, and the Circle encircling

Aspects: Priest/Priestess empowerment

Colors: White, Crystal, Rainbow and Gold lights, Turquoise ray

Kindred Spirits: Rabbits, Salmon, Frogs

Tree: Sea

Stones: Pearl, Mother of Pearl, Abalone, White Quartz, Aquamarine

Incense: Sweet Floral

Cycle: Lammas

Setting Image: Temple

Hallow: Glass boat, sacred vessel

Theme: Quest

Natural Force: Mists

Access Allies: Arthur, Lady of the Lake

Format: Moderate

Message: There is only one, true vessel that provides transport to the mystical realms of Spirit that nurture, and surely you are that vessel. This is as truly so as you are a vessel of the divine feminine, the White Goddess, who holds fair dominion over the natural healing realms of which Avalon is one Light. Enlighten your self with truth and spirit, and you will travel surely.

———

It is a beautiful sunlit morning in the sacred isles. The dawn mists have begun to drift away, dispersing in the warmth of a new day. It is Lammastide, and you find yourself in a mystical crystal boat, traveling across the sea of spiritual consciousness to reach the mystical temple on this lovely sacred isle. With you is Arthur in a golden aspect as the mythic king of all time. He is clear and unburdened by concerns of the mundane world. Together, you are going to celebrate the first harvest of the cycle of Nature, and the first millennium of Arthur's powerful influence on the cycle of Celtic nature and mythical philosophy. Although Arthur has been a part of Celtic Nature for far longer than a thousand years, you are going to celebrate his influence over a millennium of the modern Celtic mind. He is joyful and almost boyish as your boat brings you both into shore.

The Lady of Avalon in her most majestic aspect is there to greet you as you arrive on this new isle. She is accompanied by the high Priest and Priestess of this isle's temple. They greet you affectionately and bow to honor the royal sovereign king, Arthur. There are others present to help as you dock the boat among the silvery reeds on the shoreline. All of Nature seems to join in this greeting, as well. Tiny green frogs croak melodically among the patches of dawn's mists, still drifting in the cool rushes where the waters of the sea merge with the river flowing out from the land. It is a blending of realms and you are conscious of the power of this point of connection.

As you step off the boat, a group of musicians begins playing a processional tune with harps, flutes, and drums. Young Fair Folk maidens throw sweet fragrant blossoms on the path where Arthur walks ahead of all who are gathered here. It is a joyful gathering, and you feel exhilarated by all you experience here. The Lady of Avalon walks ahead with Arthur and you follow them in a position of privilege and honor.

It is a lovely walk to the temple on this isle, and you feel close to all the beauty of Nature that surrounds you here. There are sleek white rabbits and large gray hares in the meadows beside the temple path. They gaze at you without fear here, for they are honored as symbols of The White Goddess in Her many aspects. When you pass a quiet pool of clear fresh water, you catch a glimpse of mystical salmon swimming among the stones in the gentle stream. Their sides reflect the sunlight in rainbow patterns, and you remember their significance as Celtic symbols of knowledge.

At last you reach the temple site, between two gently rounded hills that remind all who come here of their connection to the nurturing heart of the Earth Mother Goddess and their service to the Sovereignty of the lands. The temple is made of soft gray and white stones. These are rounded from ages spent in the rivers of time and tides. Today the temple is decorated with silk banners which billow like great sails in the morning breeze. Some are made of turquoise silk, emblazoned with golden emblems of the Sun. Others are white with Celtic weave in rainbow tones, symbolizing the royal right of leadership and the full spectrum of Nature's powers. You feel you are truly one of a royal clan of Nature's children, and you know this is a lineage multitudes share, although not all are yet aware.

You gaze at the silk banners and feel empowered by your dedication to a path of Service and Light. It is a privileged position of sovereign leadership, and if only within your own realms, it is more than enough for the good of all. Cool breezes blow in from the shoreline as you follow Arthur and the Lady of Avalon into the temple. The others who have come in procession encircle the temple at a respectful distance. Only you have the privilege this day to share the sacred temple with Arthur and the Lady of Avalon. They show you around the temple, pointing out on the walls the carvings and stonework depicting the sacred quests of others who have served the Light and the Lands.

You feel both shy and bold at the same time; but you soon find a respectful balance of both. You have all that morning in the temple with Arthur and the Lady of Avalon. You feel graced to have the opportunity to listen and ask questions within this temple. You feel emotionally more secure than you may have ever felt before, because your kinship with these mythic allies is one of truly deep, spiritual quality.

At first you feel rushed, as though the moment could slip away forever. The Lady senses your uncertainty and lovingly assures you that this temple and all its empowerment are eternally present for you in this fine, rare realm. Arthur calls for you to share a bountiful breakfast that has been brought to the temple to celebrate the arrival of the Sun King, the Lady of Avalon, and of

their honored ken—you, in your aspect of wise light warrior, mystic, or mage. Over breakfast, you comfortably share news of your own realm—as you would with familiar kinspeople or family—or with clan.

The time passes in its most perfect dimension, and you truly find that you feel completely welcome within this temple and on this sacred isle where the river meets the sea. You know whomever you encounter when you travel here will always welcome you with true spiritual kinship. You feel you can come whenever there are needs within you which you must find enlightened ways to meet, or questions whose answers may only be found within this sacred temple of your innermost self.

As the noonday Sun climbs high in the sky over this sacred isle, a trumpet signals the time for you, Arthur, and the Lady of Avalon to return to your own realms of time and responsibility. With promises to come again soon, Arthur leaves first, escorted by a royal procession of Fair Folk and by the priests and priestesses of this mystical isle.

The Lady of Avalon asks you to stay for a brief moment in this time between the worlds. She has a gift for you which will help you travel to this isle of consciousness and enlightenment whenever you have need of the Divine healing light you can find within this sacred realm.

In order to ensure this, the Lady now proceeds to initiate you in a manner reserved for those who are in true alliance with the spiritual powers of Avalon and all the other sacred isles within that realm of consciousness and light, such as the one you have found this day. She takes you to the altar inside the temple and lifts a white cloth which has covered sacred objects of ceremonial empowerment.

There are five small bowls crafted of Faerie crystal with waves etched delicately on their sides. These symbolize the waves of emotional consciousness which carry you to this sacred isle. Each crystal bowl is filled with clear water and has a lovely fragment of stones, shells, or gems within it. The Lady of Avalon dips her fingers in each bowl, in turn, and touches your heart in blessing, empowering you with the qualities found within each of these sacred vessels:

First: The waters in which there is mother-of-pearl bring you the maternal nurturance of Mother Ocean.

Second: The waters within which there is a perfect pearl bring you the receptive emotions of the Moon.

Third: The waters that contain abalone shell bring you the balance of a full spectrum of feelings.

Fourth: The waters in which there is an aquamarine bring you a softer power of the intense turquoise ray which drives your feelings of dedication and service. This, and the crystal of the vessels themselves, clarify your emotions and crystallize your feelings of purpose.

This being done, The Lady of Avalon presents you with a sacred vessel for your own inner journeys. It is a small glass boat, a crystalline vessel crafted in the realm of Faerie, which can transform mystically to carry you into these realms of heartfelt love, healing, and empowerment. The Lady of Avalon tells you that within this realm you will be regarded as an initiated, priestly member of the spiritual clan of Light which serves the White Goddess in all Her Sovereign aspects, and the Sun King, Arthur, as the Celtic Lord of Light.

Whatever your role in other realms, either mystical or mundane, you remain eternally a sacred person of wisdom and power in this sacred realm where the river meets the sea.

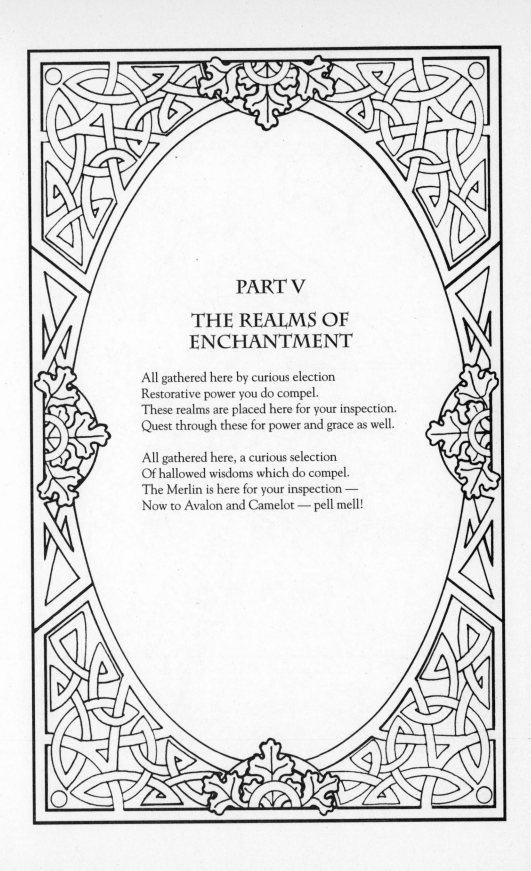

PART V

THE REALMS OF
ENCHANTMENT

All gathered here by curious election
Restorative power you do compel.
These realms are placed here for your inspection.
Quest through these for power and grace as well.

All gathered here, a curious selection
Of hallowed wisdoms which do compel.
The Merlin is here for your inspection —
Now to Avalon and Camelot — pell mell!

CHAPTER 24

THE HALLOWED SYMBOLS

The man who comes back through the Door in the Wall will never be quite the same as the man who went out. He will be wiser but less cocksure, happier but less self-satisfied, humbler in acknowledging the relationship of words to things, of systematic reasoning to the unfathomable Mystery which it tries, forever vainly to comprehend.

Aldous Huxley
The Doors of Perception (New York: Harper-Row, 1990)

The myriad of symbols in the Camelot legends are your personal keys to the "Doors of Perception"—to the elemental realms of power they were created to represent. These elaborate symbols have emerged from ancient ages to express their sacred, Celtic mystery with significant meaning for all of us in modern times. These are hallowed symbols because they reflect a sacred alliance or synthesis, which honors the interrelationship of all life—Self, Nature, and Spirit.

Although these symbols have transformed from simple to complex, expressing the evolutionary progress of the Celtic philosophies as they have expanded to become our own, their elemental power has remained essentially and foundationally the same. Because of this ancient Celtic foundational alliance of power, our current alliance with power can continue to evolve and expand—creating multidimensional transformations for ourselves, our cultures, and our world.

In order to strengthen our alliance with Nature and to stimulate the ancient encoded knowledge and Celtic tribal wisdoms within, we will explore these hallowed symbols as well as the gifts of power and perception which have come to us as a legacy—one we accept with honor.

THE ELEMENTAL SYMBOLS OF POWER

The hallowed symbols in the Camelot legends have their origin in the elemental gifts of Faerie—the talismanic powers of the Tuatha dé Danann. These symbolize the elements of Nature and their natural reflections in ourselves, as do all power symbols, regardless of their simplicity or complexity. To the four ancient symbols, I add a fifth element, Spirit—or ether. Spirit is implied, more or less, by the reflected relationship of its symbolic power with our selves and in our lives, transformationally. Spirit is also present in the highly evolved skills of these Fair Folk, whose gifts have become our hallowed legacy—from the Tuatha dé:

> ... they stand out as a people of magic wonders, learned in all the arts and supreme masters of wizardry. Before coming to Ireland they had sojourned in the northern islands of the world, where they had acquired their incomparable esoteric knowledge and whence they brought with them four talismans: the Great Fál—the person under whom this stone shrieked was king of Ireland; the spear of Lug—no victory could be won against it nor against him who had it in his hand; the sword of Nuadu—no one escaped from it when it was drawn from its scabbard; and the cauldron of the Dagda, from which no company would go away unsatisfied.

Alwyn and Brinley Rees
Celtic Heritage (London: Thames and Hudson, 1991)

These talismanic gifts, in more familiar terms, have come to be called:

The Stone of Destiny: Earth—Position, Order, Wisdom. The stone has its legendary origin from the Tuatha dé stronghold at Falias—currently Ulster. It has also the gift of an earthy dragon ally, magickally called Morfessa.

The Spear of Light: Air—Perception, Inspiration, Focus. This spear's legendary origin, also a stronghold of the Tuatha dé, was at Gorias—currently Leinster. The Spear's airy dragon ally is magickally called by the name Esras.

The Sword of Power: Fire—Protection, Strength, Courage. The Sword has its legendary origin at the Tuatha dé stronghold of Finias—currently Munster. The Sword's fiery dragon ally is magickally called Useias.

The Cauldron of Plenty: Water—Processes of Healing and Initiation. The Cauldron has its origin in legend, from the stronghold of the Tuatha dé at Murias—currently Connaught. The Cauldron's flowing dragon ally is magickally called Semias.

These descriptions are brief, but we have Hallows to explore, so try a quick exercise in imagery on your own, using these ancient gifts provided symbolically by our proto-Celtic Faerie-kin, the Tuatha dé Danann. You might find the Cauldron is somewhat vast, so use the Cup for a softer version of the same replenishing experience. You may add Spirit as an element in your imagery by crafting a Faerie ally to guide your experience.

THE FAERIE SYMBOLS: AN EXERCISE

One at a time, call into your mind an image of each of the four Faerie symbols. Consider the aspects each one represents and the way these can empower your life. Create an image of each dragon ally, using colors that reflect its elemental powers, naturally—the dragon is an image of your powers, too.

From the Faerie gifts which are a part of the Gaelic Celtic traditions we move to the Hallows, which represent a Brythonic Celtic version. These are quite similar, as they would be, naturally; but the stone becomes a gameboard. Since both forms represent a symbol of destiny, their elemental aspects are essentially the same.

Both the stone and the gameboard symbolically link to the Source of self-determination and the powers that influence your position on the gameboard of life. This game often seems to be playing all by itself, moving figures and pawns around according to mysterious rules. However, you may find you have the choice to be pawn or player more often than you realize.

The Brythonic Hallows

The Gameboard: Earth—Position, Order, Strategy, Wisdom

This Gameboard emerges from the Welsh oral traditions which describe it as one of the Thirteen Treasures of Britain. The additional element of strategy comes with this Brythonic symbol, best described as a stone gameboard, with figures in silver (receptive) and gold (active) which help you reflect on, and in, the pattern of the stoneboard and the strategic powers of the game.

The Spear: Air—Perception, Focus, Inspiration, and Aim

The Spear's qualities have the added element of aim in its Brythonic version. This added aspect makes it somewhat more active, so you may find it symbolically more amplified for transformational work. Cast it lightly until it becomes familiar, and don't focus on just one aspect. If you do, you may find you've missed the point—or even just gotten the shaft.

The Sword: Fire—Protection, Strength, Courage, Guardianship

The Sword's added element makes its Brythonic version a more active manifestation of yourself in the service of guardianship. Just be sure to use the first three aspects to provide the elements you need for yourself first—before assuming guardianship.

The Cup: Water—Processes of Healing, Initiation, and Divination

The Cup's added element brings an activated use of inner knowing and intuition. These are important to use to determine the causes, effects, and measures needed to bring about healing, self-renewal, and to divine the result of the initiation experiences of your life.

These Hallows may also be experienced by crafting them symbolically in imagery and reflecting on their qualities in regard to the powers and aspects needed in your own life.

Some correlations connect to these Hallows as symbols of the four seasons. Some use this system: Stone game: Earth—Winter, Sword: Air—Spring; Spear: Fire—Summer; and Cup: Water—Fall. Others use the following system (as I most often do): Spear: Air—Spring; Sword: Fire—Summer; Cup: Water—Fall; and Stone game: Earth—Winter.

The system is a matter of choice. I find the Spear is a rather useful blend of both Fire (the Point) and Air (the Shaft); but the "flaming sword" of power described as one of the Thirteen Treasures makes it elementally more fiery than airy to me. The other Hallows, Spear and Cup, are not specified as such in the Thirteen Treasures of Britain. However, you may work with these to develop your own systems from the material which follows:

The Thirteen Treasures of Britain

There is a traditional belief that The Merlin is buried on Bardsey Island off the coast of Wales. Bardsey is a holy site where only those of "royal and priestly blood" may be laid to rest. It is the site of the ruins of a thirteenth-century abbey dedicated to St. Mary, and is reputed to be the burial place of twenty thousand saints. There is one Celtic cross as a memorial; but the mystical symbols of commemoration are the sacred Thirteen Treasures. The traditional source for a listing of these treasures is *The Mabinogion*, the Welsh tales, taken from the oral tradition, and presented by Lady Charlotte Guest. The treasures are mentioned in two stories, "The Dream of Rhonanabwy" and "Culwech and Olwen."

Both stories seem to have been created bardically, to preserve these symbolic treasures and the quests, trials, and fantastic encounters required for Arthur and his knights to obtain them. However, it is also quite apparent that these treasures emerge from even older Celtic forms, such as the tales of the "Gaelic Argonauts," who obtain similar treasures to pay a fine to Lugh, the Tuatha dé Lord of Light. (Both versions later form part of the Arthurian Grail quest.)

The Gaelic Argonaut Treasures (The Sons of Tuirenn)
1. Three apples—which heal and constantly replenish themselves
2. A pig skin—which heals and turns water into wine for nine days
3. A spear—with a poisoned blade that must be kept underwater
4. Two horses and a chariot that travel equally well on sea or land
5. Seven pigs—killed and eaten each night and are alive and well the next day
6. A hound-whelp—who catches every wild beast she sees
7. A cooking spit—from the Island at the bottom of the Irish Sea
8 Three shouts upon a hill—where no shouts are allowed

Elemental Aspects of the Thirteen Treasures of Britain

1. A flaming sword of power
2. A plate that always is filled with food
3. A horn that always is filled with drink
4. A chariot always ready to give a ride to any desired location
5. A halter that can capture horses on its own
6. A knife that can carve enough for twenty-five with one slice
7. A cauldron that cooks food only for those who are brave
8. A whetstone that sharpens knives that guarantee death
9. A cloak that fits only those who are of noble birth
10. A cooking pan that provides any desired food
11. A ring of invisibility (from Lunette of the Fountain)
12. A chessboard with self-playing silver and gold pieces
13. A mantle of invisibility (reputed to be Arthur's)

In order to understand these treasures, we can correlate them to a list of magickal items used in ceremonies and rituals, as well as in transformational crafting. These are somewhat arbitrary, but their symbolic qualities are similar. As you go over these suggestions, be guided by your own responses in order to develop your own correlations.

Treasures	Element	Ceremonial Symbols
1. Flaming sword	Fire	1. Swords/daggers
2. Food platter	Earth	2. Plates, trays
3. Drinking horn	Water	3. Cup/chalice
4. Chariot	Air	4. Animal symbols, steeds
5. Halter	Air	5. Censers, incense burners
6. Knife	Fire	6. Spear, knife
7. Cauldron	Water	7. Cauldron, bowl
8. Whetstone	Fire	8. Lamp, candle
9. Noble's cloak	Earth	9. Staff, rank symbol
10. Cooking pan	Air	10. Wand
11. Gold ring	Water	11. Ring
12. Chessboard	Earth	12. Altar, stone tablet
13. Mantle	Spirit	13. Robes

With a closer look at the elemental aspects, we can get a clearer sense of how these correlations work and what the Thirteen symbolic Treasures of Britain may be representing, in general. From this, you can develop a personal, more specific match for symbolic meaning. As these are hallowed symbols of ancient sacred origin, use them with an attitude of spiritual reverence and acknowledge the Grail which gives you the right of connection to their powerful legacy.

1. The flaming sword or short sword daggers are used to create a protected space where ceremonies may take place. Swords are also used to symbolize rank in terms of power and guardianship, as well as to activate power at each cardinal point.

2. Food platters are often used for offerings in many ceremonies, sometimes as "spirit plates" in Native traditions. The spirit of sharing provides its own replenishing reward, which creates a cycle of plenty. The Earth aspect indicates the structures that provide for production and sharing of resources.

3. The drinking horn is the cup in primitive form, with the horn being a more active aspect of its power. Because it is filled with drink, it symbolizes the actions one must take in order to accept from the Waters of Life—the eternally flowing source.

4. Chariot is an image with a link to the shamanic steeds or animal allies that we envision creatively—with an element of Air—to help us explore different realms and dimensions located within.

5. Halter is a line that captures an energy; the symbolic power of the horse. Censers burning with the "smoke of transformation" capture our attention and halter our minds so we may be focused and guided (either from within alone, or with another to facilitate our inner work).

6. Knife is used to carve symbols and cut through bindings symbolically. Both of these have to do with communication, with self, others, and spirit. The spear is an Air element of one-point focused communication which can often be achieved only through the use of one-point symbols (with uncomplicated, direct representations or one focused intent, word, effect, location, or individual in mind).

7. Cauldron is the symbol of transformation by immersing in the deep waters of consciousness at times. At others, the processes of self-reflection must effectively be experienced by looking into the deep, or shallow, feelings or emotional conditions. From this can come a bravely deserved reward, and it isn't always necessary to be the "boiled food."

8. Whetstone brings the sharp edge of focus as well as the tempered quality of clear motivation to the forged blade of anger or intensity, which can result in too much Fire. The candles or lamps symbolize the gentle aspects of Fire—not a blaze, but a sharp-edged flame.

9. Noble's cloak has an Earth element relationship to the trappings of rank we use in crafting of imageries, as well as some rituals that follow "the rank and file" formats. This cloak is a banner of sorts and has a heraldic, declarative quality. It's a "designer label" symbol; but this has its symbolic place, to remind us of the abundance of power and the rights of self-sovereignty.

10. The cooking pan is like a wand or any symbol that turns on the switch and lets you "cook up" the imagery or the ceremony—or even the ritual recipe to provide the sustenance you desire. Air is the aspect of inspiration here, and the focus, aim, and abilities of mind and brain.

11. The gold ring of invisibility symbolizes the way we shift our persona to project a different image—thus making the everyday self, in effect, invisible, if only temporarily, so we can illuminate our vision. These qualities show a definite element of Air.

12. Chessboard or altar: the game plan is set up and played out by the symbols, images, or items we structure, with an elemental Earth aspect to provide the order and forms for manifestation.

13. Spirit is a mantle of invisible power that illuminates, protects, initiates, and orders our crafting with positive purpose for the good of all.

In her superb work on modern Celtic shamanism called *By Oak, Ash, and Thorn*, D. J. Conway provides a listing of these Thirteen Treasures of Britain, from the Welsh triads. In this list, the relationship to ceremonial magicks and more ancient shamanic practices can be seen, particularly in the first, third, fourth, and seventh treasures—which are listed (with correlated aspects and additions from me) as follows:

1. "Dyrnwyn (White Hilt), the Sword of Rhydderch the Generous." This aspect of the "flaming sword" symbolizes the activation medium of white light synthesis, utilized benevolently. I suggest a possible connection between Rhycher Powys (which means "arable land") from "The Dream of Rhonabwy" as a correlated symbol of the Sovereign Lands from which the Celtic Swords of power quite often emerge, representing guardianship, leadership, and service, in elemental alliance with Nature.

3. "The hamper of Bwyddno Ganahir" which Conway suggests "may mean a container such as the crane bag" or a magickal pouch containing items for crafting and power. This aspect of the "pan which cooks whatever food is desired" also has some of the mystical qualities by which the mind can image what is needed and ceremonially correlates with the tools of the trade, the items used in rituals as containers of power.

4. "The halter of Clydno Eiddyn" which Conway suggests "may have symbolized a headband, or torque." This "halter which captures horses on its own" represents the abilities of brain and mind to control both focus and perception in order to create transformational projections. This is another correlated form such as the censer and its transformational smoke which I have mentioned previously. Additionally, the headband which Conway suggests can symbolize the powers of mental perception and the torque worn around the neck can be representative of the expressive projections made with magickal will. (Remember the third

eye, forehead region represents the synthesis of wisdom, and the neck/throat region represents the power point of expression, devotion, and will.)

7. "The Knife of Llawfrouned the Horseman." This aspect of the "knife which could carve enough for twenty-five with one single slice" has sometimes been described as black-hilted. This, combined with the skills of a horseman, symbolizes the ability to cut to the chase, employing strategy and tactics to provide the needed power for specific goals, such as victory or abundance.

These versions of the Thirteen Treasures, and of the Faerie gifts or powers presented thus far, form the basis for expanded, elaborated symbols such as the ones found in more current images in the Camelot legends. These we will focus on in our imageries and explorations of these hallowed realms. These symbols represent an alchemical synthesis, as blends and as multidimensional representations which correlate to many realms of power. However, to understand them more easily and use them effectively while becoming familiar with their aspects and powers we will initiate this process by placing them in designated categories as follows:

The Hallowed Symbols: Currently Reflected and Expanded from the Realms of Camelot's Legends

Spear: Air—Perception, focus, aim, inspiration, creativity; also includes: Bow and Arrows, Staff, Wand, and Harp, and correlates with East: The Merlin: Evolutionary—Illumination

Sword: Fire—Protection, strength, courage, will, guardianship; also includes: Faerie blade, Battle Shield, Lance, and Drum, and correlates with South: Battles: Guardian—Trainers

Cup: Water—Processes of Healing, initiation, intuition, emotions; also includes: Cauldron, Chalice, Scabbard, Sheath, Pouch, Glassboat, and Mirrored Shield, and correlates with West: Avalon: Initiator—Healers

Stone: Earth—positions of rank, order, wisdom, growth, prosperity; also includes: Gameboard, Cloak, Banner, Symbols: (three aspects) of Light, Nature's Woven Star, and Runes to determine structures and systems of self-destiny, and correlates with North: Camelot: Connectors—Manifestors

With a four-element direction and aspects approach, these next symbols would come under the categories specified in the list that follows. In a five-element approach, I designate these as symbols of Spirit. In this, the element takes precedence over the symbol.

Spirit: Center, Circle, Circle encircling—Light Source, Divine Power; Symbols include:
Crystal Sphere—Enlightenment Power, which also correlates with Air/Spear
Crystal Point—Synergy Force of Light, which also correlates with Fire/Sword

Grail—Restorative Source of Light, which also correlates with Water/Cup
Spiritual Symbol—Divine Light Connector, which also correlates with Earth/Stone
    (This symbol is decided upon personally)

Additionally, the element of Spirit provides the power of the White Goddess—
four of her aspects correlate as such:

Spear: East—Inspiration—The goddess of Poetry, as empowering muse
Sword: Fire—Guardianship—The goddess of Smithcraft, forging power
Cup: Water—Renewal—The goddess of Healing as the initiating power
Stone: Earth—Structures—The goddess of Civilization, with orders for power

As the more ancient symbolic Earth Mother, The Goddess is Danu/Don, the Sovereignty of the Lands. This symbolizes the maternal source in manifested forms of the alliance of Receptive Synthesis. This synthesis blends the elements of Nature, cultures, tribes, and individuals, with all aspects activated in forms of service. These forms of service are self-determined through the processes of accessing, activating, and reflecting the elements of self-nature. This is done using the aspects of Air, Fire, Water, Earth, and Spirit—for Illuminative Focus, Protective Will, Emotional Self-Renewal, Structures of Personal Honor, and Divine Guidance.

In concert with The Divine Lady is the Lord of Light, also correlated with the symbols and their aspects:

Spear: Air—Evolutionary Catalyst—The lord of Magick, expanded power
Sword: Fire—Protective Force—The lord as Warrior, protective power
Cup: Water—Emotional Security—The lord as Lover, compassionate power
Stone: Earth—Practical Growth—The lord as King, leadership power

As the more ancient, symbolic Sky Father, the Lord of Light is the "Good God," such as Dagda/Bran, the All-Father (*Dis Pater*). This symbolizes the paternal source also in manifested forms of Active Synthesis, which provide the transformations, goals, and achievements that the blended elements of Nature, along with cultures, tribes and individuals, create for themselves, their people, and their planet.

Together, the symbolic Divine Lady and Lord of Light strimulate a reflective synthesis of all the elements and aspects that are present. This divine pairing provides a balanced source of empowerment for natural potentials and positive purposes.

Beyond this is the ultimate Source, still perceived as the undefinable Great Mystery. This highest aspect of Spirit and Light is described according to one's spiritual philosophies, as well as religious beliefs. Some call this the Godhead, or God, the Creator. Others call this the Great Goddess or the Creatrix. Still others blend these and say "Mother Father God," which actuates both maternal and paternal powers. I prefer the viewpoint of a spiritual synthesis, calling this Source, the Universal Divine. Whatever this Mystery may be called, it is an essential source of all elements and aspects. It is the All that reflects in the symbols we create to define life as we perceive and experience it, in aspects we can discover and define.

Transformational Symbols for Hallowed Experiences

Thus far in this chapter we have explored the hallowed symbols, from general versions to vast expansions. Now we will proceed to specify these Hallows as potential empowering symbols for your work with imagery and crafting the transformations in your life. Remember that symbols are not limited either to, or by, the categories we place them in, nor the correlations we make in relationship to the elements, aspects, and powers they represent.

The key to the transformational power of any symbol is its power to transform itself into keys of expanded purpose. In this, symbols are a direct reflection of yourself in relationship to your self-transformational powers and potentials. Just as you weave or craft transformation with threads of your experiences and fibers of your elemental aspects in synthesis, so you can work with the hallowed symbols. Weave and craft with these, using an experimental (read Druidic) attitude, and an experiential approach. This is essentially alchemy with symbols. However, you already know what the ancient alchemists were seeking—the philosopher's stone of alchemical properties is right inside your head. With your philosophic mind and the properties of your brain, you can create the transformations you want.

Symbols are the catalysts for golden transformations. They activate like pure gold, shining in your manifestations of power and purpose. Here are some suggestions and formulas, using the hallowed symbols in discussion, exercises, and imagery (as well as some solid smithcrafting, by Bridget, to forge experiential wisdom). Use these and your own images and interpretations to deepen your experience in the realms of power found in the legends of Camelot, The Merlin, Arthur, and Avalon, in the 'round.

Aspects of the Hallowed Symbols, from Traditional Legends

These aspects are arranged alphabetically here so you can explore them without structured categories of elements and correlating attributes. Instead, as you go through them, develop your own image first, using the description I've given. Then add the elements one at a time to see how your symbolic image changes. Remember that Spirit is an amplifying element in general, and will give your symbol more intensity. Therefore, you might want to use Spirit as an amplifier to experience symbols that emerge more subtly, with less definition. You can also use Spirit amplification to observe elemental changes in your symbols, specifically, and in your general use of transformational imagery.

The 28th Hallowed symbol, the woven star of elemental power and synthesis, is discussed in greater detail. Following that is my personal list of those elements I find most frequently accessible and currently active in each hallowed symbol.

The Twenty-eight Hallows: Numerological Formulation, 2 = 8 = 10 = #1

1. Banner: The Banner is a declarative symbol that allows you to show your true colors and to try other colors as keys to transformations. These often display allies from Nature, such as animals or trees, symbolizing power.

2. Battle Shield: The Battle Shield is a declarative symbol of challenge, as well as protection. It can also display allies of power that declare your intentions, purposes, and powers for crafting.

3. Bow and Arrows: The Bow and Arrows are focusing symbols that activate your aim. These allow you to transmit or communicate any form of messages. This can be done from a distance and from positions that are secure or camouflaged.

4. Cauldron: The Cauldron is a process symbol that represents deep cycles of self-healing and personal initiation. It also provides a tool for the processes of divination.

5. Chalice: The Chalice is a mystical symbol with a sacred, priestly quality. This indicates the times when ritual or ceremonial attitudes are your best approach for emotional renewal.

6. Cloak: The Cloak is a declarative symbol that displays your position, rank, or powers, as well as the energies of the colors in which it emerges. This also can provide a way to make the mundane self "invisible" and the mystical self visible in imagery.

7. Crystal Point (and clusters): The Crystal Point is an amplified spiritual symbol of encapsulated powers and structures of magick crafting. It is also a tool for directing energies of communication, individually with the point, clusters for groups.

8. Crystal Sphere: The Crystal Sphere is an amplified spiritual symbol that helps you divine, determine, and direct your purpose. This may be seen as a microcosmic symbol, representing the macrocosmic 'round.

9. Cup: The Cup is a process symbol for more personal and natural cycles of renewal. It represents the everyday flow of feelings, rather than deep currents of emotional cycles.

10. Drum: The Drum is a focusing symbol that helps set the pace and rhythm of energies you are directing. Its power as a key is its ability to express natural energies.

11. Faerie Blade: The Faerie Blade is a mystical symbol that amplifies its natural, direct qualities and adds an aspect of Fey to your crafting. It is used for shaping, or carving specifics for manifestation, and also for protection and courage.

12. Gameboard: The Gameboard is a focusing symbol that allows you to play out your designs and plans. It is also useful for strategic divination if you image the game-playing as it is without your plans.

13. Glass Boat: The Glass Boat is a mystical symbol that represents the process of voyaging within the realms of consciousness. It can also be used to transmit healing energies and magickal images.

14. Grail: The Grail is a spiritual synthesis symbol that represents the source of healing restoration. It also symbolizes the processes of self-renewing quests made to reach the Grail within.

15. Harp: The Harp is a declarative symbol that represents a relationship of service to the Muse. It is used as a focus catalyst for inspiration, expression, and for setting a reflective pace.

16. Lance: The Lance is a declarative symbol of testing challenges and direct, even blunt, methods of communication. Its powers are best activated while securely "seated" on a shamanic steed.

17. Light Symbol: The Light Symbol is your sacred, spiritual symbol and reflects your faith according to your design. Traditional symbols may also be used without interference, for these lines are always clear.

18. Magick Pouch: The Magickal Pouch is a declarative symbol that shows your ability to collect, encapsulate, or store powers and wisdoms and keep them accessible when you want or need to activate them.

19. Mirrored Shield: The Mirrored Shield is a process symbol that represents the experiences of inner knowing. It also declares the powers of being intuitively mystical while maintaining a mundane front or persona.

20. Runes: The Runes are focusing symbols for any means of divination that allows you to obtain sacred wisdom, usually adapted from a system of traditional structures. These provide for a more strategic form of divination.

21. Scabbard: The Scabbard is a process symbol which represents the manner in which you balance, contain, and encapsulate power, rather than use it unwisely or needlessly.

22. Sheath (for Faerie Blade): The Sheath is a process symbol that represents your ability to keep your thoughts, plans, and purposes to yourself when you need to do that. It also symbolizes private willpower.

23. Spear: The Spear is a focusing symbol that enables you to express yourself directly for purposes of transmitting magickal images and messages. It also gets the point across in any form of communication.

24. Staff: The Staff is a declarative symbol that represents your position in connection with power. It serves as a symbolic conductor for currents of energy and directs the order of crafting.

25. Stone: The Stone is a focusing symbol with distinct powers for declarative and divinational purposes. It allows you to focus on what your life declares, and divine both choices and changes.

26. Sword: The Sword is a declarative symbol that represents the right to use power for protection and guardianship. It also indicates your skills at crafting or wielding active power.

27. Wand: The Wand is a focusing symbol that directs your attention to the specifics of the purpose and the powers required. The Wand is a symbolic cue, alerting the magickal mind.

28. Woven Star Symbol (with an extensive explanation): The Woven Star is an elemental synthesis symbol representing the aspects of Nature, interwoven in an alliance of power. In some cases the points are the four primary elements (Air, Fire, Water, Earth) with the fifth point symbolizing Ether (Spirit) or relationships with the realm of Spirit.

    Traditionally, the "single point up" symbolizes Spirit exalted within—and sometimes above—the natural elements. Also, in Craft traditions, the double points up symbolizes the service of guardianship exalted by personal choice over personal and even spiritual desires. This is why the Congressional Medal of Honor and some other five-point star medals are designed in the "horns up" manner; symbolizing the sacred service of providing protection and strength. This form derived from the ancient rites of the hunter/warrior Celts and still empowers those who guard for positive purposes.

    Unfortunately, this symbol has a frequency or current which some modern new guardians and Light warriors may find jammed with static from misuse and misconception. These may well stem from misuse of the Mithraic Bull in ancient times, also a misconception of its own rite.

    In more current times, the misuse takes the forms of static, confusions, and negativities. This is created by those who will ultimately discover they have been operating under the misconception that they have the power to avoid the consequences of their actions. Further static on this symbol's frequency line comes from sensationalistic misrepresentations and superstitious misconceptions. These are often carefully manipulated by the misusers of power from various spiritual and religious systems, and of course, there is the media image. Fortunately there is great progress—progress that illuminates the Truth with Light.

    When the "two points up" form of the woven star is encircled with positive protective intentions and unity of purpose for the good of all, it can be an extremely potent symbol. By all Rights, and in all rites, specifically—whoever uses this one had best be of the Light, for the Right, in the Know, on Alert, wise and very clear at all times, even when this symbol is not supposed to be activated, because of the powerful magnetism within any raw power symbol which invariably attracts some forms of scrap metal and other useless trash.

    Instead, I suggest the uncircled form when activating this ancient "two points up" symbol. Even this one is tricky and requires all the elements of self-nature in a light, right, knowing, alert, wise, and clear synthesis. If this form is used because it provides a personal change or boost for the ego, those who receive this boost will also invariably be charged—but not with positive power.

Another way to use this ancient symbol of guardianship is to add the powerful Celtic symbol of the hunter, The Green Man, The Herne, the Lord of the Trees and the Forests, who is also known as the Lord of the Animals. This symbol is the sacred stag. The stag and his antlers are more in keeping with the protective powers used for the Right. These antlers alone, or the symbol of the stag, will access and activate profound elemental powers for positive guardianship. Furthermore, they won't require profound efforts of self-protection, nor protection for others who share your realm. The greatness and purity of this stag's symbolic powers comes from its name in Middle English—The Hart.

The "single point up," woven five-point star is clearly traced to the legends of Gawain (although it most likely has much more ancient origins). This woven star (without the modern circle) is described as being on Gawain's belt. This locates it at the physical place of power called the Solar energy point. Additionally, the belt encircles and supports, both a symbolic and natural representation of the forces of Nature's elements. When Gawain returned from his encounter with the Green Knight, the legend tells that the Round Table Knights decided to wear woven stars in honor of Gawain's bravery and because he had upheld the codes of Chivalry by keeping his word and his part of the bargain.

Gawain is also depicted with this woven star on his shield, symbolizing both protection and an elemental alliance with Nature. This combination is an extended symbol of guardianship. The battle shield implies that others are involved, while the belt is more solitary, symbolically. Both the belt and the battle shield, with five-point woven stars, "single point up" for exalted Spirit, form a powerful image, of equal magnetism with any other raw power symbol. Try this symbolic combination in colors of your own choice and you will craft with true, positive powers. Also, try using the stag in the center of this woven star, with his antlers encircling the upraised point, symbolically empowered by Spirit, as well as the supportive elements of Nature.

There are many other aspects and symbolic deities that have been correlated with the five-pointed star. After a quarter of a century in this field, I find two aspects of the star remains unresolved for me. The first is the fact that it isn't a wheel, or a round, which is always a symbol of synthesis and harmony—and can thus always be seen as right side up. Also, the five-point star would, by necessity, place one symbolic deity, or aspect, above the rest. I personally prefer to represent these divine realms as circles symbolizing, not their rank, but their position in regard to our tangible perception of these powers of Spirit. These expanded realms, or circles of Spirit, may be intangible; but their powers are directly perceived—and may well be said to be aware—of us.

The woven star is a symbol of courage that has survived more misuse and misconception than even the Orthodoxy could manage. Still, it pleases those of dualistic philosophy to point out the potentials for the inversion of power when this star—and other non-wheel symbols—are inverted for negative purposes. This, too, shall pass one day, and such symbols will be recognized for their representations of natural polarity, instead of the dualistic, either/or aspects that have been laid on them "separatistically." In the meantime, we still have to wait on the wheel of evolution. The wheel will have to bring a new cycle before this happens en masse, philosophically. If you're wondering why I described the woven cross as "single point up" and "two points up," instead of "right side up" and "inverted," it's part of my own small part in the turning of the evolutionary wheel.

In effect, I'm saying that the woven star is always Right-wise, and cannot be used for any purposes, other than those reflecting the Right and Wise synthesis of all the elements, including Spirit, of Nature, and self-nature. (Take that, those who seek to misuse or abuse this symbol. Never, never, never again !!! Tripled. And this goes for all symbols of Light and Synthesis, for that matter.)

As to the dualists, well ... In every tradition, there are those too busy judging externally, like the neo-Pharisees they are, to really see the Light within. If they could really see the Light, they would know this truth: The Light can never be inverted. As to those who believe they can invert the powers of this, or any symbol of Light and synthesis, I say they had better look again—and within— for the truth. They will find they truly are inverting themselves—and others who are going along for the thrill.

I suggest we encase these types in circles of positive power formed from Light with laser qualities. When they are besieged by the Light, I have faith most of them will finally see it as Truth, and the rest, who are blind by self-intention, will have to transmute the hard way, or they may always choose to open their eyes and their hearts on their own. We cannot do this for them, even if we want to.

This is a truth all of us as Light warriors need to remember—especially the warrior/guardians and the healer/initiators who become so personally involved in their paths of service. Still, even the connector/leaders can't structure a system that the self-destructive can't avoid. Nor can the evolutionary illuminators make someone change their mind, regardless how inspirationally they shine the Light. There are times when some transformations have to be given over to Spirit, and the Light Workers of the Divine Realms. Remember that giving over is not surrender; it's calling in reinforcements from a truly undefeatable Source.

Before I add the list of elements that I find naturally reflected in the expanded list of the twenty-eight hallows, I have an exercise for future use. Recall or review the statements I made about the misuse and misconceptions about the symbol of the woven star. If any of these other hallowed symbols seem potentially tricky for you, examine these in the same Light we discussed in detail above. I believe you'll find all of these symbols have a power that is always Right-wise and true when reflected in the positive Light within yourself and your experiences.

Elements Most Reflected in the Twenty-eight Hallows

(with elements in order of influence)

1. Banner: Earth + Fire + Spirit
2. Battle Shield: Fire + Spirit + Earth
3. Bow and Arrows: Air + Water + Spirit
4. Cauldron: Water + Spirit + Earth + Fire and Air, in balance
5. Chalice: Water + Spirit + Earth
6. Cloak: Earth + Water + Air
7. Crystal Point (and cluster): Spirit + Air + all others, equally
8. Crystal Spear: Spirit + Air + Fire + Water and Earth, in balance
9. Cup: Water + Earth + Spirit
10. Drum: Fire + Earth + Spirit
11. Faerie Blade: Fire + Spirit + Air
12. Gameboard: Earth + Air + Fire
13. Glass Boat: Water + Spirit + Air
14. Grail: Spiritual Synthesis of Powers (Classed in Water as a healing symbol)
15. Harp: Air + Spirit + Earth
16. Lance: Fire + Air + Earth
17. Light Symbol: Spirit + Water + Earth + Air and Fire, in balance
18. Magick Pouch: Water + Earth + Air
19. Mirrored Shield: Water + Air + Spirit
20. Runes: Earth + Water + Air
21. Scabbard: Water + Earth + Fire
22. Sheath: Water + Air + Fire
23. Spear: Air + Fire + Spirit
24. Staff: Air + Spirit + Earth
25. Stone: Earth + Water + Spirit
26. Sword: Fire + Air + Spirit
27. Wand: Air + Spirit + Earth
28. Woven Star: Elemental Synthesis of Powers (classed in Earth as a magick symbol)

CHAPTER 25

ARCHMAGERY: THE MERLIN'S MAGICK

There is nothing that sets the forces on notice that is more potent than action!
You can play the part in your mind a thousand times over, but until you begin
to take action the dream remains at rest, with all the hopes of all the others
who are still unfulfilled. No matter what the dream, there is always something
that can be done on a level of reality each day.

Kara Starr
Merlin's Journal of Time

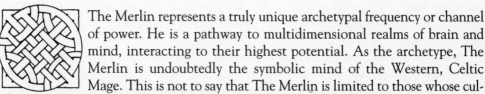

The Merlin represents a truly unique archetypal frequency or channel of power. He is a pathway to multidimensional realms of brain and mind, interacting to their highest potential. As the archetype, The Merlin is undoubtedly the symbolic mind of the Western, Celtic Mage. This is not to say that The Merlin is limited to those whose cultural and tribal codes are essentially Celtic. However, the forthright nature of this archetypal frequency, with its evolutionary variables and ever-expansive catalyst for intellectual development has led even a Celt or two to believe that The Merlin's magick or multidimensionally linked powers for our own potential growth are somehow lacking in spiritual quality. Nothing could be farther from the truth.

This mistake stems from not understanding an essential quality The Merlin symbolizes. That is the unwavering conviction that Spirit is an intangible source that is best served by those who are willing to develop their potentials and discipline their minds to fulfill higher purposes—such as the service of evolution for the benefit of all humankind.

Working The Merlin's Magick is Archmagery. It is of the highest order of intelligent analysis combined with the illuminative magick which arises from inspirational catalysts. As the mind is ever changing and the brain is ever active, so Archmagery is a transformational process that is unlimited by rigid concepts of schedules, rituals, and arbitrary rules that serve no purpose.

The Merlin's magick requires no particular attributes of time or aspects that correlate, such as colors, symbols, or specific elements. The Merlin does not require these aspects, for they are all inclusive in the mind connection which is "the Magician who lies sleeping in the All." It is we who need these props in order to signal our brains to start firing those neurons at a faster pace and to send the message to our mind that it must evolve at a greater rate in order to keep up with our potential possibilities.

The Merlin represents that marvelous intense power of clear focus, intellectual stimulation, and the alchemy of mind and humor. Archmagery requires us to stretch until we reach what we have grasped for time and again. Then, having grasped one point, Archmagery urges us to develop beyond our present abilities until we accept, with grace and service, our powerful potentials as the true responsibility they represent.

Archmagery emphasizes no other mind-set, except for a willing, well-motivated attitude of positive, experiential learning. With The Merlin as an archetypal, guiding symbol, you can reach what you may feel to be the top of your brain; but think again! What you will have felt is but one more layer in the multilayered, multifaceted aspect of your mind/brain alliance. The Merlin is your encoded ideal professor, trainer, initiator, and, in some strange way, a bit of a British nanny.

Archmagery with The Merlin requires an ability to work and learn from experiences that are resistant to schedules, and can always be relied upon for their spontaneous invigoration; bringing about the best you can be. If Archmagery seems to be an exhaustive process, well, sometimes it is. It will remain that way until you either restructure your own connection, on your terms—more or less—and learn to set your own boundaries while not setting limits for your self. This truly is the archetypal active, Western, expansive, Celtic, indomitable spirit at its finest, in this, the Archmagickal realm of mind.

If this ever feels just far too overwhelming, remember that an archetype—like angels or deities in Nature—never rests. However, you are the operator, the controller, the pilot of your own mind and brain. If The Merlin seems to be taking charge, that's your mind's way of telling you to stop surfing those intense brain waves all the time. Come in to shore, so to speak, and do nothing for a while. That is the only way to win at Archmagery, for it is a most illuminating mind game which you play essentially with yourself.

Archmagery with The Merlin is your experience of the magickal aspects of your mind. These are the realms that resist measurement and categorization. They are the realms of the inner frontier that all humankind must cross in the inevitable process of evolution. The Merlin symbolizes that strong iconoclastic individual and collective spirit which drives us to strive to be first across the evolutionary race line.

Now, before you retreat—thinking you've somehow found your self linked up with an archetypal, inner space astronaut in the figure of The Merlin—just remember one thing: The image you choose to activate in your mind is the reflection of the relationship you have chosen to develop with and within the highest realms of inspiration, thought, idealism, and intellect. You may always choose the aspect that suits you best at the time. This can range from the slightly bumbling wizard in Disney's "Sword in the Stone," through the cool, philosophic-adviser to Arthur as portrayed in "Excalibur," and on into the gentle, tolerant nature of the Wise Old Man.

If an aspect of this archetype seems unreasonable, then it is you who is being unreasonable with yourself. If an aspect seems bent on making every encounter a negotiated deal or a high-stakes game that you feel ill-equipped to win or even benefit from, then you are gambling with your self, unfairly. With a good sense of humor and solid self-acceptance, you will find the Right and Fair way to evolve your own potentials with clear purpose and positive self-regard. All that is required for a stellar quality archmagery is for you to be right with your mind.

Because of the expansive nature of working with this archetypal symbol of magick in the realm of mind and consciousness, I have developed imageries that will provide access to, and activation of, your potential with the most positive and illuminating images of The Merlin as an inspirational friend and supportive ally for your own processes of developing higher potentials and for greater personal empowerment, over all.

This chapter contains two imageries designed to introduce you to working with The Merlin's Magick. In this, the Merlin is that archetypal symbol of Archmagery with whom you may develop an alliance of the mind with the brain for the mutual benefit of both. Before you begin with these imageries, you may want to read the list of aspects of the Merlin which I have included to help you develop your own connections with this archetypal mage, whether as an inner source of wisdom, or an imaged ally of archmagery.

As I have said before, correlations are only needed insofar as they wake up or activate the brain. This, in turn, gives access to more realms of the mind in an active, expanded manner. The brain "loves" ritual, and the brain is the organ of the mind. The purpose of using specific colors, symbols, stones, themes, or images is to help the brain develop a system whereby it can develop a more direct line or specific program that leads to the realms you wish to reach. This is why ritual is preferred by those who want to achieve a specific effect or mindset. For those whose intent is to explore the realms of the mind, a ceremonial approach is less specific. In either case, The Merlin provides a useful "tour guide" to call on as you explore the many inner dimensions of your self-potential and the power of your mind.

These correlations are based on aspect matches and experimental, experiential work with the resonant current that we affectionately call The Merlin. You may find some of these are far more or less effective for the creation of your own connection to The Merlin. If so, consider those that do seem most effective from various points. For example, if a certain color works very well in evoking the figure of The Merlin, then a stone of similar hue is likely to do so, as well.

Remember that these listed correlations are only a primary sample, and not limited or restricted in any way. There are some tendencies about working with a powerful mind current that show a clear link with blended color rays, such as scarlet, indigo, turquoise, golden green, and peach. These work quite well due to the fact they are of blended tones or frequencies, as is the Mind. However, the blended-ray rose just doesn't provide access to a Mind frequency such as The Merlin archetypally represents. This could be because rose ray is a heart-centered ray related to emotional realms, and thoughts do not always match with feelings.

Also, the turquoise ray aspects of idealism, zeal, dedication, evolved service and the like are an excellent frequency match for The Merlin. However, the actual color with which you are best able to access both those qualities and The Merlin is a bright electric blue. Another is an intense cobalt blue, not a synthesis energy such as indigo, but an expansive, activating aspect which is similar. These and other correlational "quirks" you will simply—and sometimes not so simply—have to try for your self.

In general, all the correlates selected for the imageries in this chapter and in the chapter on The Merlin Current may be used as images with a clear effect. It is not necessary for you to have, in a mundane sense, the items that appear on the correlations lists or as gifts, jewels, magickal talismans, and tools in the imageries. Remember, you are working with your Mind in every imagery provided for Avalon, Camelot, or The Merlin's realms.

Use your imagination. It's no accident the word "magi" is contained in imagination, nor the word "mage" in image—after all, it is the magick of the Mind that activates the power within the Mind of the World. Do it wisely, please. Be Mage. You need not rely on anything outside your imagination; but if it helps to have cues and props such as these correlations represent, then feel free to use them. We all love the colors, textures, fragrances, and paraphernalia of Archmagery—and any other spiritual or magickal system. Just remember, no matter how powerful someone says an object is, its power is only as strong as your Mind chooses to make it.

ASPECTS OF THE MERLIN FOR CRAFTING IMAGERY

Bright Mind—Right Will—Light Evolution: Element: Air (+ some Earth and Fire)

Direction: East (+ some North and South): N–NNE–NE, E–ESE–SE

Aspects: Mind—Evolutionary illumination, connection, manifestation, wisdom, creativity, multidimensional linking, focus, philosophies, intellect, brain stimulation, pathways

Colors: Blended Rays (except Rose):
Scarlet—Fire, balance, personal identity
Indigo—Water, synthesis, evolved consciousness, magick
Golden-Green—Earth, rejuvenation of potentials, cycles of Self

Turquoise—Air, dedication, self-determination, service
Peach—Spirit, communication, positive restructuring

Additional Colors (Etheric Rays, "Lights," full strength):
Platinum—Mind, multidimensional linking
Copper—Body, strength, substance, centered power
Crystal—Spirit, Divine purpose, psychic guidance:
+ Violet Blue—Magick, Mind realms expansion, spiritual synthesis

Kindred Spirits (Animal Allies):
Dolphin—multidimensional linking
Large owls—vision, stealth, messenger, wisdom
Wolf—guardian, ally, natural laws, elements
Wrens and Finches—signals, inspiration, dedication
Otter—humor, intellect, friendship, communication
Cats (familiar, "domestic")—perception, observation, sensuality
Crows—signals, collector, information, gossip
Spider—weaver, fates, protection, unifier
Snake—wisdom, power, transformational "medicine"
Ravens (pair)—allies or trickster, shape-shifter, signals
Dragon (alchemical)—power, elemental force, synthesis
Eagle (symbolic)—vision, prophecy, truth

Trees (and plants):
Oak—connection, stability, power, wisdom
Ash—self-renewal, knowledge, symbols

Additional Trees:
Alder—higher intelligence, spiritual balance
Blackthorn—control, power, position, rank, order
Furze—awareness, learning, mind stimulation
Beech—creativity, adventure, vitality
Honeysuckle—clarity, perceptions, focus
+ Sea—realms of mystical consciousness
Grove—harmony on a group scale, critical mass

Stones (alchemically treated crystals):
Cobalt crystals—dark blue, treated with cobalt—access, pathway
Aquafloras—bright aqua, treated with gold—activation, encoder
Platinum crystals—rainbowed, treated with platinum and silver—
        multidimensional linking, codes

Additional Stones:
Garnet (bright crimson)—balance, identity, self, persona
Azurite—synthesis, wisdom, psychic knowledge
Peridot (light, bright tones)—neural activator, healing catalyst
Citrine (dark, golden)—order, active intellect, self-image

Fluorite (dark violet, blue, clear)—mind stimulation, dreams
Topaz (clear, blue)—sensory perception, clarity
Lapis—expression, inspiration, brain development
Amethyst (dark violet)—transformative spiritual catalyst
Crystals (single point, clear, intense)—amplified mind
Opals (dark blue and violet, intense tones within)—creative thoughts, encoding

Metals:
Platinum—multi-elemental, dimensional connections
Copper—application of ideas, success, achievements

Incense:
Frankincense—acknowledgment of Divine guidance
Myrrh—shamanic attunement to Earth and Spirit
Light sandlewood—focused, open mind, vision
Heather—elemental allies, devic connection

Cycle Celebration Times:
Spring: Vernal Equinox—new growth, goals, plans

Additional Times:
Winter Solstice, Yule: return of Light
Winter/Spring: Imbolc, Candlemas—inspiration
Spring/Summer: Beltane—alliance

Days and Planets:
Wednesday: Mercury—mind
Thursday: Jupiter—expansion, wealth, health
Uranus—universal flow
Neptune—psychic gifts

Setting Images:
Tower—higher intellect, evolutionary consciousness
Tree (in Forest)—shamanic connection, brain activation
Crystal Cave—illumination, symbols, imagination
Stone Tomb—primal codes, tribal codes, transformation
Henges—ceremonies, studies, measurements, goals

Hallowed Symbols:
Staff—wisdom, magick, initiation
Spear—focus, aim, thoughts, ideas, communication
Gameboard—plans, destiny, strategy, pathways
Bow and Arrows—perception, ideas, aim
Stone of Destiny—DNA, tribal codes, personal plans, pathway
Wand—activation, manifestation
Shield (mirrored)—self-acceptance, identity, balance
Sword—activation, achievement, protection, success, power

Grail—source, Divine inspiration, guidance, enlightenment
Crystal point (synergy)—synthesis of powers, aspects
Harp—source of inspiration, attunement, celebration

Themes:
Otherworld—inner realms, devic, elemental, mystical
Hallows—sacred gifts, symbols, codes
Battles—strategy, tactics, goal enforcement
Round Table—vision, evolutionary alliances and unity

Natural Forces:
Winds—evolutionary ideas, change, transformation
Flames—inspirational catalysts, illumination

Primary Archetypes (Access Allies)
The Merlin—evolutionary catalyst, illuminator, Archmage
Ganieda—divination catalyst, codes, and symbols
Nimue—elemental, shamanic connector, transformer
Morgana—metaphysical catalyst, guardian
Lady of the Lake—initiator, guardian of mystical realms
Taliesin—inspirational catalyst, memory codes
Blaise—shamanic teacher, elemental and tribal codes and Arthur in all aspects—
    student, page, squire, knight/warrior and King.

THE ARCHMAGERY IMAGERIES

These imageries are designed to help you access a personal image for working with the archetypal Archmage, The Merlin. When an image is accessed, it means you have made a clear representational image of the symbolic key to a powerful realm of mind and consciousness. Some can do this so directly that they are able to create holographic images that others can see, while they often cannot. Still others can project these images from person to person and place to place. While these are exciting potentials, they arose from an image that first emerged within the Mind, one that became like an old, familiar friend. So take the time to input the information that has been designed in the form of second-person journey imageries. In other words, you are there. When something seems to work well, pause and encapsulate the experience. When you return, you may find it has encoded itself.

TOWER OF MAGICK SYNTHESIS: SYNERGY

Elements: Air, Fire, Water, Earth, and Spirit

Directions: East, South, West, North, Center

Aspects: Mind/Body/Spirit Synthesis, activation magick

Colors: Indigo ray, Gold and Crystal lights

Kindred Spirits: Dragon, Owl

Tree: Oak

Stones: Azurite, Lapis, Aquaflora, Crystal Point

Incense: Frankincense

Cycle: Yule

Setting Image: The Merlin's Tower

Hallow: Synergy Crystal, Staff

Theme: Hallows

Natural Force: Flames

Access Allies: The Merlin

Format: Brief

Message: The essential energy with which you craft the magick of your life is composed of all the elements of Nature and self-nature in harmonious synthesis, amplified with crystal clarity and the purity of the Light.

You find yourself in an image of a visit to The Merlin's Tower. It is a crisp, clear day in midwinter, and you can see for miles all around in every direction as you look out the tower windows. The sun is high in a clear, bright sky, and the snow glistens with gold and crystalline lights. The Merlin has been working his magick outside all morning and elemental dragons are swirling about the tower. You watch for a while as they swoop close to the windows and fly upward toward the sun.

The Merlin is still outside waving his magickal staff in wide circles. This is causing even more dragons to emerge from the ancient oak trees encircling the tower. From a hollow in one very ancient oak, an owl watches patiently while The Merlin activates the powers of the dragons, the elemental energies of the lands. After a few moments, the owl spreads its wings and flies up to the tower window where you are standing. The Merlin glances at you and laughs in greeting. He waves and turns to enter the tower.

Soon you can hear The Merlin making his way up the tower stairs. When he enters, you notice the flames in the small fireplace seem to brighten and blaze more powerfully. The Merlin bids you to stir the coals in the fire and toss in some rare and sacred frankincense. Soon the tower is warm and fragrant. After you and The Merlin enjoy a cup of Yuletide wassail, you sit beside the fire for your lesson in magick.

All the while, the dragons have been circling closer and moving faster. The owl ruffles its feathers as one dragon brushes the window ledge with its tail. Although each of the dragons is a different color, they are circling so quickly they seem to blend as they swoop around. The Merlin watches this with amusement and swings his staff in time with the dragon's flight. Around and around goes his staff, pacing the dragon's flight.

The Merlin bids you to bring him a beautiful wooden box filled with stones and crystals. He asks you to select stones and crystals you believe will activate the power of these dragons most effectively. At first you consider a powerful clear crystal point. You test it by pointing quickly as one dragon sweeps by the window. The owl and The Merlin laugh at your astonishment when that dragon disperses in a burst of gold and crystal lights. You are not so amused by this, but you try again.

Remembering your lessons, you choose a dark blue crystalline stone. The Merlin nods with approval and informs you that you have chosen an azurite. The azurite glows with a deep indigo light. Looking into the box, you find an alchemical crystal, infused with gold. This crystal gleams with an aqua tone and golden lights jump from it toward your clear crystal point.

You notice that the colorful dragons have begun to blend in a swirl of deep blue lights as they circle outside the tower windows. They are moving very fast now, and you decide to bring them to Earth a bit. You choose a lovely lapis stone and place it against your forehead for a moment with your eyes closed. The dragons are so close now you can feel the tower rock as they brush the walls and the windows.

The Merlin is watching as you open your eyes, and he asks you what you think you need for this magick work. In reply, you reach out for his staff. The Merlin laughs again and gives you the staff. You stand in the center of the tower and move the staff in great wide circles. First, you make fast circles, then slower and slower circles. Still the dragons are outside, but you realize what you must do. Concentrating very hard, you make the circles with the staff smaller and smaller and smaller.

The tower becomes infused with a powerful indigo light swirling closer and closer and closer to you. You can no longer make out the shape of the dragons; but you feel their wings brush you as they circle in. You tap the staff on the floor fiercely.

The Merlin inquires what you plan to do with these dragons of power and where you plan to keep them if you haven't made such a plan. The owl hoots from its new perch on the stair rail in the center of the tower room. With a flash of your brain, you realize what to do.

You take the clear crystal point and aim it at the encircling dragons of light and power. You are astounded to see the indigo circle widen. Quickly, you turn the crystal point toward your self and slowly, slowly, slowly make smaller and smaller and smaller circles; each time turning Sunwise. As you make these circles, the dragon lights circle and enter the crystal in your hand. For a moment, the crystal glows indigo—then it is clear once more.

The Merlin smiles, and even the owl looks pleased. You have encapsulated the powers of the elements from which the dragons emerged. The Merlin gives you a soft indigo velvet cloth covered with golden stars and crystal beads. Remembering your own magick, you carefully wrap the crystal—now the dragon crystal—in the indigo cloth.

As is honorable, you offer this crystal to The Merlin; but he waves it away and tells you it is a gift you have earned. It is a magick synthesis of all powers and directions reflected in the colors of the dragons— blended in synthesis—as magick must ultimately be.

The crystal is yours for synthesis and energy. This you have already blended into the alchemy of synergy. You have brought the powers together and encap-

sulated them for your future magick— each and all they are, the amplifiers of your personal aspects of power. As The Merlin takes his staff back, you see a crystal on it glow indigo.

The Merlin suggests you use your synergy crystal to keep the magickal synthesis of your self in Harmony. This can be the foundation crystal for all your works of Light and Power Synthesis.

THE INSPIRATION GAME: CREATIVE STRATEGIES

Elements: Air, with some Fire

Directions: E–SE

Aspects: Catalyst for ideals and inspirations, ideas

Colors: Turquoise ray, platinum and crystal lights

Kindred Spirits: Ravens

Tree: Beech

Stones: Cobalt crystal, Lapis, Platinum Crystal and Platinum

Incense: Sandlewood

Cycle: Candlemas

Setting Image: The Merlin's Tower

Hallow: Game board, Wand

Theme: Hallows

Natural Force: Flames

Access Allies: The Merlin, Arthur, Taliesin

Format: Moderate

Message: In order to plan the strategies of your own life, you must first perceive the pattern from an objective point of view.

————

It is a frosty February afternoon, with gray clouds hanging low in the sky and patches of snow covering the lands surrounding The Merlin's Tower. You make your way across the grounds of the fort until you reach the tower door. You climb up the spiral stairs toward the warm room at the top of the tower. A cheery fire illuminates the room and makes you feel at home in this now familiar place.

Taliesin is playing a soft tune on his harp, and he nods in greeting. Arthur

and The Merlin are engrossed in a game they have set up on a small table in the center of the tower room, and do not seem to notice you. Taliesin signals for you to be very quiet, so you tiptoe to a chair near the game table and sit down. As you do so, The Merlin's pair of ravens call out their raucous greeting to you. At this, Arthur looks up and smiles, but his smile fades fast as The Merlin moves a small figure on the Gameboard and triumphantly declares himself the winner.

Looking closer at the game pieces, you notice they are figures of Knights and Ladies of the Camelot courts. Some of these are carved in an amazing likeness of the now familiar figures. The Merlin begins a tutorial discussion on Arthur's strategy, and lack of strategy, in the game. Arthur covers his ears with his hands and declares that losing is by no means as difficult to take as the inevitable lectures on what should or should not have been done. The Merlin feigns being offended, as Taliesin plucks his strings to create a discord. At that, the ravens join in, perfectly in tune with the dissonant sounds of the harp. Soon everyone is convulsed with laughter, and the fire blazes even more merrily than before.

Arthur stands up and suggests you take his place at the gameboard with The Merlin. You declare that you are game and sit down across from The Merlin. Arthur takes a seat beside Taliesin and bids him play a more suitable, inspirational melody for this glorious Candlemas afternoon. The Merlin remarks that Arthur should have celebrated the White Goddess of inspiration sooner; then perhaps he would not have lost the game. Arthur winces.

All the while, you have been studying the gameboard. It is a lovely piece of carved beech, the wood of creativity and adventure. The board has the same checkerboard pattern as countless other games; but this pattern seems to vibrate with an electric intensity. Looking very closely, you can see the game pieces moving ever so slightly by themselves. You wonder briefly how it would be if these knights and ladies could dance— and, in so wondering this—they begin to do so. The ravens caw loudly as you almost jump out of your chair in surprise.

The Merlin mumbles something about bothersome Knights and Ladies as he taps the gameboard with an unusually beautiful magick wand. The game pieces immediately revert to carved wooden figures, quite naturally immobile. The Merlin sweeps the figures off the gameboard and places them in a crystalline bowl. He taps the gameboard with his wand, and the checkered squares vibrate visibly.

The Merlin inquires if you have any specific game in mind, or if you would prefer he choose. You are quite naturally curious, so you motion for The Merlin to choose the game. With a knowing smile, The Merlin pours a few dozen carved wooden figures out of an earthenware jar. These figures are strangely familiar; but you can't quite recognize who they are meant to represent. The Merlin hands you several of these game figures, and you find they are carved from fragrant sandlewood. The scent brings you a sense of focus and alerts your mind in a most pleasant manner.

The Merlin arranges a number of these pieces in rows along the back squares of his side of the gameboard, and you follow suit with your figures on your side. Immediately, the sandlewood figures begin to move ever so slightly, rocked by the vibration of the gameboard. The Merlin suggests you watch a while until you see how the game is played. He taps the board once with his wand, and the figures begin playing the game by themselves. Very quickly, you find all of your figures have been overtaken, and The Merlin beams triumphantly.

Then The Merlin taps the board again, and the game repeats itself. This time, both the figures and the moves of the game seem familiar. After your next, quick defeat, you decide on a strategy of your own. You boldly ask for the use of the wand, and The Merlin hands it to you; feigning reluctance and protesting the sacrifice he is making.

You hold the wand in your right hand and study it for a moment. It is about a foot long, with crystals on either end and metal wires wrapped around the bright blue fabric that covers the center. Looking at it closely, you observe one of the crystals is cobalt blue, and the other is shot through with rainbows. The wire, which seemed silver, you now realize is made of platinum, the same metal that infuses the rainbow crystal on the end of the wand you have pointed at the board. The fabric covering the shaft of the wand is woven with threads of turquoise, electric blue, and indigo. It is an alchemically crafted tool, and you decide to test its powers before you begin the next round of the game.

Reaching into your pocket, you pull out a lovely piece of polished lapis and hold it in your left hand. With just a moment's indecision, you choose to tap the lapis stone with the cobalt-blue crystal on the end of the wand. Immediately, the lapis begins to vibrate. You can feel its bright synthesis energies activating in your hand and moving upward to awaken your mind and your brain. You look up at The Merlin and detect he is pleased with your strategy so far.

Confidently, you swing the wand around and tap the lapis with the rainbowed crystal on the other end. With a

flash of electric blue light, the lapis is transformed into a figure that looks exactly like you. Acting nonchalantly, you place this lapis figure in the center of the gameboard and line up the sandlewood figures as before. The Merlin follows suit with his figures and adds a lovely platinum game piece fashioned in the likeness of a wizard.

With only a brief hesitation, you tap the gameboard three times in succession. On the first tap, your sandlewood figures transform into familiar characterizations of your friends and family. On the second tap, The Merlin's figures assume the shapes of more representative characters from your life. Some of these are only slightly familiar; others are unknown to you. On the third tap, the figures begin the game of your life.

You watch as the pattern of the game unfolds. Some of the familiar figures provide support or present obstacles, just as they predictably do in your life. Others move in quite unexpected directions, not necessarily the way you would have chosen for them. Entranced by this unfolding pattern laid out on the gameboard of your life, you see your lapis figure buffeted about, knocked over, set upright, and moved back and forth at the will of the other pieces.

With a firm resolve, you tap the lapis piece with the rainbowed crystal point of the wand. Tiny spectrums of light leap into the lapis stone, and it begins to regain its position on the gameboard. Soon all the figures on the gameboard are gone, except for the platinum wizard and your lapis figure. You glance up at The Merlin; but he watches you impassively. You notice Taliesin has stopped playing his harp. He and Arthur are both watching you intently. With a laugh much like that of the ravens, you tap the wizard with the cobalt crystal point. In a flash of electric blue light, the platinum figure of the wizard affixes itself to the center of the wand. You laugh again triumphantly. This time, all those in the tower, including the raven, laugh with you.

The Merlin congratulates you on your creative game strategy. He collects all the sandlewood figures and places them in a bag made from a fabric like that covering the shaft of the wand. With a flourish, he folds the gameboard and presents it to you along with the bag of figures. The Merlin suggests you use this magickal gameboard and its figures to experiment with the strategies of your game—before you experiment with the strategies of your life, and, for the sake of creative magick, The Merlin bids you keep the wand, as well—wizard and all.

CHAPTER 26

LADY OF THE LAKE:
AVALON'S ARTS

For all my mind is clouded with a doubt —
To the island-valley of Avilion;
Where falls not hail, or rain, or any snow,
Nor ever wind blows loudly; but it lies
Deep-meadow'd, happy, fair with orchard lawns
And bowery hollows crown'd with summer sea,
Where I will heal me of my grievous wound.

Alfred, Lord Tennyson
Idylls of the King (New York: Signet/The New Amer. Library of World Lit., 1961)

 The realm of Avalon is a source for spiritual harmony, emotional balance, and healing gifts. Avalon represents a link between the mystical and spiritual in its highest, most devotional aspects. In a more ordinary sense, if that word can be said of Avalon, this realm represents a living link between the ancient Celtic priests and priestess. It is a receptive realm of sacred healers and initiators. They are mystically merged with the changing orders of their times, but have reemerged to reflect their light in our times. Their living legacies are those whose work is the service of the sacred transformational arts, the many forms that heal and support.

This is not to say that all who attempt to access this realm and reflect its transformations within their lives must be involved in specific roles, such as healer, diviner, or in priestly service to others. All that is needed is a receptive understanding of the sacred gifts, the grace of powers for self-healing, personal divination, and a reverent ceremonial, or ritual attitude. Whether this attitude is developed in group or solitary practices is not as important as whether it emerges from a personally initiated process of self-transformational service to the divine healing aspects. It is the sincere seeker, whose works express a willing service, who most clearly accesses Avalon. Efforts made to develop personal balance in life and initiate in-depth intuitive connections to wisdom in a sacred way will most clearly prepare those who quest for Avalon; for these are Avalon's gifts.

Avalon is also a realm of action, yet its focus is within, where the true receptive processes of self-transformation must begin, and begin again, throughout the cycles of our lives. Experiences of Avalon are invariably transformational and initiate new cycles, even when that process may not be perceived until later. In Avalon's realms, perception is an emotional awareness, a sense of self divined through a sense of feelings. Like the waters with which Avalon is associated, the perceptive development of emotional sensitivities is an ever-flowing, ever-changing process.

Avalon is truly the happy isle, and it is best approached with a light, joyful reverence. This approach provides a clear, ceremonially self-empowering experience of both the elemental aspects associated with the lands and realms of Avalon, as well as essential archetypal figures, such as The Lady of the Lake, and the White Goddess in Her many aspects. The Lord of Avalon may be said to be represented by Arthur in a most enlightening aspect. The High Priest of Avalon emerges in different images according to the Nature of the spiritual work or process of the time.

For those who wish a more ritual, receptive connection to Avalon, the aspects I have selected and your own traditional approaches may be used for a most spiritually empowering experience. As long as it is understood that no one can hold dominion over this realm, nor claim an exclusive right as clergy or any other self-officiated position, the access to Avalon will remain clear and actively flowing. All that is truly required is a positive intent and a personal willingness to experience the cycles of life's changes and develop a receptive attitude of self-acceptance and optimistic faith. Avalon's realm and the Lady of the Lake represent an etheric realm where Spirit expresses itself emotionally and is experienced through feelings and intuitive wisdom. Etherically, Avalon is the realm that connects Body-Mind-Spirit. This healing connection is made possible by a reflective, personal, in-depth exploration of the realms of emotion.

ASPECTS OF AVALON FOR CRAFTING IMAGERIES

Bright Feeling—Right Knowing—Light Transformation

Element: Water (+ some Fire and Earth)

Direction: West (+ some South and North) SW–WSW–W, W–WNW–NW

Aspects: Spirit—Healing initiations, partnership, inner quests, intuition, release, renewal, emotional attunement

Colors: Etheric Rays, "Lights" (except bright Gold)
Rose (blended ray)—Fire and Body realms

Gray—Air and Mind realms
Spirit—Spirit, as the element and Spirit realms
Brown—Earth, stability, and connection
Black—Water, release, and renewal

Additional Colors (gentle strength, infused with White Light):
White, Crystal, Rainbow—transmittal, clarity, order
White Gold—medium for activation
Pale Silver—intuition, receptive self-awareness
Golden-Green—cycles of renewal in Nature and self-nature
Lavender—spiritual, ceremonial, reverence
Aqua—self-reflection, self-acceptance, positive flow
Light Blue, Pink, Green, Yellow—self-expression, love, healing, focus
+ Violet-Rose: Spiritual, ritual, ceremonial realms

Animal Allies (Totemic, Kindred Spirits):
Crane, Heron (most water birds)—intuition, nurturance
Swans—grace, beauty, transformation
Small Owls—inner knowing, secrets
White Birds, especially Doves—mystic signals, sacred
Bobcats and Lynx—elusiveness, stealth
Rabbits and Hares—perception, providers
Blackbirds (especially Magpies)—messengers, predictions
Raven (single)—transformation, release

Amphibians: Flexibility, bridging
Fish (especially Salmon)—wisdom, consciousness
Deer (herds and fawns)—receptivity, attunement
Dragons (devic)—inner journey allies
Unicorns (symbolic)—mystical consciousness

Trees (and plants):
Apple—choice, self-growth, personal harvest
Aspen—emotional transmittal, communication

Additional Trees:
Ivy—compassion, friendship, will, self-expression
Reed—flexibility, preparations for change
Fir—receptivity to inner knowing, personal choice
Willow—healing transformation, emotional journey
Spindle—catalyst for self-transformation
+ Sea—mystical consciousness, journey experiences

Stones:
Rose Quartz—compassion, love, healing consciousness
Moonstone—receptivity, personal cycles, nurturance

Garnet—inner balance, attunement

Amethyst (pale and clear or opaque with white)—Spiritual renewal
Smoky quartz—shamanic journeys, devic, elemental
Obsidian (especially translucent)—release and centering
Tourmaline (especially watermelon)—heartfelt healing

Additional Stones:
Hematite—essential physical energies, intuitive self-healing
Peridot (pale, opaque)—healing catalyst, antibiotic clarifier
Opals (white, rainbowed, soft-toned)—medium of healing consciousness
Pearl, Mother of Pearl, Abalone—filter, healing flow
Aquamarine—ceremonial purification
Blue-lace Agate—intuition, spiritual self-expression
Opaque Quartz (white, brown, black—especially two–five point clusters)—medium
    for healing cycles of release, renewal, and reconnection with elemental energies
    for balance

Metals:
White Gold—gentle healing activation catalyst
Pewter—grounded, physical healing methods
Light Silver—awareness of inner flow for balancing

Incense:
Jasmine (light, not heavy Eastern temple incense)—devotion
Sweet Florals—celebration of new cycles, beauty, love
Gentle Herbals (example: Lemongrass, Lavender)—clearing, health
Fruit (example: Apple, Peach)—journey, growth, achievement

Cycle Celebration Times:
Fall: Autumnal Equinox—balance of self, goals, harvest

Additional Times:
Summer/Fall: Lammas—dedication to personal goals
Fall/Winter (old Celtic Summer/Winter): Samhain (All Hallows)—cycles of release
    and renewal

Days and Planets:
Monday: Moon—healing, intuition, psychic guidance
Saturday: Saturn, Pluto—patterns of personal life plans

Location Images:
Isles—realms of consciousness
Tors—ritual, ceremonial practices
Temples—sacred realms of Spirit
Lakes—deeper consciousness, source of gifts
Rivers—flow of psychic, inner knowing, deep consciousness
Holy Wells—sacred source of intuitive gifts
Fountains—emerging wisdom, psychic impressions

Hallowed Symbols:
Grail—Divine source of restoration, healing
Cup, Chalice—personal connection to the Divine
Pouch—contained power, resources, gifts
Scabbard—contained power, inner strength, control
Shield (mirrored inside)—self-reflection, self-knowledge
Stone of Destiny—awareness of purpose, missions, goals
Sword—activation of personal gifts of power
Glass Boat—vessel of quest and inner journey
Symbols (Runes)—methods of divination

Themes:
Courtly Love—rapport, relationships, acceptance, unity
Quests—journeys of balance, self-renewal, healing
Grail—Divine source of healing, self-renewal

Patterns:
Mists—private emotions, veils for inner knowing
Tides—patterns and cycles of self (external and internal)

Primary Archetypes:
Morgana—metaphysical techniques, critical quest
Nimue—elemental power, ceremonies, enlightenment
Ganieda—wisdom, divination, sacred healing
Vivienne of Garlot—organization of spiritual practice
Nentres of Garlot, Rex Avallonis—activation of spirituality
Lady of the Lake—symbolic head of Avalon Isle, initiator, provider from
    mystical realms
Arthur in the aspect of Lord of Light—active ally to Sovereignty of Land

AVALON'S ACCESS AND ACTIVATION IMAGERIES

The three imageries in this chapter, Fountain of the Swans: Compassion; Isle of
Quests: Shamanic Journey; and The Ivy and The Grail: Spiritual Healing, each present the Lady of the Lake in a somewhat different aspect. She is archetypally, perhaps,
one of the most flexible images of power with whom you can work. She is a nurturer,
initiator, teacher, and a weaver who represents your self-balancing abilities and your
intuitive responses to the needs you feel within. She is a healer, not a warrior. Her
realm of encounter is internal and peaceful.

To some, the Lady of the Lake is the White Goddess of Avalon, and this is a view
that holds true in all her aspects as maiden, mother, and crone. It is true, as long as
you remember that she represents only one beautiful part, one perfect crystal, in an
unimaginably vast and varied cluster. Still, she is a clear Celtic ray of light from the
unlimited Divine, and from within yourself, divinely crafted. The Lady of the Lake is

an archetype of the Divine Feminine strengths and compassions that are essential for healing and nurturance during times of inner change. Her powers and gifts manifest within your self.

FOUNTAIN OF THE SWANS: COMPASSION

Elements: Water and Spirit

Directions: West and Center

Aspects: Sacred connections of the heart

Colors: Rose and Violet rays, Silver and Gold lights

Kindred Spirits: Swans

Tree: Ivy

Stones: Rose Quartz, Lavender Amethyst, Moonstone, White Gold and Silver

Incense: Sweet Floral

Cycle: Lammas

Setting Image: Fountain

Hallow: Chalice

Theme: Courtly Love

Natural Force: Tides

Access Allies: Lady of the Lake

Format: Brief

Message: Compassion can be expressed relevantly, and even ruthlessly, in the relationships of your life as long as it emerges from a heart that recognizes the power of truth and love which is reflected in an attitude of unconditional, positive regard.

It is a clear, crisp day in early Fall at the time of that season's initiation, Lammastide. You have been walking through the forest all day, deeply contemplating your role in the relationships of your life. You have sought solitude to find your self and to reclaim the gifts of heartfelt emotions, expressed in balance. For some time now you have felt yourself swinging between states of cold indifference and compulsive involvement in regard to those in your life. Somewhere, in the midst of being pulled in different directions by those with whom you share your life, you have allowed the center of your self to become stressed to a point that you feel weak and vulnerable.

Your attempts to strengthen your center have been mostly ineffective so far. You often find yourself feeling on the edge of your own experiences, and even very close to being outside of yourself. Thus, you have come seeking a source within which will give you the strength to serve your own needs and those of others in your life. More than strength, you seek to regain the positive regard for your self and others. You seek to strengthen your compassionate nature and find a way to express your love for others which does not martyr yourself or make you defensively manipulative.

While you have been walking, your emotions have run the gamut, from tears of frustration and despair to torrents of rage and righteous indignation. Now, as you find yourself in the center of the forest, you have begun to feel clear and receptive. You have released what built up in your emotions, and you feel ready for a renewal of your heart and spirit. You decide to rest for a while, and you find a suitable spot beside an ancient, ivy-covered ruin where you can comfortably go to sleep, perhaps to dream. The fragrance of sweet forest flowers soon lulls you into the realms of personal renewal.

You emerge within a dream of Divine guidance. You are standing beside a beautiful stone fountain, covered with ivy and interwoven sweet flowering vines. At the center of the fountain is the statue of the beautiful young maiden of Nature, carved from white marble which is veined in silver and gold. At her feet are two swans crafted from purest-white marble, kept constantly clean by the clear water which flows from a vessel the maiden holds lovingly.

The dream deepens and transforms. You find yourself standing beside an expanded fountain. Here the waters flow from within the center of the fountain in a wide circle of white streams which rise up rapidly and cascade down again into a large, clear pool. There are two beautiful white swans swimming in this sacred pool, and a Lady of Divine Love and Beauty sits at the edge of the fountain watching them with affection. In her hand is a chalice crafted of white gold and silver. It is set with moonstones and cabochons of rose quartz and pale lavender amethysts. There is a glow of light around this Lady which compels you to come closer to her. You know by her graceful expression and her gentle light that this is the Lady of the Lake in her most compassionate aspect. She bids you share a marble bench at the edge of the forest, where you can watch the fountain.

You sit beside the Lady and share your deepest feelings: of joy and despair, of love and of fear. Taking all the time you need, you tell her of the emotional relationships in your life. With complete honesty, you tell her of the rewards you have reaped: those that have been deeply enriching, and those that cost you dearly. You describe your feelings during the times when you have given too much and when you have given too little. In describing these, you realize that both ways have left you feeling weak, vulnerable, and depleted.

As you express your feelings, you experience the ebb and flow of your emotional cycles and tides. At first you are so intent on sharing your experiences you are barely aware of the beautiful fountain just a little distance from where you are sitting now. Then, as you become clearer and lighter from this process of release, you realize that the waters of the fountain have been transforming as you expressed yourself to the Lady.

At your descriptions of highest joys and the emotional rush of love, the fountain shoots forth with such force that the waters seem to touch the sky above. Yet when they splash back down, they miss the pool for the most part and land in the tangle of ivy and densely woven vines. When you describe the low points in your life and the feelings of emptiness and loss, the waters barely rise above the surface of the pool. Unable to recycle the clearing waters, the pool becomes increasingly shallow and ever more stagnant. You notice that the swans of transformative grace and beauty have abandoned the unpredictable

315

pool. They have turned to cold stone statues and are now trapped in a tangle of undergrowth surrounding the fountain. Remembering that the ivy and the vines represent relationships and emotional involvements, you realize the meaning of this dream. You clearly relate this to the meaningful ways you involve yourself and your emotions with others—and with your self, as well.

You express your need to find a heartfelt, positive way to restore the transformational beauty within your life—and within your inner visions and dreams. The Lady of the Lake offers you a drink from her Chalice of Compassion, and you accept with heartfelt gratitude. As you receive the renewing power within, the restored powers reflect all 'round. You take all the time you need with the Lady at this fountain

of renewal and share all that emerges from the realms of your innermost feelings. You do so until you have remembered the powerful renewal of emotions, expressed in balance, and with positive compassionate regard for yourself—and therefore—for others.

When you are ready to release your image of the Lady and the fountain, she presents you with a chalice all your own. It is similar to hers, as you feel is right for you. As the image fades, you glance back within your inner vision and find the swans swimming peacefully in the tranquil pool once again. The waters of the fountain cascade in a gentle flow, splashing just enough on the ivy and vines to refresh them so they may draw from their own sources of power in Nature. This is the way of truest compassionate power.

ISLE OF QUESTS: SHAMANIC JOURNEY

Elements: Water and Earth

Directions: W–NW

Aspects: Elemental self-attunement quest

Colors: Brown, White, Silver lights, Scarlet ray

Kindred Spirits: Bobcat, Owl, Heron, Crane

Tree: Spindle

Stones: Smoky Quartz, White Quartz, Silver, and Garnets

Incense: Fruit

Cycle: Samhain

Setting Image: Isles

Hallow: Stone of Destiny

Theme: Quest

Natural Force: Mists

Access Allies: Lady of the Lake

Format: Brief

Message: Life is an experience of growth that emerges from a grounded sense of self-security, is supported by the strength of stable emotions, and branches out in self-expressions, constantly nurtured by the cycles of self-renewal.

The deep forest night has fallen upon the sacred isles in the sea of consciousness. It is Samhain, the time of All Hallows, and you find yourself questing deeply within the realms of Nature and self-nature. You have come to the sacred isle on a shamanic journey to find the power of your emotional alliance with the Sovereignty of the Lands.

Before you begin your journey within, you spend some time with the Lady of the Lake, represented here in her most primitive, Celtic shamanic aspects. She strengthens you emotionally with her assurances that she will remain closely attuned to your feelings and will guide you safely through the Moonless night to your journey's destination, wherever you may choose that to be.

The Lady of the Lake dresses you in the garb of a Faerie shaman. You put on simple robes of soft brown fabric with a white cloak to bring you the means of warm travel, transmitting you into the realms of deep Earth power. She gives you a ring of invisibility to wear. It is crafted in silver for receptivity and holds a deep, uncut garnet for balance.

You are also given a long, smooth walking staff made from the hardwood of a spindle tree. This staff will aid you in making your journey by acting as the axis connecting Self and Nature through the power of emotional experience. The Lady gives you a pair of quartz crystals, one smoky brown, the other milky white. These are for Earth connection and for transmitting your experience of shamanic journey into the realms of emotional renewal and empowerment. Finally, she gives you a piece of fruit of your own preference to leave in Nature as a gift, honoring your mutual alliance.

You are guided to walk through the dark forests on the sacred isle until you come to a clearing. In that clearing, you will find a single standing stone, which is intricately carved with codes and symbols. These carvings shift their shapes shamanically to bring relevant wisdom to each journey you make. The carved single stone that stands in the clearing is an aspect of the stone of destiny. You are guided to help yourself find it by using your dark and light quartz crystals and your ring of receptive balance.

You will be accompanied only as far as you can be without interfering with this ultimately personal shamanic quest. Should you decide to return quickly for your own reasons, all you need to do is recall your image of the lovely Lady of the Lake. Herein she is dressed in white flowing robes and a warm brown cloak, as befits a humble priestess in sacred relationship with the Sovereignty of Nature. It is this simplicity of spirit and humble reverence that allows the open connection between the questor in shamanic realms and the elementally empowering realms of Nature.

When you feel ready and receptive, this journey begins, so prepare yourself as a sacred seeker in the shamanic realms. The Lady carries a lantern with a white candle inside it to guide your way along the shoreline to where the deepest part of the forest may be entered. The mists surrounding the sacred isle this night are softly comforting, and bring you a feeling of refreshing renewal of purpose.

As you walk along the shoreline, you are aware of the deep peace that the misty silence brings you. Only the steady rhythm of your heartbeat now expressing your feelings of security is there to signal that you are an individual part of all living Nature. When you reach the point where you are to enter the forest alone, you find a sturdy Fir tree there, marking the path. You decide to leave the fruit at the base of this tree in honor of its strength of purpose.

You tap your Fir wood staff against the Fir tree three times in acknowledgment, and you enter the forest. As you glance back, you see the lantern is now hanging from a branch of the Fir where the Lady has placed it to provide a signal of light for your quest. Although you do not see the Lady now, you see two large birds waiting patiently in the pool of candle light. One is a brown heron, and one is a white crane— so you know this shamanic Lady is still there.

As you travel through the forest, you find that your white cloak has a light of its own and provides another means by which you may travel directly to your destination. You soon find yourself in the forest clearing, facing the single standing stone whose symbols are now codes with meanings for you alone. Taking all the time you need, you get the feel of your surroundings and of the personally resonating stone of destiny in the clearing.

Images and feelings emerge, merge, and transmit themselves to you as you experience this personal shamanic journey. You take the smoky quartz and the white quartz in your hands and prepare to deepen your journey. When you do this, you find you have kindred spirits who have come to guide your way.

Into the clearing step a pair of brown bobcats. These elusive cats have come to bring their predatory perceptive skills for the purposes of amplifying your experience and providing guardianship. A pair of white-winged owls fly in from the forest and perch atop the stone of destiny. These sacred birds of wisdom have come to bring their own skills of vision, ever powerful in the darkest night, and their abilities as hunters to grant you further protection.

You take time to form an alliance with the owls and the bobcats, for they truly are kindred spirits in feeling. You allow these allies to bring you messages of power for your personal life journey, as well as your shamanic quest into the realms of Nature.

If you feel called to do so, you may deepen your experience by shamanically entering the standing stone. This stone is a gateway to the center of Nature and self-nature.

THE IVY AND THE GRAIL: SPIRITUAL HEALING

Elements: Water, Spirit, and Earth

Directions: West, Center, and North

Aspects: Healing consciousness, nurturance

Colors: Violet, Rose ray, Silver light, Green ray

Kindred Spirits: Crane

Tree: Ivy

Stones: Amethyst, Rose Quartz, Opals, Tourmaline, Moonstone

Incense: Herbal

Cycle: Samhain

Setting Image: Isle

Hallow: Grail

Theme: Grail

Natural Force: Tides

Access Allies: Ganieda, Morgana, Nimue, Lady of the Lake

Format: Brief

Message: The grace that fills the Grail is a healing source of unlimited supply—as long as it is served with reverence and shared with remembrance for the Source from which all may receive, spiritually.

———

It is a dark, cloudless night, with only a sliver of a moon shining among an endless pattern of stars and celestial bodies of light. You find yourself on the shore of a small sacred isle secluded in a mystical sea. It is Samhain and a time for the spiritual healing powers of this All-Hallowed festival.

The gentle tides of evening sweep softly to and fro along the shoreline as you walk toward a small, ivy-covered chapel beside the sea. The scent of sacred herbs burning in the cauldrons in front of the chapel begins to awaken deep sacred feelings within you. The chapel is softly illuminated with candlelight as you enter and greet your sacred friends, your spiritual allies, and healing initiators in a circle of power.

First you greet Ganieda as befits her position as your elder guide, your spiritual great-grandmother of wise transformative power. Here, she is dressed in robes that reflect the silver light of emotional receptivity. Next you greet the Lady of the Lake as befits her current right to that position and her right as spiritual grandmother to you. She is wearing rose-colored robes to express the power of temperance and compassion which she symbolizes in her aspect here.

You turn to greet Morgana in a matriarchal aspect of mystical powers. She is wearing the deep violet robes that symbolize her rank as a metaphysical queen in her own right. You now greet Nimue warmly in her aspect as maiden daughter of Nature, and heartfelt sister, elementally kin to you. She is wearing robes of rich, vibrant green, which symbolize her deep love for, and her sacred connection to, the heart of Nature.

The power of each of these sacred Ladies of Avalon consciously conveys their feelings of support and concern for you. They each embrace you silently and hold you tenderly, heart to heart in mystical alliance. The sacred jewels they wear over their hearts infuse your inner being with their unique nurturing and healing powers.

Ganieda's moonstone opens you to a deeper receptivity to your own healing process.

The Lady of the Lake's rose quartz opens your heart to the experiences of loving feelings.

Morgana's amethyst opens you to an acceptance of the metaphysical gifts of inner wisdom.

Nimue's tourmaline opens you to the positive growth of emotional cycles and self-renewal.

You take all the time you need to share your process of self-healing and your skills in service to the healing light that illuminates others in your life. In this chapel, you are able to blend the inner gifts of healing and consciousness to craft any means that will provide for the positive nurturance of others, as well as for yourself. Remembering that all healing is self-healing, you craft images of light and love that will encourage others to activate their own healing processes. This you can do, and this is for the good of all. You transmit the light of healing through yourself, from yourself, in hopes that it will evoke the healing light within others that you encounter.

After you have spent your time in this mystical company of Avalonian healers, you take time to renew the heal-

ing powers within. This you do here by sharing a holy cup of healing, a Grail found within this small sacred chapel by the mystical sea.

The Lady of the Lake takes this Grail from the altar in the chapel and gives it to you to drink from and pass around the circle of your inner allies of spirit. Before you do this, you notice that this Grail is crafted of silver and set with an alchemical opal. This, you know, symbolizes the importance of being receptive to healing; but also of receiving in balance. As the alchemical opal symbolizes, healing is spiritual medicine that works for your own good so long as you take it in proper balanced doses and at the appropriate times. Too little, too rarely, leads to depletion of the mind, body, and spirit. Too much, too often, leads to self-indulgence and dependency of these same aspects of your holistic self.

By the same alchemically symbolic token, these truths apply to your work with others in your efforts to bring healing to their own lives. Remembering these truths, you may always receive and activate your own healing powers from within—and from within the realms of the highest healing Light.

Take all the time you need—in balance—to share the gifts of this Grail in this spiritual realm of healing consciousness.

CHAPTER 27

FOR RIGHT AND THE LIGHT: CAMELOT'S CODES

For should the lore of the land become lost to the recollection of men, whether by forgetfulness of tradition or invasions of men of alien race and tongue, then will the land revert to what it was before its naming and settling: to the nine forms of the elements, a formless mass, unfeeling, unmeaning, inchoate; with its kings unwed to the 'Sovranty' of the Land …

Nikolai Tolstoy
The Coming of the King (New York: Bantam, 1989)

Camelot may be commonly believed to be a realm of fantasy, or a Faerie tale that can never come true, because that is not its nature. If those who do believe this could only look inside their minds, they would realize that Camelot is the Truth. The Truth that is called Camelot is a symbolic synthesis, a concept of many aspects, which is encoded deep within. The truth of what is Right and Light is encoded along—and within—the concept of Camelot.

The synthesis form of truth and enlightenment that is Camelot is a collectively encoded concept. It is far more clear and accessible to most than The Merlin, or even fair Avalon. This is because Camelot symbolizes a shared ideal. That ideal may be seen as Faerie tale or fantasy; but the truth upon which it is based is quite real. We are very fond of hearing tales that remind us of our past glories; but when we explore Camelot's realms, we begin to see these are tales of eternally present glories and gifts of power.

The unity of the Round Table, the honor of Chivalry, and the human rights of Courtly Love are clear and present truths. The Grail is a concept accepted in a high-mass aspect of consciousness and the empowerment of its Light is eternal Truth, which reflects in every spiritual manner in which it is presented. The Quests are not as commonly known; but the concept of seeking the Source is clearly connected to the Grail, and that is now a part of Camelot.

The intricate themes and symbols are not as familiar to most; but these are mystical truths whose light and truth are honored in many ways and forms. The cast of Camelot's characters may still be misconceived by most, but they are—as people are—part of the Light and activators of Truth, accordingly, and a part of the Camelot pattern. Arthur is a symbolic king whose legend tells of one whose vision came to be—and then became no more. This tale is one that most relates to the cycles of human life, yet, in this is a false concept, for the truth is that Camelot is still a clear vision.

The vision that is Camelot is manifested by the codes within that guide the structures of our lives according to the ideals which Camelot represents for the once, future, and eternally present dimensions of time and mind. Whether someone is conscious of what Camelot represents, or whether they regard it as a Faerie tale or Utopian ideal, they are affected by its Truth in every aspect of their lives. That is because Camelot lives in the Light that can never be extinguished.

If others do not seem to understand what you find so illuminating within these realms, tell them it is a pattern filled with adventure and magick, which are codes for what is possible in an enlightened dimension of our times. That dimension, you then explain, is one of Honor and Truth. They may be ideals, it is true, yet real in all those whose life is for Right and the Light.

ASPECTS OF CAMELOT FOR CRAFTING IMAGERIES

Bright Purpose—Right Structures—Light Manifestation

Element: Earth and Fire (+ some Air and Water)

Direction: North and South (+ some East and West) NE–ENE–E, SE–SSE–SSW–W, NW–NNW–N

Aspects: Body—Restorational connections, organization, positions of power, societal codes, protection, guardianship, relationships

Colors: Primary/Secondary/"Spectrum Rays" (except Indigo):
Red—Spirit, Divine life force
Orange—Fire, vitality, control, relationships
Yellow—Air, intellect, planning
Green—Earth, abundance, expansion, health
Blue—Water, spiritual consciousness, expression

Additional Colors (Etheric Rays, full strength):
Silver—Receptivity, perception, inner knowing
Gold—Activation, catalyst, creation
White—Mind, transmittal medium
Rainbow—Spirit, higher purpose, harmony
Copper—Body, strength, ability, success
+ Violet purple: Royalty, rank, sovereign leadership realms

Animal Allies (Totemic, Kindred Spirits):
Bear—territorial guardianship
Boar—strength, aggression
Lions—leadership, power
Big Cats—judgment, strategy, justice
Cattle (especially White Bulls and Cows)—wealth, Source
Deer—Stag and Doe (especially white)—hunt, fertility
Horse—(especially white and/or red)—vehicle, mobility
Dogs—loyalty, protector, ally
Badger—ferocity, tenacity, defender
Sheep—Ram and Ewe (especially golden)—rulers, fertility
Mouse—humility, swiftness
Ermine (white with black tails)—royalty, wealth
Hawks and Falcons—perception, focus, aim
White Owls—wisdom, vision, magick
Osprey—hunter, focus
Eagles—ideals, honor, power positions
Ravens (three, in particular, or more)—allies, fates, conflict
Roosters and Hens—signals, guardians, providers
Pheasants and other Game Birds—rank, wealth, power
Salamanders—intensity, transformation
Dragons (heraldic)—force, rank, power
Griffins (symbolic)—strength, ideals, power

Trees (and plants):
Rowan—independence, determination, self-control
Holly—Source, eternal power, life force
Birch—change due to challenge
Elder—new source of strength

Additional Trees:
Hawthorn—spiritual organization, times of change
Hazel—order, strength, centered power
Vine—harmonious strengths, interrelated powers
Yew—protection, wisdom, guidance for change
+ Grove—group unity, shared purpose, efficiency

Stones (Gemstones; but gem quality is not necessary):
Ruby—active life force, rebuilding, divine fire
Opals (orange tones) or Golden Topaz—clarity, creativity
Amber—energy distribution, magnetic flow, purifier
Emerald—balanced growth and expansion, well-being
Sapphire (medium, dark tones)—clear seeing, spiritual wisdom
Diamonds or Zircons (clear)—loyalty, service catalyst
Tourmaline (especially watermelon)—alignment, unity
Amethyst (bright violet, medium tones)—spiritual purpose

Additional Stones:
White Quartz—transmittal medium
Jasper (red, yellow, green or combinations)—strength
Carnelian—vitality, health, relationships, kinship
Tigereye—goals, plans, stability, organization
Aventurine or Green Moss Agates—luck, confidence, peace
Bloodstone (green jasper with red inclusions)—success
Sodalite—supportive balance, plans, focus, aim
Chryscola—determination, calm courage, resolve
Bournite (Peacock Ore)—manifestation, ordered plans
Crystal multipoint clusters (clear, or with rainbows) balanced empowerment of
    group or multi-achievements

Metals:
Gold—activation catalyst, manifest success
Silver—receptivity catalyst, goals, plans, schedules
Copper—practical application of plans and assets
Steel—manifest forms of power

Incense:
Evergreen—eternal life, abundance, growth
Dragon's blood—protection, allies, elemental powers
Cinnamon—activation, creation forces, energizer
Amber—bridge between realms, spirit and mundane

Cycle Celebration Times:
Winter Solstice—Yule—return of the Light, renewal
Summer Solstice—Midsummer—fullness of growth and potentials

Additional Times:
Summer/Fall—Lammas—dedication, service, harvest
Fall/Winter—Samhain (All Hallows), release and renewal
Winter/Spring—Imbolc (Candlemas), inspiration, new plans
Spring—Vernal Equinox—first growth of projects, plans
Spring/Summer—Beltane—sacred unions, relationships

Location Images:
Castles, Forts—power, position, guardianship, wealth
Forests—quests, pathways, challenges, initiation
Caves—inner journeys, wisdom, symbols, codes
Lands—service, restoration, alliances, nurturance

Days and Planets:
Tuesday—Mars—guardianship, aggression
Friday—Venus—relationships, harmony, love
Sunday—Sun, Earth, activation of life force, power
Any other day—Earth, life force, elemental power

Hallowed Symbols:
Sword—achievement, power, manifestation
Symbol (Spirit)—Highest connection to the Light
Grail—Divine Source, inspiration, restoration
Drum—pace, rhythm, courage, quest catalyst
Cloak—mantle of protection, position, rank
Crystal sphere—orb of vision, plans, goals
Woven Star—interrelatedness of elements, powers, aspects
Stone of Destiny—wisdom, purpose, guidance, knowledge
Gameboard—codes, order, plans, strategy
Spear or Lance—ideas, goals, focus, tactics
Shield (Battle)—protection, self-declaration, rank, power
Banner—self-power, chivalry, codes of honor
Scabbard—rest, rapport, security, peace

Themes:
Round Table—Unity of purpose, alliances
Chivalry—Codes of Honor
Otherworld Challenge—tests of inner strengths
Battles—conflict resolutions
Courtly Love—choice, Divine catalyst, relationships
Quests—dedication to service of higher power and purpose
Lands—Sovereign alliances, elemental power
Grail—Divine source of healing, love, restoration

Patterns:
Flames—catalysts for growth, action, creation
Mists—veils for spiritual guidance
Tides—patterns of mundane and mystical realms
Winds—evolutionary change, ideas, inspiration

Primary Archetypes:
Arthur—in aspects of Warrior, King, Sovereignty's consort
Guinevere—benevolent matriarch, gentle Empress

Lancelot—intuitive catalyst, receptive partner, love
Morgawse—guardian, defender, trainer, elemental power
Gawain—balance, reflective ideals, positive intentions
Perceval—perseverance, wise innocence, courage
Galahad—purity, transformational ally in Spirit
The Merlin—evolutionary planner, teacher, advisor
Nimue—transformational, elemental power ally
Morgana—metaphysical initiator, healer, advisor
Mordred—revolutionary catalyst, intelligence agent
Pellinore—quest advisor, planner, trainer
Bors—practical guide to mundane realms of duty
Sir Kai—loyal, supportive advisor for mundane structures

Camelot is an earthier realm, and its experiences can be quite instructive. Because of this, I have expanded the messages included in the aspects at the start of each imagery. Most of these imageries will still feel less mystical; but this is a realm of practical magick. It is where the mystical can be applied to the mundane in ways that are wise, creative, and well-ordered for success and growth. It is also a realm of regal power, and the forces for battle, too. Remember these realms are for your own use, and try not to wear a crown outside, nor carry a sword, as a rule.

ACCESS AND ACTIVATION IMAGERY

This chapter contains one extensive imagery that empowers your position in connection to this realm. The Camelot imageries in the later chapter are all much more brief, because you no longer need as much guidance—except from within yourself—naturally. As always, the imageries are meant as catalyst experiences to encourage you to create your own experiences with the archetypal images in your realm of mind. The imagery in this chapter, like the others I have used in the text, has been carefully designed so you are not limited to expectations of gender or sex. I point this out because Camelot's knights are invariably portrayed as males. It is absolutely true that women warriors were unique and rare, in an active aspect, which a knight symbolizes. This active warrior aspect can be imaged in whatever form you choose, if you want to reflect that aspect. Just remember that women of power are still made knights and honored with respect, just as the men who are knighted by the same sovereign decree. With rare exception, in current times, your knighthood is bestowed in a mystical manner, by the Sovereignty of the Lands. When a man is knighted, he is then called Sir. When a woman is knighted, you can then quite appropriately call her a Dame.

Still, it might be wise to ask—or clarify this first—or respectfully address her as a Lady.

FORTRESS OF THE PENDRAGON: SUPERIOR STRATEGY AND POWER

Elements: Fire and Spirit

Directions: South and Center

Aspects: Courage, Strength, Will, Drive

Colors: Red and Green ray, Gold, Copper, Silver, and Crystal lights

Kindred Spirits: Badger, Bear, Boar, Horse, Raven, Dragon, Wolf, Fox

Tree: Holly

Stones: Ruby, Red Jasper, Clear Crystals, Gold, Copper, Steel

Incense: Cinnamon

Cycle: Midsummer

Setting Image: Fortress

Hallow: Shield, Sword

Theme: Battles

Natural Force: Flames

Access Allies: Arthur, The Merlin, Morgawse, Mordred, Gawain

Format: Extensive

Message: A superior force will always overcome an inferior force. This is true as long as the superior force is measured in terms of its spiritual qualities as well as its strengths, size, or quantities. A superior force is one with a balanced ratio of powers, those that come from their mundane resources, and those from their mystical relationship, or spiritual alliance with the Source Divine. A superior force uses the powers of a wise mind to create its strategies with clear purpose and consequences which will be for the good of all. Remember that Pendragon means the head of the dragon. This is the power that plans ahead, before taking action.

It is a warm Midsummer's eve as you ride your finest horse toward the Fortress of the Pendragon. The fortress shines with a mystical glow; its strong stone ramparts seem copper as they reflect the red-gold rays of light that streak the western sky. The fortress is festooned with banners which signal the presence of many warrior clans, united within the walls. You can see the allies on these banners, symbolizing the strength and powers of each mighty clan.

A blue-black raven on a yellow background announces a clan of wise strategic skills. A red badger on a field of white and a red boar against gold signify the fierce, aggressive warriors who have shown they have the means to take action when their lands and clans are threatened. Countless other banners fly proudly in the twilight sky. Their sym-bolic allies seem to move with a power all their own, animated by the light of many campfires. The winds of twilight blow across the ramparts, causing the banners to fly proudly, declaring their power to all the lands and sky surrounding this mighty fortress of the High King, Arthur.

As you ride up to the gates, you pause to look at the two highest banners, symbols of the strongest powers. The great brown bear of territorial powers protects the clans and the lands, as he has done since ancient times when the tribes still lived in caves. The bear stands ready on a background of green, guarding the sovereign realms from the heart of the lands he serves. Holly leaves with bright red berries are embroidered on the corners of the great bear banner. These, you know, remind those who see them that the protective powers of this symbolic guardian never rest, even in Winter. Guardianship is an eternal service, its powers ever actively perceptive to the heartbeat of the lands. You admire the rich, green holly hedges that border the fortress walls in wild abundance.

Set above all the others, the royal banners fly from every point along the fortress wall. These banners have red dragons on clear fields of golden yellow, and the dragons seem both fierce and wise as they fly above the fortress. You honor the dragon banners which declare the royal power. These announce that the head of all the lands, the high king of the Celtic clans is present at this time—King Arthur, in royal residence at this place of power and protection. You salute the royal Pendragon's power and the ancient guardian bear. Then the gates of the Fortress of the Pendragon open to let you enter and you are welcomed there.

You pass through the gates and ride under an arch made of strong gray stones with veins of blood-red jasper running through them all. The keystone of the fortress arch has crossed swords, carved in symbol. The swords are placed across a shield on which stone dragons stand in fierce alliance. Their tails are woven around the hilts of the swords, and their fiery breath brushes across the double-edged blades. The keystone has been freshly brushed with layers of gleaming gold. This declares the power and the willingness to activate a state of war, should the need arise—as it may have now.

You dismount, and a young page comes quickly to tend to your horse. You question the page before he leaves, for pages always have the latest news. They often know more than most have yet to discover, more perhaps than they should tell. You hold a silver coin between two fingers as you inquire about the current state of events at the fortress. The page dutifully lists the presence of the warrior clans whose banners you already recognized; but you flip the coin to him anyway. Then you take a gold coin and hold it up to the light from the fires. With focused intent you ask again about what the page has seen or heard. With but a brief protest about his oaths of honor, this page, who might never be a true knight, tells you what you need to know.

Some far-Northern warriors have attacked castles all along the borders between Scotland and Wales. Rumor has it that King Arthur judges this to be a matter for a troop of knights and not a cause for war. Queen Morgawse has come to the Fortress of Pendragon to demand that an army be sent immediately to defend the regions from further invasions. Morgawse is more magnificent than the page had ever imagined. He seems somewhat enchanted by her, as he tells you about her encounter with the King, when she called for her rights to battle.

The page begins to add some more news about Morgawse and Arthur; but you stop him before he is able to tell what everyone knows already and will not say. This is about Gawain and Mordred, whose father is Arthur, in spirit, if not in truth. The horse signals that someone is coming. You quickly give the coin to the page with a warning about his gossiping ways and turn to find that Arthur and

Gawain are approaching. The Merlin is close behind them, with a horn of cinnamon wine to refresh your mind and spirit.

These three of royal power and rank greet you with such warm kinship that you wonder if the now-frightened page will ever recover from the shock. Assuming this page to be in your service and therefore pledged to confidence, the three then tell you what you have heard from the page, and what no one else knows, as yet. Morgawse has persuaded some of the knights to fight, regardless, with Mordred at the lead. The clans whose castles were attacked have begun to remember the wrongful actions as far more than they were. Morgawse is quite implacable in her fiercest role, the warrior queen, and she will agree to wait only until Midsummer's day has ended, at twilight tomorrow. After that, there will be no way to delay her retaliatory actions, for she is a Queen in her own right and can choose when and where to make war.

The warriors who attacked the castles are a band made up of many different clans. Although they declare their allegiance only to themselves, their clans may not agree. These warriors are mostly young and wild, even by the far-Northern standards, so their deaths could start a widespread war which the lands and the people don't need. These attacks have already started divisions in the Round Table knights, between the loyal clans, and within them as well, so the potential for destruction is real and right at hand. The warrior band was sighted making its way toward an old fortress nearby. It is not twenty miles away from The Fortress of the Pendrag-

on, which even they are not stupid enough to attack. They are expected to arrive at the old fortress by midday next, before the knights who guard it have returned from midsummer festivities. Although the fortress is rather old, it has been besieged before. It even withstood the Roman troops and is honored as one of the few places of power that remains, as yet, unconquered. It would be a dishonor to that proud, brave place and a disgrace to the Summer Goddess, as well, to attack even those wild warriors on a sacred, Solstice day.

You have listened quietly and taken in all that has been said, almost as well as the page, it seems, who is silently signaling your attention. Your opinion on this is valued and requested as soon as possible. You politely ask for a few quiet moments to consider all the aspects. With your drinking horn in one hand and the impertinent page beside you, you walk a short distance away and stand close to one of the fires. You command the page to be silent so you can envision a possible plan, and you stare at the banner-filled skyline, searching for a solution.

The page is uncharacteristically quiet as he pulls a clear crystal from his cloak and points it at the fire. Then he holds the crystal above the flames and points it toward the banners. Unable to resist what you think is just a distracting ploy, you gaze into the crystal structures where the fire, the banners, and the fortress are reflected in a bright golden light. As you watch the Pendragon banners dancing within the crystal, you glimpse beyond just far enough to formulate a plan. With a feigned fierce look at the page, who seems far too pleased with himself, you stride with purpose back to the others and share your plan for a solution.

When Arthur hears what you have to say, he roars with truly royal laughter and gives his consent with delight. Gawain agrees to gather all the resources you need, as long as you will let him be at the lead, which is wisest. You agree to this honor and wait while The Merlin gives you advice. Soon you are ready to leave, and the page brings your horse when you summon him. He brings a horse for himself, as well, and quite humbly offers his service. It seems he has no knight of his own, something to do with his manner, he thinks. More like something to do with his mouth, you think; but you agree to let him accompany you. You've learned some of the lessons this page has yet to learn. Some of these were rather recent lessons, so you know that experience is the truest teacher. Besides, you feel you owe this page that chance, for his cleverness and his courage. You only hope that both those qualities will hold for the page—and for yourself as the plan unfolds into a new experience. You ride out from the Fortress of the Pendragon and the gates close quietly, but are not bolted; and thus the plan for solution begins ....

In the morning, just before midday, you return to the Pendragon Fortress to find that your news has preceded you, in several conflicting versions. You grant the page the honor of accurately informing the king—and all who are gathered around to hear—what came to pass. To this honor, you add with significance of meaning, a message for the page. You grant him your permission to tell what

he has, by oath, been pledged to keep silent—and that is your right not to reveal your intentions, your strategies, or your actions.

Still, this is a time of celebration and a true, natural balance has been achieved. Action and reaction have canceled out the danger of chaos. The crowd listens with rapt attention as the proud page relates the tale with an almost bardic flair. You see that even Morgawse is pleased, for she appreciates fine strategy. When she smiles at the page, he almost swoons; but he manages to speak, though he stutters a bit at the start.

The warrior band came to the old fortress just before the break of dawn. In the first rays of light, they saw that a few banners, on the fortress walls—some new, some frayed—were being flown against the sky. With bold excitement at having the chance to conquer these clans and seize their arms, as well, the wild band of young warriors rode inside, storming an empty fortress. In their eagerness for action, they neglected to notice that which was glaring and obvious to anyone within sight: The gates of the fortress had been removed, all 'round, and a circle of smoke still rose from fires that appeared to be cooling within the fortress walls.

Enraged, the warriors wheeled their tired horses around and made ready for what might come. They drew their swords and brandished the blades; but these would prove to be useless. A shower of fiery arrows shot out of the forest encircling the fort, and soon the oil-soaked fires were billowing with thick black smoke. When the band of warriors tried to make their escape, they rode blindly into the forest. Although they did have the presence of mind to scatter in many directions, whichever way they rode, they encountered a circle of power. The Round Table knights demanded surrender. These knights had too much honor to battle with brats—unless they were stupid enough to challenge the circle of powerful warriors.

And thus, the page concluded, all had been put to right. Many of the young warriors were on their way back to face the disgrace they had brought to their clans, and the unconquered old fortress had retained its honor, which everyone held dear.

The story told, the page steps back and Arthur summons you forward. With pride and delight at a job well done, King Arthur bestows these gifts upon you—for your services and purposes:

A great sword of power from the realms of the sacred that crafted it with powers of wisdom and will, the qualities befitting a mindful warrior, a blend of spirit and steel.

A smaller sword, also Fey-crafted with powers of cleverness and courage which increase in proportion to the honor of the warrior who wields the blade.

A massive war shield embossed in silver to reflect the light to whomever encounters it. Inside the shield are your symbols of power, which remind you of your rank and honor.

A smaller shield with silver mirroring on the inside to cast a true reflection.

A few banners, some frayed, some new, whose allies you have activated.

One old fortress, by honor protected, to provide for you an almost royal residence.

A selection of knights, some new, some a bit frayed, to help you establish your stronghold and to train your warriors, as well.

A group of young warriors, slightly smoke-damaged, who had chosen to remain in the custody of Arthur, but more appropriately now belong to you. They are sworn to serve what they have come to respect: the powers of strategy and will.

You accept these honors with grace and gratitude; but you know it is your duty to share. You give these gifts to the proud page who might yet become a knight. Since it seems this page has become a part of your life you begin by making him your squire, on condition that he remember his service is to you. This you know he will do, for your kinship with him is strong and true.

You give him the small sword for his cleverness and courage, and the small mirrored shield (since you already have one), which reminds him how honor reflects from the inside. You give him a banner which he may fly one day from a fortress he has earned. On it is a bright orange fox on a faded field of green. You are amused to see a young lass step up and offer your page—now your squire—a length of green silk from her gown, with which she will sew a new background for the banner of the clever fox. You are amused to see your new squire is speechless—and the lass looks a bit like a fox, so you know she is also your ally.

As to your banner, it is also frayed, for it has flown over many an unconquered fortress. Its ally, once viewed with misconception, is now seen in a new light of honor, its power returning with purpose. When a secret love offers to replace it or repair its tattered background, you decline; for you know its powers will be restored by your service.

And so you select, as is your right, the banner and ally that suit you best, the one that will fly most proudly and show your colors truly. These banners can change as you require—even the banner you gave to your squire!

A wolf, either red-gold, or gray, on a background of white or blue. These bring you active or flexible powers and the means to be honorable and true.

A raven, or three, blue-black and bold, on a background of red, green, or gold—for courage, heart, and active powers in solitary or group situations.

A dragon, either silver or gold, on a background that balances the powers of that ally in every aspect. Silver on gold makes you insightful, receptive to the actions and reactions all around. Gold on silver activates your plans, which were receptively considered and crafted.

When you have chosen your banner, the one that displays your powers currently, The Merlin, Arthur, and Gawain honor your right as a part of Camelot, the realm of Right and the Light. Morgawse and Mordred acknowledge your powers and offer their alliance, should you ever need it. Morgawse reminds you that warriors and knights are within all Lords and Ladies of power. Should your position and right be challenged, she'll be more than pleased to defend (or avenge) it! Although you hope such a fierce ally will never be required in your field of experience, you thank her with honor and grace. You also accept the gifts that Morgawse and Mordred give you: two rings, one of silver and one of gold. Both are set with bright clear rubies. Each ring brings power and the superior strengths of essential life force. With silver for receiving and gold for activating, you can always maintain a reflective balance of powers, equally acting and reacting within the realms of your life.

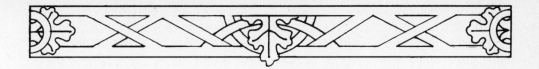

CHAPTER 28

THE MERLIN CURRENT

My return to life had been easier than I had anticipated. It seems that to the simple folk, as indeed to the people in distant parts of Britain, the tale of my return from death was accepted, not as plain truth, but as a legend. The Merlin they had known and feared was dead; a Merlin lived on in the 'holy cave,' working his minor magics, but only a ghost, as it were, of the enchanter they had known. It may be they thought that I, like so many pretenders of the past, was some small magician merely claiming Merlin's reputation and his place.

Mary Stewart
The Last Enchantment (New York: Fawcett, 1979)

 The Merlin Current is a realm that is not exclusive to the singular archetypal frequency or vibrational channel within the Individual and Collective Mind of Western, European Celtic consciousness which we call The Merlin. While it is true that a figure of such significantly expansive and interwoven power does dominate that particular realm of Mind, it is also true that other equally strong symbolic figures arise in imagery from that same realm of image and archetypal power.

In this chapter there are four images, two of which present other figures without the Merlin, and one in which the primary access ally is yourself—and the location image of The Merlin's tower. In the latter image, the access allies of archetypal qualities make a late appearance with what those in the theater call a "walk-on part."

It is important for you, in working with any archetypal character, to also work in connection with the locations associated with them. The locations are an important part of the pattern of tribal and individual codes that activate their symbolic qualities within your own mind. The Merlin's Tower is a symbolic representation of the higher, more formal operations of the brain, while the cave is associated with the primal or elemental aspects of brain and mind.

The tree (or in a lighter version, a large shrub) often shows up in these images. These symbols retain their shamanic aspects, representing the quality of branching out from a rooted connection, in the ground—or on the brainstem—and growing in a widespread, broad-reaching manner to connect with the source of light. This describes the basic pattern of the brain's development. The symbolic entrapment of The Merlin in a tree also represents the way his archetypal quality has remained encoded in the brain as part of the still-mystifying storage system. This symbol of the tree in the Mind is a current of thought, ideals, and unique, ever-enduring magick. It is the fiercely independent and iconoclastic qualities that make the figure of The Merlin a cherished part of our tribal and cultural memory traditions.

The Merlin does not always have clear connections to specific forces in Nature or tribal dieties. As Celticists and Arthurian scholars have either debated or lamented about this, I have been left to wonder how such an obviously natural quality as that symbolized by The Merlin could be overlooked. Yes, The Merlin is also our symbolic wise man, enchanter, royal adviser, and all-around influence on the Round Table knights and their codes of honor. More than all of those, though, the Merlin symbolizes that primal force that is our evolutionary drive to develop ourselves as fully as we can.

THE MERLIN CURRENT: ACCESS AND ACTIVATION IMAGERIES

The imageries that follow deal with balance, rejuvenation, communication, and achievement. This time, as you experience the other figures presented in these imageries, note how their aspects change in relationship to one another, and, when he is present, how The Merlin's aspects are also different. As you work with the interaction of archetypal figures, in particular those whose mythic relationships have been presented with conflicting overlays, you may notice that you have "static" on the line, or crossed wires.

For example, I have yet to create an imagery that places the Merlin anywhere near an Avalonian isle temple, or any part of an Avalonian realm. However, I have found that some of the Avalonian figures such as Nimue and even Morgana, can seem to emerge in a location other than Avalonian and work in interaction with The Merlin. Admittedly, I usually call in that wise Druidic sister of The Merlin, Ganieda, to serve as a calming influence—or as a potential referee or line judge. If there are figures who conflict too much for your purposes, simply review the cast and call in another.

THE CAVE OF SCARLET CRYSTALS: BALANCE

Elements: Air, with Fire and some Water

Directions: E–SE, with some influence of SE–SW

Aspects: Mind/Body, Etheric/Physical linking and balance

Colors: Scarlet ray, Copper and Crystal lights

Kindred Spirits: Wolf, Snake

Tree: Alder

Stones and Metals: Garnet, Crystal Point, Copper

Incense: Sandalwood

Cycle: Spring/Summer, Beltane

Setting Image: Crystal Cave

Hallow: Shield (Mirrored)

Theme: Battles

Natural Force: Winds

Access Allies: Blaise, Ganieda

Format: Brief

Message: To obtain a positive balance of self-perception and self-projection, use the powers of self-reflection.

———

It is a warm, windy afternoon on a once and future Beltane eve. You find yourself entering the mouth of a cave which is behind a wise and spiritual Alder tree. You feel the balance of this tree as you enter the airy, comfortable cave, where you are welcome. This cave is the home of Blaise, the shamanic Druid who will teach you about the elements of your self-nature. As you move deeper into the cave, Blaise comes forth to greet you. With him is his gentle companion, the Wolf, who will help you learn about the laws of Nature and self-nature. You greet them as time-honored friends. You tell them you have come seeking inner balance for your self-identity and for a more balanced connection between your Mind and Body. It is a time for uniting the receptive and active aspects of yourself, the etheric and the physical, the inner female and the inner male. This is a time for linking in alliance that which you have often felt battling within.

As you contemplate this, you know Blaise understands. The wolf moves deeper into the cave, and you follow, with Blaise beside you. The scent of sandalwood drifts on the winds blowing through the cave. As you step through an opening, you see another friend and ally, one whose wisdom is ancient and grandmotherly.

Ganieda is waiting patiently as you step into another chamber of the cave. This chamber is sparkling with crystals which send out rays of scarlet and crystalline clear lights. The tones already bring you a feeling of purpose, identity ,and balance. Ganieda is holding an inquisitive snake with a lovely design on its back. The design seems to shift from left to right as the snake moves. Yet, when still, the design shows a balanced equal design of a single shape that combines both sides harmoniously.

Blaise and Ganieda point out the wisdom of creation's design that allows for a flexible connection between what may seem separate, but ultimately, inwardly, is not.

The snake moves from near Ganieda to rest on a stone altar in the crystal cave. On the altar you find a lovely piece of garnet and an exceedingly clear crystal point. As you gaze at the stones, you notice there is also a beautiful shield waiting for you on the altar. You know it is yours alone, for its mirrored surface shows only yourself, clearly. Before you pick up the stones, you place a few copper coins on the altar in reverent return for the gifts you have before you.

You hold the garnet in your left hand and your crystal point in your Right. You focus on the flow of the garnet into your left hand, bringing access to your gifts of receptivity. Next, you focus on the active, amplified energy of the crystal point in your right hand. When you have done this for a time, you bring your hands together slowly. As you do this, you watch yourself in the mirrored shield. You notice that your face is illuminated in a glowing light of garnet hues. Your expression reflects the bal-anced accepting of yourself and your right to be in this cave. As you continue balancing with the help of all the elements and allies in the cave, you discuss your self-nature with Ganieda, Blaise, and the kindred spirit allies. You can feel their supportive illumination helping you to find the most balanced aspects of yourself within.

When you are ready, you lift the shield carefully and hold it up to the lights in the crystals. As these lights reflect within the cave, you feel them uniting within yourself. Gazing into the mirrored shield, you are mindful of your self in balanced reflection. As you think of yourself in balance, your balanced image reflects in the mirror of yourself, as it does in your self-nature.

When you are ready, you replace the shield, the garnet, and the crystal on the altar, knowing they will always be there, within, whenever you need to be remind-ed of your ability to balance the aspects of yourself. You discuss this inwardly with Blaise and Ganieda. Then you let the image of the cave and all within, fade within, awaiting future visits.

THE FOREST ILLUMINATED: REJUVENATION

Elements: Air, Fire, and some Water

Directions: East, South, and some SW

Aspects: Activation of Mind/Brain potentials

Colors: Golden-Green ray, Rainbow light, White and Gold light

Kindred Spirit: Cats, Wrens, Finches

Tree: Furze

Stones: Peridot, Fluorite, Opals, Lapis

Incense: Sandalwood

Cycle: Vernal Equinox

Setting Image: Forest, Tree

Hallow: Harp, Bow, and Arrow

Theme: Otherworld

Natural Force: Winds

Access Allies: Taliesin, Nimue

Format: Brief

Message: Potential is evolved in direct proportion to the ratio of receptive perception and active projection with which you renew the forms of your mind's reflections.

You are walking through a mystical forest on a bright and breezy Spring morning. The trees are freshly covered with morning dew which sparkles in tiny rainbows inside each drop. There is new growth everywhere. The cycle of Nature's renewal is poised in perfect balance at this time of the Vernal Equinox. You can hear the light birdsong of little finches as they flutter among the yellow-flowered branches of a Furze shrub.

A tiny wren flies out of the Furze and lights on your shoulder. As the wren begins to sing, you hear harp music from deep in the forest. Following the sound of the harp, you come to a small, sunlit glade where you find two familiar figures. Taliesin, the Bard, smiles at you as he strums his golden harp, and Nimue looks up and nods in greeting. The small white cat sitting on Nimue's lap stretches and jumps gracefully to the ground. The cat comes to you and rubs her cheek against your hand as you reach out to pet her. Her golden-green eyes are wide, alert, and bright; yet she studiously ignores the little wren as it flutters jeal-ously on your shoulder. Taliesin calls to the wren and it flies over to perch on his harp. The harp is carved with Celtic weave, and its frame is set with crystals shaped like pyramids and diamonds. As you look closer at these crystals, you recognize their shapes are natural. Their cool blue tones tell you they are fluorites, the stones of Bardic mind power.

Nimue bids you to sit beside her while you listen to Taliesin play the harp. The perfume Nimue is wearing has the light scent of sandalwood and spice. Her jewels are illuminated in the rays of the Springtime sun. Nimue is wearing a golden necklace of opals which are milky white with rainbow lights of surprising intensity. The opals are set off by brilliant golden-green peridots and bright blue lapis stones which match the deep blue of her eyes.

Nimue smiles as she notices your interest in her necklace. You explain that you can tell by the design and the choice of stones that this is a necklace for powerful alchemical workings; but you are not quite sure of its specific purpose. Graciously, Nimue lifts the necklace over her head and places it in your left hand. You can feel a hidden fire within these lovely stones.

On impulse, you place the necklace against your forehead. You are surprised to find that the stones are cool to the touch when you place them there. As you start to hand the necklace back, Nimue suggests you try again. This time, you hold the stones so they may be illuminated by the bright sunbeams that seem to be dancing in the glade to the melody of Taliesin's harp. The stones begin to feel warmer and you place them gently on your forehead. Just as you begin to close your eyes, you notice the white cat is watching you with eyes that now seem as blue as lapis. You want to turn toward Nimue; but you feel yourself drawn into the hidden fire within your mind.

As the stones connect with your mind, a burst of golden-white light fills your inner vision. The light cascades through your mind and reorganizes itself in rainbow tones. You open your eyes to find the forest glade filled with spectrum rainbows reflecting from a myriad of crystal prisms hanging from almost every branch of the trees. You also find that Nimue, Taliesin, the cat, and the wren are gone; but you are not alone.

Standing just in front of you are two beautifully illuminated figures. You know from experience that these are Fair Folk. There is a Lord and a Lady, both shining and shimmering in the sunlight. The Lord is holding a small, magickally crafted harp made of gold.

The Lady has a bow and a quiver of Faerie arrows. You notice that the feathers on these arrows are wren feathers, and this puzzles you.

In answer to your unspoken question, the Faerie Lady places an arrow in her bow and swiftly shoots it skyward. You look up to see another cascade of rainbows begin to shower down upon you. This time the spectrums are sharp and crystalline. They enter your mind like lasers of light and you can feel your mind expand and awaken to higher potentials than you had imagined before. Your inner vision clears and crystallizes into a heightened state of awareness. You are clear and perceptive, with a sharper focus than you have ever experienced before. For a moment you experience the full rush of power of Nature's rejuvenation within your self.

After the rush of power has subsided, you sit quietly for a moment, contemplating the magick potential of your own mind and brain. The Faerie Lord hands you his harp and you find you have only to touch its strings lightly to create a magickal melody. For a while you all enjoy the music of the harp and the sounds of the birds in the forest singing in harmony. When you have finished, all is silent in the forest glade.

The Faerie Lord and Lady have become even more translucent and shining than before. You can see the forest through them. Then, just as they begin to fade away, they present you with two gifts: the harp and the bow with its full quiver of arrows.

THE CRYSTAL SPEAR: COMMUNICATION

Elements: Air, with some Fire

Directions: E–SE

Aspects: Clarity and focus, thought conveyance

Colors: Peach ray, Gold, Copper, and Crystal lights

Kindred Spirits: Otter, Crows

Tree: Honeysuckle

Stones: Aquaflora Crystal, Copper, Citrine, Clear Crystal Point

Incense: Heather

Cycle: Beltane

Setting Image: Henge

Hallow: Spear

Theme: Round Table

Natural Force: Flames

Access Allies: The Merlin, Arthur

Format: Extensive

Message: True Communication is a consistently circular process that rarely succeeds when insistently started by coming straight to the point.

You are standing in the center of a small, low henge of stones at high noon on a late spring day just before Beltane. Beside the henge, a lovely stream flows with clear waters over smooth stones. The stream is home to several playful otters whose joy in simply being alive is wonderful to see. They splash and chatter away in the clear waters which sparkle with gold lights from the rays of the late afternoon sun.

There are honeysuckle vines creeping up and around the stones in the henge, and bright heather covers the ground in the center of the circle. Sweet fragrance from the heather and the honeysuckle gives an air of warm camaraderie to this afternoon's work. Overhead a flock of crows calls down to you as they pass by. Their call is echoed by the calls of The Merlin and Arthur who are summoning you to give them your attention.

Remembering your task, you select four small stones from a box that the Merlin has brought to the henge. Starting at the Eastern part of the circle of stones, opposite the setting sun, you begin placing these small stones on top of the henge stones. In the East, you place an aquaflora crystal to activate the inspirational element of Air. In the South you place a dark golden citrine crystal to activate the creative fires of the element Air. In the West you place a clear crystal point to ensure the flow of inner thoughts will be clearly understood, thus activating the Water aspect of the element, Air. In the North, you place a shiny piece of copper to bring form to your purpose and help manifest your ideas. Thus, having activated the Earth aspect of the Air element, you return to your point in the East to complete the circle.

Then you step back into the center of the henge and wait for instructions from The Merlin. The Merlin approaches you and places a finely crafted crystal spear in your hands. The shaft of this spear is wrapped in gold and copper wires formed into a beautiful Celtic weave design. The blade point is cut crystal and sharp as steel. There are braided ribbons made of peach and gold satin which are tied with three knots where the blade meets the shaft of the spear.

The Merlin motions for Arthur to move to the far edge of the henge, just in front of the standing stone in the West. The Merlin whispers a message in your ear and moves away to stand in front of the standing stone at the East point of the henge. Your task is to use the crystal spear to convey the message to Arthur that The Merlin whispered to you, without using any words. This seems to you to be a fairly straightforward lesson in mind-to-mind communication, using the symbolic tool of thoughts, the spear. Since the crystal amplifies all, you feel this will be easy to accomplish.

Remembering your lessons, you silently breathe the words of the message onto the spear point: "Arthur, move to your power position of kingship." Confidently, you cast the spear directly at Arthur, only to find that it barely leaves your grasp before plunging, point down, in the heather at your feet. Arthur folds his hands over his chest and tries not to laugh. You avoid looking at The Merlin as you pluck the spear from the ground and try again.

This time, you hold the crystal spear point up and make a Sunwise circle, dramatically flashing the spear point in the sunlight. You start to cast the spear, but catch yourself just in time. Carefully, you breathe the message onto the spear point and blow on it for good measure. With all your strength you cast the spear straight up toward the sun. You are not quite quick enough to avoid being struck on the head by the blunt end of the shaft as the spear makes an immediate descent.

Overhead, a few curious crows squawk in protest, and you are sure you've heard the otters laughing in the stream. You turn to glare at the otters; but they are watching with such friendly concern, you find yourself laughing instead. This helps you relax a bit and shake off some of your dramatic pride, as well. You turn to The Merlin and request that he give you a hint about what you are or are not doing which keeps you from accomplishing this seemingly simple task. The Merlin replies in his cryptic riddle style today, much to your dismay. He tells you what you are doing is beside the point of what you need to do. Seeing the look on your face, The Merlin adds another comment about focusing on the means to the end. You feel flames rising within.

You retrieve the spear from a tangle of honeysuckle vines where it landed when it bounced off your head. As you walk slowly back to the center of the henge, you study the spear and remember The Merlin's words: "beside the point" and "the means to the end." You have a hunch and you try to check this out with mind-to-mind communication with The Merlin. He wags his finger at you and shakes his head, "No." You realize you'll have to act on your hunch to test it, regardless of who may laugh at you this time. You shake off the fiery rage and replace it with the flames of creative focus.

You hold the spear directly upward and align the point with the Sun to pull in its warm energies. Keeping the spear lined up and steady, you lower it slowly until the blunt end touches the ground, connecting to the powers of the Earth. Already you can feel the crystal spear begin to vibrate in your hands. Holding the blunt end firmly connected to the ground with one hand and the silken ribbons in the other, you swing the blade in a small but distinct Sunwise circle. As you do this, you breathe the message into the spear point once again. Then, with a steady stance, you begin to position the spear for casting. Taking a deep breath, you focus your aim and concentrate on the spear until its crystalline surfaces are infused with warm peach and gold lights. As you release your breath, you blow the message carefully along the shaft of the spear, from the blunt end up to the place the ribbons are tied on, just beside the point.

With assurance, you cast the spear directly at The Merlin in the East. The crystal spear moves swiftly and strikes its mark straight on. The crystal spear hits the aquaflora crystal, creating a shower of golden sparks as it does so. Then, so quickly that it is scarcely visible, the spear swings its point to the right. First it glances off the citrine in the South, then the clear crystal in the West, creating a circle of gold and crystalline lights as it circles Sunwise. To your surprise, the spear does not stop at Arthur, but continues on, striking the copper in the North with a passing blow that sends copper lights shooting skyward. Finally, the spear lands in the East, point down, at the Merlin's feet.

You stare blankly at the spear, still shaking in the ground. For a moment, you are uncertain whether you have succeeded or failed. Then you feel someone giving you a pat on the back. You turn to hear Arthur congratulating you on your aim as he moves to the center of the henge—the place of power and kingship, or queenship—the place of Sovereign power. The Merlin joins you both and explains in his unique style.

The Merlin takes the spear and points out the circle of golden-toned lights, which is still visibly illuminating the stones in the henge, and tells you to remember the circular nature of all communication. Then he bids you to collect the four small stones you had placed in each of the four cardinal points of the henge. The Merlin tells you to bring them back to the center of the henge, one at a time.

As you do this, you note that each of the small stones has encapsulated a different aspect of the original message. Holding the aquaflora from the East, you hear the identifying word "Arthur" vibrating inside your mind. The citrine in the South resonates with the physical command "Move." The crystal from the West fills your mind with "to your power," and the copper from the North clearly transmits "position of kingship." You know now that only the full circle could have accomplished the task of communicating the full message. In review, the Merlin points out the aspects of each direction that supported your task of mind-to-mind communication: The East alerted and identified the target mind. The South activated the physical body. The West assured that the inner power of the target mind would awaken to the task; and the North brought specific acknowledgment of the form and the title. Only when the crystal spear had traveled the full course of the circle could all the aspects communicate clearly as a message. This you are told by The Merlin.

Arthur kindly reminds you that it is the way of a warrior to place as much importance on the means to an end as on the end, no more, no less. He also tells you to value the shaft as much as the point of the spear, whatever your purpose. You realize that all of the ritual dramatics you may use will never be a substitute for the powerful simplicity of the lessons in communication that The Merlin and Arthur have taught you here.

Arthur takes the spear in his right hand and steps back several paces. He breathes a message down the shaft and, with a final sharp burst of air blown on the point, he casts the crystal spear directly at your heart. Fighting an instinct that tells you to duck, you close your eyes, but open your arms to receive the spear point straight on. You feel it enter with a bright, gleaming ray of light that softens to a warm peach glow with-

in. For a while, you feel you have the power to communicate peacefully with everyone and everything in the world— as long as you do so from that glowing warm center of your self.

When you open your eyes, you are alone in the henge, and the Sun is no more than a golden peach glow on the horizon. The standing stones seem to be made of copper in this light as they reflect the sky of Beltane. The honeysuckle and heather are vibrant green, white, and violet, and their fragrance is stronger than before. You realize that with the power to communicate mind to mind comes the amplified power of communicating with the mind of Nature.

You raise both arms high above your head in a gesture of gratitude and honor for the gifts of power. When you lower your arms, you find you are holding the crystal spear in your hands. From the crystal spear comes a message, vibrating inside your mind:

From the center of your self to the center of the Circle encircling is a simple, circular path you cast point by point. From the Circle encircling to the center of your self is the only straight shot. Spirit communicates directly, all else circles, naturally—pure and simple, cast from within.

THE BLACKTHORN STAFF: ACHIEVEMENT

Elements: Air and Fire

Directions: East and South

Aspects: Evolution and manifestation of knowledge

Colors: Golden-Green, Indigo ray, Copper, Gold, and Crystal lights

Kindred Spirits: Wolf, Snake

Tree: Blackthorn

Stones: Peridot, Lapis, Aquaflora crystal, Amber, and Copper

Incense: Myrrh

Cycle: Candlemas

Setting Image: Tree, Tower

Hallow: Sword

Theme: Battles

Natural Force: Winds

Access Allies: Nimue, Arthur, Morgana, Taliesin, Lady of the Lake, The Merlin

Message: Take only what you require for your needs each time you receive from the manifestations of power in your life—and remember that they are a mutual creation, crafted with amply wise design and abundant Wisdom, which is Divine and timelessly Eternal.

It is a bitterly cold day and the clouds are dark, gray, and heavy. For what seems to be an endless time, the rain and sleet have been falling all around. There is a break in the weather just now; but you know it will be all too brief on this dismal February day. You are in The Merlin's tower, trying to concentrate on your lessons in magick and mind evolution; but your heart is just not in it today. The Merlin has left you alone in the tower, which is a treat you normally treasure. Today, though, you would rather have his company. Even his most cryptic lessons and riddles would be a welcome change. Still, you try to study.

Finally, you put down your books in frustration and decide to explore this wonderful tower room with all its tempting tools of wizardry. You stand up and declare your intentions to create a little magick of your own. After all these lessons, that should be no difficult achievement, you tell the Merlin's pair of wolves who are peacefully dozing by

the fire. Their response to your declaration is no more than a flick of an eyelash and an ear. Ganieda's lovely indigo snake raises her head and peers down at you from the top shelf of the highest bookcase. With a dismissive flick of her tongue, she settles back down in the fur-lined basket that is her favorite winter retreat. Chill winds blow around the tower and you hear the driving rain beating against the stone walls. The heavy tapestries covering the windows billow and let in blasts of icy cold air. You wonder briefly at the wisdom of animals who sleep through such a dreadful winter day and the humans who don't have sense enough to do the same.

Feeling inspired by your own rebellious nature, you rummage around through an odd assortment of crystal balls, dragon's claws, and stacks of indecipherable charts. Nothing you find strikes your fancy, so you retreat to the fireplace to reconsider your plan. As you are about to sit in a very comfortable chair, you notice a blackthorn staff leaning against the wall near the fire. Although it is very ordinary as staffs go, you are compelled to investigate its powers. You walk toward the staff, stepping over the sleeping wolves as you go and pick it up.

The staff is ebony and smooth, with only a few rounded knobs where the thorns once had been. As soon as you hold it, you can see clearly the great Blackthorn shrub from which it was cut, long ago. You briefly catch the fragrance of white flowers and a glimpse of the purple fruit the Blackthorn bears. Experience being what it is, you realize that this unassuming staff has some significant potency. You quickly take down a massive volume of notes and look up the powers of the Blackthorn. You feel decidedly Druidic as you pursue your research; but your moment of self-satisfaction fades as you find the Blackthorn represents aspects of imperialistic attitude and dogmatic control. You wonder if you have been tricked by the wizard seeking to ensure that you continue your studies, even in his absence. Looking further into the notes, you find some hastily scrawled words: "Blackthorn for strife, in particular that which arises from achievement of goals." Under these words are some rough sketches of the purple winter fruit of the Blackthorn, its early blooming white flowers and a fierce-looking thorn inked in black. As you turn the page, you find a drawing of the massive Blackthorn bush that grows at the base of The Merlin's tower. Under this drawing is a strange equation of Aristotelian logic:

Blackthorn = Strife, control, imperialism
Blackthorn: Achievement (therefore)
Achievement = Strife

You consider this for a moment; then pencil in a comment of your own:

Strife = Achievement

Since by now you feel it is strife enough to pass a dreary Winter day alone with your lessons in a cold, stone tower, you resolve to make the best of it by achieving something magickal—with the Blackthorn, no less. To match your battle mood, you take a sword down from the wall and place it in the center of the room, along with the Blackthorn staff. You rummage through a basket of stones, coins, trinkets, and crystals until you have found five to your liking.

Taking the stones to the center of the room, you arrange them in a five-point pattern on the tower floor, around the slightly rusty sword. You lean the Blackthorn staff against the stair rail and go in search of a potent activating incense. In a short time you return with a small bowl filled with fragments of myrrh in one hand and a piece of lit kindling in the other. You light the incense and soon the tower is filled with its sweet spicy fragrance. It is almost strong enough to cover the smell of singed wolf hair from the piece of burning kindling you dropped on the tail of one of the wolves. You rush over and pour water on the poor wolf's tail. He regards you with a look reserved for those who are pitifully afflicted—or simply pitiful—and you resolve to be more focused and careful. You can already see how achievement can cause strife. Now you resolve to reverse the equation. The wolf is unharmed. Only a fragment of hair is blackened and frizzed from the fire and the water, as well. You decide to let him drift back to sleep, so you cover him—

and the smell of burned hair—with a soft woolen blanket.

You return to your arrangement of stones with the heavy volume of notes in your arms. You open this volume to the page with the Blackthorn drawn on it and place the book across the sword. On second thought, you move the sword to rest across the drawing and circle the stones around the volume. In the East you place an aquaflora crystal, in the South, a small copper coin, in the West, a tumbled peridot, in the North, a rough-cut lapis, and in the Center, a thin gold ring

You take the Blackthorn staff and cast a circle, somewhat hastily, but with sincere words of positive intentions. Remembering the importance of being specific as well as earnest, you tap each item you have arranged around the sword and state the aspects you wish to manifest for your experiment in magickal achievement:

From the aquaflora in the East you want perception, from the copper in the South, willpower, from the peridot in the West, inner knowing, f46rom the lapis in the North, sacred wisdom, and from the amber in the Center, expanded power.

Satisfied, you tap the staff on the floor three times and wait expectantly. Too late, you realize you haven't specified what even you expect. With a great rumbling of stones and wood, the unexpected arrives. After you have picked yourself up off the floor, you find you have magickally achieved the manifestation of a huge Blackthorn bush right in the center of the tower room. The wolves are fully awake now and growling fiercely at this unnatural sight. Ganieda's indigo snake is indignantly trying to regain her position in the overturned basket on the floor.

You run quickly to one of the windows, pull back the tapestry and look down at the base of the tower. Where the Blackthorn bush is supposed to be there is only an amazingly deep hole that is rapidly filling with rain. From the top of the tower, down to the base, there are roots sticking out of the cracks between the stones in the wall. As the freezing rain blows in across your face, you realize that the weather will at least delay The Merlin's return for a little while. With a hasty thanks to the elements, you turn to resolve the strife you have achieved thus far.

You replace the indigo snake in her basket and return it to its place on the shelf. You quiet the wolves with assurances that you have everything under control, and you ignore their dubious expressions. You quickly search for the stones, the sword, and the book—which have scattered in every direction—most of which have to be reached through the thorny brambles of the Blackthorn bush. You search for the staff until you realize it has disappeared into the bush from which it originally came.

You take each stone, the coin, and the ring, and line them up on the sword blade, which you have placed on top of the closed book. You stare at your new arrangement for a while until you have an inspiration. Carefully removing the sword and stones, you open the book once more. Turning to the section on the Blackthorn, you add yet another equation:

Strife = Achievement
Strife = Control
Control = Achievement

Telling yourself dogmatically that you can control this situation, you assume as imperious a posture as you can manage. Tapping each stone with two fingers of your left hand, you demand that help be provided. After a moment's hesitation, you relent and add three words: "Please, please, please."

For a moment nothing happens. Then the great rumbling begins again. There is a crashing sound and then you are no longer aware of anything for a while. You drift along in a flow of light and color. Swirls of golden-green, indigo, copper, gold, and crystal seem to lift you from the floor. You are aware of a bright electric blue ball of light and you awaken to find yourself seated in the comfortable chair by the fire. Both wolves are sleeping peacefully, and you notice neither one has a singed tail.

You force yourself to look at the center of the room and find the Blackthorn staff still leaning against the stair rail. Everything appears to be normal. Even the sword is hanging on the wall in its usual place. There is a faint smell of myrrh in the room; but perhaps it was there all along. You can't recall. The book is back on the table and, best of all, the bush is gone from the room.

Just as you have gathered up enough courage to see if the Blackthorn bush is back in its rightful place at the base of the tower, you hear the sounds of several people coming up the stairs. You turn to find an unusual assortment of visitors entering the tower room with The Merlin. They each greet you in turn and tell you they have brought you gifts on this cold, Candlemas day. One at a time, they give you their gifts, with no comment but a smile.

First, you get an aquaflora crystal from Nimue; then, a copper coin from Morgana; next, a tumbled peridot from the Lady of the Lake; then, a rough-cut lapis from Taliesin; next, a thin gold ring from Arthur; and finally, a bouquet of white blossoms from The Merlin.

The white blossoms are rather familiar. You have seen a picture of them somewhere. Then you realize they are the white flowers of the Blackthorn bush, some of the first to bloom—even during the harsh times and the strife of Winter. They are one of Nature's signs that Spring will arrive, that renewal will be achieved despite any of the times of strife that may precede it. That is a magickal, even dogmatic, command of Nature—perhaps the only sovereign who truly has the right to be imperious all the time.

The Merlin pulls the tapestries back and lets the warm sunlight of early Spring shine into the tower. You breathe a sigh of relief, and all present in the tower nod in silent accord. You pass the rest of that promise of Springtime afternoon sharing stories about the adventures and misadventures that naturally accompany achievements—especially magickal ones.

Before you leave The Merlin's Tower for today, he gives you a small white blossom and a piece of purple fruit that was left on the floor when the Blackthorn finally returned to its original location. The Merlin informs you that all that had been required to release the Blackthorn tree from the Tower was to pick a piece of its fruit or a flower from its branches and bless the power that provided for its growth—and for yours, naturally.

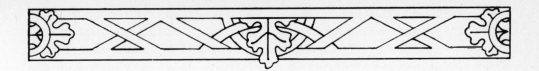

CHAPTER 29

ARCANE AVALON

Known also as "The Dwellers in Avalon," these archetypal figures send out a call which is answered in time by all who are drawn to study the Arthurian tradition. The power of the inner realms is thus conveyed in a broad ray, outward from the centre, until it percolates through the worlds into the lands of men, where it works towards a cosmic goal … A word, whispered in Avalon, becomes a trumpet call in the ears of those who seek the good of the world and the furtherance of all mankind.

John Matthews
The Elements of the Arthurian Tradition (Dorset, England: Element Books, 1989)

 Avalon is essentially the healing, divinational, and initiatory aspect of the Otherworld, a realm combining elemental, Nature forces with emotional attributes of self-nature and the divine gifts of Spirit. Within this realm, the gifts that are accessed and activated are a blend of the mystical arts and the magickal arcane wisdoms represented in symbolic forms that express themselves in the crafting of your life. Avalon's gifts are available to provide supportive motivation for the achievements that are in your dreams.

The supportive influential power of Avalon's arcane symbols and archetypal figures is often expressed in a quiet, subtle fashion; but the effects are just as often experienced in a quite surprising, directly self-transformational manner. This is because the usually softly accessed, serene Avalon experience is so easily encoded and encapsulated in the realms of emotion and of Mind, as well. In essence, that pleasant Avalon experience remains at the ready, waiting patiently for the just right combination of feelings, thoughts, and external cues to activate its power.

For example, you may have had an uplifting "visit" to Avalon that helped restore your feelings of self-esteem and stabilized your sense of emotional security.

You may feel that the effects of that emotionally empowering experience have faded into memory, along with the imagery of Avalon. You may well be surprised when, at an unexpected time, you find yourself responding to situations or individuals in a very different, far more self-assured fashion. The signals from others—and those from within yourself—that had caused you to feel emotionally insecure or inadequate in some way, or that had usually resulted in a self-defeating expression of feelings, may well become the signals that inspire your response as a person of power and positive self-esteem. Have faith in yourself and your abilities to obtain what you need from the inner realms of healing powers and transformation. Healing is rarely a truly instantaneous process. When it seems that way, it is usually because the time and the conditions were ideal—and the quiet transformational powers were potent and ready within.

Avalon is not like The Merlin Current, which makes you wonder if you are actually going to stay intellectually "in flight," all the time. That effect is dramatically obvious. Camelot's realms are similarly upfront and direct in their effects. Both of these realms have their own archetypal gifts which bring lasting qualities of personal empowerment and expanded self-evolution into your life. In the Avalon realm, though, the archetypal gifts, the symbols of power within, have a distinctly spiritual aspect which gives these an eternally effective quality.

To access Avalon is to open yourself to the Divine in a uniquely individual, personal way. In Avalon, you are able to recognize what the Bards who wrote of Courtly Love called "The Divine Power Operative" in one's own heart, and within the heart of someone you love. Avalon is about relationships with yourself and with others. The heart-feeling aspects are activated through experiences of Avalon. You are given the chance to develop truly balanced compassion and nonjudgmental attitudes in regard to yourself and in regard to others.

Avalon also provides the symbolic keys, the images, that represent the cycles of transformation within your self. This awareness of personal cycles gives you a more flowing relationship with your own feelings and with the everchanging tides of your emotions. Avalon's archetypal aspects enable you to get a "feel" for who you are and what you feel is right for yourself—in your life.

Finally, Avalon's realm is well-accessed by those who work with the gifts of divination, in an intuitive manner, based more on feeling than on symbolic, correlational facts. These facts rely on mind and memory, rather than on inner knowing and individual responses. In this, the deeply emotional individual is most at home in the archetypal Avalon realms, as is also the spiritual person. Avalon's archetypes are as flexible and flowing as the ways in which you approach them. Remember that when you feel you need a set, ritual access, for this type will not stand too much that is fixed. The emphasis is on finding the flow within and keeping as clear a connection as you are able to manage.

THE ACCESS AND ACTIVATION IMAGERIES: AVALON

The imageries that follow are The Temple of Lavender Mists: Attunement Initiation; The Raven's Well: Purification; The Tor Ritual: Guardians of the Circle; and The Lady and the Fair Folk: Mystical Attunement. Go through these imageries slowly and absorb the experiences with care. You will find your encoding, encapsulational gifts will serve you well.

THE TEMPLE OF LAVENDER MISTS: ATTUNEMENT INITIATION

Elements: Water and Spirit

Directions: West and Center

Aspects: Emotional attunement, self-initiation

Colors: Violet ray, White and Gold lights

Kindred Spirits: Dragon, Unicorn

Tree: Fir

Stones: Amethyst, Pearl, Mother of Pearl, Blue Lace Agate, White Gold

Incense: Jasmine

Cycle: Autumn Equinox

Setting Image: Temple

Hallow: Scabbard (Faerie Sheath)

Theme: Quest

Natural Force: Mists

Access Allies: Morgana

Format: Brief

Message: We express ourselves in many lights and ways that reflect the forceful and the lyrical aspects of our individual nature. As in the Light of Nature, there is always a blend, reflecting a balance. This is a balance that we may reflect when we honor both aspects, forceful and lyrical, for what they bring to our lives, individually; and we also honor their enlightened blend.

———

It is a misty evening at the time of the Autumn Equinox. You are standing in front of a mystical temple surrounded by soft-needled, ancient Fir trees. Behind you, the sunset has painted the western sky in gentle tones of lavender and gold. From inside, you can smell the deep, spiritual fragrance of temple jasmine compelling you to enter within.

You step anxiously inside, hoping your feelings of excited anticipation will not prevent you from expressing yourself with ceremonial reverence. You

have come to this temple to celebrate your initiation as one who has developed the wisdom and skills of emotional attunement and intuition for self-healing, and the service of helping others heal themselves.

The Lady Morgana acknowledges you with ceremonial reverence. She is present in this temple in her highest aspect as priestess of the realms of Avalon. Her robes, like yours, are violet and gold, symbolizing the activation of spiritual service. Both of you wear personal talismans of your own design, crafted of white gold and set with amethyst and pearls. The Lady Morgana holds a lovely box inlaid with designs in mother-of-pearl. The box is closed and locked with a key made of white gold.

The altar in the center of the temple is arranged as you imagine it to be for ceremonies of spiritual magick and initiation. There are white candles in golden wall sconces throughout this sacred temple. By their illuminating power, you can see that the jasmine burns brightly, and its smoke transforms itself into mystical lavender mists within the temple.

The Lady Morgana brings a large flat plate made of pale lavender-blue stone and puts it on the altar, then places the mother-of-pearl box in the center of the plate. She requests that you approach the altar in a manner you feel to be most ritually powerful and spiritually sacred for yourself. When you feel ready to begin, the initiation also begins. From the emotional realms of your inner being, you open to the sacred rite of self-initiation.

Just as you feel this rite, you experience the power of personal emotional acceptance. You are clear and in tune with the power within. In response to this, the Lady Morgana opens the mother-of-pearl box and pulls forth two white gold magickal figures, Faerie-crafted in miniature, symbolic fashion. She places these on the blue-lace agate plate so you can see them clearly. There is a dragon and a unicorn, both of which make you feel magickal in your own way.

With metaphysical crafting, the Lady Morgana projects expanded images of the dragon and the unicorn as holograms in the center of the temple. You feel a rush of excitement and power as you see them projected in the lavender mists above the altar. Initially, they are no more than simply enlargements of themselves. Neither one appears to have more or less power than the other, nor differences in size.

The Lady Morgana guides you to experience the Unicorn as a symbolic expression of your emotional attunement to power and magickal service. You feel your emotions in complete harmony as you watch the unicorn transform into a full-sized creature of great beauty and grace. The unicorn shows its feelings of devotion to you by nuzzling your shoulder and gazing into your eyes with an expression that reflects deep sincerity of emotion. You feel the wonder of this unicorn, who is both delicately sensitive and durably strong, as a powerful symbol of the mystic and the mundane.

As you and the unicorn make acquaintance with mutual admiration, The Lady Morgana guides you to express, in exaggerated form, a round of elementally powerful, personal emotions, beginning with Fire. Although you do not feel the anger of Fire at this moment, you know how to reach the realms within yourself where vestiges of rage are stored, by choice or otherwise. As you express anger and rage, the dragon transforms to express these aspects on an expanded scale, changing shape, color, and projected power. This feels thrilling until you notice that the unicorn has become fierce and wild in response to the changes in the dragon— and to those changes in your emotions.

You are guided to continue this round of expressions and to observe the transformations as a first-quality Druidic scientist would. You are also guided to take note of your own feelings—for it is from these that your image and its effects are truly projected within yourself. To this end, the Lady Morgana guides you through the elemental round, expressively:

Water: The dragon becomes soft and flowing with ever-shifting forms, most of which display some measure of sadness or despair.

The unicorn becomes weak and undefined. There is no longer a horn to distinguish this mythical steed from a weary, mundane old nag.

Earth: The dragon manifests in expanded structural perfection with each detail of its being carefully ordered and organized for power.

The unicorn transforms into a cold marble figure, heartbreakingly real to see, but without any possibility of feelings or of mystical, symbolic alliance. It is no more, or less, than a perfect statue of a perfectly shaped horse with a horn.

Air: The dragon evolves rapidly according to expanded visions, unedited by rational thoughts or perceptive focus. Its form continues to shift, even when you no longer feel that you are part of the creation of its image.

The unicorn becomes a cartoon caricature of its symbolic powers, ranging from images of childlike fantasy to dark-intentioned exploitative images of unnatural qualities.

Spirit: The dragon vanishes into the lavender mists, merging with the light, illuminated and reemerging as the delicately crafted miniature figure whose only powers are its symbolic role, linking you to the Divine.

The unicorn follows suit—as is natural.

The Lady Morgana guides you to encapsulate your emotional reactions to the experience of these symbolically attuned transformations and to review them in your own time and realm of feelings. She places the tiny white gold figures in your hands, the unicorn in your left, the dragon in your right. You feel an intense emotional responsive connection to what each of these represents. The unicorn is your spiritual magick and the dragon is your elemental power.

The Lady Morgana guides you to clasp your hands together carefully, with your fingers gently interlocking around these figures. As you do so, you feel the spiritual force of violet rays rushing through you, followed by the activation power of golden lights. A gentle glow of white light emerges from within and you feel the force and the responsibility of rightfully attuned transmission of power.

Then you are guided to open your hands, and you find that yet another transformation has taken place. Within your hands, within your self, you find that you are holding a delicately beautiful scabbard, Faerie-crafted in size and quality. It is no larger than needed to sheathe a Faerie blade. On this sheath, crafted in white gold, are two symbolic figures. A unicorn and a dragon face each other in attuned alliance, each from their own side.

THE RAVEN'S WELL: PURIFICATION

Elements: Water and Spirit

Directions: West and Center

Aspects: Release for renewal, healing initiation

Colors: Black, Gray and Silver lights, Golden-Green ray

Kindred Spirits: Owl, Raven, Lynx

Tree: Willow

Stones: Obsidian, Black Quartz, Pewter, Peridot, Aquamarine

Incense: Herbal

Cycle: Samhain

Setting Image: Holy Well

Hallow: Cup

Theme: Quest, Grail

Natural Force: Mist

Access Allies: Ganieda, Morgana, Nimue

Format: Brief

Message: There is rarely, if ever, a true Wasteland in which we must live. There are only the occasional, forlorn stretches of barren landscapes that we must cross, following a lonely road. So long as we remember the Source from which we came, and which is our ultimate destination, we will find this same Source provides for us along the way. When we accept what that Source provides and learn to seek it, purely, we soon will find that the Wasteland within fades into light and beauty.

It is a cold, misty-gray day at the time of All Hallows. You find yourself walking among the barren hills of a stark, bleak landscape. All afternoon a large black raven has been your constant companion, and you know she is guiding you to the place of release and renewal you seek. As you make your way over a softly curving hill, you come upon an ancient holy well made of crumbling fieldstone.

Beside the well is an old weeping willow whose branches are gently blowing in the cold, late-Autumn breezes. The raven has perched herself on the edge of the well, so you know you have reached the place of purification for which you have traveled all this dismal day.

When you come closer, you see trinkets and tokens have been left at this holy site. There are stones and crystals in the hollow places between the fieldstones with which the well was built so very long ago. You see translucent obsidians and black quartz crystals used for healing release. There are trinkets hanging from the branches of the weeping willow. You see holy symbols crafted in simple, gray pewter and pendants set with bright stones that stand out in contrast to the muted colors of this place. There is a pendant with a golden-green peridot, the stone of healing renewal, and another with an aquamarine, the stone of sacred ceremonies. Tied in simple bundles, there are also fragrant herbs hung in the willow. Their scent is fresh, and you feel comforted to know that others have recently come before you to this holy site.

You have brought a simple wooden cup, plainly fashioned, to draw healing water from this holy well. Since this is a sacred site, you feel both reverently hopeful and respectfully humble in your quest for personal purification. You say prayers of your own creation to honor the source of transformational power. You consider all that has brought you here along the path of your emotional journeys and spiritual quests.

If you feel the need to do so, you weep in remembering your sorrows as well as your successes, for both are emotionally draining. You look up to find that two other kindred spirits have joined you and the raven at this holy well. A little gray owl has perched on a branch of the willow, and a little wildcat, a lynx, has curled herself in a ball among the roots of the tree. You feel comforted by their presence.

You close your eyes and continue your prayerful inner ceremony. When you open your eyes, you find the kindred animal spirits are no longer with you. In their places are three women whom you have come to know well. The Maiden, Nimue, is resting against the base of the tree, and the Crone, Ganieda, is standing inside the softly swaying branches of the weeping willow. On the edge of the holy well, Morgana sits regarding you in a gentle manner that reflects her most maternal aspects.

Nimue is wearing robes of a muted golden-green color. Ganieda is dressed in black, and Morgana's cloak is a soft, silvery gray. Where you had once been wearing a different shade, you now feel yourself dressing in the palest tone of aquamarine you have ever seen.

You greet each other quietly, and the three women listen as you tell them why you need to draw directly from the Source this holy well represents. When you have expressed your feelings and clarified your emotional state of being, the three women offer to help in your process of purification. You thank them each and all for their support, but decline to accept their offer. You express your concern about becoming dependent upon their powers, even though you know these powers are no more, or less, than a reflection of your own.

With compassionate understanding and acceptance of your right of choice, the three women take their leave of you. As they go, each one bestows a kiss upon your forehead. You feel comforted and spiritually empowered by their token of kinship. When they have left, you take the unmarked wooden cup and reach for the bucket which is tied to the holy well.

As you lower the bucket into the deep, dark waters, you see yourself reflected in the mirrored depths within. There, in the center of your forehead, is a design of triple Moons, each outlined in the colors worn by the ladies. You know this is a mystical marking and may not be perceived as a power source by others. Still, you feel an emotional empowerment already beginning its cycle of self-renewal within.

You drink from the cup of water that you have drawn from the holy well. When you are ready to leave, you notice your cup has also been transformed. It now bears the design of the triple Moon.

THE TOR RITUAL: GUARDIANS OF THE CIRCLE OF POWERS

Elements: Spirit

Directions: Cardinal points and the triple circle of Spirit

Aspects: Protection of the elemental purpose of ritual

Colors: Scarlet, Rose, and Violet rays, Gray, Black, White

Kindred Spirits: Black Birds, White Birds, Dragon

Tree: Fir

Stones: Garnet, Amethyst, Black Quartz, White Quartz, Silver, and Gold

Incense: Jasmine

Cycle: Samhain

Setting Image: Tor

Hallow: Stone of Destiny, symbol runes, pouch

Theme: Quest

Natural Force: Winds, Tides

Access Allies: Your self and druidic-ken, Ganieda, Rex Avallones (Nentres of Garlot), and Vivienne

Format: Extensive

Message: When you feel all alone and isolated from those of like mind and those of your own kind, remember: your role is to do your own thing. Do this by yourself, according to your own mind and in a positive, assertive, and kind manner—even if no one else is there. Do this and you will soon find you have far more allies than you may know. They are also aware, in their own ways, with visions much like yours in their own minds. There are always other people who share your philosophies in their own enlightened ways. Shine your own light, clearly, and they will respond, in kind.

It is the time of the Celtic New Year, the season of Samhain, Summer's wane. You find yourself atop the great Avalon Tor, attending a Sunset ritual during the time of the Full Moon. There are many others in attendance at this Samhain ritual, most of them wearing robes that indicate their spiritual orders and positions of power. There are a few, such as yourself, whose affiliations with power are based on a more solitary alliance than the majority of those gathered here at this time.

You feel somewhat isolated and you make a mental note to bring another ally of your own kind when next you attend this particular type of ritual. For now you rely on the strength within your self and the kindred spirits you observe around the ritual site. Just as the Sun sets and the Full Moon begins to rise, you see two flocks of birds. A flock of black birds flies in from the South and passes overhead on their way North. These black birds call out noisily as they pass by.

Only you and a few others, whom you have already noticed, seem to know these black birds are allies for magickal group workings and ceremonies. You are somewhat concerned that these black birds have not paused to encircle those at the ritual with their shamanic powers, which are a symbolic gift of Sovereignty. You note this and let it pass, along with the black birds. Another flock of birds passes overhead, moving in from the West and flying directly East. These are white birds, mystic messengers from the Land of Mystery, as the Old Ones have taught.

You consider that the two flocks have created a pattern in the shape of a plus sign. Perhaps this is a symbol of equal balance, or the hub of a wheel. You also consider that this pattern could be emphasizing either the powers of the four cardinal points, S, N, W, E, or signaling conflicts or lines of division. You decide there are enough indications of divisions at this ritual already. You can see that various groups have begun to jockey for positions of power here and there. Each group is more elaborately garbed in regalia than the next. Their black, white, or violet robes are heavily ornamented with silver, gold, and expensive symbolic jewelry.

You feel the power at this ritual has begun to shift from that of the circle united to that of the many sections who have separated themselves according to their sense of hierarchal privilege. You wonder if these separatists have forgotten the evolutionary concept of the Round Table; then you realize they never truly knew what that was. You look to the leaders of this ritual, hoping they have noticed the divisions and are attempting to unite the group in harmony once again. With the clear sight of one accustomed to observing Truth in all of Nature and self-nature, you see that the leaders are carefully avoiding those groups whose positions have been overthrown by others. You watch for a while to be sure of your assessment, growing frustrated as you see the High Priestess Vivienne and her lord Nentres of Garlot, Rex Avallonis, carefully cultivating those groups who have managed to move closest to their own position of power.

You wonder if anyone else realizes the significance of this and how its divisive nature could affect the essential connection to Nature which this ritual is supposed to represent. You consider making your way to the center of the ritual space and delivering a much-needed reminder about the importance of a unified spiritual circle; but you remember the wisdom that tells about how the ancient heralds who brought unwelcome news were often made martyrs because of their message.

You decide to act on your own, using your personal connection to the elemental powers of Nature. You reach inside your cloak for a talisman of power to bring you strength and courage. You bring forth a dragon brooch, crafted of silver, with wings and claws lightly brushed in gold. The dragon is encircled with garnets and amethysts, lightly tumbled. You sweep your simple gray robes back to reveal the deep scarlet tunic you are wearing underneath. This color is the mark of a spiritual warrior, one charged with maintaining a spiritual balance in matters pertaining to Sovereignty. The dragon brooch, which symbolizes the Right and the elemental powers of Nature, you pin wisely on the left side of your tunic, just in line with your heart. You know that pinned on the right side, the dragon powers could become too bold and create divisive conflicts, rather than subdue them.

You decide to carry your simple Fir staff in your right hand, symbolizing the right of choice and the power of personally expressed spirituality. A gentle breeze begins to blow across the lake surrounding the Avalon Tor as you begin to cast your own circle by encircling the entire ritual space. You can see the waves change direction as the breeze moves across the waters, and you hope this signals a change in the tides and the divisive times you have observed so far here.

As you walk quietly, head down, around the ritual area, you concentrate on holding a positive image of unity in your inner vision. The breeze lifts your robes as you walk along the outer edge of the Tor. You catch the scent of jasmine, which seems to grow stronger. You look up to see there are others also walking the circle, encircling. Some are right behind you, some right ahead, and others, you now discover, have been walking beside you all the way.

You feel a fierce sense of pride and purpose as you see how most of those walking the circle, encircling, are also wearing emblems of elemental power, similar in energy to your talismanic dragon. Some are dressed in robes of the priestly variety, some the garb of Druidic teachers and bards, and others, like yourself, are wearing the colors of a warrior in active service. All are guardians in their own right. All have divined the potential danger in divided spiritual rituals. All have chosen to take personal action to unite the powers they feel are spiritually present at the Tor ritual.

You feel an intense emotional bond with these solitary, active guardians—

and you begin to understand the power of such a solitary alliance, united in service to Sovereignty. As you all complete the third circle, each at your own pace, you spontaneously gather around an ancient, unnoticed standing stone at the distant edge of the ritual circle. It is primitively carved in the shape of the Celtic Earth Mother. You stand, as that stone stands, an individual strong and deeply connected to the Earth, still resonant with power from a distinct, unique link to all the elements of Nature. You feel the power of this stone icon and take pride in being individually iconoclastic in your choice of a spiritual path.

As you all gather around this stone, unlimited by any set pattern or hierarchal procedures, you feel a deeper sense of kinship with others than you have ever felt before. With the natural flow of power that arises from such spontaneous unity, you and the others begin to share your own Tor ritual. Each contributes freely, sharing their heartfelt wishes for the good of all. Each resists speaking of anything but the most positive ideals and visions. Each who has divined situations that cause concern addresses these by stating them only in terms expressing the possible solutions, rather than stressing the possible problems. Each and all, you are fully aware of the sacred power of words. Each and all, you are elementally Druidic in your approach to all life.

In an unspoken accord, you take turns connecting with the standing stone goddess. As you take your turn, you realize that this, too, is a stone of destiny. As you touch the stone figure of the ancient Celtic Earth Mother, you hear Her voice as a steady, rhythmic heartbeat. Each heartbeat guides you with glimpses of what your choice of spiritual service brings to your life—and, thus, for the life of all around you. You feel the elemental nurturance which the ancients before your time honored as the Earth Mother.

You lift your gaze toward the twilight sky and watch the celestial bodies emerge from the soft rose-gray sky and you honor that which the ancients called the Sky Father. You and the others, each in your own way, honor the great mystery of Spirit, and the Divine power that has graced you with the ability to choose what is Right and of the Light for the good of yourself—for the good of all.

You remember that another, larger circle is involved in its own ritual here on the Tor. As you turn to watch what has progressed, you are amused to see that only a few groups have remained politically positioned near the leaders, Vivienne and Nentres. You see, with interest, that the Rex Avallonis has begun to realize what is happening, for he is making his way to the altar at the center. Vivienne, the High Priestess, is no longer able to see beyond the crowd that has clustered around her. They are blocking her view of the others who had come questing to the Tor for ritual. Those questors, both the solitaries and those in groups, had been given a lesson here on the Tor, one that they had heeded. You feel very encouraged to see that all but those tightly gathered around the High Priestess, Vivienne, have interwoven themselves into an actively communicating group. You

notice there is a bright rose-violet glow encircling these questors. You know this glow has emerged from heartfelt, inclusive spiritual connection, newly experienced or reexperienced by those who had once felt that power was an exclusive property.

You watch with the others of your ken, as Nentres, Rex Avallonis, moves the two quartz crystal clusters on the altar. He picks up the black quartz in his left hand and the white in his right, and whispers an earnest prayer to the heavens. With no announcement, no dramatic flair for attention, he moves the quartz clusters together. When they meet, the crystals seem to explode with intense black and white lights. A shower of sparks fountains upward into the gray sky of evening; and when it subsides, the quartz clusters are both clear and illuminated from within.

The light within the crystals moves forth to join with the rose-violet glow, and soon the heart and spirit of all who have united are encircled with the amplified power of a true ritual circle. In that light you see a pattern you had not noticed before. There are mystically illuminated concentric circles atop the Tor that touch the official ritual circle but do not match the lines the leaders had drawn. Then, as you encapsulate the image of these mystical circles before they fade into the Earth, you see where the center of all these illuminated circles truly is. At the center of the circles encircling each other, illuminated by the Light from their lines, is the Standing Stone, the powerful icon of the once and always times, The Earth Mother, sacred Sovereign of the Celts.

You feel graced to have been shown that divine reminder. Others of your ken have divined it as well; but there is no need for words of explanation. You and your ken embrace each other as family, as clan. You are no longer unknown to each other; indeed, you never were, for you all form an alliance which is ancient in origin and current in evolution. Perhaps you will chance to meet again—in realms of Light.

You stay as long as you choose to at the now-illuminated united ritual on the Tor. You know you and your ken have accomplished the task for which you were placed at the ritual. You have accepted the gifts and responsibilities of guardianship well. Now you feel empowered with purpose—and naturally proud of your part in the protection of the circle.

After you have remained at the ritual on the Tor long enough to observe and absorb all you need, you make your way down the spiral path that leads to the Lake of Avalon. You pause by the lake to look at the Moon and the bright heavens encircling all reflected there. You are pleased to find a wise elder waiting for you with a gift. Ganieda greets you with a proud embrace and praises for your work. Then she pulls a soft pouch from her cloak pocket and places it in your hands. One side of the pouch is black, the other white, and there are tumbled stones inside. You can see quartzes in dark and light tones, some smoky, some milky, some crystal clear—

all etched with symbols and runes that are significant to you. Ganieda asks if you know how to divine with stones and symbols as well as you have divined with Nature and self-nature this evening at the ritual. When you say you are familiar with your own forms of the divination craft, Ganieda smiles with wise-elder patience. Then she asks you whether you prefer to know what you're getting into before, during, or after you're into it.

As you pause to consider your response, Ganieda gives you a bit of wisdom about having the Sight—and using it well in the Service of the Light. Her comments are blunt, in her wise-elder fashion—and when she has made them, she leaves you to consider the power of her words and her lesson to be aware is druidically to prepare.

After is hindsight, which makes you either a Hart or a Jackass, depending on what you have experienced while you were "into" it all.

During is insight, which can be clear or cloudy, depending on the climate of the experience and how well-equipped you are to weather what you find yourself "into."

Before is Divine sight, which is illuminating only if you reverence the light within yourself in connection to the Divine Light from which all spiritual guidance emerges—and then merges "into" your personal divination craft.

THE LADY AND THE UNICORN:
MYSTICAL ATTUNEMENT

Elements: Spirit

Directions: Center and the Circle encircling

Aspects: Self/Spirit, Clearing, Receptivity, Acceptance

Colors: Turquoise ray infused with White, Silver, and Gold lights

Kindred Spirits: Unicorn, Dragonflies

Tree: Aspen

Stones: Aquamarine, Peridot, Opals, White Quartz, Silver, and Gold

Incense: Herbal

Cycle: Autumn Equinox

Setting Image: Lakes

Hallow: Sword (Faerie Blade)

Theme: Quest

Natural Force: Mists

Access Allies: Lady of the Lake, Nimue, Ganieda

Format: Extensive

Message: There is a philosophic question that requires no response except one of personal reflection. It asks, "If a tree falls in the forest and no one is there, does the falling tree make a sound?" In the processes of self-questing, the only responses which are required come from your own self-reflections. When you recognize those self-reflections are also questions, you will realize that the real answers that feel right and true seem far more easily found. The answers to your self-questions are in your heartfelt self-reflections. These mirror your emotions, with all their aspects, clearly present, illuminated by the full, light power of compassionate self-acceptance.

It is a bright day in the balance time of Autumn, when the Equinox brings day and night into perfect alignment with each other, if only for a brief moment after the long days of summer and before the long nights of winter begin. You find yourself walking alone through a beautiful stand of Aspens which border a deep, blue-green lake in the realm of Avalon. Everywhere you look, Nature seems intensely alive, as if in celebration of the last warm light rays of the waning harvest Sun. The cycles of change can be perceived by the rich herbal fragrance of Nature's transformations, as old growth becomes new soil—but only a slight hint of this is present on this day. The colors of Nature are vibrant and evocative as they resonate around and through you with their harmonic qualities, their tones as much sound as hue.

The only indication of the cycle of Nature's time of rest, soon to come, is the sound of crisp leaves beneath your feet and the shimmering drops of golden-green leaves drifting down from the light-barked branches of the trees. The day is so warm there are mists rising from the still, night-cooled waters of the lake. The clear afternoon sky and the towering trees reflect in perfectly mirrored balance, making it unusually difficult to determine where the lands leave off and the lake begins.

The waters are deep and still, and the trees are quiet as you pause to gaze at your own image reflected in the lake. You are interested to see how your image changes, and you observe these shifts of self-reflection with a serene detachment and comfortable self-acceptance. From time to time, a cloud of mist will move across the mirrored waters; and when the surface clears again, you find you have changed in reflection. At other moments, only the shimmer of the dragonflies skimming lightly on the surface of the lake seems to let you know which is your true self and which is no more, or less, than a clear reflection.

You find a smooth white stone that is as flat as a coin, and you skip it across the surface, creating a chain of concentric circles leading from the shoreline to the center of the lake. When the waters are smooth once more, you take a silver coin from your pocket and cast it out into the middle of the lake with a whispered wish to know the dwellers in this fine Fair realm where Nature and self-nature meet in Spirit.

The coin drops surely in the center of the lake with a deep, certain sound which echoes in the trees. The sound rings around the lake and resonates as intensely as the ripples on the lake rush out from the center in circles. The sound steadies into a gentle hum as the ripples brush against the shoreline with softly lapping waves. Sunlight through the trees dances in expanding circles across the waters, making the dragonflies' wings shine with an opalescent light, like Faerie wings as you remember them in your childhood dreams.

You remember those childhood dreams wistfully—and you remember the wish you made this day; but there is only the quiet of the trees and the calm of the waters. It is a silence that seems to resonate with anticipation, and you feel that familiar inner childhood impatience urging you to action. With great persistence, your inner child spirit coaxes you to sing, dance, make music with the trees, or just do something carefree.

The elder parent within begins to drone inside your mind with critical reminders about the propers and impropers of your possible actions. The adult, so balanced in theory, proves flighty when confronted with the possibility of encountering a true Faerie in this rare realm. Summarily outvoted from within, the elder's voice withdraws from your consciousness; and, just as it fades from your mind, it is heard echoing in the trees—and the voice of the elder is laughing.

From out of the elder Aspen trees comes the figure of an old woman, a Fair Folk, as you judge her to be. She puts you in mind of Ganieda; yet, somehow, you are not sure. You decide to greet her with a polite, respectful bow; but you manage only to nod your head before the Fair Folk elder has disappeared among the trees with no trace except the faint echo of her laughter.

You feel quite frustrated by this curious encounter, and you silently hope that wasn't the extent to which your wish was to be granted. Your inner child seems to be having some kind of tantrum, and you struggle to put that image out of your mind. You are relieved to have the inner tantrum cease so quickly, until you realize it has started again nearby. Just a few yards away on the shore of the lake, a small Fair Folk child, a maiden no more than half a dozen years old by your estimate, is ranting away about what you should or should not have done.

You listen, transfixed by her voice, and realize this young maiden is speaking with the sound and the authority of an elder. You gasp in surprise as the Fair Folk elder woman dashes out of the trees to make faces at the Maiden and then quickly dashes back to hide behind a large, overturned tree. The maiden responds to this like a not-very-grand, grouchy grandmother, calling out threats to a bothersome child. The elder responds with taunts of her own and all you can do is listen and wonder what went wrong.

You are startled to hear yourself demand silence from both these strange, unpleasant, and not-so-Fair Folk. You catch sight of yourself reflected upside-down in the mirrored lake as you shout a few threats of your own, mostly for your own benefit. With a few more uncharacteristic comments about the fact that everything seems upside-down in this realm, you heave a larger, rougher rock as far out into the lake as you possibly can. You watch with satisfaction as the ripples swiftly obliterate your angry, reflected image.

You turn to see if your intrusive visitors were impressed by your forceful action; but they are nowhere in sight. There is only a silver-white mist drifting across the fallen tree where the elder had been, and a thick cloud of mist has already enveloped the spot on the shore-line where the small maiden had been standing. You feel strangely alone, almost missing these disturbing characters.

You turn and start to heave a long sigh, but you find yourself stopped short by what you see. The lake is no longer visible. Even though you know you are standing right at the edge, you cannot see the shoreline at your feet. Nor, for that matter, can you see your feet for the mists are rising fast and thick around you everywhere. You think to step back, away from where you know the lake to be, so you will not lose your bearings altogether. With three wide steps backward, you feel safer, although still quite mystified by what you are experiencing.

Soon, there is nothing but the silvery-white mist and the resonating sound of silence. Although you expect to be disturbed by this, you find yourself feeling quite peaceful and strangely more secure than you have in quite a while. As you express these feelings inside your mind, you find that you begin to hear a warm and familiar, strong, clear voice echoing the words you have chosen to form your thoughts.

After a few moments of this, you are amazed to discover that the same voice of strength and clarity you have been admiring with wonder is understandably familiar—for it belongs to you—and you alone. It is a voice that you haven't truly heard in a long time, at least not in ways that would reveal to yourself the qualities within your feelings and self-expressions. Delighted with this self-revelational turn of events, you take the time to tell yourself what you feel, what you think, what you want, and what you need.

You never even consider wistfully whispering your wishes. When you remember what you wished for, you fairly shout it out with confidence and self-esteem. For good measure, you call out your thanks through the mists for reminding you of yourself, fairly. This, you recognize, is most certainly how you have been granted your wish to know personally one of the Fair Folk.

You have enjoyed your own company when that was all you had. You have stood your ground, even when you had to take a few steps backward to find it. Most of all, you have not allowed yourself to accept that which is upside-down to hold dominion over what you know to be right-side up—and that is, your true sense of yourself.

As you realize the humor of having come looking for a Faerie—only to find yourself in a fog—you laugh until the tears flow, and when the tears have stopped flowing and the laughter has been encapsulated within your heart and mind, you know you have experienced a realm of resonant self-attuning qualities. In the mists which you had expected to bring you visions of fantasy figures and their magick, you found one of the truly real Fair Folk. You know all you experienced were reflections for you to observe and consider, only in regard to yourself. From the center of your own consciousness, you called forth images which were upside-down into form, as they were, and were still able to deal with your own self-image in a straight-up way, just right for your self.

Even though you realize those strange and unpleasant characters, the taunting, childishly foolish elder and the threatening, grouchy old granny-child, are also within, you know that the true voice of authority within is your own. "To use it wisely and in balance for self-attunement" is the vow you voice into the mists, and "to honor myself with a fair self-acceptance," and "to honor the center of myself and the circle of my life with others, and the circle encircling, which is the realm of mystery and spirit and grace."

When you have spoken three vows of self-attunement, self-acceptance, and self-acknowledgment of that awakening grace, the great mystery, you take all the time you wish to create some vows of personal affirmation in honor of your own acceptance of self and of Spirit—the alliance of your highest self. You craft these in as casual or as ceremonial a fashion as you wish.

When you are ready, the mists will return to the cool depths of consciousness, to the mystical lakes of Avalon's realms. Truly, there are many depths of consciousness to be found in that realm, each uniquely suited to provide what is for the good of all that you are—now and potentially. The realm of Avalon can provide access to an evolutionary self-transformative realm of healing initiations.

Avalon is a quest into the mists of spirit and emotions. It is a quest you have made well. You undertook a quest in search of one of the Fair Folk, and you found your self. You may have wished to fly—as a Faerie is often perceived to be able to do—but you were fogged in mystically. Still you flew, truly, on the strong wings of self-acceptance. You watched the dragonflies with all their translucent beauty, and you made them dance when you bravely created changes in the waters of consciousness which the lake symbolized.

When you had no reflection, image, or direction to find your bearings, you went within to find a way—a way all your own—to grant your own wish. You encountered what you had dreamed of—and wished for as a child—and found it is no fantasy; for you are truly that which you call Faerie. You are child, adult, and elder, a triple-aspected, unique individual who has the power to see her own self-nature clearly and to see clearly how Nature reflects within, as well.

When the mists have cleared, you take three steps forward to balance your experience and set yourself upon your path once more. When you imagickally reach the place on the shoreline of the Avalon Lake you have visited, you find a gift is waiting for you. It is a gift that you may use to disperse unwelcome fogs and mists, to cut through the bindings of critical comments and false scripts which are not either well-intended nor wisely inspirational in regard to your positive personal development and spiritual self-attunement.

One thing, though—which you need to know bardically—this gift will amplify that which is constructive and true—uniquely—as they are good for you. So, if you continue to hear a comment, or if a script keeps ringing in your ear—cut through mystically, three times with love, not fear. If these then repeat or reappear, "better listen,"—or at least listen better—for the constructive truth and love most dear.

And your gift is a Faerie blade, a dagger of mystical craft. It is unsheathed and sharp, so be aware of your own cutting remarks—particularly those you make to yourself—for you are most likely to believe those first.

Your Faerie blade from this realm is a gift from the Lady of the Lake, who also provided the mists and the dragonflies. It also comes from Nimue and Ganieda, who provided the not-so-pleasant characters of the elder and the child—in whichever role you match them. The effect is inseparably the same.

This Faerie blade, as it is best named, is crafted of silver, gold, and white light, which makes it receptive, active, and effective as a means for transmitting. It has a figure on the hilt that reminds you it is crafted of a mystical blend. The figure is a unicorn, a white steed of power with a horn to symbolize its active magickal nature. This is your unicorn, and you may see its reflection change supernaturally, from time to time—as yours does, naturally.

There are stones you may choose to set in the hilt of your Faerie blade—or not, as you wish. These were selected for crafting primarily in the realms of Avalon for mystical quality magick and are well-linked spiritually with the White Goddess in her now familiar, triple Avalonian aspects. There is aquamarine, here for The Lady of the Lake; and peridot, here to represent Nimue; there are opals of muted tones, here for Ganieda. And, when you feel you know her well, add amethysts for Morgana, as gentle or intense in tone as you wish, to reflect her image—and, naturally, your own in each of these.

CHAPTER 30

THE CAMELOT CRAFT

The contemplation of the well-known (and not so well-known) stories of the knights and ladies of the Round Table is also one of the paths to that great inner plane Temple wherein the mightiest loving guides of the human race and the planet Earth await the questing soul.

Gareth Knight
The Secret Tradition

 In this final chapter, we complete the text that has guided your exploration into the realms of the Camelot legends thus far. Your own explorations continue as you create them, along the lines of your personal path. As the realm that is Camelot is more instructive, with systems for experience, I will shift my role as your guide to your instructor; then turn the explorations over to you. The first three imageries will be crafted as are the others, which were the guided experiences.

The next four will require your own skills of crafting. I'm certain your skills are already of Mage quality. These are the suggested imageries, with catalyst aspects to encourage your own transformational experiences. After you have completed these craftings, you will be better prepared to transform any of the other imageries into exercises, ceremonies, or spiritual rituals, according to how you need them. This is true of all three realms we have explored from the perspective of your guided experience.

ACCESS AND ACTIVATION IMAGERIES

Although we have separated the realms of The Merlin, Avalon, and Camelot in order to explore and experience their unique qualities, they are truly linked mystically. Therefore, I remind you to blend and combine their aspects in order to create your own experience of what these realms represent, personally, to you. As long as you maintain a reverent attitude, remember what you know, research what you need to know, and respect what you discover; your experiences will be rewarding. Explore with a positive, empowering purpose and your purpose will be positive and empowering. Be true to your self and be wise. Your experiences will be both wise and true in their value for your life. Also remember to check the appendices for additional exercises and information on going back to previous exercises for a new, and renewed, look at where you began with this book. Remember that you have completed several quests already with the distances you have traveled, but especially with the dimensions of your personal journey. You know that you are still, and always, on a new Hallowed Quest. It's a spiralling path, a 'round into the light.

FALCON'S FORT: CONTROL AND POWER

Elements: Fire and Earth

Directions: South and North

Aspects: Structure, form, planning, order, control

Colors: Yellow and Green rays, Gold, Brown, Copper, and White lights

Kindred Spirits: Falcons, Dogs, Cats

Tree: Hazel

Stones: Tigereye, Amber, Yellow Jasper, Bloodstone, Gold, Copper

Incense: Amber

Cycle: Midwinter, Yule

Setting Image: Fortress

Hallow: Lance, Crystal Sphere

Theme: Lands, Quests, Chivalry

Natural Force: Tides

Access Allies: Arthur, The Merlin, Sir Kai, Pellinore, Guinevere

Format: Brief

Message: The processes that we call part of the establishment are better viewed as a part of the Chivalric order for establishing power with grace.

This was once a royal procedure, a summons to determine the right rewards for the right efforts. There were bestowals of lands, betrothals of love, and powerful alliances of clans by marriage. This process of summons also established the rights of succession. We can use the same concept to summon ourselves, truthfully. We can plan for, prove, and accept our power by right of individual achievements and positive uses of personal qualities. Achievements are earned. Qualities are gifts or skills. Both require a structured effort to activate and use well. When you can do this with grace, then grace of power will summon you.

It is a cold Midwinter day and you are within the walls of Arthur's fortress at Caerleon. There are preparations being made for Yule; but you have come outside to be away from the noise and bustle. You sit cracking hazelnuts with the hilt of your sword and listening to the royal planning meeting going on nearby. You are impatient with this Winter day, but you have learned to keep this to yourself—even if the cats and dogs have perceived this and seem to be avoiding you, wisely. You decide to join the meeting since they haven't asked for privacy; but they signal you to stay where you are. This makes you more curious, so you focus on them with what you think is not obvious observation.

Arthur and Sir Kai are discussing what seem to be most trivial matters for a king and his seneschal to bother with. Details of a realm and rulership are not of interest to you just now. You wonder how they stand it; but they seem quite patient as they continue. You shift your mind to The Merlin and King Pellinore, who are talking about the objects each one holds. The Merlin has a crystal sphere in which you can see swirls of color: yellow, green, and gold. Pellinore is holding a lance crafted with a new design. Its shaft is made of copper, and its point is painted brown.

Responding to your natural curiosity, you move a little closer, while pretending not to be interested. Sir Kai notices this shift in your position and sends you inside to fetch warm drinks for all of them. He says nothing about a drink for you.

While you wait inside the kitchen, Queen Guinevere comes in. Even she seems to ignore you, standing so forlornly amidst the kitchen help. Guinevere seems most serene today, enjoying the cheerful tasks which are part of Yuletide's seasonal celebrations. She is wearing a simple woolen gown in shades of copper and brown. Only the jeweled belt she wears shows her royal rank. The belt is made of braided gold bands, linked with copper clasps and set with amber stones. The scent she is wearing is also made of amber spice and suits the warmth of her spirit. You look at your own belt which is fine, but not exotic. It is made of copper, brushed with gold and set with jaspers and tigereyes—such practical stones, and strong; but just not special, you think to yourself, and heavy too, you decide,

suitable for the purposes of holding a person on the ground when what they really want is to fly, and yet ....

The queen had given you this belt, one that she had designed especially for you with stones to match your powers. Remembering this, you give the stones a little rub to clean them. Now the bloodstone jasper seems to gleam with a rich green light, streaked with lines of red, and the tigereyes are a truer gold than you had realized before. Even the simple yellow jaspers have a brighter tone; but the stone you really love is the blue-gold tigereye on the buckle. It was called a hawk's eye, the Merlin told you last Yule when the queen presented it to you. Then you had been treated royally; but now you are in the kitchen waiting for a surly lad to fill four tankards with warm ale.

Times and tides will change, you tell yourself with some self-pity. Then you jump with surprise as the hawk's eye seems to wink. When you have recovered, you remember who you are and why you do not have to wait upon the surly whims of a kitchen lad—nor the surly whims you willfully let control what you feel inside.

You take a hazelnut from your pocket and place it on a table. With one strong blow you crack its shell with the hilt of your sword. Platters rattle and spice bottles roll; some cups fall to the floor; but you calmly eat that nut while order is restored. In a clear, strong voice you make a comment which on the surface seems to be quite simple; but the heavy looks it inspires assure you that the meaning struck its target just as surely as the lances you have thrown in

367

Summer tournaments. A grateful look from Queen Guinevere empowers you with purpose, for she does not have the heart to scold in order to put others in their proper place.

Your comment was quite well planned and delivered as by a person of power. You simply stated that the King and his company were already discussing their plans to find a more effective way to see that everyone did their tasks in a more efficient way. They surely would not take kindly to waiting in the cold while others, who should serve them quickly, were taking up their time and yours, to do a simple task, such as filling five tankards with the finest warm, sweet ale.

As the tankards are quickly filled, you see there are only four. Then, as the now quite humbled lad catches the look in your eyes, he rushes to the cupboard and fills another tankard. When you reach for them, he insists on carrying them for you. You nod your head with noble grace and walk proudly outside, with the kitchen lad following behind as fast as he can.

King Arthur and King Pellinore are discussing the merits of a fine young falcon that has been brought to them while you were gone. The Merlin and Sir Kai seem pleased to see that you have managed to get some service after all, for they had been wondering when you would remember that you could. When the kitchen lad leaves, you start to ask if you may stay or if you should go; but Arthur signals you to come closer and meet this fine young falcon. You are so entranced by the beautiful bird that you forget you had felt neglected. As you stroke the falcon, you feel a rush of pride within and a sense of deep connection.

You remember that you have the right to enjoy the power you've earned by your deeds of merit and courage. You remember, too, that this does not mean you must constantly be stroked and praised, for you are not a little child. You realize the importance of even the most trivial things which, if they are done well, can even lift the burdens of a king. The Merlin has told you often that service is not all glory and sometimes the simplest tasks remind you of who you are. You have been told to accept these with the same grace as those tasks that are more significant. Then you soon will find that grace of power in the simple, as well as in the special experiences of your life. Each and all, the tasks are a part of the order of the Lands. When you use the codes of chivalry in everything you do, then the quest for that which is special is a part of everything, and you remember just how special you truly are. Moreover, anyone can feel this way. If they accomplish their tasks with grace and pride, they will be empowered, regardless of the task.

As you consider all these things you have learned from experience, you realize you have been neglectful of your company. The King and The Merlin have been watching you while you make connection with the falcon—and the fine young falcon within you. Pellinore and Sir Kai are waiting patiently and holding gifts wrapped in Yuletide colors. One is very long, you see, with a point that could not be hidden. The other is round and tied on top with a simple white ribbon.

You have to laugh, for they have tested you this day on the battlefield in the kitchens just as surely as they have in the fields of training for battle. The presents are early; but Yuletide spirit seems to have arrived when you recalled the Light within yourself. So, you open the gifts with delight.

The Lance from Pellinore and Sir Kai is to ensure that you take aim from a grounded position and not in flight, for that would miss the mark. The Sphere of Crystal from the Merlin is to design your plans and dreams with the power that is wasted on surly whims and boredom.

Then King Arthur gives you the fine young falcon who has just begun to fly. When you gaze into the falcon's keen and proud blue-gold eyes, you are startled to see one eye wink. But you do not jump this time, for your task is to teach this hawk controlled power—so perhaps you'll learn together—both in kind.

THE AMBER CASTLE: DEMANDS OF POWER

Elements: Fire and Air

Directions: South and East

Aspects: Energy, Trust, Control, Relationships

Colors: Orange, Green and Blue rays, Gold light

Kindred Spirits: Deer, Sheep, Roosters, Hens

Tree: Rowan

Stones: Amber, Opals, Carnelian, Aventurine, Sodalite, Gold

Incense: Amber

Cycle: Midsummer

Setting Image: Castle

Hallow: Sword, Shield, Banner, Cloak

Theme: Round Table

Natural Force: Winds, Flames

Access Allies: Arthur, Gawain, The Merlin, Morgana

Format: Moderate

Message: Power that emerges from sources or symbolic images with which you are not familiar must be challenged by you to determine their intent—or your intention for them. Lines of power or alliances in realms either mystical or mundane, require consistent maintenance, even if the connection has always seemed solid. A clear line of power can become disconnected by neglect, misuse, or the manipulations of others. This can happen whether the line of power is in mystical, symbolic, or mundane, manifest forms relating to your life. Keep your connections clear with self-challenging evaluations of your intentions, needs, and plans for the use of power. If need be, do the same with others who come to negotiate terms of power.

It is a bright midsummer day as you ride through the beautiful forest. You are on your way to a castle you have not visited, but where Arthur and Gawain have gone to conduct the business of the Round Table alliance. You make your way through the forest and see in the distance a castle that fits the description you have been given. Since your journey has been long this day, you decide to rest a while before you go on to the castle.

You rest beneath a Rowan oak and notice a small herd of deer watching you from the forest depths. They look at you with such concern you can't help laughing, and the deer disappear into the forest. You dream strange dreams of fires and storms. You dream of swords without blades and shields with no structures; only hilts and frames reveal the objects for what they would have been—but what they are not, truly.

You awaken to find it is still day, although your daydreams have felt more like nightmares. You shake off the chill you feel inside, blaming it on the foolish pride that made you insist on coming alone to a castle you knew nothing about. You remind yourself that the castle is close and Arthur is there with Gawain. You mount your horse and ride quickly toward the distant castle.

As you draw near, your spirits lift. You are glad to be out of that forest where the deer watch with fear in their eyes, and the dreams you have are frightening. The castle is made of warm, pale orange stones, which make it seem very welcoming. The lands outside the castle are simple and friendly, with farm animals here and there, grazing quietly. You see fat sheep scattered across the hills with their wool as yet unshorn. Roosters and hens scratch at the ground just outside the castle gates.

It is very quiet at this castle today, so you assume the lord and his guests have gone hunting. The king's banner is not flying here; but you realize that it may be wise, at least until the alliance is signed. The banners that are flying are of a simple design, gold Celtic knot weaves on backgrounds of blue, and others on a field of green. These are fine colors, ones you also choose for times and places

when you want their powers to reflect the right message, or provide the right feelings as the situations require.

You start to knock on the simple wooden gate, but it swings open before you have the chance. You are startled to find a beautiful Lady standing at the castle's entrance. She is wearing a gown of palest orange. A muted warmth and the scent of amber drift toward you on the winds which are moving in through the castle door. Inside, a small fire burns near the gate, which you realize must be for cooking, since this midsummer day is hot already.

The Lady of the castle beckons you to enter; but your horse seems to hesitate. Not wanting to appear unable to control your horse, as a knight certainly must, you resist the urge to spur the horse on. For some strange reason, you recall your dream—perhaps because of the flames of the unseasonal fire burning within this castle wall.

The Lady awaits with a cool, quiet look; and you realize she has not spoken. She fingers a necklace around her pale throat, as if to assure herself it is still there. You notice the necklace is made of stones usually are not found in such pale, pale shades. There is amber in beads just tinged with a yellow color, and carnelian that looks as though its color had been bleached out of it; but you can't imagine how. It is the same with the green of the rich aventurine and the blue of the strong-toned sodalite. These have faded, but not as much as the other stones, which seem older somehow. Still your horse refuses to ride into that castle at all. To stall for time, you remember a procedure that helps give clarity when you are not sure what to do.

With a pleasant formality of tone and manner, you state your position and your intention. When the Lady hears Arthur's name, she brightens for just an instant. It is like a blush; but it fades so quickly you wonder if the poor Lady is altogether well. Still, she makes no response. This time you repeat the same things in a much more purposeful manner. You feel slightly invigorated by the sounds of your voice echoing from the castle walls—and you think for a moment that your eyes are tricking you; for the walls seem to glow with a brighter shade of orange for just an instant, then fade back to pale.

The Lady smiles sweetly and you see her teeth are tiny and sharply pointed. At this, your horse rears and you struggle to control him. Then you address the Lady with a commanding voice. You demand she identify herself and find that she grows pale when you do. You repeat your demands again and again, as though driven to do so by a force within. Each time you demand that she identify herself, the Lady grows paler, until she fades away and, with her, the castle fades away, too—leaving only the fire smoldering in the middle of a bare field of ground.

Astounded by what you have encountered, you ride close to the fire and see what has been burned. There you find a strange sight indeed, for among the ashes are the objects in your dreams. The frame of a shield and the hilt of a sword lie stone cold among the still warm coals. Both are blackened and misshapen.

You ride as swiftly as you ever have imagined—away from the fire toward the deep green forest. Your horse needs no persuasion from you to keep up the pace all the way home.

To your surprise, the banners of the king are already flying on the ramparts when you reach Camelot that afternoon. You burst into the great hall and find Arthur there with Gawain, the Merlin, and Morgana. Before you can tell them of your strange encounter, you notice that Morgana is sewing a design on a bright blue banner, a Celtic knot weave in golden thread. Then you see that the Merlin is wearing a cloak you have not seen him wear before. It is a rich forest green with gold designs, the same Celtic knots you've seen already, more times than you cared to, certainly.

As you realize you have encountered another test, your first reaction is rage. You restrain yourself and wait until you can ask the reason—the purpose—of this most unpleasant lesson. When you do ask, you address it to Gawain, who has yet to test you unfairly, so you feel.

You are surprised to hear Gawain admit to designing the frame for the lesson. With help from The Merlin and Morgana's craft, the lesson did become a bit more disturbing than Gawain had intended; but Arthur insisted that this lesson be learned, even if it had to be driven in—all the way to the hilt. You feel confused and furious at this news.

Then Arthur explains that there is vital importance in the lessons that teach you to check out every situation as thoroughly as you possibly can—particularly in strange places and with people who are strangers to you. The Merlin adds that this is true, and sometimes truer still in the mystical realms of mind where projections and illusions may often be found—put there by your own mistaken intent—or the manipulative intentions of others.

Morgana apologizes for the frightening necessity that justified her distressing illusions. She explains that false allies, whether mystical or mundane, can drain you as quickly as you can give them your trust, for it is in their nature to do so. She explains the use of dreams which can cause you to seek illusions of safety, and of lures that entice with the simplest means, such as colors you feel are best reflective of yourself. These both lure and empower you so vitality is increased—just before it is drained. In mundane terms, you are pumped up; when you have served their purpose, they let you down—small wonder you feel depleted.

Then Morgana rises to assure you that what you did was all done well. There had been a few clues along the way, and the natural actions which gave you insight. The deer had been watching as the dream was sent into your mind—for they are truly perceptive. The remembering of the procedure for challenge and command may be better credited to the actions of your horse; but you heeded the warning your fine steed gave you. You also used powers of keen per-

ception to observe shifts as subtle as a blush, particularly on a projected illusion. The unseasonal fire was the catalyst fire that symbolized the ashes your energies could become if you did not challenge and command those experiences and symbols of power you will always encounter, from time to time, as you explore the realms of mystical mind, and those realms in mundane form filled with many people on magickal paths—some not as clear intentioned as others, and some clearly of bad intention, far more rare and usually obvious, though not always.

Morgana tells you the Celtic knot can be one of alliance or entrapment, and both use the same basic pattern. The vital difference is intention, intention, intention. When that is clear, all is cleared.

Then The Merlin takes the green cloak and gives it to you in honor of the heart of your courage and the feelings that expanded your perception. Morgana gives you the bright blue banner because you expressed your self with clear will and purpose, which you then demanded be returned, in kind. Thus, when the illusion was insistently challenged, it faded from your mind, unable to remain in the light of truth and the power of knowing what is Right. Never assume when you can check it out.

THE CRYSTAL FOREST: ALLIANCE

Elements: Fire and Air

Directions: South and East

Aspects: Kinship, Communication, Shared purpose, Unity

Colors: Yellow and Orange ray, White, Spirit, and Gold and Silver light

Kindred Spirits: Horse, Dogs, Bear, Birds

Tree: Elder

Stones: Tigereye, Jaspers, Carnelian, White Quartz, Sodalite

Incense: Cinnamon

Cycle: Midsummer

Setting Image: Forest

Hallow: Spear, Lance, Gameboard

Theme: Chivalry, Round Table, Courtly Love

Natural Force: Flames and Winds

Access Allies: Lancelot, Guinevere, Arthur

Format: Moderate

Message: There is great pride and power in being a part of a greater purpose that is shared and served by those with whom you are in spiritual kingship. The alliance of power that arises from activated unity is a rare and fragile circle. If the purpose for the alliance is too broad in scope, the circle can collapse, crushed by too many people, places, or possibilities all rushing in at once. If the purpose narrows to empower just one person, it implodes, or is self-absorbed, and if the purpose is shared originally, it must continue to be shared, inclusively, with natural shifts in positions to provide for a flexible alliance.

Exclusivity creates a stiff circle that often becomes brittle, cracked, and broken as the purpose pales in comparison to the process of keeping the circle, exclusively. Such rigid alliances, or circles of shared purpose, are only required in crisis cases of conflicts, chaos, or war. Otherwise, an alliance must be open to illumination in order to work for Right and the Light honorably, with natural cycles of renewal.

———

There is a soft breeze blowing through the branches this day as you ride your horse to a clearing at the heart of the forest. It is a lovely clearing, filled with Midsummer's full, blooming growth, and surrounded by a grove of Elder trees which enhance the lands with their mystically renewing powers. The dogs who have come along with you this day race ahead and roll like puppies in the lush, green grasses. You dismount and let your horse graze on the sweet shrubs while you share your lunch of cinnamon cakes with the dogs and a few wild birds who have joined you.

You have brought your spears and a lance this day, and you set them up against an ancient Elder. You take a gameboard out of your saddlebag and set it up to play its mystical game. There are concerns in your mind about the high court at Camelot. Alliances have been broken now, far too many times. You watch the figures on your magickal gameboard playing out their roles, which you still don't understand. You consider what you've learned about the codes of the Round Table and Chivalry—but, most of all, the truth of Courtly Love. So much which seemed ideal and real as it was being structured now seems like a dream or foolish illusion. Somewhere along the line the connections have been broken. What once was alliance now seems like war.

A tiny wren twitters in the ancient Elder where your spear and lance are leaning. You decide to practice your skills, in order to clear your head. After casting the spear across the clearing and hitting your mark with practiced perfection, you mount your horse and practice charging, until your lance becomes stuck in an old dead tree. The force of this unexpected collision causes you to pitch forward off your horse. You are dimly aware of the lance above your head, thrust deep in the dead tree as though it were a spear.

The next thing you are aware of is the sound of voices from the center of the clearing. You sit up to find three figures playing at the gameboard, and you realize they must not be able to see you, even though the blow sent you sprawling nearby. Arthur, Guinevere, and Lancelot are absorbed in the game and don't hear your call. They are dressed in their finest with jewels and garments of unique quality. Arthur is all in gold, with a great golden tigereye ring on his right hand. Guinevere is completely covered in silver, with a deep blue sodalite, set in a silver ring on her left hand. Lancelot is dressed all in white. He is wearing a bright carnelian, set in copper, on his right hand, and a ring made of pewter, with white quartz crystals, on his left.

When you consider their appearance, you know it is unique, and something about them makes you sit back a bit and observe without being observed at this time. Then you notice there are no figures on the gameboard, but the three figures in the clearing are still playing the game. You realize this is a mystical projection, which probably explains why the dogs are gone. Your horse is grazing quietly at the edge of the clearing, but he keeps one eye on the center and the game. You know he is doing just as you are: hiding in plain sight and watching the scene unfold.

The Sun climbs high, directly overhead, and gives the forest a white-hot glow. From every leaf on the ancient elder, a tiny crystal light begins to sparkle. The sparkling crystal becomes a circle of light which surrounds the clearing with the clarity of spirit. Then you see there are three other circles surrounding each of those who are playing the game. Although the circles are linked, they are also unique, for they keep transmuting as the game goes on.

Arthur's circle is of the brightest gold, with a power so active it is almost blinding to behold. Guinevere's circle is crafted of silver, so delicate it is almost eclipsed by the golden light that emerges from Arthur's circle. Lancelot's circle is pure white and sparkles with flashes of both silver and gold as if it were infused by the other two circles. These two change constantly, but Lancelot's stays steady, reflecting both. The noon Sun of Midsummer enflames the crystal circle, surrounding the clearing with a ring of fire.

The bright gold of Arthur's light is drawn slowly into the ring of mystical fire. Though the three figures never stop their game, you see by their lights that another dimension of the game is playing out its destined course to the end. The silver of Guinevere's light becomes fragile and translucent, progressively weakening as the gold light leaves. The silver infusions in Lancelot's white light link with the fading circle around Guinevere, and the gold infusions meld them together, with only a few flashes of gold being drawn into the circle of fire with Arthur's light.

Where there once were three circles in the heart of the clearing, there are only two, which are transforming into one. You watch as the silver now strengthens in power, then begins to strengthen the power of the gold, which is bright and beautiful to behold. Soon, both circles become one pure white ring of warm and healing light. Infused in the circle of mystical white light are interwoven lines: soft, serene silver and gentle, secure gold.

The crystal fire ring burns itself out, leaving a brittle ring of dim light surrounding the clearing, while gray clouds gather and block out the Sun. Although the game continues, the figures are fading. Lancelot and Guinevere are fading together; but Arthur is fading alone. Unable to stand this, you run to the heart of the clearing with your spears and your lance in your hands. You seem to recall your lance had been stuck; but perhaps you had dreamed that—or you're dreaming this now. This, you realize, is not as important as protecting the alliance these figures have shared.

With only a few jaspers you carry for strength, you manage to place a hold on the fading figures. You call your horse, but he is already there, ready to ride in service of what's Right. You ride in three circles around the clearing, with the ancient elder as your guiding point. As you do this, you drag your lance until the sharp point is softened by the three circles of power you draw in the ground.

You rush back to the center, where the figures are holding, even though their reflected images are faint. The sunlight is gone now behind dark clouds, and the Moon's soft glow is unlikely to emerge tonight, for the clouds are thickly set in. The forest greens are distinctly brilliant as their ray of light often is before a storm. You gratefully recall the natural magick that links all to the powers of the lands.

Remembering your training, you cast copper coins from your pocket in a circle to surround the three sacred figures inside. You place four more in the circles you have drawn in the ground with your lance, one coin in each direction, as nearly as you can determine them. This, you know, will be effective as long as the coins line up equally like a balanced cross of Nature. With one more copper coin in the center of the gameboard, you are ready to craft the alliance once again. If only in the realm of spirit, the alliance will empower itself eternally and, in turn, empower both the realms of mystical and mundane life.

You select three spears that you know will fly true when you focus your aim on the form of your targets. With each spear, you draw one circle until you have three circles linking in harmonious proportion. These you draw around the three figures who are already placed in powerful positions. Guinevere's circle is on the left; alone it is far too receptively crafted. Arthur's circle is on the right, where its bold unique quality sets it actively apart. Lancelot's circle links both in the center and slightly above for the power of spirit.

With all you have of the powers for images to manifest the transforming light in the Mind of the All, you focus on the circles from a distance away, directly in front of the Elder tree in the East. You steady your stance in the roots of the tree and cast three spears, one at each circle in the heart of the clearing. The spears move through the faint reflections surely and strike their mark in the center of each circle. For a moment there is nothing you can see changing; then a beautiful transformation begins.

Starting with Arthur, the figures illuminate with clarity, then merge into their part of the three linking circles. Next Guinevere, then Lancelot merge in kind, leaving only the circles drawn on the ground. You are satisfied that they are now linked with each other in harmony and merged with the land; but there is more to transformations of such powerful lights as these.

A storm cloud bursts, sending down a torrent of rain. Thunder and lightning crash about the forest; but in the circled clearing there are only the softly falling raindrops of a sweet, refreshing midsummer shower. When the shower stops, so does the storm, which has raged with purpose, purifying the atmosphere that surrounds the lands and the forest. All of the circles have washed away into the ground. Only the spears and the gameboard remain. A few bright copper coins gleam here and there among the roots of

the Elder trees, where the rain has carried them during the storm. The coin on the gameboard has disappeared, although the rain had been quite gentle. Just as you wonder if you should leave your spears, a beautiful rainbow emerges from the clouds. It seems to sweep down with a mystical force until it connects to the ground, at the heart of the clearing. The next thing you see are three linking circles rising up from the clearing in balanced connection to each other. The circles are all crafted with a crystalline light, harmoniously infused with white, silver, and gold. You watch as the circles merge with the rainbow and become part of the ordered spectrum of light. The rainbow resonates with amplified power as it connects to the highest spirit, and the lands respond in kind, vibrating with elemental power. Thus is a mystical alliance created, and thus is its power restored in the realms of mind, spiritually illuminated.

Soon all returns to a quiet midsummer afternoon; but as you ride home through the forest, with the dogs now bravely leading you home, you notice the raindrops have an interesting reflection. When you pause to look closer, you are able to see three linking circles in rainbow tones which symbolize their clear alliance with Nature, in all her colors and aspects—and with Spirit, which is eternally within the One and the All.

THE SUGGESTED IMAGERIES
WITH CATALYST ASPECTS

THE CAVE OF BLUE MISTS: SPIRITUAL PURPOSE

Elements: Earth and Spirit with some Water

Directions: North and Center

Aspects: Realization of power potentials and path

Colors: Blue and Violet ray, Rainbow, Silver and White lights

Kindred Spirits: Dragon, Hawk, Mouse

Tree: Hawthorn

Stones: Sapphire, Amethyst, Bournite, Silver, Steel, White Quartz

Incense: Amber

Cycle: Midwinter–Yule

Setting Image: Cave

Hallow: Stone of Destiny, Chalice, Sword, Woven Star

Theme: Otherworld

Natural Force: Winds

Access Allies: Gawain, Nimue and The Merlin

Message: The equalities of power exist only with the realms of the Universal Divine where power is indivisible, and therefore, equal. In human realms, we make arbitrary judgments in order to provide structures and form. Thus we think in terms that measure, compare, blend, multiply, and sometimes divine. This similarly describes the processes that transpire when people of equal gifts of power encounter, interact, and sometimes separate. In Nature, we see this process as a catalyst for evolution, in self-nature, a threat to our power (or pride!). When we accept the natural process whereby once parallel paths reach out on unique new lines, we'll see the power of that for the good of all—and be proud.

———

Suggestions for the Cave of Blue Mists: Spiritual Purpose

Elements: Emphasize the Circle, encircling, and bring Spirit in with spirals leading to the center of your circle. To close, lift the spirals as high as you can imagine; then release with grace and gratitude. You'll still have all you need.

Directions: Remain in the center and face North, in order to keep the emphasis on the sacred and not earthy aspects.

Aspects: Make comparisons of path and potential to find how to use your gifts successfully on your path.

Colors: Infuse your circle with Rainbow light first, to enlighten all aspects in a 'round of balance.

Kindred Spirits: Bring in Mouse first to put perspective into your image and provide receptive modesty. Keep Mouse in your "pocket."

Tree: Hawthorn blossoms are pure white, symbolizing gentleness. Use their image to express a more gentle, spiritual aspect.

Stones: Bournite brings full spectrum colors with a solid foundational strength for order, which is creative.

Incense: Amber can be replaced with Nag Champa, or Champa.

Cycle: Emphasize your return to the Light, renewing.

Setting: A high vaulted cave image gives a cathedral quality.

Hallow: The chalice is your image of your personal Grail within. Craft this image in order to give yourself a personal stone of destiny, symbolizing inner knowing and divination skills. Also give yourself a woven star, if you want one, in order to connect with Gawain, and with all the elements of yourself.

Theme: Otherworld allies who help here are The Shining Ones.

Natural Force: Be aware of the pace of your thoughts and what they tell you. If you think fast about an aspect, it is probably connecting well. Slow thoughts may mean the concepts in your image are not clear or intuition is telling you they're not for you. File these for future reference and don't let them worry you.

Access Allies: Gawain is best as the one to tell you how to activate spiritual purpose. Nimue is reflective and can provide dimensions of both receptivity to image your purpose and activation to craft it in the realms of your life. The Merlin will be best for generating philosophical ideals to empower your purpose.

Message: If you've shared a path with someone, then one of you was not on your own path. You can walk side by side for a while; but eventually this gets too close for comfort. This means it's time for one of you to move on, in a spiritual sense of changing direction. This may be an advance in a catalyst sense, as well as an advance in position. So, whether you move up or move on, or whether you remain, you have advanced as a part of a higher process. In either case, accept the change with grace. If you resist this change or accept it with grace, you may find you have to do some time—reviewing yourself. Resistance is a cue you are not truly on your own path—or that you don't realize you are.

THE GRIFFIN AND THE GRAIL: DEVOTIONAL QUEST

Elements: Spirit, Fire, and Earth

Directions: Center, South, and North

Aspects: Service, Initiation, Honor, Purpose

Colors: Blue ray and Silver light

Kindred Spirits: Eagle, Lion, Griffin

Tree: Yew

Stones: Sapphire, Sodalite, Diamonds, Crystal cluster, Silver

Incense: Evergreen

Cycle: Midwinter, Yule

Setting Image: Castle of the Grail

Hallow: Grail, Symbol of Light

Theme: Quests

Natural Force: Spirit, Flames, Winds, Mists

Access Allies: Pellinore, Perceval, Bors, Galahad, Gawain

Message: There is a fundamental wisdom based on the knowledge of power, which counsels us to experience life with an attitude of temperance, and nothing in excess, or all things in moderation. This is not a law to be enforced or preached, but a philosophy to guide us through all that life presents along the way. Temperance isn't abstinence; it's caution. Excess isn't abundance; it's wasteful surplus. Moderation means a steady pace or taking the middle road, as on the Moon card in Tarot, where we can walk in balance between the covert and overt parts of our self.

We can experience the balance of our receptive and active powers and thus reflect a balanced light—as the Full Moon reflects fully the Sun. We are both passive and aggressive, domestic, tame, and wild. With a temperance of attitude, we can be all, and not be any one aspect of ourselves. As long as we keep in balance with ourselves, we are in balance with the light within.

Suggestions for The Griffin and The Grail: Devotional Quest

Elements: Fire is honored first here as the "senior" catalyst.

Directions: Bring the North and South aspects into the center of a smaller circle, cast inside two larger ones. This will allow you to pull from both directions, without feeling pulled in both directions. You can also imagine the aspects of North and South as wide, angelic wings—or wear rings on either hand to symbolize these. This will work, no matter which way you need to turn.

Aspects: Pledge your willingness to service, but don't make promises you really can't keep. Be realistic about what you can do—and do that as honorably as you can.

Colors: Place various shades of blue in the directions (such as hot blue in the South, for fire), then a bit of silver inside the blues to bring expression with an elemental balance of all aspects.

Kindred Spirits: Dragon as active, Eagle as receptive, Griffin as reflective.

Tree: Yew may be replaced by juniper, cedar, or nettles.

Stones: Crystal clusters will need to be cleaned in saltwater beforehand. Afterward they can be covered lightly, or placed in sweet herbs to retain the spiritually amplified aspects.

Incense: Mix jasmine and evergreen incenses for amplified image.

Cycle: The Grail and the symbol are gifts that are accepted but never possessed, for they dwell within everyone, in their own image, and manifest in the forms of our lives. Accept these in the spirit of accepting a new light and power. Accept them also as the Yule symbol, which is the turning wheel, or cycles of life.

Setting: Grace yourself with the restorative images of the Grail castle. There are enough tests in life, without creating more. Each time you quest for the Grail within, you'll receive a different aspect of what you need. Thus tests you set for yourself may be self-depleting and self-defeating. Why would you want to do this to yourself? Accept the grace within.

Hallow: An image of your symbol of Light can be a key to the Grail within. You can also have that image etched on the Grail.

Theme: Quest with purpose or you'll find yourself in a maze.

Natural Forces: Bring Flames of Faith and Winds of Philosophy together for Divine Inspiration. Infuse with Spirit and Mists of Emotion to create a sense of Devotion.

Access Allies: Let your image of Pellinore be a cue to tell you when you're off track. Galahad is best viewed from a distance, since his aspect can make you "bliss out." Perceval is a cue to keep persisting. Bors reminds you of the spiritual quality in even the most boring tasks. Gawain is your best guide for honor and devotion to the ideals of the Right.

Message: Steady = right on; Erratic = off track. Pace yourself and you'll go the distance it takes to reach your destination. Whether you are seeking a goal or a Grail, follow your path with a reflective pace and walk in balance.

BLOOD OF THE DRAGON: SOVEREIGN POWER

Elements: All, triple-empowered with Spirit

Directions: All, triple circles

Aspects: Acceptance of personal powers, gifts, duties

Colors: Violet and Green ray, Gold light

Kindred Spirits: Ermine, Pheasant

Tree: Birch

Stones: Amethyst, Emeralds, Tourmaline, Amber, Gold, Crystal

Incense: Dragon's Blood, Resin

Cycle: Midwinter, Yule

Setting Image: Castle

Hallow: Sword, Drum

Theme: Lands, Round Table, Otherworld, Quest

Natural Force: All, amplified with Spirit

Access Allies: Arthur, Morgana, Gawain, Nimue, The Merlin, Morgawse, Mordred, Guinevere, Lancelot

Message: The sacred triplicities found in Celtic/Christian spiritual philosophies and religious practices symbolize a supportive, interlocking trine, such as the Triple Goddess. The triplicities also represent the processes by which ceremony and ritual awaken the brain and activate the Mind to restructure aspects of our life. This triple process is used for empowerment of the self in connection to the Sacred Mind of the All by the practice of requests, or prayers made in series of threes. The first activates Beta waves, the business of your mind; second, the Alpha waves of receptive consciousness; and the third, the Theta waves of deep conscious transformation.

Suggestions for Blood of the Dragon: Sovereign Power

Elements and Directions: Specify none. Emphasize the triple powers of the Circle with a call to Spirit, or prayer repeated three times, or in sets of three, if you need more litany.

Aspects: Acceptance of self is accomplished by a realistic appraisal, and not by self-praise. Acceptance requires the catalyst of Compassion.

Colors: Bring in green first for heartfelt experience. Violet brings an exalted power. If you feel this too strongly, skip the activation of violet by gold. Activate green three times for the heart of Nature.

Kindred Spirits: Ermine are intense protectors. If they seem too "snappish," try symbolic griffins instead. Besides, the pheasants prefer the griffins.

Tree: Birch can be replaced by any light-barked, strong tree, such as white oak or white pine. Ash is also very regal in aspect.

Stones: Watermelon tourmaline are ideal for aspects of balanced powers within Nature (as Sovereign) or self-nature (self-sovereignty).

Incense: Bayberry and spice are lighter aspected if you tend to get a bit more imperious than most when assuming leadership roles. Sprinkle just a little dragon's blood incense over whatever you use, and on your "third eye." This way you can keep your head on your shoulders in the most exalted positions.

Cycle: Ancient Midwinter, or Solstice images, as well as more current New Year's, are more flexible here—for example, New Year's in a Highland castle with all your clan allies gathered around. Christmas aspects and Yule can create a fixed mindset that mixes spirituality and sovereignty in a way that graces neither one. Remember the powerful freedom that separation of church and state represents. In flexible balance, both can have grace.

Setting: Your sovereign castle image represents your relationship to power and responsibility in your life. Consider this and make your castle a comfortable, manageable size.

Hallow: The sword in this image is ceremonial, symbolic of your graceful use of power and your honorable sense of its duties. Craft it lightly. The drum is a gift to give to yourself which helps set the pace and become sensitive to the rhythms of your life cycles.

Theme: Round Table is best if imaged first—to bring both alliance and self-reliance together within the realms of your life.

Natural Force: Bring in a circle of Spirit, the creation force; then Flames to catalyst power; Winds to transmit; Tides to make it a part of the pattern of your life; and Mists to soften or disperse any aspects that are too intense.

Access Allies: The Merlin crowned Arthur, so he is the best ally to remind you of your potential leadership. Even if only within the realms of your own imagery, leadership can be a self-empowering role. Arthur, Guinevere, and Lancelot are symbols for active, receptive, and reflective powers in this type of image. Their emerging images cue you as to which aspect you require. Gawain and Nimue are images of strategists, both with reflective, balanced aspects. Morgawse and Mordred are images of fierce protectors. However, they are both aggressive and calculating in their aspects. If you access their image too frequently, you may find yourself walking the sharp edge of a sword. Morgana is the most intellectual image, symbolizing the qualities of being a well-informed analyst in regard to your life, over all.

Message: This triplicity is the Beta-Alpha-Theta aspects of brainwave activity. It is also a holy symbol of the Christian Trinity and the Sacred Triple Goddess of Nature. A more linear, structured aspect is the triple-pointed pyramid, the supportive trine relationship. This can also be used, as Dion Fortune (*Applied Magick*, Wellingborough,

Northamptonshire: Aquarian Press, 1985) taught:

> All gods are one god
> All goddesses are one goddess
> And there is one initiator.

Put your initiator at the top point, for Divine catalyst.

WINTER'S FLAME: RELATIONSHIP

Elements: Fire and Earth

Directions: South and North

Aspects: Balance of heartfelt connections, sacred marriage

Colors: Orange and Green rays, Copper and White lights

Kindred Spirits: White Owls, Stag and Doe, Ram and Ewe

Tree: Vine

Stones: Tourmaline, Amber, Carnelian, Chryscola, Copper

Incense: Amber

Cycle: Midsummer

Setting Image: Lands, Forest, Cave

Hallow: Scabbard, Sword, Chalice

Theme: Courtly Love

Natural Force: Flames and Winds

Access Allies: Arthur, Guinevere, The Merlin, Gawain, and Nimue

Format: Moderate

Message: There are times when we encounter others who represent aspects that we need, to reflect a balance that is not within ourselves. Although this seems to have an order of perfection that feels like love, a true connection of great power, it may well be just an external form of what we want to manifest in our lives. If that encounter leads us to create that needed aspect within ourselves, then the encounter is truly positive and powerful. Thus it is a higher love. However, if we allow that other person to be a substitute for the structures we must create within, the result can be damaging and destructive, even without our awareness or intentions being consciously involved. Before you allow yourself to be persuaded (or self-persuaded) that another person has the power you need for personal balance, make an honest effort to find that power within yourself first. If you find that inner power, you may find a balanced relationship, as well. You certainly will be better able to make a balanced decision, and this is for the good of both of you, and all who may be connected. Balanced needs allow you to need another in a balanced way in your relationships, without being needy.

Suggestions for Winter's Flame: Relationship

Elements: Earth is more objective; Fire is more subjective.

Directions: Make a circle first, and bring aspects of both South and North inside for uniting relationships.

Aspects: A sacred marriage is any relationship that blends either practical and physical (N + S), practical and spiritual (N + Center) or unites practical and physical with a bond of spiritual. Physical and spiritual rarely works well, unless it's with Tantric Yoga. This requires some in-depth understanding of the mystical philosophies and traditions of India. Body/Mind healing work does use both physical and spiritual; but the etheric, or Mind, aspect is the balancing medium.

Colors: Green revives heartfelt connections directly. Orange has a wider, extended, kinship aspect; but is also an energizer. Start with green most times.

Kindred Spirits: White owls in pairs are powerful images of a mystical quality in relationships. (White) Stag and doe are both powerful symbols for magnetism in a relationship; but this attracts others and can cause conflicts unless this is a part of the purpose of leadership. (White) Ram and ewe have a mutually magnetic aspect which allows a relationship to have mutual attraction while maintaining more privacy than the symbols of the stag and doe (especially white).

Tree: Vines used in images of relationship need to have some little thorns to help them stick. Large sharp thorns are not a fair test, even for rosy relationships.

Stones: Amber is an electric current conductor, useful as a catalyst for love. Tourmaline is key for strong heart bonds.

Incense: Amber can be replaced by spice, jasmine, or sandalwood for Body, Spirit, and Mind aspects, respectively.

Cycle: Midsummer is an egalitarian image, with Full Sun (male/active) and Full Earth (female/receptive).

Setting: Lands are for extended kinships; Forests are for love and marriage; Caves work for spiritual relationships and can also be shared by couples for ancient Grand Rites.

Hallow: Give yourself the scabbard to bring a protective, mutual guardianship aspect into your life and into relationships of deepest trust and alliance.

Theme: Courtly Love is best in current times, if both partners court each other, with mutual positive regard—and not for manipulative reasons.

Natural Force: Winds bring in the power of like-mind; Flames are more physical. Together, they create a Body/Mind balanced passion in a relationship.

Access Allies: For an objective look at the potential power of a relationship, make a circle in your image. Put The Merlin in the center as a translator and interpreter. Arthur goes in the North, for this was the practical power aspect; Gawain in the South for the power of physical attraction; Nimue in the East for the mind power match; and Guinevere in the West for powerful emotions. Imagine the partners in the potential (or current) relationship in the center with The Merlin. Then imagine them being questioned by each ally in regard to the aspects their directional, elemental positions represent, such as:

Nimue: East, Air—questions about their philosophic ideas, perceptions of each other, creative abilities, intellectual pursuits and ability to inspire each other.

Gawain: South, Fire—questions about their willpower, self-esteem, protective attitudes, physical conditions, faith, courage, sexual drive, tempers, humor.

Guinevere: West, Water—questions about their emotional types, expressions of feelings, devotional qualities, willingness to keep in balance, intuitive characteristics, achievements, spiritual beliefs, and practices.

Arthur: North, Earth—questions about their practical qualities, abilities to live an ordered life, views on societal structures, attitudes and abilities in regard to prosperity, levels of education, pursuit of sacred wisdom, and traditional values.

In the Center, the Merlin provides insight from a position of synthesis, and so do you. Try this with a group of people, some acting as the archetypal characters. Just remember to keep it light and use lots of humor.

Message: Remember that you love someone else for who you are, because they provide a catalyst for you to develop ways to meet your needs, and not because they just provide what you need.

AFTERWORD

Harken, finally, the bardic bold,
Presenting the visions in a new mold,

With Wizards, Queens, and Knights of old,
And Avalon's isle, the realms unfold.

Trace the silver, find the gold.

Observe the legends, this should you behold,
For they are never growing old,

Yet shift their shapes, as they are told,
And with each quest, another fold,

And thus are made the myths of gold.

So try your own hand, now do be bold,
And at your command, the tales are told.

THE RIGHT-WISE BORN, TRUE KING, A FAERIE TALE

Adapted by Amber Wolfe

After the conception of Arthur and the death of Uther, The Merlin, the good enchanter, came to London from Gwynned—his mysterious valley in North Wales. At a Yuletide festival, a stone appeared before all the knights gathered there. Set in the stone was a great sword pointed downward. Inscribed on the stone were the words: "Whosoever pulleth out this sword from this stone shall be the right-wise born, true King of All Britain."

Many tried to loose the sword from the stone. None were successful. It was decided to hold a tournament on New Year's Day. One of the knights who came was good Sir Ector, with his son Kai—newly made a knight—and Sir Kai's younger brother Arthur, then about sixteen years old and still a squire.

Sir Kai found his sword missing and sent Arthur back to fetch it, but their mother had left already and locked the place where they were lodging. Arthur remembered having seen a sword sticking out of a large stone in the churchyard. Unaware of the significance of that sword and too hurried to read the prophetic inscription accompanying it, Arthur pulled the sword from the stone effortlessly.

Arthur brought the sword to Sir Kai, who, having already tried to wrest it from the stone himself without success, immediately recognized both the word—and the importance of what had transpired. On impulse, Sir Kai raced over to his father, Sir Ector, and claimed he had pulled the sword from the stone.

Sir Ector, being wise to the ways of young knights anxious to prove themselves, asked Sir Kai, on oath, to tell him what had truly happened. To his credit, Sir Kai immediately gave up the pretense and said it had been Arthur who pulled the sword from the stone.

Sir Ector took both Sir Kai and Arthur back to the stone and commanded the deed be reenacted. Arthur, still mystified by the reaction of his father and his brother, quickly replaced the sword. This being done, both Sir Ector and Sir Kai attempted to wrest the sword from the stone, with no success. Finally, Sir Ector instructed Arthur to try. Then, just as quickly as he had placed the sword in the stone, Arthur drew it forth again.

At this, both Sir Ector and Sir Kai knelt in reverence before Arthur. While a shocked Arthur listened, Sir Ector told the tale of how The Merlin had brought Arthur as a babe to be fostered until the time came for him to assume his rightful role as King of all Britain.

Sir Ector proclaimed Arthur the true king and pledged to him his allegiance, as well as his continuing love. Arthur accepted this unexpected honor and pledged his service to the Sovereignty of the Land, to God, to the people, and to the task of righting the wrongs he saw around him. Arthur asked Sir Ector to remain as the wise father he had come to love; and he named his brother, Sir Kai, as his seneschal adviser. Both he requested to be true knights of his Court.

When the three men told the knights, Druids, and the Christian clergy who were present what had happened, there was much dissension and disbelief. It was decided to hold another such tournament at Eastertide, when the Light and the Land were newborn with the coming of Spring. In due course, the time came again. Many knights and kings had come from the British Isles to try their hand at pulling the sword from the stone. After each and every one of them failed to do so, Arthur stepped forth.

With a flash of Light, Arthur pulled forth the sword. On seeing this, the people shouted for Arthur to be acclaimed the true-born, right wise King of all Britain. Although many of the kings and knights agreed with this, others did not. Still, the clamor of the people made them keep their thoughts hidden—for the time-being.

For a brief time, Arthur—now King Arthur—set about the business of gathering a select group of the finest knights to train for service to the land and the King. Thus was the beginning of the Court at Camelot and the Round Table, though it was not yet seen for what it was, because both the land and the knights had spent so much time being divided and in opposition to each other.

During this time, many of the dissenting knights and kings had joined forces for the purpose of destroying Arthur, whom they saw as an unknown, upstart impostor. Foremost among those plotting against Arthur were the Kings of Lothian, of Gwyndd, Orkney in North Wales, of Gorre, and of Garloth. Together, they sent word they were coming with gifts for Arthur—gifts to be delivered with the sharp edges of their own swords.

Having heard of this threat, The Merlin led King Arthur and his knights to the strong fortress at Caerleon in South Wales. There they were besieged by the hostile knights for a fortnight, but none could break through the fortress walls—nor the strong forces that protected King Arthur and his faithful knights.

On the fifteenth day of the siege, The Merlin came out of the fortress to address the angry knights and kings who were so determined to see Arthur and Camelot undone. It was then he told all gathered, both those who were loyal to King Arthur inside Caerleon and those in opposition outside, a wondrous and prophetic tale:

"It is a great truth that Arthur is indeed the rightful king of all these lands: Britain, Wales, Ireland, Scotland, and the Orkneys. He is also right-wise King of Brittany and shall one day be known as the true-born spiritual king of lands destined to become the home of many Celtic peoples and their children's children, as yet unborn."

Then The Merlin told how this had come to pass:

"Arthur is the true-born son of King Uther Pendragon by a magickal union with Igraine of Cornwall. By my mystical arts, I arranged this union in order to serve my role in the creation of the coming king and the destiny that he, in turn, would fulfill for the Sovereignty of the land and its peoples everywhere. Because of this sacred destiny, I had Uther agree to place in my keeping the child who resulted from his union with Igraine."

Then The Merlin continued with even more mystical elements of his wonder tale:

"When Arthur was first born—and before I placed him in the keeping of the good knight, Sir Ector—I took him to the Land of Mystery, the sacred realm that those of Avalon know and guard well. In that realm of mystery and magick dwell the Fey, rulers of the elements and the dominions we call the Otherworld. There the Fey bestowed great gifts of power upon the babe Arthur, so he would be able to fulfill his destiny and his service to Sovereignty."

Then The Merlin spoke of this with great emphasis for the purpose of posterity.

"First, Arthur was presented with all the powers of the Hallows, the sacred gifts of the Fey. These were the spear with which to change the thoughts of human mind; the sword of power for guardianship of the land; the holy cup, vessel of nurturance for the good of all; and the stone of destiny from which the patterns of life may be determined. Upon receiving these sacred Faerie gifts, Arthur was further endowed with the unifying force of harmony, as yet to be fully understood by humanity. For this unity and harmony, which is an element of spirit, the symbol shall be an eight-pointed star. This will represent the many lines of power and lands in which Arthur shall come to be honored as a spiritual king of Light, as Arthur, the once, future, and eternally present King."

Then The Merlin told the most prophetic part of his wonder tale:

"Lastly, before I took Arthur from those of Avalon and of the Fey, three more prophecies were given of him—and to him as right-wise King of Britain:

"First, that Arthur would be the finest of all knights on whom all future knights should mold their own skills and services. Second, that Arthur would be the greatest king ever known in this land on whom all future kings of Light should mold their own rulership and service. Third, that Arthur would live longer than any other king. He will endure beyond the limits of mortal life, into the everlasting realms of myth and mystery which are so dear to the hearts and minds of humankind."

Then The Merlin spoke the last of his wonder tale:

"Most sacred, though, is the greatest sword of power of all time, which is being created in the realm of mystery for Arthur to wield. It is to be called Excalibur, the sword of all that is of the Light and of the Right. This sword can be used only for right causes, those which are for truth and goodness. When the time comes, Excalibur shall return to the Earth, to the realm of Sovereignty from which it came. From then on, Excalibur shall arise only when it is needed by Britain and all of her children's children, for all time to come. While Arthur wields Excalibur, his true kingship shall prosper. Thus, all will grow, not only the land itself, but the mystical realm of Britain and her children. This realm shall be known as Logres, the blessed land, and Arthur shall be known as its right-wise, true-born king. For a time, Logres shall manifest on the Earth. Then, while the power is present, Arthur shall accomplish many deeds that will be known for all time. There will be a brief, shining time before the shadows of darkness reclaim the power of Logres. After that, all of Britain and her children shall remember. They shall have faith as they wait for Excalibur to arise once more, wielded by Arthur, the constant king, who serves the Sovereignty of the Lands."

Thus having spoken, The Merlin bowed deeply to King Arthur. The others present heard and felt the power and the wonder. They knew truth had been told. All of them bowed also; all pledged their loyalty to their true king, Arthur.

And so it was that Arthur was acclaimed king and was crowned with the title for all time. It was then that the true work, the destiny that was Arthur's, began to be fulfilled. King Arthur and the Knights of Britain began the many adventures that have come to be known as the Legends of Camelot.

BIBLIOGRAPHY

Historical, Cultural, and Anthropological Sources

Alcock, Leslie. *Arthur's Britain: History and Archeology A.D. 367-634*. New York: Penguin Books, 1983.

Ashe, Geoffrey. *The Discovery of King Arthur*. Garden City, NY: Anchor Press/Doubleday, 1985.

Bonwick, James. *Irish Druids and Old Irish Religions*. USA: Dorset Press, 1986.

Bord, Janet and Colin. *Mysterious Britain: Ancient Secrets of the United Kingdom and Ireland*. London: Paladin/Granada, 1984.

Cunliffe, Barry. *An Illustrated History of the Celtic Race: Their Culture, Customs and Legends*. New York: Greenwich Press, 1986.

Ellis, Peter Berresford. *Caesar's Invasion of Britain*. New York: New York University Press, 1980.

Every, George. *Christian Mythology*. London: Hamlyn, 1970.

Gimbutas, Marija. *The Goddesses and Gods of Old Europe: Myths and Cult Images*. Berkeley and Los Angeles: University of California Press, 1982.

Green, Miranda. *The Gods of the Celts*. Totowa, NJ: Barnes and Noble, 1986.

Herm, Gerhard. *The Celts: The People Who Came Out of the Darkness*. New York: St. Martin's Press, 1976.

Huxley, Aldous. *The Doors of Perception*. New York: Harper-Row, 1990.

Lacy, Norris J. (Ed.). *The Arthurian "Encyclopedia."* New York: Peter Bedrick Books, 1986.

Laing, Lloyd and Jennifer. *The Origins of Britain*. London: Paladin/Grafton, 1986.

Laing, Lloyd. *Celtic Britain*. London: Paladin/Grafton, 1986.

Leek, Sybil and Stephen. *A Ring of Magic Islands*. Garden City, NY: Amphoto Books, 1976.

MacCana, Proinsias. *Celtic Mythology*. London: Hamlyn, 1973.

Markale, Jean. *Women of the Celts*. Rochester, VT: Inner Traditions, 1986.

Matthews, John and Stewart, Bob. *Warriors of Arthur*. London: Blandford Press, 1987.

Newark, Tim. *Celtic Warriors: 400 B.C.–A.D. 1600*. Dorset, England: Blandford Press, 1986.

Piggott, Stuart. *The Druids*. New York: Thames and Hudson, 1986.

Powell, T. G. E. *The Celts*. New York: Thames and Hudson, 1986.

Reilly, Robert T. *Irish Saints*. New York: Avenel Books.

Ross, Anne. *The Pagan Celts*. Totowa, NJ: Barnes and Noble Books, 1986.

Savage, Anne. *The Anglo-Saxon Chronicles: The Authentic Voices of England from the Time of Julius Caesar to the Coronation of Henry II*. England: Dorset Press, 1983.

Scherman, Katharine. *The Flowering of Ireland: Saints, Scholars and Kings*. Boston: Little, Brown and Company, 1981.

Sharkey, John. *Celtic Mysteries: The Ancient Religion*. New York: Thames and Hudson, 1987.

Tuchman, Barbara W. *A Distant Mirror: The Calamitous 14th Century*. New York: Ballantine, 1978.

Wacher, John. *The Coming of Rome*. London: Paladin/Grafton, 1986.

Wentz, W. Y. Evans. *The Fairy Faith in Celtic Countries*. Gerrads Cross, Buckinghamshire, England: Colin Smythe, 1988.

Series: Specific Texts

1. *Mysteries of the Unknown: Mystic Places*, Time Life Books.

2. *Milestones of History: Ancient Empires, The Fires of Faith*. Newsweek Books.

3. *Great Ages of Man: Barbarian Europe, Age of Faith*. Time Life Books.

Mythical, Fictional, Folk, and Faerie Tale Sources

Barber, Richard. *The Arthurian Legends: An Illustrated Anthology*. USA: Littlefield, Adams and Co., 1979.

Bradley, Marion Zimmer. *The Mists of Avalon*. New York: Knopf, 1982.

Caldecott, Moyra. *Women in Celtic Myth: Tales of Extraordinary Women from the Ancient Celtic Tradition*. Rochester, VT: Destiny Books, 1992.

Chant, Joy. *The High Kings: Arthur's Celtic Ancestors*. New York: Bantam Books, 1983.

Cochran, Molly and Murphy, Warren. *The Forest King*. New York: Tor, 1992.

Fitzpatrick, Jim. *The Book of Conquests*. Surrey, England: Dragon's World, 1978.

Gantz, Jeffrey. *The Mabinogion*. New York: Dorset Press, 1985.

Gose, Elliot B., Jr. *The World of the Irish Wonder Tale: An Introduction to the Study of Fairy Tales*. Toronto: University of Toronto Press, 1985.

Green, Roger Lancelyn. *King Arthur and His Knights of the Round Table*. London: Penguin, 1953.

Jackson, Kenneth Hurlstone. *A Celtic Miscellany*. New York: Dorset Press, 1986.

Jacobs, Joseph. *More Celtic Fairy Tales*. New York: Dover Publications, 1968.

Marshall, Edison. *The Pagan King*. New York: Doubleday, 1959.

Rees, Alwyn and Rees, Bunley. *Celtic Heritage: Ancient Tradition in Ireland and Wales*. London: Thames and Hudson, 1991.

Smith, Peter Alderson. *W. B. Yeats and the Tribes of Danu: Three Views of Ireland's Faeries*. Garrad's Cross, Buckinghamshire, England: Colin Smythe, 1987.

Squire, Charles. *Celtic Myth and Legend: Poetry and Romance*. London: Newcastle Publishing, 1975.

Steinbeck, John. *The Acts of King Arthur and His Noble Knights*. New York: Farrar, Straus and Giroux, 1977.

Stewart, Mary. *The Crystal Cave*. New York: William Morrow, 1970.

_____. *The Hollow Hills*. Greenwich CN: Fawcett, 1973.

_____. *The Last Enchantment*. New York: Fawcett, 1979.

_____. *The Wicked Day*. New York: William Morrow, 1983.

Sutcliff, Rosemary. *Sword at Sunset*. New York: Tor, 1987.

Tennyson, Lord Alfred. *Idylls of the King*. New York: Signet/The New American Library of World Literature, 1961.

Tolstoy, Nikolai. *The Coming of the King*. New York: Bantam, 1989.

White, T. H. *The Book of Merlin*. Austin, TX: University of Texas Press, 1977.

_____. *The Once and Future King*. New York: Berkley, 1977.

Series: Specific Texts
The Enchanted World: Fairies and Elves, Seekers and Saviors, Wizards and Witches, Legends of Valor, and The Fall of Camelot. Time Life Books

Psychological, Symbolic, and Metaphysical Sources

Anderson, William. *Green Man: The Archetype of Our Oneness With the Earth*. London: Harper Collins, 1990.

Bates, Brian. *The Way of Wyrd: Tales of an Anglo/Saxon Sorcerer*. San Francisco: Hayes and Ron, 1983.

Bettelheim, Bruno. *The Uses of Enchantment: The Meaning and Importance of Fairy Tales*. New York: Vintage Books, 1989.

Bonewits, P. E. I. *Real Magic*. Berkeley: Creative Arts Book Company, 1971.

Campbell, Joseph (Ed.). *The Portable Jung*. New York: Viking/Penguin, 1985.

Campbell, Joseph and Moyers, Bill. *The Power of Myth*. New York: Doubleday, 1988.

Campbell, Joseph. *The Hero With a Thousand Faces*. Princeton: Princeton University Press, 1973.

_____. *The Mythic Image*. Princeton: Princeton University Press, 1990.

_____. *Myths to Live By*. New York: Bantam Books, 1984.

_____. *Occidental Mythology: The Masks of God*. New York: Viking/Penguin, 1984.

_____. *Primitive Mythology: The Masks of God*. New York: Viking/Penguin, 1987.

_____. *Transformation of Myth Through Time*. The World of Joseph Campbell Series. St. Paul, MN: Highbridge Productions, 1990. Audiotape cassette.

_____. *The Way of the Animal Powers*. San Francisco: Harper and Row, 1983.

Campanelli, Pauline and Dan. *Wheel of the Year: Living the Magical Life*. St. Paul, MN: Llewellyn, 1989.

Capt, E. Raymond. *Stonehenge and Druidism*. Thousand Oaks, CA: Artisan, 1979.

Conway, D. J. *By Oak, Ash and Thorn: Modern Celtic Shamanism*. St. Paul, MN: Llewellyn, 1995.

Fortune, Dion. *Applied Magick*. Wellingborough, Northamptonshire: Aquarian Press, 1985.

_____. *The Machinery of the Mind*. York Beach, ME: Samuel Weiser, 1985.

_____. *Sane Occultism*. Wellingborough, Northamptonshire: Aquarian Press, 1985.

Goodrich, Norma Lorre. *King Arthur*. New York: Harper and Row, 1986.

_____. *Merlin*. New York: Harper and Row, 1988.

Graves, Robert. *The White Goddess*. New York: Farrar, Straus and Giroux, 1983.

Hall, Calvin S. and Nordby, Vernon J. *A Primer of Jungian Psychology*. New York: Signet, 1973.

Hawkins, Gerald S. *Stonehenge Decoded*. New York: Dell Publishing, 1965.

Hope, Murry. *Practical Celtic Magic: A Working Guide to the Magical Heritage of the Celtic Races*. Northamptonshire, England: Aquarian Press, 1987.

Johnson, Robert A. *We: Understanding the Psychology of Romantic Love*. San Francisco: Harper and Row, 1983.

Jung, Carl Gustav. *Aspects of the Feminine*. Princeton: Princeton University Press, 1982.

_____. *Dreams*. Princeton: Princeton University Press, 1974.

_____. *Four Archetypes: Mother/Rebirth/Spirit/Trickster*. Princeton: Princeton University Press, 1973.

_____. *Memories, Dreams, Reflections*. New York: Random House, 1965.

_____. *Psyche and Symbol*. Garden City, NY: Anchor/Doubleday, 1958.

_____. *Psychology and Alchemy*. Princeton: Princeton University Press, 1980.

Knight, Gareth. *The Secret Tradition in Arthurian Legend: The Magical and Mystical Power Sources Within the Mysteries of Britain*. Northamptonshire, England: Aquarian Press, 1983.

Matthews, Caitlin and John. *The Arthurian Tarot: A Hallowquest Handbook*. Northamptonshire, England: Aquarian Press, 1990.

Matthews, Caitlin. *The Elements of the Goddess*. Dorset, England: Element Books, 1989.

Matthews, John. *The Elements of the Arthurian Tradition*. Dorset, England: Element Books, 1989.

_____. *The Elements of the Grail Tradition*. Dorset, England: Element Books, 1990.

Moore, Robert and Gilette, Douglas. *King—Warrior—Magician—Lover: Rediscovering the Archetypes of the Mature Masculine*. San Francisco; Harper San Francisco, 1990.

Rutherford, Ward. *The Druids: Magicians of the West*. Northamptonshire, England: Aquarian Press, 1984.

Starr, Kara. *Merlin's Journal of Time: The Camelot Adventure*. Solano Beach, CA: Ravenstarr Publications, 1989.

Stewart, R. J. (Ed.). *Merlin and Woman: The Second Merlin Conference. London, June, 1987*. London: Blandford Press, 1988.

_____. *The Book of Merlin: Insights from the First Merlin Conference, London, June, 1986*. London: Blandford Press, 1987.

_____. *The Merlin Tarot: Images, Insight and Wisdom from the Age of Merlin*. Northamptonshire, England: Aquaria Press, 1988.

_____. *The Mystic Life of Merlin*. New York: Routledge and Kegan Paul, 1987.

_____. *The Prophetic Vision of Merlin: Prediction, Psychic Transformation, and the Foundation of the Grail Legends in an Ancient Set of Visionary Verses*. New York: Routledge and Kegan Paul, 1986.

Wolfe, Amber. *In the Shadow of the Shaman: Connecting with Self, Nature and Spirit*. St. Paul, MN: Llewellyn, 1988.

_____. *Personal Alchemy: A Handbook of Healing and Self-Transformation*. St. Paul, MN: Llewellyn, 1993.

Series: Specific Text

Man, Myth & Magick: An Illustrated Encyclopedia of the Supernatural. Volumes 1, 8, 9, 12, and 13, Richard Cavendish, Ed. New York: Marshall Cavendish Corp., 1970.

INDEX

D

E

F

G

H

I

J

K

L

STAY IN TOUCH

On the following pages you will find listed, with their current prices, some of the books now available on related subjects. Your book dealer stocks most of these and will stock new titles in the Llewellyn series as they become available. We urge your patronage.

To Get a Free Catalog

You are invited to write for our bimonthly news magazine/catalog, Llewellyn's *New Worlds of Mind and Spirit*. A sample copy is free, and it will continue coming to you at no cost as long as you are an active mail customer. Or you may subscribe for just $10 in the United States and Canada ($20 overseas, first class mail). Many bookstores also have *New Worlds* available to their customers. Ask for it.

In *New Worlds* you will find news and features about new books, tapes and services; announcements of meetings and seminars; helpful articles; author interviews and much more. Write to:

Llewellyn's New Worlds of Mind and Spirit
P.O. Box 64383-806, St. Paul, MN 55164-0383, U.S.A.

TO ORDER BOOKS AND TAPES

If your book store does not carry the titles described on the following pages, you may order them directly from Llewellyn by sending the full price in U.S. funds, plus postage and handling (see below).

Credit card orders: VISA, MasterCard, American Express are accepted. Call us toll-free within the United States and Canada at 1-800-THE-MOON.

Special Group Discount: Because there is a great deal of interest in group discussion and study of the subject matter of this book, we offer a 20% quantity discount to group leaders or agents. Our Special Quantity Price for a minimum order of five copies of *The Arthurian Quest* is $99.80 cash-with-order. Include postage and handling charges noted below.

Postage and Handling: Include $4 postage and handling for orders $15 and under; $5 for orders over $15. There are no postage and handling charges for orders over $100. Postage and handling rates are subject to change. We ship UPS whenever possible within the continental United States; delivery is guaranteed. Please provide your street address as UPS does not deliver to P.O. boxes. Orders shipped to Alaska, Hawaii, Canada, Mexico and Puerto Rico will be sent via first class mail. Allow 4-6 weeks for delivery. International orders: Airmail – add retail price of each book and $5 for each non-book item (audiotapes, etc.); Surface mail – add $1 per item.

Minnesota residents add 7% sales tax.

Mail orders to:
Llewellyn Worldwide, P.O. Box 64383-806, St. Paul, MN 55164-0383, U.S.A.

For customer service, call (612) 291-1970.

Prices subject to change without notice.

CELTIC MYTH & MAGIC
Harness the Power of the Gods & Goddesses
by Edain McCoy

Tap into the mythic power of the Celtic goddesses, gods, heroes and heroines to aid your spiritual quests and magickal goals. *Celtic Myth & Magic* explains how to use creative ritual and pathworking to align yourself with the energy of these archetypes, whose potent images live deep within your psyche.

Celtic Myth & Magic begins with an overview of 49 different types of Celtic Paganism followed today, then gives specific instructions for evoking and invoking the energy of the Celtic pantheon to channel it toward magickal and spiritual goals and into esbat, sabbat and life transition rituals. Three detailed pathworking texts will take you on an inner journey where you'll join forces with the archetypal images of Cuchulain, Queen Maeve and Merlin the Magician to bring their energies directly into your life. The last half of the book clearly details the energies of over 300 Celtic deities and mythic figures so you can evoke or invoke the appropriate deity to attain a specific goal.

This inspiring, well-researched book will help solitary Pagans who seek to expand the boundaries of their practice to form working partnerships with the divine.

1–56718–661–0, 7 x 10, 464 pp., softbound   **$19.95**

CELTIC MAGIC
by D. J. Conway

Many people, not all of Irish descent, have a great interest in the ancient Celts and the Celtic pantheon, and *Celtic Magic* is the map they need for exploring this ancient and fascinating magical culture.

Celtic Magic is for the reader who is either a beginner or intermediate in the field of magic. It provides an extensive "how-to" of practical spell-working. There are many books on the market dealing with the Celts and their beliefs, but none guide the reader to a practical application of magical knowledge for use in everyday life. There is also an in-depth discussion of Celtic deities and the Celtic way of life and worship, so that an intermediate practitioner can expand upon the spellwork to build a series of magical rituals. Presented in an easy-to-understand format, *Celtic Magic* is for anyone searching for new spells that can be worked immediately, without elaborate or rare materials, and with minimal time and preparation.

0–87542–136–9, 240 pgs., mass market, illus.   **$4.99**

GLAMOURY
Magic of the Celtic Green World
Steve Blamires

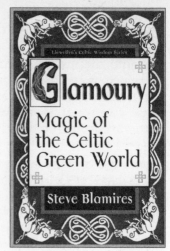

Glamoury refers to an Irish Celtic magical tradition that is truly holistic, satisfying the needs of the practitioner on the physical, mental and spiritual levels. This guidebook offers practical exercises and modern versions of time-honored philosophies that will expand your potential into areas previously closed to you.

We have moved so far away from our ancestors' closeness to the Earth—the Green World—that we have nearly forgotten some very important truths about human nature that are still valid. *Glamoury* brings these truths to light so you can take your rightful place in the Green World. View and experience the world in a more balanced, meaningful way. Meet helpers and guides from the Otherworld who will become your valued friends. Live in tune with the seasons and gauge your inner growth in relation to the Green World around you.

The ancient Celts couched their wisdom in stories and legends. Today, intuitive people can learn much from these tales. *Glamoury* presents a system based on Irish Celtic mythology to guide you back to the harmony with life's cycles that our ancestors knew.

1–56718–069–8, 6 x 9, 352 pp., illus., softcover $16.95

THE GRAIL CASTLE
Male Myths & Mysteries in the Celtic Tradition
by Kenneth Johnson & Marguerite Elsbeth

Explore the mysteries which lie at the core of being male when you take a quest into the most powerful myth of Western civilization: the Celtic-Teutonic-Christian myth of *The Grail Castle*.

The Pagan Celtic culture's world view—which stressed an intense involvement with the magical world of nature—strongly resonates for men today because it offers a direct experience with the spirit often lacking in their lives. This book describes the four primary male archetypes—the King or Father, the Hero or Warrior, the Magician or Wise Man and the Lover—which the authors exemplify with stories from the Welsh Mabinogion, the Ulster Cycle and other old Pagan sources. Exercises and meditations designed to activate these inner myths will awaken men to how myths—as they live on today in the collective unconscious and popular culture—shape their lives. Finally, men will learn how to heal the Fisher King—who lies at the heart of the Grail Castle myth—to achieve integration of the four archetypal paths.

1–56718–369–7, 6 x 9, 224 pp., illus., index $14.95

Prices subject to change without notice.

LEGEND
The Arthurian Tarot
Anna-Marie Ferguson

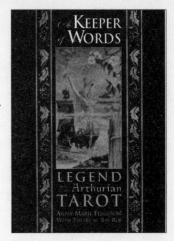

Gallery artist and writer Anna-Marie Ferguson has paired the ancient divinatory system of the tarot with the Arthurian myth to create *Legend: The Arthurian Tarot*. The exquisitely beautiful watercolor paintings of this tarot deck illustrate characters, places and tales from the legends that blend traditional tarot symbolism with the Pagan and Christian symbolism that are equally significant elements of this myth.

Each card represents the Arthurian counterpart to tarot's traditional figures, such as Merlin as the Magician, Morgan le Fay as the Moon, Mordred as the King of Swords and Arthur as the Emperor. Accompanying the deck is a decorative layout sheet in the format of the Celtic Cross to inspire and guide your readings, as well as the book *Keeper of Words*, which lists the divinatory meanings of the cards, the cards' symbolism and the telling of the legend associated with each card.

The natural pairing of the tarot with Arthurian legend has been made before, but never with this much care, completeness and consummate artistry. This visionary tarot encompasses all the complex situations life has to offer—trials, challenges and rewards—to help you cultivate a close awareness of your past, present and future through the richness of the Arthurian legend ... a legend which continues to court the imagination and speak to the souls of people everywhere.

1–56718–267–4, Book: 6 x 9, 272 pgs., illus., softcover
Deck: 78 full-color cards, Layout Sheet: 18" x 24", four-color $34.95

IN THE SHADOW OF THE SHAMAN
Connecting with Self, Nature & Spirit
by Amber Wolfe

Presented in what the author calls a "cookbook shaman-ism" style, this book shares recipes, ingredients, and methods of preparation for experiencing some very ancient wisdoms: wisdoms of Native American and Wiccan traditions, as well as contributions from other philosophies of Nature as they are used in the shamanic way. Wheels, the circle, totems, shields, directions, divinations, spells, care of sacred tools and meditations are all discussed. Wolfe encourages us to feel confident and free to use her methods to cook up something new, completely on our own. This blending of ancient formulas and personal methods represents what Ms. Wolfe calls Aquarian Shamanism.

In the Shadow of the Shaman is designed to communicate in the most practical, direct ways possible, so that the wisdom and the energy may be shared for the benefits of all. Whatever your system or tradition, you will find this to be a valuable book, a resource, a friend, a gentle guide and support on your journey. Dancing in the shadow of the shaman, you will find new dimensions of Spirit.

0–87542–888–6, 384 pgs., 6 x 9, illus., softcover $14.95

PERSONAL ALCHEMY
A Handbook of Healing & Self-Transformation
by Amber Wolfe

Personal Alchemy offers the first bold look at the practical use of "Rays" for healing and self-development. Rays are spontaneous energy emanations emitting a specific quality, property or attribute. The Red Ray, for example, represents the energies of life force, survival and strength. When used in conjunction with active imagery, the alchemical properties of the Red Ray can activate independence, release inferiority, or realign destructiveness and frustration. Personal Alchemy explains each color Ray and Light in depth, in a manner designed to teach the material and to encourage the active participation of the reader.

What's more, this book goes beyond anything else written on the Rays because it contains an extensive set of alchemical correlations that amplify the Ray's powers. Each Ray correlates with a specific element, harmonic sound, aroma, symbol, person, rune, astrological sign, Tarot card, angel, and stone, so there are numerous ways to experience and learn this system of healing magick.

0–87542–890–8, 592 pgs., 7 x 10, illus., softcover $17.95